DATE DUE

NOV 3 0 1994	
MAY 7, 1996	
SEP 1 7 1996	
OCT 2 2 2000	
GAYLORD	PRINTED IN U.S.A.

ANALYZING
QUANTITATIVE BEHAVIORAL
OBSERVATION DATA

ANALYZING QUANTITATIVE BEHAVIORAL OBSERVATION DATA

Hoi K. Suen
University of Connecticut

Donald Ary
Northern Illinois University

LEA LAWRENCE ERLBAUM ASSOCIATES, PUBLISHERS
1989   Hillsdale, New Jersey   Hove and London

BF
76.6
O27
S84
1989

Lawrence Erlbaum Associates, Inc., Publishers
365 Broadway
Hillsdale, New Jersey 07642

Library of Congress Cataloging-in-Publication Data
Suen, Hoi K.
  Analyzing quantitative behavioral observation data / Hoi K. Suen
and Donald Ary.
    p.   cm.
  Bibliography: p.
  Includes index.
  ISBN 0-89859-945-8
  1. Observation (Psychology)—Statistical methods. 2. Psychology—
Research—Methodology. I. Ary, Donald. II. Title.
  BF76.6.027S84 1988
  300'.72—dc19   88-1507
                                                          CIP

Printed in the United States of America
10 9 8 7 6 5 4 3 2 1

Contents

Preface

This book is an attempt to provide a comprehensive and up-to-date summary of recent developments in theories and techniques in three important analytical stages of quantitative behavioral observation research: sampling, measurement, and statistics. On the one hand, these developments have improved the quality of observation studies. On the other hand, they have generated some confusion and have widened the gap between theory and practice.

Direct observation of human and animal overt behaviors as a research technique has been widely used in most behavioral science research. To improve the efficiency and to reduce the obtrusiveness of direct observation, behavioral scientists in the 1920s developed some of the early behavioral sampling techniques. Various refinements and developments in the techniques took place between 1929 and 1974. These have been summarized in primatology and applied behavior analysis journals. Since 1974, the sampling techniques have become increasingly sophisticated and complicated. Many of the new approaches involve advanced statistical techniques, whereas others involve elaborate coding systems. Some of the developments were not inherently new approaches but were statistical controls designed to minimize systematic and random sampling errors.

In the early history of behavior observation, little regard was given to such psychometric concepts as reliability and validity. It has since been shown that such psychometric issues also pertain to behavior observation, and appropriate techniques for the assessment of reliability and validity have been developed for use in observational research. The Generalizability Theory of measurement, which is possibly the most sophisticated approach to the assessment of the quality of observational data, has also been gaining popularity among behavior analysts.

The analysis of observational data has until recently depended primarily on classical statistical procedures, which are built upon the assumptions of random sampling and subject independence. During the past decade, it has been shown that observational data are frequently autocorrelated. This discovery has rendered many classical inferential statistical techniques inappropriate for a large portion of observational studies. Many alternative methods have been suggested, ranging from visual inspection of graphic data to the highly sophisticated Autoregressive Integrated Moving Average (ARIMA) approach.

At least four practical problems, which necessitate a comprehensive text on the psychometric and statistical analysis of observation data, were created as a result of these developments. First, these developments often took place in a piecemeal fashion without the perspective of a unified theory. For example, some procedures in sampling techniques were based on a normal sampling theory, whereas others were based on other forms of probability distributions such as the Poisson process. Some developments in data analysis techniques were based on the assumption of independence of data, whereas others accounted for the autocorrelations inherent in a large portion of behavioral observation data.

A second problem was created as a result of the basic orientation of the researchers. Some new methods or refinements of existing methods were evolved by individuals with a strong orientation toward field application. These methods were often based on recognizable patterns in empirical or simulated data. Others were developed by theoreticians and statisticians and were frequently based upon pure mathematical theories. The application of the field-developed methods was often frustrated by an inherent lack of external validity because of the limited range of data from which these methods were derived. The application of the theoretical methods, however, frequently encountered problems of practicality.

The third problem is one of communication. Because behavioral sampling, measurement, and data analysis techniques are utilized in so many different disciplines, improvements in techniques were made independently within each discipline and usually communicated only to those within the same discipline. This lack of cross-references among different disciplines has generated problems of parallel developments, rediscovery of ideas known in other fields, and the lack of a coordinated direction. These problems further exacerbated the absence of a unified theory.

The fourth problem is perhaps the most serious. The development of the language of behavioral analysis has not kept pace with the rapid development of techniques and concepts. Consequently, there is a great deal of confusion within as well as between the disciplines as to the exact definitions of various terms.

These problems point to the need for a comprehensive text through which the theories, techniques, and language can be summarized and unified within one general frame of reference. This book represents an attempt to provide such a gathering of various theories, concepts, methods, statistics, and terminologies in quantitative behavior observation.

Acknowledgments

Many individuals have contributed to the development and completion of this book. We wish to express our deepest appreciation to our editor at Lawrence Erlbaum Associates, David Boynton, for his many constructive comments and helpful suggestions. We are also indebted to Bruce Biddle, Donald P. Hartmann, Thomas R. Kratochwill, Johnny L. Matson, and Steve V. Owen for their excellent ideas and guidance on the earlier drafts of this book. Our students, Leslie Welsh and Elizabeth Worden, also provided numerous useful suggestions. We are especially indebted to Patrick S. C. Lee for his review of an early draft of the chapters on time series analysis. Additionally, we are grateful for his generous permission to print an original statistical table compiled by him and his students (Appendix C).

The completion of this book would not have been possible without the support provided by the Provost's Office and the Office of Special Projects at Northern Illinois University and the Bureau of Educational Research and Service at the University of Connecticut. We are especially grateful for the support and encouragement given by Alfonzo Thurman, Robert Gable, and Lida K. Barrett. We also would like to thank Sandy Bland and Monica Weaver for their valuable clerical assistance provided throughout this project.

We wish to express our gratitude to our wives, Barbara Suen and Sheila Ary, for their consistent support, encouragement, and understanding throughout the entire preparation of the text. Additionally, Barbara Suen provided the much-needed proofreading of the various drafts of the book, and Sheila Ary provided editorial assistance.

Hoi K. Suen
Donald Ary

CHAPTER 1
Introduction

Holmes: "You saw this?"
Dr. Mortimer: "As clearly as I see you. . . ."
Holmes: "How was it that no one else saw it?"

—Sir Arthur Conan Doyle
The Hound of the Baskervilles

WHAT THIS BOOK IS ABOUT

In this book, we discuss various measurement and statistical issues involved in studies where data are acquired throuth direct observations of human or animal behaviors. Specifically, the focus is on quantitative methods through which the quality of the observational data can be assessed and the observed behavioral phenomenon can be described.

This is not another how-to book for researchers who are engaged in the direct observation of human or animal behaviors. For those who are interested in a how-to field guide, there are a number of excellent applied texts available for specific audiences today. To name a few, Haynes (1978) provided many case studies in his text on behavioral assessment in clinical psychology. Martin and Bateson (1986) have provided an introductory guide to observational studies in animal behavior. Bakeman and Gottman (1986) have provided an introductory text on the observation of interactions. Additionally, Hartman (1982) edited an overview of issues to consider when using human observers in a scientific investigation.

These applied texts typically tell readers what sampling, psychometric, or statistical technique is superior under what circumstances. Missing from these "guidebooks" is a clear explanation of the whys of these measurement and statistical techniques. This book is intended to fill this gap. As such, this book is primarily conceptual and theoretical in nature. Our intention is to bring together a large array of fragmented *theoretical* information, which has been scattered throughout the literature spanning various disciplines.

THE IMPORTANCE OF THEORETICAL CONSIDERATIONS

A careful review of contemporary literature on the methodological issues in such disciplines as behavioral assessment, behavior therapy, behavioral medicine, behavioral psychopathology, ethology, primatology, and applied behavior analysis strengthened our conviction that a quantitative theoretical text such as this is not only needed for theoreticians, but it is particularly important to clinical or applied practitioners.

This is because the development of quantitative behavioral observation techniques is at a critical juncture. There is a considerable amount of confusion, particularly in the applied literature, as to what technique should be used under what conditions. Many of the recent developments in the applied literature have been based only on recognizable patterns among empirical data without a sound underlying theoretical foundation. Consequently, many of these "discoveries" are inherently ad hoc in nature and are unique to specific sets of data gathered under specific circumstances.

The development of these ad hoc techniques, without the benefit of basic theoretical principles, has gone out of control in many instances. Too frequently, ad hoc procedures are confused with fundamental techniques. Inventions of new language to disguise old wine in new bottles have led to considerable confusion of concepts. Powerful fundamental techniques are being categorically dismissed as irrelevant, without a full understanding of their enormous potential for application. Hartmann (1981) complained in his editorial note when he was first elected the editor of *Behavioral Assessment* in 1981 that the applied literature in behavioral analysis had become xenophobic of fundamental measurement and statistic theories to the point that they had attempted to "re-invent the wheel."

We hope that the sources of these confusions become clear to our readers as they progress through this text. However, to illustrate the nature of some of the more apparent confusions, consider, for instance, a peculiar applied technique called *transduction accuracy*. This technique has been simultaneously described by various leading clinical behavior analysts as a measure of reliability, as a measure of validity, and as a measure independent of reliability or validity. We show in later chapters that this is a case where a new term has been invented to describe an application of an already existing concept in the fundamental psychometric literature. By inventing such a new term, clinical researchers confuse themselves.

For another example, based on results of ad hoc applied studies alone, a sampling technique known as *partial interval sampling* has been simultaneously hailed as the best and denounced as the worst time-sampling technique. The answer actually lies within a basic understanding of the theoretical psychometric properties of time sampling. A psychometric technique known as the *multifaceted nested-design generalizability technique* was developed, keeping in mind the type of complex applied situations commonly encountered by field investigators. This technique was categorically dismissed as irrelevant or as statistical overkill by those who have not tried to understand it sufficiently well to apply it. Perfectly appropriate fundamental time series analysis techniques were dismissed as too complex in favor of new, simpler, but highly questionable applied techniques that bring in through the back door the exact techniques they are supposed to replace. Based on ad hoc applied studies, behavioral data have been described as both primarily autocorrelated and not autocorrelated simultaneously. The answer is in the understanding of the theoretical relationship among sampling strategy, sample size, error estimates, and the autocorrelation function. The list can go on and on.

In light of these confusions and contradictions, those of us who are interested in the direct observation of human and/or animal behaviors need to pay closer attention to the fundamental theory of measurement and statistics. Clinicians or applied researchers must be aware of the theoretical basis of statistical techniques. Depending on the applied situation, clinicians should modify these techniques to suit the local environment. For modifications to be meaningful, however, clinicians must be aware of the whys of the fundamental techniques.

WHAT IS DIRECT BEHAVIORAL OBSERVATION?

Observation is a very general term encompassing a large array of techniques and practices. What constitutes an observation is further complicated by the frequent use of the term *observed data* to represent any empirical data, regardless of how the data were acquired. When conducting behavioral research, observed data may be gathered with one or more of a number of tools. The more common tools include paper-and-pencil tests, such as the many aptitude tests; self-administered interest or personality inventories, such as the many tools used in career guidance; attitude or opinion scales or questionnaires, such as the many tools used to measure authoritarianism, self-concept, and other sociopsychological constructs; projective tests, such as the popular Rorschach inkblot test; and the direct observation of human and animal behaviors. The last method, the target of discussion in this book, is considered by many to be superior to other methods of data collection. This belief stems from the assumption that data gathered through the direct observation of behaviors without an intermediary test, questionnaire, or other instrument reflect those behaviors directly. It therefore requires relatively little conceptual inference to connect the data to the phenomenon.

The establishment of the linkage between the phenomenon and data gathered through means other than direct behavioral observation generally requires a large inferential leap. For instance, with a self-administered questionnaire, in order to believe that the data actually reflect some inner characteristic of the subject, the following chain of indirect inferential connections must be accepted. First, the content of each question is related to the characteristic being studied. Next, the subject's response to each question accurately reflects the subject's feeling toward the question. Finally, the way the total questionnaire is scored reflects the characteristic faithfully.

With direct observation of behavior, it is believed that such an indirect inferential linkage is not needed. What is being observed *is* in fact what is being studied. What is being studied is "there" as plainly as the eyes can see. Hence, direct observation is often assumed to be superior to other means of data acquisition. After all, seeing is believing. It becomes clear as we progress through this book that this is not necessarily true.

Whether or not the assumption of superiority is true, direct observation of behavior is a particularly useful method of data acquisition for many early childhood development studies because the subjects have not yet acquired the language skills needed to respond to questionnaires or projective tests. It is also useful for the study of the mentally retarded, who are verbally deficient. In ethology, direct observation of animal behavior is perhaps the most viable method for data collection. Other advantages of the use of direct observation are described by Fiske (1978) and by Wiggins (1973).

UNSTRUCTURED AND SYSTEMATIC
OBSERVATIONS

Not all direct observations of behaviors are appropriate for a scientific investigation. In our daily social interaction, we are consciously or unconsciously engaged in the direct observation of others' behaviors almost continuously. We observe the behaviors of other pedestrians when we are walking down the street, or we observe what others are doing when we are in a restaurant. From these observations, some, like Sir Arthur Conan Doyle's famous hero Sherlock Holmes, derive more information than others from the same set of observations. Unfortunately, most of us do not possess Mr. Holmes' superior sense of what to observe and what to ignore. For most of us, daily observations of events and behaviors are generally casual and unstructured. Given this unstructured nature, it is extremely difficult to understand the mechanism and characteristics of information gathered through this type of casual daily observation. Since we know so little about data gathered from this type of casual observation, there is very little that can be said about the measurement and statistical characteristics of these data.

As opposed to casual daily observations, behavioral observations in scientific investigations of human or animal behaviors and interactions are generally systematic and controlled. This does not mean that the subjects' behaviors are controlled. Rather, what to observe, when to observe, where to observe, how to observe, other actions taken by the observer, the method of recording events and behaviors, the method of analyzing the information gathered, and/or the environment under which observations are to be made are rigidly prescribed and the subsequent prescribed procedures diligently followed. Since the process of observation is rigidly controlled, the nature of the data gathered is well defined. Hence, systematic methods for the assessment of data quality and for data analysis can be developed. These systematic measurement and statistical methods for systematic and controlled behavioral observations are the object of discussion in this book.

QUALITATIVE AND QUANTITATIVE OBSERVATION

There are two primary approaches to the systematic direct observation of behavior. These two approaches can be categorized roughly into a qualitative and a quantitative approach. They can be mutually complementary and not mutually exclusive. In this book, we discuss only the issues involved in a quantitative observational study. However, for a proper perspective, it is important to point out some of the main characteristics of both approaches and the effectiveness of the qualitative and quantitative approaches when used in combination.

In a quantitative observational study, a complex phenomenon, behavioral or otherwise, is first conceptually reduced to a number of *measurable* and observable behavioral variables. These variables are defined and a system for measuring these variables is determined before actual observation is done. A hypothesis that tentatively describes the relationships among these behavioral variables is then postulated. These relationships, if confirmed through empirical behavioral data, provide a quantitative description or explanation of the phenomenon. These defined behavioral variables are then observed to gather information or data of their quantities. Statistical analyses are performed on these quanititative data to determine whether evidence of the hypothesized relationships indeed exist. The hypotheses are either confirmed or not confirmed.

This quantitative approach, sometimes described as a positivistic approach, contains a number of strengths and weaknesses. The main advantages are its objectivity and replicability. When properly conducted, the results of a quantitative observational study are independent of the observer; in other words, different observers following similar procedures should report similar results. This makes the results more credible to an external audience. The main disadvantage of this approach is that when a complex behavioral phenomenon is reduced to a few quantifiable variables, the phenomenon can be overly simplified. Even if the research hypothesis is confirmed, it may be that the outcome is only an incomplete and at times unjustifiably superficial and shallow understanding of the phenomenon.

As a contrast, the qualitative approach, typified by such methods as ethnography, allows an investigator an in-depth understanding of a phenomenon. With ethnography, sometimes referred to as the anthropological field study method, the observation of a phenomenon starts without prior judgments, hypotheses, or preconceptions. The participant observation method, in which the observer participates as a member of the social group being observed, is most often used and recommended. However, nonparticipant observation methods have also been used in some ethnographic studies. In either case, the entire group is continuously observed for an extended period of time, and the observer attempts to record (in handwritten field notes) virtually everything (e.g., environment, activities, interactions) that occurs. In order to gain meaningful insights from the field notes, a number of guiding principles must be followed in the observation process and, more importantly, in the interpretation of the observation record. Among others, Geertz (1973) suggested that the key to ethnography is proper cultural interpretation.

Fetterman (1982) identified four major guiding principles for data collection and interpretation in ethnography. First is that of phenomenology. Under this principle, the observer attempts to understand the social phenomenon from the perspective of an insider. To gain the insider's viewpoint, the observer would either be a participant of the social group or would interview key informants from the group. The goal is not a cold, scientific understanding but an empathetic understanding of the phenomenon. The second principle is holism. An observer maintains the larger picture, or the total cultural system, as the focal point. All observations and interpretations are attempts to identify relationships between elements and the whole system. Another important principle is a nonjudgmental orientation on the part of the observer. This requires the observers to record the total situation without superimposing their own value system, judgment, or bias. Finally, the principle of contextualization requires that all data be considered only in the context of their own environment.

The advantages of ethnography are (a) its ability to provide an in-depth understanding of the phenomenon under study and, when compared against quantitative observations, the reduced chance of overlooking important variables or phenomena; and (b) the theories or hypotheses generated through this process are "data-driven," or based on what has been observed as occurring, rather than being "armchair speculations." Because of this particular characteristic of ethnographic observations, resulting theories or hypotheses are sometimes referred to as grounded theories or grounded hypotheses.

Borg and Gall (1983) identified a number of disadvantages of ethnography. First, ethnographic methods require highly alert and sophisticated observers. Observers must have extensive training in advanced sociology or social anthropology. Second, properly conducted ethnographic studies require continuous observations over a very extended period of time (e.g., months or years). This makes them time consuming and expensive. Third, the enormous amount of written record from the lengthy observations is very difficult to organize and interpret. Fourth, there is little safeguard against observer bias, other than observer training. Fifth, although the observer is theoretically nonjudgmental, the observer has to make constant decisions as to what to record and what to ignore among the array of simultaneous behavioral occurrences. Finally, with the recommended participant observation method, the observer becomes a member of the social structure being studied. Personal emotional involvement—where, for example, empathy may turn into sympathy—may reduce the validity of the data being collected.

The qualitative and quantitative approaches need not be mutually exclusive. Indeed, they can be mutually complementary. A thorough scientific investigation is generally divided into an exploratory (or formative) and a confirmatory (or summative) stage. In the exploratory stage, an investigator is interested in the formulation of hypotheses. For this stage of inquiry, qualitative techniques have certain decided advantages. Methods such as ethnography allow the investigator to gain in-depth insight and to formulate potentially meaningful and comprehensive hypotheses. In the confirmatory stage, an investigator is interested in gathering evidence to support hypotheses. For this stage, quantitative techniques allow for the gathering of objective evidence. Without qualitative exploratory observations, quantitative methods may lead only to superficial results that may be only tangential to the phenomenon under observation. Without quantitative confirmatory observations, qualitative methods may lead to little more than the investigator's personal view of the phenomenon.

A third approach that has gained some support among applied or clinical behavior analysts should be noted here. This approach, strongly advocated by such individuals as Donald Baer (e.g., Baer, 1977b; Parsonson & Baer, 1978), can best be categorized as being between the quantitative and the qualitative approaches. The quantitative techniques are applied, but conscious attempts are made to keep these techniques to the minimal level of sophistication. The basic principle of this approach is to keep measurement and statistical procedures intuitive and simple, avoiding "cooked" numbers that may be uncomprehensible to a clinician or practitioner. It has been argued that by keeping everything simple, applied behavioral studies will become a "people's science." Additionally, important variables may manifest themselves clearly even with simple quantitative analyses. Minute treatment effects that can only be detected through sophisticated and highly sensitive quantitative techniques are considered not salient and hence are not fundamental variables of interest.

We do not recommend this approach. Although it does not gain the advantages of either the qualitative or the quantitative approach, this approach contains the disadvantages of both. And although it may lead to a superficial understanding of a phenomenon, it does not, on the other hand, provide the rigorous quantitative evidence to be confirmatory. Observer biases and other errors in analysis may not be detected through such simplistic analyses.

THE APPLICATIONS OF BEHAVIORAL OBSERVATION METHODS

As a research tool, quantitative behavioral observation is widely used across a large number of disciplines. The earliest use of systematic direct behavioral observation methods is Darwin's study of human and animal emotions (Darwin, 1872). Systematic direct behavioral observation has been used in the vast majority of published studies in many behavioral journals (Kelly, 1977). Its application is particularly popular in psychology, biology, anthropology, medicine, and many social sciences (Martin & Bateson, 1986). More specifically, its application can be found in the literature in anthropology, behavior therapy, biology, business, child development, clinical psychology and psychiatry, comparative and cross-cultural psychology, ecology, education, entomology, ethology, experimental psychology, genetic psychology, guidance and counseling, neurophsiology, primatology, psychophysiology, social psychology and sociology, and special education. Table 1.1 identifies a few examples of the application of direct behavioral observation methods in each of these areas of scientific inquiry.

QUANTITATIVE BEHAVIORAL OBSERVATION AS A BODY OF KNOWLEDGE

Many have referred to systematic direct observation of human or animal behaviors as the *sine qua non* of science (cf. Ary, Jacobs & Razavieh, 1985;

TABLE 1.1
Examples of the Use of Direct Behavioral
Observation Methods in Various Disciplines

Discipline	Example
Anthropology	Whiting and Whiting (1973), Borgerhoff-Mulder and Caro (1985).
Behavior Therapy	Swan and McDonald (1978), Wade, Baker, and Hartmann (1979), papers in *The Behavior Therapist* and the *Journal of Applied Behavior Analysis*.
Biology	Davies (1982), Michener (1980), Chatfield and Lemon (1970), Altmann (1965).
Business	Brown, Solomon, and Stephen (1977).
Child Development	Cairns (1979), Lytton (1971), Mitchell (1979), Gelfand and Hartmann (1975), Arrington (1939, 1943), Brazelton (1973), Wright (1960), and papers in *Child Development*.
Clinical Psychology and Psychiatry	Fiske (1978), Cone and Foster (1981), Conners (1969), Hartmann and Wood (1982) papers in *Behavioral Assessment* and the *Journal of Psychopathology and Behavioral Assessment*.
Comparative and Cross-cultural Psychology	Longabaugh (1980).
Ecology	Krebs and Davies (1981), Dice (1945).
Education	Boyd and Devault (1966), Rosenshine and Furst (1973), Smith (1985), Flanders (1970), Hawkins, Axelrod, and Hall (1976), Herbert and At-tridge (1975), Frick and Semmel (1978).
Entomology	Symonds and Unwin (1982).
Ethology	Hutt and Hutt (1970), Martin and Bateson (1986), Sackett (1978), Aldrich-Blake (1970).
Experimental Psychology	Jones (1924), Watson and Raynor (1920).
Genetic Psychology	McDowell (1973), Sorosky et al. (1968).
Guidance and Counseling	Gottman, Markman, and Notarious (1977), Patterson and Maerov (1978), Raush (1972), Roberts and Renzaglia (1965), Tinsley and Weiss (1975).
Neurophysiology	Rosenthal and Rubin (1978), Aschoff (1981).
Primatology	Altmann (1974), Rhine and Flanigon (1978), Rhine and Linville (1980), Griffin and Adams (1983), Suen (1986a).
Psychophysiology	Johnson (1975).
Social Psychology and Sociology	Weick (1968), Fassnacht (1982), Bakeman and Dabbs (1976).
Special Education	Berk (1979), Francis (1966), Meier-Koll et al. (1977), Prehm (1966).

Gelfand & Hartmann, 1975). It has been hailed as the hallmark of applied behavior analysis (Ciminero, Calhoun & Adams, 1977) and as the greatest contribution of behavior modification to the treatment of human problems (Johnson & Bolstad, 1973). It has often been considered virtually bias free and axiomatically valid (Cone & Foster, 1982). Behavior observational data are often used as the yardstick against which the validity of data from other measurement procedures are judged.

However, in the past decade or so, it has become increasingly clear that the superiority of behavioral observation data over other means of inquiry cannot be axiomatically asssumed. Although observational data require a smaller inferential leap from data to reality, their validity is threatened by their own unique set of problems, such as observer obtrusiveness and subject reactivity. Although "seeing" may be "believing," different observers observing the same phenomenon may indeed "see" different things. Observational data are, in fact, not exempt from error, and questions concerning the quality of the data must be addressed. Many of these reliability and validity questions are the same as those that are addressed with other data.

A number of specific developments in observational methods in the past decade or two have challenged the assumption of superiority of observational data: First, it was found that some of the most popular time-sampling methods used in behavioral observation tend to produce inherently biased data. This has led to the rather disturbing question of the validity of the data of many of the earlier behavioral observation studies. Second, the most popular psychometric indicator of data reliability in behavioral observation—the percentage agreement index—has been discovered to tend to be spuriously inflated in value. This questions what the actual level of reliabilities were for many earlier studies. Third, since observations are generally made over time, the time dimension is a much more intimately relevant variable for behavioral observations than for other research methods. Matters are considerably complicated by the presence of the time dimension, in that much behavioral data collected from observations over time tend to contain a specific statistical characteristic known as autocorrelation or serial dependency. The existence of autocorrelation in a set of data renders most of the conventional statistical analytic techniques, commonly used in earlier observational studies, inappropriate for data analysis. This questions the appropriateness of the conclusions of some of the earlier studies.

In earlier years, single, or molecular, behavior observation has become the exception rather than the norm. Increasingly, more than one molecular behavior is observed in a study within a sophisticated scheme. For instance, a number of related molecular behaviors (e.g., hit, kick, pull hair, etc.) may be observed within a study to measure an overall molar behavior (e.g., violent aggression). In other situations, a single or a number of molecular behaviors are observed to reflect an abstract variable or construct. For example, the occurrences and nonoccurrences of eye contact, appropriate speech, and so on may be observed to assess a subject's "heterosexual social skills." The type and manner of speech between a husband and a wife may be observed to assess "marital discord." The body language as well as the speech of a subject may be observed as measures of "depression." With these types of observations, the object of measurement and inquiry is no longer the simple overt molecular behavior being observed. Rather, it is much less tangible. The earlier direct connection between the observed behavior and the object of inquiry no longer exists. Data validity cannot be automatically assumed.

With increased complexity in the object of measurement and in the sophistication of the observation process, as well as a number of fundamental psychometric and statistical developments, quantitative behavioral observation has evolved into a distinct body of knowledge. Many of the recent developments in quantitative observation methods have occurred in primatology and a specific field of methodological inquiry known as behavioral assessment. The term *behavioral assessment* was originally used to distinguish treatment-related assessment procedures in behavior therapy from "traditional" assessment procedures such as the projective Rorschach testing procedures. Most subsequent growth in behavioral assessment proved to have wider applications in the general area of behavioral observation across disciplines than originally intended.

OVERVIEW OF THE BOOK

In this book, we present the fundamental process as well as some of the more recent developments in quantitative behavioral observations, particularly as they relate to measurement and statistical issues of observational data.

In a scientific quantitative study, a researcher generally follows a number of specific and forever on-going steps. First, a theory is formulated to explain or predict some natural event or behavior. Next, based on this theory, a research hypothesis that specifies the relationships among the events and/or behaviors of interest, which are called variables, is postulated. This hypothesis may be generated through an in-depth ethnographic study, an "armchair speculation," or deduced from the collective knowledge gained from previous research. Next, a general scheme for data collection and variable manipulation, called research design, is selected. In behavioral observation studies, there are two primary designs: naturalistic observations (called *ex post facto* study in nonobservational jargon) in which behaviors are observed as they naturally occur and experiments (including variations such as quasi-experimental studies and single-subject studies) in which one or more variables are deliberately manipulated. After a research hypothesis has been formulated and a research design chosen, a sample of subjects from whom data are to be collected are selected. After data have been collected through procedures as prescribed in the research design, the quality of data is assessed through the appropriate reliability and validity procedures. Once the quality of data is ascertained, the data are analyzed through appropriate statistical procedures. A conclusion is drawn based on the results of the statistical analysis. The research hypothesis is either confirmed or not confirmed.

The formulation of an appropriate research hypothesis and the selection of a proper research design are primarily conceptual processes. The various conceptual and epistemological problems and cautions in hypothesis formulation and research design are outside the quantitative analytic focus of this book. Discussions of these issues can be found in numerous research texts (e.g., Ary, Jacobs, & Razavieh, 1985; Kerlinger, 1986) and many books on scientific epistemology. Campbell and Stanley (1966) wrote the classic text on research design. Martin and Bateson (1986) devoted one third of their book to the specific problems of hypothesis formulation and research design in behavioral observation.

We assume the reader has already generated a behavioral hypothesis and selected an appropriate research design. At this juncture, the reader is confronted with numerous decisions, which can be divided into two major types: data collection and data analysis. For data collection, the investigator has to select the appropriate sampling method in terms of what to observe, whom to observe, and when to observe. The sampling issues involved in "what to observe" are addressed in chapter 2. In chapter 3, the issues of subject sampling, or "whom to observe," are discussed; and in chapter 4, the issues of time sampling, or "when to observe," is addressed. Data collection is not complete until there is evidence that the data collected are reliable and valid. The methods for the assessment of the reliability and validity of behavioral observation data are discussed in chapters 5, 6, and 7. An array of statistical methods appropriate for the analysis of behavioral observation data exist. These can be divided into "classical" methods and time series methods. We assume that readers are familiar with classical statistical methods, which can be found in any introductory statistical texts. For those who have not utilized classical statistics for some time, we have provided a brief refresher in Appendix A. Chapters 8, 9, and 10 provide a survey of time series statistical methods.

CHAPTER 2
Behavior Sampling and Recording

"Would you tell me, please, which way I ought to go from here?"
"That depends a good deal on where you want to get to."

—Advice from Cheshire Cat to Alice in Lewis Carroll's
Alice's Adventures in Wonderland

Prior to the actual observation of behavior, three different aspects of observation must be determined. These aspects correspond to the answers to the questions what to observe, whom to observe, and when to observe. What to observe involves behavior sampling. Whom to observe involves subject sampling. And the question of when to observe is one of time sampling. In this chapter, we concentrate on the question of behavior sampling. Subject sampling and time sampling are discussed in chapters 3 and 4, respectively.

What behavior to observe is also closely related to the question of what physical tool needs to be used to aid the human senses and memory in the observation and recording of the behavior. The tool to be used is determined by the behavior or behaviors to be observed. This close relationship between target behavior and tool is most pronounced in the physical sciences. For example, if the target behavior is the movement of distant galaxies, minimally, an optical telescope would be needed. Similarly, if behaviors of a certain virus are to be observed, a powerful electronic microscope or a spectroscope would be needed.

The issue of target behavior selection is complex. Furthermore, mechanical and electronic aids available for observing and recording behavior rapidly become obsolete with the current advances in computer technologies. Unlike subject sampling, time sampling, and all the various issues, discussed in later chapters of this book, that have quantitative and statistical bases, behavior sampling or the determination of target behaviors and recording technology is primarily determined by conceptual, theoretical, and ethical considerations. Although nonquantitative in nature, the determination of target behavior and associated recording technology may actually determine the appropriate quantitative techniques for time sampling, reliability and validity assessment, and statistical data analysis.

BEHAVIOR SAMPLING

The first and most obvious question in an observational study is what overt behavior to observe. Any single human or animal subject will display countless behaviors, ranging from the most readily observable gross motor movements to behaviors not readily detectable, such as the release of adrenalin in fright. The potential repertoire of behaviors is further enlarged in observing the interactions among a number of subjects. In this situation, not only must the target behaviors for each subject be determined, but also the various combinations of behaviors across subjects as the potential targets of observation.

Research Question and Target Behaviors

The most obvious aid in selecting what to observe is the research question. It defines the general area of a subject's behavioral repertoire as the potential target area. For example, if the research question is concerned with a pupil's interaction with a teacher, obviously one would not observe the pupil's eating behavior at home. The research question helps define what *not* to observe. However, the number of potential behaviors to observe may remain substantial.

For basic research in which a researcher seeks answers to conceptual problems, the identification of target behaviors can be facilitated through a carefully delineated research question. For example, the question of "how well can a mouse run through a maze after 20 practices in a laboratory under normal lighting and room temperature" reduces the possible target behaviors to a small set of behaviors that may include the amount of time for the mouse to run through the maze, the number of times the mouse approaches a dead end, the amount of time spent at each intersection, and so on, under the specified conditions. The more precise the research question, the smaller the number of possible behaviors to observe.

For applied research or clinical evaluation of treatment outcome, the ability to focus on a very small set of potential target behaviors is severely limited. One of the major complexities of defining target behaviors in applied and clinical situations is the difficulty in defining a research question that is clearly related to the presenting problem. For example, a male client who complains that he has consistently failed to maintain a relationship with a female may lead a clinician to hypothesize that the problem is a lack of heterosexual communication skills. From this, the clinician would then observe such behaviors as eye contact, voice volume, and physical gestures of the client in heterosexual social interaction. The connection between the target behaviors such as eye contact and the original complaint of failure to maintain a relationship is a hypothetical one, bridged through the intermediate hypothesis that the actual problem is one of communication. This intermediate hypothesis may in fact be an erroneous one, and the target behaviors chosen may not be related to the presenting problem at all.

The selection of target behaviors for observation in applied or clinical situations can be viewed as a continuous process (Kanfer, 1985). A presenting problem is converted into a research (or measurement) question. Based on this research question as well as other considerations, a number of target behaviors are selected. A treatment program is designed to change these target behaviors. If evidence indicating that the target behaviors are in fact not related to the presenting problem emerges during the treatment program, then the research question needs to be reformulated, a new set of target behaviors identified, and the treatment program altered to fit the new target behaviors.

Otherwise, the original target behaviors are observed prior to and after treatment to determine any change of these behaviors. If the target behaviors are indeed related to the presenting problem, change of these behaviors in the desired direction should eliminate the problem. If the observational data show evidence that the selected target behaviors have changed and yet the presenting problem persists, it is indicative of the inappropriateness of the selected target behavior. At this point, the research question must be reformulated and a new set of target behaviors selected. Because we can never be certain that a selected set of target behaviors is indeed the cause of, or even simply related to, the presenting problem, we can never be certain that the selected target behaviors are appropriate until the presenting problem is eliminated through treatment.

Single Versus Multiple Behaviors

After certain behaviors have been eliminated as potential target behaviors through an examination of the research question, there may still be many possible behaviors to observe. For effective observation, these need to be reduced to a manageable number of behaviors. There are at least two approaches to the selection of the final set of behaviors. The first approach is to concentrate on a single most salient behavior as the target of observation. More recent researchers tend to favor a second approach that suggests that an interrelated "constellation" of behaviors should be observed simultaneously.

The former approach, sometimes referred to as the monosymptomatic approach (e.g., Evans, 1985; Lazarus, 1966; Meyer & Crisp, 1966), represents the conventional wisdom expounded by researchers with a strong orientation toward the operant conditioning paradigm. It attempts to identify the single most salient behavioral manifestation of the variable as the best representation of the variable. The behavior identified is the target for observation, and inferences are made from it to the variable.

Alternatively, the single most salient target behavior selected does not just represent a variable in observable terms; rather, it *defines* the variable. This is closely analogous to defining intelligence as "whatever is being measured by an IQ test," rather than questioning whether an intelligence test in fact measures the abstract underlying construct called intelligence. In other words, instead of defining a variable and then attempting to identify its overt manifestations for observation, the variable is defined based on what is observable. In many situations, this single behavior approach is quite sufficient and appropriate. For instance, to treat alcoholism, we may decide not to attempt to identify possible underlying causes such as depression and seek to alter these causes. Rather, we observe the drinking behavior and attempt to alter that behavior only. This approach can be summarized by Eysenck's (1960) statement: "get rid of the symptom and you have eliminated neurosis."

The single target behavior approach, whether as a symptom or a variable by itself, has the decided advantages of a clear focus and a relatively uncomplicated statistical measurement and analysis process. It lends itself to a relatively clear experimental treatment because the treatment is designed to change only one behavior, and the validity of the experimental outcome is better confirmed. If the variable of interest for a study is defined as a specific target behavior, or if the variable of interest can be appropriately represented by a single behavior, the observation of the single target behavior is adequate and efficient. For example, to test the effectiveness of a treatment for drooling, the observation of drooling as the single target behavior is adequate.

However, if the variable of interest is a complex one for which a single selected target behavior is only one of the many possible manifestations, the use of a single target behavior is inadequate. A complex variable may be one or various combinations of three different types of variables. The first type is sometimes referred to as a *composite behavior*, whereas the second and third types are sometimes referred to as *syndromes*.

With a composite behavior, a variable may have many parallel behavioral manifestations, none of which can singly define the variable. However, collectively all the behavioral manifestations do completely define the variable. A medical analogy for this type of variable is the common cold, which manifests itself in a number of simultaneous symptoms. Eliminating any single symptom is insufficient to eliminate the cold. However, when all symptoms are eliminated, the common cold is "cured." A behavioral example of this type of variable is "compliance in the classroom." Compliance or noncompliance in the classroom takes on many behavioral forms for each subject, and the behavioral forms are different from subject to subject. Changing one particular noncompliant behavior of a subject does not necessarily change other noncompliant behaviors of the same subject in the classroom. However, when all forms of noncompliance in the classroom for a subject are changed, the variable "compliance in the classroom" is changed from noncompliance to compliance. The type of complex variables exemplified by compliance in the classroom is a collective variable that conveniently summarizes a number of behaviors of similar nature. The variable is defined as the sum of all the behaviors.

A different type of complex variable is one that is more profound and manifests itself, among other things, in a variety of overt behaviors. These syndromatic behaviors, however, are only partial manifestations, in that the sum of these behaviors does not define the variable. Collectively, these behaviors form a syndrome that reflects but does not define the variable. A medical analogy for this type of variable is the contraction of certain venereal diseases, such as herpes and gonorrhea, which manifest themselves in a variety of symptoms. Elimination of these symptoms, however, does not indicate the elimination of the disease. For a behavioral example, if one wishes to assess the amount of "self-control" among prison inmates, the frequency of violent behaviors is only one of the many symptoms. Even if all such symptoms are identified and eliminated, it does not conclusively indicate the existence of self-control.

Another example is "marital concord versus marital discord." This variable manifests itself in a large variety of behaviors. The frequency of situations in which a spouse laughs, raises voice, clarifies, disagrees, is sarcastic, mimics, and so on during a conversation between a couple are some of the verbal behavioral signs of the variable. However, these signs may only be partial indicators of marital concord or discord. For this type of variable, it is important to identify the constellation of behavioral manifestations of the variable (Kazdin, 1985). The final selected behaviors should be representative of the overall constellation.

In applied or clinical situations, a third type of complex variable may occur. In these situations, a client may complain to a clinician about a number of simultaneous problems. The clinician may determine that the problems are interrelated. For example, Evans (1985) presented the following hypothetical example, which is dramatic but not unrealistic: A client complained of depression, social anxiety, poor child behavior management, and tension headaches. The therapist examined the situation and determined that the severe tension headaches were related to the disruptive behavior of the child. These headaches in turn limited the client's ability to manage the behavior of the child. These headaches also led to nonparticipation in social activities, leading to social anxiety. The social anxiety led to a lack of social contacts and opportunities to establish friendships, which led to loneliness and depression. Finally, the depression further limited the ability to control the behavior of the child, which in turn further compounded the problems.

If the original problems are viewed as four separate problems, we would have to postulate at least four variables and identify a number of target behaviors for each of the variables. However, if the interrelatedness of the problems can be hypothesized, the four problems become elements of a network of events with a clear sequence. The most effective point of intervention can then be determined. The selection of a target behavior is then much simplified because we can concentrate on the behavioral manifestations of a single point in the sequence of events. In the previous example, it may be postulated that the management of the behavior of the child may be the critical point of the sequence. The necessary treatment for the client may then constitute a training program on behavioral management principles and techniques, as well as assistance in reducing the disruptive behavior of the child. Under this scenario, behavioral manifestations of other problems such as depression and social anxiety can be temporarily ignored.

Selecting a few target behaviors at strategic points of an interrelated system of behavioral problems has the advantage of efficiency. However, there is also considerable risk that the hypothesized causal linkage among the behavioral problems may not exist. The a priori postulation of the interrelatedness of a number of presenting problems is subjective and judgmental. Yet the appropriate selection of target behavior hinges upon the accuracy of the judgment. As an objective basis for the postulated relationships, Kazdin (1985) suggested the initial observation of a large variety of potentially related behaviors and empirical evaluation of the existence and nature of the covariations among the behaviors. Through such a process, we can obtain an objective basis for the identification of the key target behaviors. The additional advantage of this approach is the ability to identify negative changes in other behaviors as a result of a possible change in a particular target behavior. For instance, Becker, Turner, and Sajwaj (1978) found that although a decrease in ruminative vomiting of a young girl led to desirable changes in a number of other behaviors such as a decrease in crying and an increase in smiling and social interaction, it led at the same time to an increase in stereotypic behaviors and head-slapping.

The issue of whether the selected target behavior or behaviors constitute the variable of interest by themselves or are manifestations of an underlying variable has important implications for the assessment of the validity of behavioral data. These implications are discussed in detail in chapter 7 on the validity of behavioral observation data.

Dimensions of Behavior

For quantitative observations of behavior, it is not sufficient to identify the target behaviors. Along the time continuum, a behavior exists in a number of either mutually independent or dependent dimensions. For a particular target behavior, some dimensions may be more appropriate measures than others. Therefore, it is important to identify the dimensions to be observed in the target behaviors.

Definitions

Because behavioral observation methods are used in a multitude of scientific disciplines, the fundamental dimensions and their numerous mathematical combinations and derivations have been described in a large overlapping and confusing body of terminologies. Depending on the discipline, quantitative behavioral dimensions have been expressed through duration of occurrence, duration of nonoccurrence, prevalence of occurrence, prevalence of nonoccurrence, frequency of occurrence, frequency of nonoccurrence, pattern, incidence, rate, relative frequency, mean bout duration, mean interresponse time, and so on.

Despite this confusing array of behavioral quantities, there are only three fundamental dimensions of behavior. Other measures of behavioral quantities are derived from ratios of various combinations of these three quantitative dimensions and time. These three fundamental quantitative dimensions are duration, frequency, and pattern.

Observations of occurrences and nonoccurrences of a target behavior are recorded over a specific period of time. The specific time span during which observations are made is called the observation *session. Duration* (or duration of occurrence) is the total amount of time occupied by the occurrences of the target behavior within the observation session. *Frequency* (or frequency of occurrence or incidence) is the number of times the target behavior occurs within the session. A more precise definition of frequency is the number of times the target behavior is *initiated* by the subject within the session. *Pattern* is the trend of behavioral occurrences and nonoccurrences over time.

A *bout* is a single occurrence of the behavior, starting at the initiation of the behavior and ending at the termination of the behavior. A *bout duration* is the amount of time occupied by a bout. Hence, duration (or session duration) can also be defined as the sum of all bout duration times in a session. Frequency is the total number of bouts in a session. On the other side of the coin, duration and frequency may also be expressed in terms of nonoccurrences. An *interresponse time* is the amount of time from the termination of a bout to the initiation of the next bout. The duration of nonoccurrence is then the sum of all interresponse times within a session. The frequency of nonoccurrence is the total number of interresponse bouts.

Duration and frequency are basic dimensions that describe the quantitative nature of a behavior within an observation session. However, for the purpose of comparison across sessions, subjects, or groups of subjects, they are rather inconvenient expressions of the quantity of behavior. This is because the absolute quantitative values of duration and frequency are influenced by the length of the observation session. Two subjects with the same quantities of behavior will show different durations and frequencies if the length of the observation session for each subject is different. For example, let us say that both subjects display the behavior every 10 minutes and each bout lasts 3 minutes. Subject A is observed for 30 minutes and Subject B is observed for an hour. The results of the observations will show that Subject A has a duration of 9 minutes and a frequency of 3 (i.e., behavior occurred 3 times each time lasting 3 minutes in a 30-minute session) whereas Subject B has a duration of 18 minutes and a frequency of 6 (i.e., behavior occurred 6 times each time lasting 3 minutes in a 60-minute session). The difference is not due to a difference in the corresponding quantities of behavior; rather, it is due to the difference in the length of the observation sessions.

Hence, it is often more convenient for comparison and statistical analyses if duration and frequency are expressed in standardized units. These two dimensions can be standardized on a specified observation session length. To standardize duration, we can first convert both the duration and the observation session length to the same unit of time (i.e., days, hours, minutes, or seconds). A standardized duration can then be obtained by dividing duration by session length. This becomes the proportion of time in which the behavior occurs. To facilitate interpretation, we can further multiply this proportion by 100%, yielding the percentage of time the behavior occurs. This standardized duration has often been referred to as *prevalence, relative duration,* or simply *duration.* The term *prevalence* seems to capture the proportional nature of this measure. The term *duration* leads to confusion about whether it refers to the absolute total length of occurrences or to the relative standardized duration. For these reasons, *duration* is only used in this book to refer to the absolute total length of behavioral occurrences. *Prevalence* is used to refer to the relative standardized duration.

To standardize the frequency measure, we first select a meaningful standard unit of time. The observation session can then be converted to the standard units of time. Dividing frequency by the standardized observation session would yield a relative frequency per standard unit of time (e.g., 14 occurrences per hour, 2 occurrences per minute, etc.). This standardized frequency is *relative frequency*, or *rate*. The term *rate* appears to capture the element of time in the measure more effectively. Therefore, *rate* is used in all subsequent discussions.

Duration of nonoccurrence and frequency of nonoccurrence can be standardized through identical processes. The results are then prevalence of nonoccurrence and rate of nonoccurrence. The behavioral quantities may also be expressed in terms of *mean bout duration* and *mean interresponse time*. Mean bout duration is the average length of a bout, and mean interresponse time is the average length of time in which there is a continuous nonoccurrence of behavior. Mean bout duration is assessed by dividing session duration by frequency. Mean interresponse time is obtained by dividing duration of nonoccurrence by frequency.

The exact mathematical computations of all these measures of behavioral dimensions is shown in chapter 4, which discusses time sampling. Depending on the target behavior selected, one dimension may be more appropriate than others. For example, if the target behavior is the attention span of a child, mean bout duration of attention may be more appropriate than either prevalence or frequency of attention. If the target behavior is cigarette smoking for a smoking cessation program, frequency may be more important than duration. If one wishes to observe the grooming behavior between two chimpanzees as a sign of affection, both duration and frequency expressed in the forms of mean bout duration and rate may be important. Hence, it is insufficient to identify the target behavior or behaviors. We also need to identify the appropriate dimension or dimensions for each target behavior.

Levels of Generality

A target behavior may be operationally defined at various levels of generality or exactness. For example, we may define a variable called "friendliness" through a vaguely defined target behavior, "friendly gesture," or a more exact target behavior, "smiles," or even a very precise behavior, "the simultaneous contraction of the zygomaticus and caninus muscles resulting in the uplifting of the two lateral ends of the lips." The level of generality of a selected target behavior has no direct bearing on the appropriateness of a behavior as a manifestation of a variable or as the variable. However, a very general behavioral definition requires much interpretation and inference on the part of the observer during actual behavioral observation. These uncertainties of observer interpretation and inference pose threats to the quality of the data. In general, the more exact the definition of a target behavior, the better the quality of observational data. However, the use of extremely specific and detailed behavioral definitions requires extensive observer training.

RECORDING METHODS

After a set of target behaviors has been identified and an appropriate amount of observer training has been provided, we can proceed to actual observations of the behaviors. To facilitate subsequent data analyses, it is essential that a record of the behaviors be kept. Coding systems reduce the task of an observer to either assigning the behavioral occurrences to categories or assigning a numerical value to each behavioral occurrence.

If it has been determined that the variable of interest either is a single target behavior or can be adequately represented by a single target behavior, the recording of the data is relatively simple. If the study involves only a single subject, we may observe the occurrences and nonoccurrences of the behavior and record the clock times at which the target behavior is intiated and terminated. This method is called *real-time recording*. Alternatively, if frequency is the dimension of interest, the number of times the behavior is initiated is counted. This method is called *frequency tally*. We may also divide the observation sessions into smaller intervals of equal length and assign either a score of 1 to an interval to represent occurrence of behavior or a score of 0 to the interval to represent the nonoccurrence of behavior. This method is known as *time sampling*. The nature, variations, advantages, and disadvantages of real-time recording, frequency tally, and time sampling are discussed in detail in chapter 4. The choice of recording method may determine the quality of the observational data.

When a study involves the same single target behavior for a number of subjects, the real-time recording method may be extended to accommodate multiple subjects. All subjects are observed simultaneously, and initiation and termination times of each behavioral bout of each subject are recorded. The important consideration in this case is to keep the record for each individual subject separately by either recording the times for each subject in separate columns (or rows) or on separate sheets of paper.

It is often impossible to simultaneously observe multiple subjects through real-time recording because of time pressure. Many tasks need to be performed by an observer within a short period of time. In these situations, it is more practical to use a *multiple-subject time-sampling* method. With multiple-subject time sampling, the observation session is divided into equal intervals of time. The occurrences and nonoccurrences of the behavior can be recorded either with a contiguous method, a sequential method, or an alternating method. These methods are discussed in detail in chapter 4. These three multiple-subject time-sampling methods are variations of recording the behavior of each subject in turn from interval to interval. There is no clear frequency tally method for multiple subjects. If frequency is the dimension of interest, one of the multiple-subject time-sampling methods may be used and an estimate of frequency for each subject extracted from the time-sampling data.

When more than one target behavior is involved, a variety of recording methods is available. Depending on the complexity of the target behaviors, the number of subjects observed, the extent to which the target behaviors are interrelated, and the interest in the interaction between subjects, appropriate recording methods may range from relatively simple to highly complex. Methods for recording multiple-target behaviors can be broadly categorized into either rating scales or those that are based on a time-sampling structure.

Time–Sampling–Based Methods

For single-subject, multiple-behavior observations, direct conversions of the multiple-subject, single-behavior recording methods can be used. For real-time recording, instead of recording the initiation and termination times of a behavior for each subject, record the initiation and termination times of each behavior for a single subject. For time sampling, concentrate on one of the behaviors of the subject in turn from interval to interval and record its occurrence or nonoccurrence accordingly.

For multiple-subject, multiple-behavior situations, the recording of a code of 1 or 0 in time sampling is no longer adequate. Instead, assign a unique and simple code to represent the occurrence of each behavior of interest. The subjects are then observed in a manner similar to the multiple-subject, single-behavior time-sampling scheme. That is, concentrate on one subject per interval in turn. Then either record all the target behaviors that occur within that interval for that subject by recording corresponding codes or record the single major ongoing behavior that is most representative of the behavior of the subject during that interval by recording the corresponding code. For example, if the interest is in the "reading," "writing," "listening," and "speaking" behaviors of a number of children in a classroom, use the symbol R to represent read, W to represent write, L to represent listen, and S to represent speak. The first subject is observed during the first interval. During this interval, the subject listened and spoke. Record the codes L1 and S1 for the interval representing listen and speak for subject one. In the second interval, attention is turned to the second subject, who was observed to be engaged in reading only. Consequently, the second interval is coded R2. The process is repeated for each subject. When all subjects have been observed for one interval, attention is returned to the first subject.

For a multiple-subject, multiple-behavior situation in which the interactions across subjects are of interest, or for a single-subject, multiple-behavior situation in which the relationships among the behaviors are of interest, it is important that all occurrences of all potentially interactive or related behaviors be recorded for all subjects in the multiple-subject situation or for the subject in the single-subject situation. Hence, all the target behaviors of the individual subject or all the subjects are observed simultaneously and the occurrence of each behavior for each subject is recorded interval by interval. The key in this situation is that if behavioral occurrences are omitted due to the use of simpler time-sampling schemes in which only one subject or one behavior is observed per interval, relationships between the behaviors within or across subjects may not be evidenced. These relationships may include a temporal sequence of behaviors between two subjects, such as "mother praises" is followed by "child smiles," or a covariation of behaviors, such as when "subject watches TV" is generally accompanied by "subject rocks." Due to the limitation of time within an interval, the simultaneous observation of a large number of behaviors for a large number of subjects without some type of electronic aid is difficult. Without access to an electronic aid such as a videorecorder, this method is appropriate only for the recording of a small number of behaviors of a small number of subjects.

To illustrate, one may use $B+$ to represent "brother makes positive statement," BO to represent "brother does not speak," $B-$ for "brother makes negative statement," $S+$ for "sister makes positive statement," and so on. For each interval, the speech of both brother and sister are observed and recorded. For instance, if brother made a negative statement and sister did not speak in the first interval, the codes B-, SO are assigned to the first interval. If brother did not speak and sister made a positive statement in the second interval, the codes BO, S+ are assigned to the second interval, and so on.

There are different variations of the above basic scheme for the recording of related behaviors. For instance, Haynes (1978) suggested an approach in which the sequence of behaviors within each interval are recorded. In his example, a code of $CTAN$ is used to represent "child has a tantrum," $C-$ to represent "child makes negative physical contact," $M+$ to represent "mother praises," and M- to represent "mother makes negative physical contact." If, within an interval, the child has a tantrum that is immediately followed by a negative physical contact by the mother that is in turn followed by a negative physical contact by the child, and finally followed by a praise by the mother, the interval would be coded CTAN, M-, C-, M + ."

There are many established behavioral observation coding systems for a variety of types of target behaviors. These range from coding systems for mother–child interaction to those for classroom behavior of hyperactive children to those for marital interaction to those for the assessment of anxiety during speeches. Haynes (1978, pp. 119–120, Table 4.2) provided an extensive inventory of some of these standard coding systems.

Another variation of the time-sampling scheme is a recording method known as the *interaction matrix*, which is also referred to as the *response-class matrix* (Mash, Tedral, & Anderson, 1973). In an interaction matrix, sequential interaction between two subjects is of interest. Specifically, the reaction, or response-consequence, of the second subject to various behaviors of the first subject is the focus. The behavior categories of the first subject are cross-tabulated with the reaction categories of the second subject to form a matrix. Table 2.1 provides an example of an interaction matrix. In this example, the child's behaviors of "laugh," "play," and "cry" are cross-tabulated with the mother's reactions of "smile," "ignore," and "attend." The child's behavior and the mother's reactions are observed simultaneously within each interval. For each interval, the interval number is recorded in the cell corresponding to the child's behavior and the mother's reaction, which are representative of the actual combination of behavior and reaction. For the example in Table 2.1, the child cried and was ignored by the mother in Interval 1. Hence, 1 was entered in the cell corresponding to cry and ignore. In Interval 7, however, the child laughed and was followed by the mother's smile. Thus, 7 was entered in the cell corresponding to laugh and smile. The limitation of the interaction matrix method is that it is applicable only to interactions that consist of only a two-event sequence—behavior and reaction.

Another time–sampling–based recording of interaction is the *interaction analysis categories system* developed by Flanders (1970) for analyzing teacher–pupil interactions. Unlike the response-class matrix in which the behavior of one subject constitutes one dimension and the reaction of the

TABLE 2.1
An Interaction Matrix

		Mother's Response		
		Smile	Attend	Ignore
Child's Action	Laugh	7, 10, 11, 21	3, 22, 23	9, 24, 28, 29, 30
	Play	4, 5, 12, 20	14, 15	6, 8, 25, 26, 27
	Cry	13	2, 18, 19	1, 16, 17

other subject constitutes that other dimension of the matrix, in the inter-action analysis categories system the behavior of both subjects at each interval constitutes one dimension and the behavior of both subjects at the following interval constitutes the other dimension. Within each cell in this matrix, the number of times a particular behavior of a subject is followed by either a particular behavior of the other subject or the same behavior or different behavior of the same subject is indicated. To apply this recording system, it is thus important that all the target behaviors selected for both subjects be mutually exclusive within and across subjects. That is, if Behaviors A, B, and C of Subject 1 and Behaviors X, Y, and Z of Subject 2 are to be recorded in this system, it is necessary that when Behavior A of Subject 1 is occurring, neither behaviors B and C for Subject 1 nor behaviors X, Y, and Z for Subject 2 can be occurring.

With Flanders' system, the behaviors of both subjects are observed simultaneously within a time-sampling structure. Within each interval, the most dominant behavior is coded. The matrix is then constructed based on the code for each interval as one dimension and the code for the immediately following interval as the other dimension. For example, to record the behaviors of a teacher and a pupil, 10 mutually exclusive and exhaustive behaviors of either the teacher or the pupil can be coded through a numeric system, as shown in Table 2.2. The behaviors of the teacher and the pupil and then observed interval by interval. At each interval, the single number representing the predominant behavior is recorded. For instance, if Interval 3 is dominated by the teacher lecturing, the score for Interval 3 is 5. The result of this time-sampling process is a sequence of numeric codes representing the predominant behavior at each interval. For example, the chain of codes may appear as:

5, 5, 5, 4, 8, 2, 9, 3,. . . . ., 6, 10, 7.

The value for each interval is then cast on a 10×10 matrix based on the value of the following interval. Figure 2.1 presents a resulting matrix in Garrett's (1972) study using the coding system in Table 2.2. In this matrix, the column totals show how often each behavior was observed, and each cell shows how often a behavior is preceded or followed by any other behavior. For example, Figure 2.1 reveals that in the 8,367-interval observation session, "pupil talk—response," coded 8, was the most prevalent behavior (2,375 intervals); that in 1,365 intervals, it followed another interval of pupil talk—response; in 800 intervals it followed an interval of "teacher response—asks questions" coded 4; and in 207 instances it preceded "teacher talk—praises or encourages" coded 2.

An important advantage of the Flanders' system over the response-class matrix or Haynes' system is that the Flanders' system lends itself directly

TABLE 2.2
Flander's Interaction Analysis Categories (FIAC)

TEACHER TALK:	
	1.★ *Accepts feeling:* accepts and clarifies an attitude or the feeling tone of a pupil in a nonthreatening manner. Feelings may be positive or negative. Predicting and recalling feelings are included.
	2.★ *Praises or encourages:* praises or encourages pupil action or behavior. Tells jokes that release tension, but not at the expense of another individual; nodding head or saying "Um hm?" or "go on" are included.
Response	3.★ *Accepts or uses ideas of pupils:* clarifies, builds, or develops ideas suggested by a pupil. Teacher extensions of pupil ideas are included, but, as the teacher brings more of his own ideas into play, they shift to category 5.
	4.★ *Asks questions:* asks a question about content or procedure, based on teacher ideas, with the intent that a pupil will answer.
	5.★ *Lectures:* gives facts or opinions about content or procedures; expresses his own ideas, gives his own explanation, or cites an authority other than a pupil.
	6.★ *Gives directions:* gives directions, commands, or orders to which a pupil is expected to comply.
Inititation	7.★ *Criticizes or justifies authority:* makes statements intended to change pupil behavior from nonacceptable to acceptable pattern; bawls someone out; states why he is doing what he is doing; extreme self-reference.
PUPIL TALK:	
Response	8.★ *Pupil-talk—response:* talk by pupils in response to teacher. Teacher initiates the contact, solicits pupil statement, or structures the situation. Freedom to express own ideas is limited.
Initiation	9.★ *Pupil-talk—initiation:* talk by pupils that they initiate. They express their own ideas; initiate a new topic; have freedom to develop opinions and a line of thought, like asking thoughtful questions; go beyond the existing structure.
Silence	10.★ *Silence or confusion:* Pauses, short periods of silence, and periods of confusion in which communication cannot be understood by the observer.

to an informative statistical analysis technique known as the Markov Chain, which is discussed in detail in chapter 10. To use Markov Chain with data recorded through the response-class matrix or Haynes' system, data modifications are needed. The limitation of the Flanders' system is that it is applicable only when all the target behaviors of both subjects are exhaustive and mutually exclusive.

It should be noted that all time–sampling–based recording methods are fundamentally similar. Their differences are primarily in the format of

FOLLOWING BEHAVIOR

		1	2	3	4	5	6	7	8	9	10	
P	1											
R	2		44	29	227	78	30	5	17	28	8	
E	3		56	24	115	63	7	2	11	18	9	
C	4		2		280	44	24	15	800	251	34	
E	5		18	7	289	646	56	19	84	173	40	
D	6		4		48	42	74	8	52	46	19	
I	7		1		20	22	14	46	7	14	12	
N	8		207	203	229	165	39	14	1365	56	27	
G	9		130	41	118	239	33	20	5	846	180	
BEHAVIOR	10		4	1	54	33	16	7	34	180	69	Matrix Total
	Total		466	305	1450	1332	293	136	2375	1612	398	8367
	%		5.6	3.6	17.3	15.9	3.5	1.6	28.4	19.3	4.8	

FIGURE 2.1.   Example of Flanders' interaction matrix. From "Modification of the Scott Coefficient as an Observer Agreement Estimate for Marginal Form Observation Scale Data by C. S. Garrett, 1972, Occasional paper #6, Blooming-ton: Indiana University. Reprinted by permission.

recording and eventual interpretation of data rather than the data per se. As such, data obtained through these methods have statistical characteris-tics similar to those of a simple single-subject, single-behavior time sam-pling. Hence, they are susceptible to all the potential pitfalls, problems, and limitations of time-sampling data. These statistical problems and their solutions is discussed extensively in chapter 4.

Rating Scales

Instead of observing and recording the occurrences and nonoccurrences of each of a number of target behaviors, it is sometimes desirable to assign a value representing the magnitude of the occurrence of a single target behavior or of a group of target behaviors on a rating scale. In some situations, for instance, classifying a target behavior only in terms of the dichotomy of either occurrence or nonoccurrence may oversimplify the quantitative nature of the behavior. For example, categorizing a behavior as either an occurrence or a nonoccurrence of "awake" may oversimplify the behavior in that the data of 1 or 0 are not sensitive to the fine differentiations among "awake and alert," "awake," "dozing," and "asleep." To increase the sensitivity of the data, an observer may rate the behavior of a subject as belonging to one of these four categories. In other situations, when raters have been properly trained, it may be more efficient to rate the subject's behavior based on the rater's overall subjective evaluation of the occurrence/nonoccurrence of a number of target behaviors simultaneously. For example, Wallender et al. (1985) devised a 10-item rating scale for the assessment of social skills known as BRISS. With this scale, a rater assigns a value to each of the 10 items based on the rater's general impression, rather than using precise but tedious coding of 14 specific target behaviors. This rating scale was reported to be an effective alternative to observing and coding 14 separate target behaviors.

With few exceptions where other scaling techniques such as the Thurstone scaling technique are used (e.g., Farrell et al., 1985), most behavioral rating scales have been constructed based on a variation of the Likert summation scaling technique. A *Likert scale* is one in which a respondent is asked to express his or her feeling toward a statement by placing a mark on a multicategory scale ranging from "strongly agree" to "strongly disagree." A typical behavioral rating scale follows the same basic principle and is, hence, referred to as a *Likert-type scale*.

There are at least three slightly different variations of a Likert-type behavioral rating scale. These have been referred to as the category rating scale, the numerical rating scale, and the graphic rating scale (Kerlinger, 1973). In a category rating scale, the various degrees of a behavior are listed from one extreme to the other and a rater is asked to check one of the verbal expressions that can best describe the behavior. For example, a category rating scale item for the awake behavior discussed earlier may appear as follows:

Which of the following best describes the subject's behavior? (check one)

Awake and alert
Awake
Dozing
Asleep

In a numerical rating scale, a numerical value is added to each of the behavioral categories in the category scale. The advantage of the numerical rating scale over the category rating scale is the ability to use the data directly from the former for statistical analysis. The following is a numerical rating scale equivalence of the previous category rating scale:

> Which of the following best describes the subject's behavior? (check one)
>
> 3 Awake and alert
> 2 Awake
> 1 Dozing
> 0 Asleep

For a graphic rating scale, the categories of behaviors are expressed graphically with lines and bars. For example, the awake item may appear as follows:

    Awake and Alert   Awake   Dozing   Asleep

A rater is asked to place a mark at the location along the scale that best describes the exact behavior of the subject. Of the three types of rating scales, the graphic rating scale provides maximum clarity, retains the idea of the continuum between the two extremes, and leads to more precise data. For these reasons, it is the best of the three formats.

TOOLS TO COMPENSATE FOR HUMAN SENSORY INADEQUACY

The most basic tools for the direct observation of the target behaviors are the observers' eyes and ears. However, the human auditory and visual senses often are unreliable in the detection of certain overt behaviors. This lack of reliability can be remedied through a systematic program of observer training prior to actual observations.

Other behaviors, however, simply may not be directly observable by human observers. Perhaps because the occurrence of the behavior is beyond the human sensory range, such as attempting to count the frequency of wing flapping of a hummingbird in flight. Since each flapping of the wings takes less than $1/16$th of a second, which is the limit of the human visual capacity, the frequency is essentially unobservable by the unaided eyes of a human observer. The inability to observe may also be due to the fact that the target behavior, such as heartbeat of a subject, is inherently inaccessible to the senses of the observer. Finally, the occurrences and nonoccurrences of a target behavior, such as sexual arousal, may be hidden from the human observer due to social mores.

Another limitation of the sensory ability of a human observer is its inherently low threshold for information overload. When a large amount of target behaviors occurs rapidly within a short period of time, an observer may have difficulty detecting all the behaviors. For these and other situations, various mechanical, electrical, or electronic devices may be used either as extensions of the senses of the human observers or as tools to "stretch" time to avoid information overload.

Tools to Stretch Time

Among the recording methods, real-time recording provides the most precise and comprehensive information regarding behavior occurrences and nonoccurrences. However, because of observer information overload, the use of real-time recording can be extremely difficult, if not impossible, when there are many target behaviors, many subjects, or when behaviors are initiated and terminated very rapidly and frequently. For these situations, real-time recording can still be used with the aid of certain tools.

Two commonly used tools are audio- and videotape recorders. The speech or behaviors of the subjects can be recorded permanently on audio- or videotapes. The observer can play the tape over and over again at a later time, each time concentrating on a single behavior of a single subject. Hence, a real-time recording of the behavior can be reconstructed post hoc. In a sense, these audio- and videotapes are ways to stretch time so that the observer can observe the behaviors without the pressure of time and hence avoid information overload.

In another sense, time can also be stretched relatively. This is accomplished by so simplifying the recording tasks of an observer that minimal movements (or writing) are required of the observer. By simplifying the recording task, more time is available for the observer to observe and record other subjects or other behaviors, minimizing the problem of information overload. Tools for the simplification of observer tasks range from mechanical event recorders to portable multievent real-time microcomputer recorders. Hartmann and Wood (1982, Table 1) provided a comprehensive inventory of recording tools, ranging from simple standardized rating forms to electromechanical event recorders to audio-recording such as voice spectrometers to time-lapse photography. More recently, microcomputer softwares have been developed to convert microcomputers into sophisticated multievent real-time recorders (eg., Repp et al., 1985).

Tools to "Extend" Senses

Due to the advancement of technology, which has "extended" human senses beyond ordinary daily perceptions, many of the psychophysiolog-ical responses previously considered unobservable may now be considered overt observable behaviors. Various mechanical, electrical, or electronic tools have essentially increased our flexibility in the selection of appropriate target behaviors. To observe the variable "anxiety," for instance, we would not have to rely on relatively unreliable behavioral signs such as "nail bit-ing" or "fidgeting." Rather, we may use measures such as electromyog-raphy (EMG) to "observe" muscle tension. To further improve our observation of anxiety behaviors, we can observe nail biting and fidget-ing in addition to EMG. With the rapid change in technology, we can expect that a fast increasing number of psychophysiological behaviors will be added continuously to the list of observable behaviors.

The following are some of the more common and well-established tools for the "observation" of psychophysiological behaviors. Electroen-cephalography (EEG) has been used to observe brain activities in various situations, such as when dreaming (e.g., Johnson, 1975). Breathalyzer and urinalysis can be used to observe alcohol and drug intake. Plethysmogra-phy has been used to measure the change in penile circumference as a sign of sexual arousal (e.g., Davidson et al., 1981). Pupillometry, which meas-ures the dilation of the pupil, can be used as an indicator of general arousal. Electrocardiogram (EKG) as well as EMG can be used to observe such variables as anxiety, relaxation, and arousal.

CHAPTER 3
Subject Sampling and Assignment

Although this may seem a paradox, all exact science is dominated by the idea of approximation.

—Bertrand Russel

In the previous chapter, we discussed the various considerations in deciding which behavior to observe. In this chapter, we concentrate on the question of whom to observe. Depending on the design of a study, the subjects to be observed may be identified through subject sampling, subject assignment, or single-subject selection.

A scientific investigation may fall into one of three different categories of design. In the first design, data are collected simply for the description of the characteristics or the relationships among various characteristics for one or more populations. The purpose of most public opinion polls, for instance, is to obtain data from a sample that reflects the opinions of a larger population. Another example is to compare the behaviors of male teachers versus those of female teachers. A third example is to assess the relationship between achievement motivation and career success among employees in advertising firms. In general, for this type of study, an experimental treatment is not involved and subjects or variables are not manipulated. We simply gather data to reflect what is already out there. This type of study is generally described as an *ex post facto* study. For the purpose of an *ex post facto* study, the central consideration in subject selection is to draw a sample that is as representative as possible of the overall population.

A second category of design is called *experimental* group studies. In an experimental study, an investigator deliberately manipulates a particular variable or introduces a treatment to some of the subjects. The purpose of data collection is to gather information that assesses the effects of the treatment. In an experimental group design, subjects generally are divided into experimental and control groups. Subjects in the experimental group receive the particular treatment of interest; whereas subjects in the control group receive either no treatment or a different treatment. For an experimental design, in addition to the representativeness of the sample of subjects, the equivalence between the subjects in the experimental group and those in the control group prior to the introduction of the treatment is also of concern.

A third category of designs is called *single-subject* experiments. In a single-subject study, only one or very few subjects are involved. A treatment is given to the subject and the effects of the treatment are determined by comparing the behavior of the subject before and after the treatment or the behavior under treatment and not under treatment. With a single-subject study, the questions of subject representativeness and equivalence of experimental and control group assignments are irrelevant because only one subject is involved. Instead, the important consideration is how well the results of the treatment on the single subject can be generalized to other subjects with similar or even with different characteristics.

Depending on which research design is being used for a study, the method of subject selection will differ. With *ex post facto* studies, the central concern is how well the subjects selected represent a larger population. For these studies, *subject sampling* techniques are most appropriate. For an experimental study, the equivalence between subjects in the experimental and the control group is also of importance. For these studies, *subject assignment* techniques need to be considered. For a single-subject experiment, neither subject sampling nor subject assignment techniques are appropriate. Instead, procedures to ensure the generality of the subject selected are most appropriate.

SUBJECT SAMPLING

Subject sampling is most appropriate for an *ex post facto* study. However, it can also be used to identify an initial pool of subjects for an experimental study. Subject sampling is a process of selecting a small group of subjects from a larger group. The small group is called the sample, and the larger group is called the population. Data gathered from the sample is generalized to the population. When it is possible to observe the behavior of the entire population of interest, subject sampling is irrelevant. This occurs in the rare situation in which the population is identifiable, finite, and sufficiently small in number to include all subjects in the study. In these situations and whenever feasible, the entire population should be studied. For example, if there were only 20 of a certain severely endangered species of animal in existence and you did not wish to generalize the observed data to other species, the entire population of 20 should be observed if possible and sampling is not of concern. Additionally, the data reflect the parameters directly and inferential statistics become irrelevant.

Because the vast majority of *ex post facto* and experimental studies use sample data to infer to a larger population (i.e., from descriptive statistics to parameters), some investigators have failed to make a distinction between population and sample and have been over concerned about inferential statistics. For example, in a recent research seminar, a participant discussed a survey of the attitudes among certified professional secretaries in the United States regarding issues related to the certification examination. There was a known total of about 500 certified professional secretaries in the United States at that time, and the researcher planned to send the survey to all 500 secretaires. A question was raised as to which inferential statistic was appropriate for the analysis of the responses generated by the survey to "test for the significance of the findings." Given that the respondents would include all known certified professional secretaries in the nation, the attitudes of the entire population would be investigated. There would be no subject sampling involved. Hence, inferential statistics would not be needed.

Situations in which an investigator can study an entire population of interest are rare. This is especially true with behavioral observation. The cost and logistics of observing the behaviors of a known population of, say, 500 subjects individually are astronomic. Hence, it is almost always necessary to select only a few subjects as a sample of the larger population.

Identification of the Population

The first step in subject sampling is the identification of the population of interest. A population is all the members of a well-defined class of people, events, or objects that are the central focus of the investigation. A population may be very large or quite small in size. Frequently, the larger the population, the more resources are needed to study a sample of the population. The addition of qualifiers to the description of a population generally will reduce the size of the population. However, it also reduces the degree of generality of the final research outcome. For example, "all fifth grade students in the United States" is a very large population. On the other hand, "all fifth grade students in rural schools in the United States" is a much smaller population.

Although the size of the population is an important practical consideration, the definition of the population should be guided by the extent of generalization you wish to make from the sample data. The population to be studied should be the group of individuals to whom you wish to generalize the results of the study.

With most subject-sampling techniques, it is generally required that all subjects within the defined population be identifiable and listed. This is not always possible. In practice, samples are frequently drawn from a *sampling frame* instead of a population. A sampling frame, also referred to as an *accessible population*, is all the indentifiable and accessible members of the target population of a study. Although population refers to an abstract target of investigation and a sampling frame to the "population in practice," these two terms are frequently used interchangeably. This is because when a sampling frame is used, it is frequently treated as if it were the population. Technically, data for a sample drawn from a sampling frame can be generalized only to the sampling frame, not to the population. However, it is frequently assumed that a sampling frame is sufficiently similar to the population that sample data can be generalized first to the sampling frame and then to the population.

The distinction among population, sampling frame, and samples in behavioral observation is sometimes confusing; particularly in clinical situations. Most of the confusion arises from a lack of a clear delineation of the extent of generalization regarding a particular treatment procedure. For example, in some clinical situations, a "classroom" or a "family" has been defined as the population of the study (Haynes, 1978). In reality, this definition of population proved to be inappropriate in many of these studies, depending on the conclusion one wishes to draw from the study. For example, in the evaluation of a clinical treatment of marital discord for a particular family, the family may be considered the population only if the evaluator does not wish to generalize the effectiveness or ineffectiveness of the treatment procedures to other similar families. However, it is rare that such a generalization is not made. If we do not attempt to generalize treatment effectiveness beyond the family studied, then the practice of these clinical treatments would amount to a collection of ad hoc procedures without a generalized body of knowledge. However, when these results are generalized to other families, the family under study is no longer a "population" but a single-case cluster sample (discussed later in this chapter). In general, it is rare that a small social unit such as a classroom or a family can be the actual population to which a researcher wishes to generalize results of the study.

Once a population is defined and a sampling frame identified, a sample can be drawn. There are many different ways of drawing a sample from a sampling frame. Some are more rigorous and produce more representative samples than others. A researcher should strive to obtain the most rigorous form of sampling possible. Subject sampling can be categorized into probability sampling and nonprobability sampling. Of the two, probability sampling is more rigorous.

Probability Sampling

Probability sampling is a subject-selection process in which each subject in the sampling frame has a nonzero chance of being included in the sample. This form of sampling is generally assumed to yield an unbiased sample. Only when a sample is unbiased can inferential statistics accurately estimate the extent to which the descriptive statistics for the sample are different from the parameters of the population. There are a number of probability sampling methods. The most frequently used methods include simple random sampling, systematic sampling, stratified sampling, and cluster sampling. Within probability sampling methods, simple random sampling is the most rigorous. Additionally, the assumption of an unbiased sample is most closely approached through simple random sampling.

Simple Random Sampling

In simple random sampling, each subject within the sampling frame has an *equal* chance of being selected. This equal chance is accomplished through a total randomness of selection. Random selection means that there is no known explanation that can predict which subject will be selected from the sampling frame (Kemeny & Snell, 1960). The key difference between simple random sampling and other forms of probability sampling is that in simple random sampling, each subject has not only a nonzero probability of being selected, but this probability is the same for all subjects. Which subjects will be selected is totally governed by objective chance, with no human interference. Therefore, a simple random sample will not contain conscious or unconscious biases of the researcher.

A simple random sample can be drawn from a sampling frame in a number of ways. Regardless of the method used, the first step is to identify and list all the individuals in the sampling frame. Next, a different identification number, using consecutive numbers, is assigned to each individual on the list. For example, if the sampling frame contains 1,000 individuals, the numbers 000, 001, 002, 003, ..., 999 might be assigned to these individuals. When this is accomplished, a set of random numbers is selected through various methods. How many random numbers are to be selected is determined by the desired sample size. No random number chosen should exceed the highest number in the sampling frame list. Should that occur, the random number is discarded and the next random number drawn as its replacement. Similarly, a repeated random number is discarded and another random number chosen to replace the discarded number. Those individuals on the sampling frame list whose identification numbers match those of the final set of random numbers are then used as the sample.

There are numerous ways to produce a set of random numbers. The actual method to be used is limited only by the imagination and resources of the researcher. The appropriateness of the chosen method is determined by its ability to ensure that each number in the sampling frame has an equal chance of occurrence. The more common methods used include the use of a random number table, generating random numbers through a computer or a programmable calculator, drawing numbers from a hat (or a fishbowl, etc.), and drawing cards from a shuffled deck. Besides these common methods, various methods used in the selection of winning lottery numbers or in Bingo games can be equally or even more effective. Again, the key is to ensure that each number in the pool of sampling frame identification numbers has an equal chance of being selected.

Because, theoretically, each subject in the sampling frame has an equal chance of being selected, it is presumed that all population characteristics are represented by a simple random sample. However, the representativeness of the sample is not guaranteed. In general, the more homogeneous the population, the more likely it is that the simple random sample will be representative. Conversely, for a very heterogeneous population, it is less likely that all the population characteristics are represented by the sample.

Simple random sampling is the most rigorous of all probability sampling methods. Theoretically, the sample contains neither conscious nor unconscious biases. Furthermore, all of the inferential statistics that have been developed are based on the assumption that sample data are gathered through a simple random sampling process. When a sample is drawn through a simple random sampling process, the inferential statistical assessment of sample representativeness is most accurate. Therefore, when selecting a sample of subjects from a sampling frame, simple random sampling is the ideal process. Unfortunately, simple random sampling is not always feasible in practice. For example, one of the obstacles is the often impractical requirement of the enumeration of the entire sampling frame prior to random selection. Another problem is that when the population is known to be highly heterogeneous, or the size of the sample that can realistically be used is small, simple random sampling may not be the most appropriate approach.

When simple random sampling is not feasible, other probability sampling techniques are used. With other probability sampling, each subject in the sampling frame has a chance of being selected. However, the probabilities of being selected are not equal among subjects. Although inferential statistical techniques are based on the assumption that data are gathered through a simple random sampling process, the use of these statistics for data gathered through other probability sampling processes is justifiable in that the assumption of equal probability is approximated. Since most inferential statistical techniques are quite robust, the results are generally very close approximations of their actual values. A statistic is said to be robust when the consequences of violating its underlying assumptions regarding data and mathematical characteristics are negligible. There are three common probability sampling alternatives to simple random sampling. These are stratified sampling, cluster sampling, and systematic sampling.

Stratified Sampling

One of the situations in which simple random sampling may be undesirable is when the sampling frame consists of a number of subgroups and the researcher wishes to compare some variable across the different subgroups. Simple random sampling may, by chance, fail to select members from a particular subgroup, making the desired comparison impossible. For example, a college counselor may wish to compare the scores on a self-concept assessment instrument among white, black, Hispanic, Asian, and Native American students in the college. From the college student profile, it is known that Native American students consitute only 2% of the student population. If a sample of students were selected through the simple random process, it is quite likely that extremely few or no Native American students would be selected. This would make it quite difficult to compare the self-concept scores across the identified ethnic groups. Another example would be to compare certain behaviors between male and female nurses. In the United States, the proportion of male nurses is extremely small. A simple random of a sampling frame of nurses may not lead to any male subjects at all.

Even with a relatively homogeneous group, simple random sampling may still, by chance, produce an unrepresentative sample across an important variable. For example, in many populations, the proportions of male and female subjects are approximately equal. A small simple random sample from such a population may produce, by chance, a sample of 30% male and 70% female. Data regarding this sample would not be representative of the population along the gender variable.

An approach that increases the likelihood of obtaining a representative sample yet avoids missing an important subgroup is to draw a *stratified* sample. With stratified sampling, the sampling frame is first divided into subgroups based on a variable that is considered important. Subjects are then randomly drawn through the simple random sampling process within each subgroup. For example, in order to compare the behaviors between male and female nurses, the sampling frame of nurses would first be divided into two subgroups according to gender. A simple random sample of male and another simple random sample of female nurses could then be drawn from the two subgroups, respectively. In this manner, data for male nurses would be available for comparison.

An equal number of subjects may be drawn from each subgroup. In a study of nurses, for example, if it is desired to compare the two gender subgroups, it would be advantageous to draw an equal number of subjects from the male and the female nurse subgroups.

The number of subjects to be randomly selected from each subgroup may also be proportional to the known size of the subgroups. This procedure is known as *proportional stratified sampling*, or simply *proportional sampling*. If the purpose of a study is to produce a profile of the overall population and of the subgroups, draw a proportional stratified sample. For the college student example, to draw a sample of 200 students when the proportion of Native American students in the college population is 2%, randomly draw 4 students from the Native American student subgroup.

An advantage of proportional stratified sampling is that the condition for inferential statistics in which each subject has an *equal* chance of being selected is very closely approximated. However, if comparisons are made across subgroups, proportional stratified sampling may not produce enough subjects in certain subgroups for meaningful comparisons. Comparisons across subgroups with equal number of subjects selected are more meaningful. However, sampling an equal number of subjects for each subgroup also departs further from the idea of equal chance of selection.

Cluster Sampling

A pragmatic problem found with simple random sampling and stratified sampling is that both require all subjects in the sampling frame to be identified and enumerated. This requirement is often impractical. For example, the sampling frame of all university freshmen in the United States is so large that it would be very difficult, if not impossible, to list all members so that a sample could be drawn. Even if such a list could be constructed, the sample drawn from the sampling frame would consist of subjects scattered all over the nation. Collecting data from such a sample would be very difficult and inefficient. One solution to this practical problem is to use *cluster sampling*.

In cluster sampling, instead of individual subjects, naturally occurring clusters, or groups, of subjects are used as the basic units of sampling. For example, instead of identifying and listing all university freshmen in the United States, one may identify all universities in the United States. From the list of universities, a simple random sample of universities can then be drawn. All freshmen within each of the selected universities are then included in the sample. In this case, the universities are used as the naturally occurring clusters of freshmen. Instead of drawing a random sample of all university freshmen, we draw a random sample of clusters (universities).

It is generally recommended that once the sample of clusters are randomly selected, all subjects within each cluster should be included in the sample. However, the resulting sample size may still be too large for efficient data collection. For example, with a cluster sample of 20 universities from all universities in the United States, the total number of freshmen in the 20 universities may be as large as tens of thousands. In such a situation, a simple random sample can be drawn from each of the selected clusters.

The major advantage of cluster sampling is practical convenience. This advantage is gained at a sacrifice of representativeness. Since only a few clusters are selected, the sampling error is much greater than with either a simple random or a stratified sample with the same number of subjects. For example, if 100 subjects each are taken from 20 randomly selected universities, the 2,000 subjects would be much less likely to be representative of university students as a whole than would 2,000 students selected from a sample frame of all university students. With only 20 universities represented, the resulting sample could seriously over or under represent variables of affluence, religious belief, socioeconomic status, or other dimensions in which American universities systematically differ from one another.

Systematic Sampling

Another common probability sampling method is *systematic sampling*. Instead of drawing sample subjects randomly from the sampling frame, systematic sampling draws subjects at equal intervals along the list of subjects in the sampling frame.

Like simple random sampling, the first step in systematic sampling is to list all subjects in the sampling frame. From this list, obtain the sampling frame size (N). Next, decide how many subjects should be in the sample (sample size, n). The width of the interval (k) is then determined by dividing N by n (N/n). The first subject for the sample is randomly selected from the first k subjects on the sampling frame list. From this subject, proceed forward on the list, selecting every kth subject to be included in the sample.

For example, if a systematic sample of 100 subjects from a sampling frame of 1,000 is desired, the interval width (k) is N/n = 1,000/100 = 10. From the first 10 subjects on the sampling frame list, the 1st subject for the sample is randomly selected. Let us say the 7th subject happens to be selected among these 10 subjects. Then starting with the 7th subject, every 10th subject would be included in the sample. Hence, the 7th, the 17th, the 27th, the 37th . . . . and the 997th subject would constitute the sample.

For systematic sampling to yield results approximating those of simple random sampling, it is important that the initial list of sampling frame subjects be random. If subjects on the initial sampling frame list are arranged according to a certain order, pattern, or trend, a biased sample may result. For example, if 100 subjects were selected through systematic sampling from an alphabetically listed sampling frame of 10,000, only every 100th subject would be selected from the list. It is possible, in this case, that certain ethnic groups with characteristic surnames (e.g., Chinese names starting with "Ch") would be underrepresented or not represented at all. The most detrimental pattern in the initial sampling frame list is a cyclical pattern. Suppose the population consists of all married persons in a county and the sampling frame list is arranged in such a way that husbands and wives are listed consecutively. The list is thus cyclical in that all odd-numbered subjects are males (husbands) and all even-numbered subjects are females (wives). If the interval width for a systematic sample is an even number, then the sample is biased in that only one gender is included in the sample.

There are some situations in which a sampling frame list that is prearranged in a particular pattern may yield a representative sample. In these situations, the resulting sample is largely equivalent to a stratified sample (Babbie, 1973). An example of this is the listing of subjects by social security numbers. Since the first three digits of a social security number is indicative of the state in the United States in which the subject had initially obtained the social security number, systematic sampling from this list would yield a sample quite close to a proportional stratified sample in which the subjects are stratified by geographic origin. If the variable "geographic origin" happens to be the variable by which one wishes to stratify the sample, the systematic sample is not biased.

The major advantage of systematic sampling is convenience. This convenience may be particularly important to field investigators who are without immediate access to a random number table or random number generator. For record keeping and organization of information, a sample drawn systematically from a list is generally more manageable than a random sample from the same list. The major disadvantage is the uncertainty as to whether the sample contains systematic bias resulting from the initial sampling frame list being arranged in some pattern. To the extent that the initial sampling frame listing departs from being random, the systematic sample may not be representative of the population. If the initial list is deliberately arranged according to a particular variable by which one wishes to stratify a sample, a systematic sample from this list is equivalent to a stratified sample.

The various probability sampling methods just discussed are not mutually exclusive. Different sampling methods may be combined. Through these combinations, there are a number of variations in probability sampling methods. One variation, which has been discussed previously, is to use cluster sampling to select a number of clusters. Subjects are then selected from within each cluster through simple random sampling. In this variation, cluster sampling is combined with simple random sampling. Another variation is a stratified cluster sample in which clusters are first stratified according to a particular variable and then selected through a stratified sampling process. Another variation is a weighted disproportional sample. For this sample, a stratified sample is selected but the number of subjects in each stratum is not proportionate to the number in the population. Weights may be assigned to each stratum to ensure the overall representativeness of the sample. In subject sampling, the final sample may be derived through many stages of sampling. In this type of situation, one sampling method may be used in one stage and another in the next stage, and so on.

Nonprobability Sampling

Except for cluster sampling, the probability sampling procedures require that the entire sampling frame be identifiable. With cluster sampling, all the members of each selected cluster must be identifiable. Frequently, this requirement cannot realistically be met. In many situations, less rigorous forms of sampling methods are used. These methods are known as *nonprobability sampling*. With nonprobability sampling, not all members of the sampling frame have a nonzero chance of being selected. Some subjects in the sampling frame will have no chance of being selected.

Since some subjects in the sampling frame will never be selected in a nonprobability sampling process, the resulting sample is most likely to be biased in that it will not represent the population. Furthermore, since inferential statistics are developed with the assumption of a simple random sampling process and a nonprobability sample is a maximum departure from a simple random sample, therefore, inferential statistics will not be able to assess the possible sampling error with any meaningful degree of accuracy. Results from a nonprobability sample should always be interpreted with caution.

The more commonly used probability sampling methods include accidental sampling, purposive sampling, and quota sampling.

Accidental Sampling

Accidental sampling is the least rigorous of all sampling procedures. With accidental sampling, whichever subjects happen to be available comprise the sample. Many "sidewalk" interviews in which pedestrians who happen to be at a certain place at a certain time are interviewed are examples of accidental sampling. Other examples of accidental sampling include using as the sample the first 100 people in the telephone book who happen to answer the phone, interviewing the first 50 people encountered at a shopping mall who are willing to be interviewed, and using students in one's own classroom.

An accidental sample is quite likely to be biased. However, the degree and nature of the biases are usually unknown and cannot be assessed. Inferential statistics will not be able to assess the representativeness of the sample with any degree of accuracy. At best, the data obtained from an accidental sample can only be tentative and should be used only as a guide for possible directions to be taken in a more rigorous study. At worst, data from an accidental sample may be misleading. Accidental sampling, therefore, should be avoided if possible. When it has to be used, interpret the data from an accidental sample with extreme caution.

Purposive Sampling

With purposive sampling (also known as judgmental sampling), subjects are selected based on the researcher's knowledge of the population and on the nature of the research. The researcher uses subjects as the sample who are judged as "typical" or "representative" of the population of interest. This sampling method is most useful when many of the subjects in a sampling frame are identifiable but it is extremely difficult to identify and list all subjects in the sampling frame.

For example, a researcher wishes to observe the study habits of gifted students at a particular university. The researcher judges the students in a special honors program to be representative of these gifted students. Since the sampling frame of gifted students in the university cannot be identified, the researcher uses subjects in the honors program as a purposive sample of gifted students.

A common and more refined use of purposive sampling is found in political polls. Based on previous election results, a researcher identifies a group of voting precincts that, when combined, has produced results similar to those of the overall geographical area (city, state, or nation). Subjects are selected only from these precincts for the political poll. The assumption is that these precincts together form a representative sample of the larger population.

The crucial question in purposive sampling is whether the sample judged to be typical or representative is indeed typical and representative. If the researcher is not totally familiar with the characteristics of the population, the judgmental process in selecting the typical sample may amount to an educated guess at best or a wild guess at worst. A sample shown to be representative in the past, as in the case of the sample of precincts, may or may not continue to be representative of the population.

The general assumption is that errors in judgment are random and that they neutralize one another. For example, with the purposive sample of voting precincts, it is assumed that if a precinct has become more conservative than a typical precinct since last voting, another precinct would have become more liberal. The errors in being typical are hence assumed to be counterbalanced. This assumption is not always true. To the extent that this counterbalance assumption is violated, a purposive sample is biased.

Quota Sampling

The third type of nonprobability sampling is quota sampling. Quota sampling contains features of both stratified sampling and purposive sampling. In quota sampling, variables that are determined to be important to the research question are identified. These variables are typically demographic variables such as gender, socioeconomic status, ethnicity, age, and urban versus rural residency. Based on known characteristics of the population from such sources as the Census report, the sampling frame is divided into multiple "layers" of strata. The size of each stratum is determined by the proportion of that stratum in the population. For example, if, based on the most recent Census update, the proportion of subjects who are white, male, aged 65 or older, and residing in a rural area constitues 3% of the population, 3% is then the size for this stratum. Next, the desired sample size is determined. A quota for each stratum is derived from the desired sample size and the proportion of subjects for the stratum. With the example just given, for a sample of 500 subjects, the quota for subjects who are white, male, aged 65 or older, and residing in a rural area is 3% of 500, or 15 subjects. The final step in quota sampling is to find "typical" subjects to fill the quota for each stratum.

Except for the final step, quota sampling is quite similar to a multiple-stage stratified sampling process. The final step is, at best, similar to purposive sampling and, at worst, similar to accidental sampling. The justification for the final step is that when all "relevant" variables have been controlled through the comprehensive stratification process, the final sample will be representative of the population regardless of how each quota is filled. This justification is acceptable up to the point that all variables related to the behavior to be studied are identified and stratified accordingly. Too frequently, the stratification process is determined by available population information. Furthermore, the final step may amount to an accidental sampling process. Therefore, quota sampling, in practice, frequently leads to biased samples.

If probability sampling is not feasible, quota sampling in which the final step is a purposive sampling procedure is the most desirable nonprobability sampling process. The least desirable nonprobability sampling method is accidental sampling. The use of inferential statistics to assess sampling error and sample representativeness is inappropriate with either accidental or purposive sampling. For quota sampling, however, the use of inferential statistics may be justifiable to some extent. The results, however, are only estimates and would have to be interpreted with caution.

Sample Size, Population Heterogeneity, and Sampling Error

One of the questions frequently asked in behavioral research is how many subjects should be selected for a sample. Unfortunately, there is no single magical cutoff point between a sufficiently large sample and a sample that is too small. In general, the larger the sample size, the more accurately will the sample statistic represent the population parameter. In other words, the larger the sample, the smaller the expected amount of sampling error. Conceptually, sampling error can be considered to be the degree of uncertainty involved, assuming that the sample statistic will accurately represent the population parameter.

The relationship between sample size and sampling error is inverse and is nonlinear. For the same population, the theoretical reduction in sampling error for each unit increment in sample size diminishes as sample size increases. For example, the amount of sampling error reduced from increasing a sample from 30 to 50 subjects is substantially larger than that reduced from increasing a sample from 530 to 550. Figure 3.1 shows the relationship between sample size and sampling error with an infinitely large theoretical population. In this figure, the actual amount of sampling error for each sample size is deliberateley not indicated. This is because the actual error is determined by the degree of heterogeneity in the population as well. However, the exact trend of the reduction in sampling error as the sample size increases is the same regardless of the degree of heterogeneity. As shown, when the sample size is increased from 10 to 20, the reduction in sampling error is substantial. However, the reduction of sampling error when the sample size is increased from 410 to 420 is almost negligible.

The ability of a sample statistic to represent the population parameter is dependent not only on sample size but also on the degree of homogeneity of the population. If the population is homogeneous, a relatively small

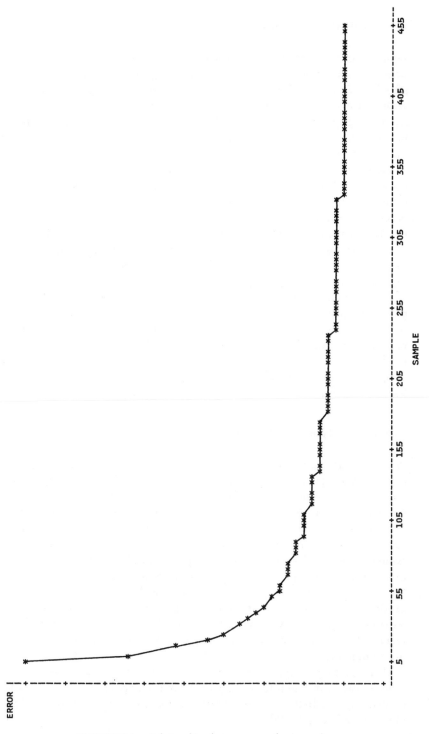

FIGURE 3.1. Relationships between sample size and error.

47

sample can yield accurate statistical representations of the population parameters. On the other hand, if the population is heterogeneous, a large sample would be needed to ensure accuracy of representation. For the same sample size, the relationship between sampling error and the heterogeneity of the population is direct and linear. That is, for each unit increment in population heterogeneity, there is a theoretically corresponding unit increment in sampling error.

Hence, in determining the appropriate sample size, a number of factors need to be taken into consideration. If it is suspected that the population is highly heterogeneous, the sample should be as large as possible. On the other hand, the larger the sample, the greater the cost and logistic difficulties. Increasing the sample size from a very small one to a moderately large one will be most cost effective. Adding subjects to a relatively large sample may not be cost effective at all. The final determination is judgmental. Figure 3.1 may aid this judgment.

The relationship among sample size, population heterogeneity, and sampling error just described exists only when the sample approximates a simple random sample. The further the sampling process departs from simple random sampling, the more uncertain is this relationship. When the sample departs from a simple random sample to such a degree that it contains sampling biases, the sample is not representative of the population regardless of sample size, and the amount of sampling error cannot be estimated.

Bias Due to Nonparticipation

When the subjects studied are human beings, no matter how carefully and rigorously a representative sample is selected from the population, there will always be some subjects who do not wish to participate in the study. Nonparticipation of subjects poses two problems to the representativeness of the data obtained from the remaining subjects. First, the sample size is reduced due to nonparticipation of some of the subjects. The smaller sample leads to a larger amount of random sampling error. Second and more seriously, nonparticipation is almost never a random phenomenon. We can reasonably assume that nonparticipants have some characteristics in common that cause them to not participate in the study. These characteristics are quite likely to be related to the characteristic being studied. Hence, the self-selection of nonpartcipating subjects renders the remaining sample biased.

If nonparticipation is a random phenomenon, the solution is simple. One simply draws additional subjects from the population to replace the nonparticipants. In this case, the desired sample size is maintained and sampling error is unaffected.

Unfortunately, nonparticipation is not likely to be random. There is no easy solution to the problem of sampling bias due to nonparticipation. The only "solution" is for the researcher to use every ethical means and incentive available to attempt to persuade or induce those who do not wish to participate to change their minds. Miller (1977) provided some tactics to maximize the participation rate of subjects in a survey research. Many of these tactics may be useful for behavioral observation with a little modification.

If the proportion of nonparticipants in a sample is relatively small, it may be reasonable to assume that the problem of a biased sample is not too severe. The results from the remaining sample may be interpreted with caution. If the proportion is large, evidence must be obtained that nonparticipants are essentially similar to participants before it can be assumed that the problem of a biased sample is not severe. One way to obtain evidence that participants and nonparticipants are relatively similar is to compare all available information regarding the participants and nonparticipants (e.g., demographic, geographic, education, etc.). If the difference between participants and nonparticipants on all available information is quite small, it is safe to assume that the problem is not severe and that the remaining sample reasonably represents the population.

SUBJECT ASSIGNMENT

With subject sampling, the main objective is to obtain a sample of subjects that is representative of a larger population so that data from the sample can be generalized to the larger population. When a study can be generalized from a small sample to a larger population, it is said to have external validity.

In an experimental study, in addition to external validity, one hopes to obtain evidence that a particular measured characteristic or change of behavior among the subjects in the study is not inherent within these subjects. Rather, it is related to the experimental treatment. To increase the likelihood that the measured characteristic or change *is* in fact due to the experimental treatment, steps are taken to remove threats to the internal validity of the study. An experiment is said to have internal validity when the observed subject characteristics or change is truly due to the experimental treatment and to nothing else. There are many possible threats to the internal validity of a study. Campbell and Stanley (1966) provided a comprehensive description of many of these threats.

One approach that tends to remove many of the threats to the internal validity of the study is to divide the subjects into two or more groups. One of these groups serves as the control group. With the control group, no treatment or a "placebo" treatment is given. Other groups receive experimental treatments. If after the treatment is given the experimental group differs from the control group on a dependent variable(s), it is assumed that the treatment has an effect on that variable(s).

Since the conclusion of treatment effectiveness depends on the observed difference between the experimental and the control groups, the critical issue is how these groups are constituted to begin with. If the two groups are established in such a way that the control group members are inherently different from the experimental group members, the observed difference cannot be attributed solely to the experimental treatment. Therefore, with an experimental study, a primary concern is how subjects are assigned to the experimental and the control groups.

In some experimental studies there are no control groups per se. The control is in the difference of treatment among the various experimental groups. To facilitate discussion, we concentrate on the situation involving only two groups: an experimental and a control group. The methods for a two-group subject assignment can be directly extended to a multiple-group situation.

In subject sampling, the ideal goal is for each subject in the population to have an equal chance of being selected. In subject assignment, the ideal is for the experimental and the control groups to be equivalent in all respects prior to experimental treatment. Individual subjects within each group obviously will be different in many respects. The ideal is to divide the subjects into two groups in such a way that the average of every characteristic for the two groups is equivalent. If this ideal could be attained, any post-treatment difference between the two groups could only be attributed to treatment effectiveness. How closely this is approximated is a major determinant of how credible the conclusion concerning treatment effectiveness is.

There are three primary methods of subject assignment that would ensure, to various degrees of certainty, that the experimental and the control groups are equivalent. These include the captive random assignment method, the sequential random assignment method, and the matched-group method. A fourth method is used to adjust for the nonequivalence between the two groups through statistical methods post hoc. A common statistical technique used for this purpose is the Analysis of Covariance (ANCOVA) procedure. These statistical control techniques are frequently considered inadequate and are used only as a last resort. Interested readers should consult more specialized texts such as Edwards (1968), Scheffe (1959), and Winer (1962).

Of the three primary subject assignment methods, captive random assignment provides the best assurance of group equivalence. The matched-group method is not recommended because it is very difficult to ensure the equivalence of the two groups.

Captive Random Assignment

Captive random assignment is used when all participants in a study are known and available at the onset of the study (Drew & Hardman, 1985; Underwood, 1966). When all subjects to be assigned to the experimental and the control groups are known and available, they are "captive." A captive random assignment of subjects is perhaps the simplest of all subject assignment methods. It is also the best approach because it best ensures the equivalence between the experimental and the control groups. The application of this method is completely dependent on the simultaneous availability of all subjects prior to the experimental treatment.

There are a number of methods used in captive random assignment. They all produce comparable effects and differ only in efficiency. Essentially, through various means, a researcher first generates a random sequence of 1s and 0s. Using 0 to represent membership in one group and 1 to represent membership in the other, the list of subjects can be assigned to the two groups according to the sequence of 0s and 1s until the number of subjects for one of the two groups is attained. Hence, if 0s are used to represent membership in the control group and 1s are used to represent membership in the experimental group and the sequence generated is 001011 . . . , the 1st, 2nd, and 4th subjects on the list of names are assigned to the control group; whereas the 3rd, 5th, and 6th subjects are assigned to the experimental group. The random sequence of 0s and 1s is generated until one of the two groups has reached the desired number of subjects. The names on the remainder of the subject list are all assigned to the other group.

This process can easily be adapted to situations involving more than two groups. For example, in a three-group study, the random number generator can be programmed to generate a random sequence of the numbers 0, 1, and 2. Group memberships can then be assigned to the three groups in a manner similar to the two-group situation. For example, if the sequence generated is 1, 1, 0, 2, 0, 1, . . . , the 1st, 2nd, and 6th subjects are assigned to one group, the 3rd and 5th subjects are assigned to the next group, and the 4th subject is assigned to the third group.

Captive random assignment methods theoretically will produce equivalent groups of subjects for an experimental study. Because group memberships are determined by objective random chance, the characteristics of the assigned groups are assumed to be approximately equal. These methods will avoid any possible conscious or unconscious bias in assignment in such a way that one group is inherently different from the other.

Sequential Random Assignment

In some situations, all subjects for an experimental study are not identifiable or available at the outset of the study. For example, the treatment for a study may be an elaborate process and can be administered to only one subject at a time. In this case, the study may be an ongoing experiment in which only a few subjects are studied each day over a period of time. Another situation is when the potential subjects for an experiment cannot be identified ahead of time and are determined by who is available at the time. For example, a researcher may advertise in the newspaper to solicit subjects for an experiment. The actual subjects for the experiment will be determined by who responds to the advertisement. In this situation, the subjects may also appear at different times over an extended period of time. For these types of situations, captive random assignment is not possible. As an alternative, the use of a sequential random assignment procedure is recommended (Underwood, 1966).

A sequential random assignment procedure is a slight variant of the captive random assignment procedure. For a two-group design, one can generate a sequence of 0s and 1s equal in length to the desired number of subjects for the study. For example, if 30 subjects are desired for the study and 15 subjects are to be assigned to the two groups, respectively, the sequence is generated until either 15 zeros or 15 ones are obtained. When this is accomplished, simply wait for the appearance of subjects. The subjects are given either the experimental or the control treatment by matching the sequence in which they appear with the sequence of 0s and 1s. Hence, if the sequence generated is 110010 . . . , the first subject who appears will receive treatment condition 1. The second subject will also receive treatment condition 1. The third subject will receive treatment condition 0, and so on.

Based on theories of chance, the groups assigned through either the captive random assignment procedure or the sequential random assignment procedure will be reasonably equivalent most of the time. There is, however, no guarantee that they will always be equivalent. In fact, a very small portion of the time the groups assigned will be substantially different and thus lead to a serious threat to the internal validity of the experiment. Although this is extremely rare, because of its seriousness the experiment should be safeguarded against its occurrence. One way to ensure that the groups are equivalent is to assess directly whether the two groups are indeed equivalent. If there is evidence that they are not, the subjects should be reassigned by repeating the subject assignment procedures.

To assess if the two groups are equivalent, one first identifies any variables that may have a direct bearing on the effectiveness of the experimental treatment. For example, if the treatment is hypothesized to have an effect on the academic performance of college freshman, one would assume that prior performance of these college freshmen may also have a direct effect the posttreatment performance,. Next, one determines an appropriate measure for the identified variables. In the college freshmen example, the freshmen's high school grade point average, Scholastic Aptitude Test (SAT) score, or the American College Testing (ACT) score may be a credible measure of the prior performance of these students. Then measure the identified variable for the subjects and compare the average values across the assigned groups. If the average values are substantially different, the group assignment process has led to biased groups, and the subject assignment procedure should be repeated to produce new group assignments.

Matched-Group Assignment

In many situations, the random assignment of subjects to an experimental or a control group is impossible or undesirable. For example, the subjects may consist of natural clusters such as students in classrooms. It is often difficult or undesirable to randomly select students from a classroom to receive a particular treatment such as an experimental instructional method while other students within the same classroom receive either no treatment or a different treatment. It would be much more efficient, and in some cases more ethical, to give all students in the same classroom the same treatment.

Another example is the initiation of an experimental program to reduce individual's stuttering behavior. If subjects are solicited with the promise that their stuttering problem would be eliminated if the treatment is effective, it would be unethical to provide the treatment randomly only to some of those who apply with hope of a cure of their problems. In these situations, if it is impossible to provide the treatment to the control group after the experiment is completed and all dependent variable measures have been obtained, a matched-group assignment method may be used.

The objective of a matched-group assignment method is to identify individuals to be in a group other than the experimental group (e.g., the control group) so that the group created is as equivalent as possible to the experimental group on variables that are deemed important to the experiment. For example, with the stuttering program, the treatment may be provided to all those who apply and then an attempt made to find a group of individuals who are similar in characteristics to individuals who apply. The first task in a matched-group assignment is to identify one or more preexperimental variables that are theoretically important to the outcome of the experimental treatment. Most frequently, the variable that is to be changed through the treatment procedure is the most important preexperimental variable to consider. In the stuttering example, the extent of stuttering is probably the most important variable to consider. Next, a measure of this preexperimental variable is administered to all experimental subjects prior to treatment. Subjects who are not in the experimental group are then identified based on the preexperimental variable. These subjects will constitute the control group and may be identified through a subject-by-subject match.

With a subject-by-subject match, an attempt is made to identify an individual with the same measured value on the preexperimental variable as has each subject in the experimental group. The final outcome of a subject-by-subject match is a control group in which every member has a "corresponding" subject in the experimental group, with the same value on the preexperimental variable. The subject-by-subject match supposedly guarantees that the two groups are equivalent on the preexperimental measure. However, it does not guarantee that the two groups are equivalent on other variables that may prove to be important. In the stuttering example, it is known that the experimental group is composed of volunteers. The control group is not. It is highly likely that when comparing a group of subjects who were motivated to do something about their stuttering with a group who are not so motivated, a group difference exists. Therefore, no amount of matching on other variables can really yield "equivalent" groups. Various other problems are inherent in the matched-group designs. One is differential loss of subjects. If treatment in our example involves aversive stimuli, subjects may simply drop out of the experiment. The experimenter now can compare only those who were willing to endure aversive stimuli with their matches who had no aversive stimuli or any other part of the treatment. Therefore, it is difficult to imagine what useful information the study has yielded.

A possible improvement is to match subjects on more than one preexperimental variable. This is feasible only if the potential pool of subjects to be identified for the control group is very large. It is difficult enough to find a matching subject on one preexperimental variable for each subject in the experimental group. With each additional preexperimental variable to be matched, the difficulty of finding a matching individual is increased exponentially. The more preexperimental variables used, the more unlikely it is that a matching subject will be found for each subject in the experimental group.

Many have extensively dicussed the potential hazards and difficulties of matched-group assignment in behavioral studies (e.g., Drew, 1969; Prehm, 1966). In general, when random assignment methods can be used, matched-group assignment methods should be avoided. When a matched-group assignment method is used as a last resort, the possible biased effects may be reduced to a limited extent through various statistical techniques such as an analysis of covariance or multiple regression. However, such techniques can only mitigate, not cure, the problems of matched-group designs. The apparent initial "equivalence" of such groups is usually an illusion.

Captive Matching

Matching can be useful when one has captive subjects. In this case, one can first match the subjects into two matched groups, then use a chance procedure to determine which will be the experimental and which the control group. In this way, there is less error in the statistical comparisons at the completion of the experiment. This can be especially important when only a small number of subjects is available.

SINGLE-SUBJECT SELECTION

In many observational studies, only one subject or very few subjects are used. For the purpose of reference, we call these studies single-subject studies. This type of study is common in clinical situations where the effectiveness of a particular behavior modification strategy on a single client is evaluated.

With a single-subject study, the source of data variation is found along the time continuum, rather than across a number of sample subjects. Additionally, the purpose of a single-subject study is to evaluate the behavioral difference between the preintervention period and the postintervention period. For these reasons, single-subject studies are a subset of *time series* designs (Glass, Willson, & Gottman, 1975), or *interrupted time series* designs (Hartmann et al., 1980). The latter are in turn a subset of *quasi-experimental* designs (Campbell & Stanley, 1966). The terms *time-series design* and *interrupted times series design* are frequently used to associate the single-subject study with a particular class of statistical analysis techniques. These techniques are discussed in detail in chapters 8, 9, and 10.

Although it is unlikely that the results of a single-subject study can be generalized to other subjects as well as across time, it is rare that an investigator does not at least hope to be able to generalize up to a point the results of the study on the single subject to a larger population. Even in a clinical situation when the purpose is simply to improve the conditions for a single client, it would be hoped that the effectiveness of a behavioral intervention strategy could be generalized to other similar clients. For example, if hypnosis is effective in changing the behavior of a client with a particular phobia, one would like to conclude that the technique is likely to be effective with other clients with identical phobias.

Generalization Through Replications

Unlike subject sampling, the ability to generalize results from a single-subject study to other subjects cannot be determined through the "representativeness" of the sample. Nor can a generalization be justified through controlling all extraneous variables, as in subject assignments. Rather, the generality of a single-subject study is determined by replications of the study with other subjects having similar or different characteristics and under similar or different conditions (Hersen & Barlow, 1976; Homer & Peterson, 1980). The more replications using similar and different subjects under similar and different conditions that show the same results, the more confidence can be placed on the generalizability of the intervention strategy. On the other hand, replications that show different results help a researcher to better define the types of subjects and conditions to which generalizations cannot be made.

Replications that show different results are as important as those showing similar results. It is unreasonable to expect that an intervention strategy leads to the same results with all subjects under all conditions. Replications that show different results define the boundaries of generalization and provide a spur for future research (Sidman, 1960).

Specification of Subject Characteristics

Replications of a study using similar and different subjects is an ongoing and everlasting process. The subject selected for the original single-subject study had many characteristics. Systematically replicating the study with subjects who differ in each of the identified characteristics alone is an unending task. Furthermore, new characteristics may be identified or considered important as knowledge in the field progresses. Given the enormous demand on time and resources, a single researcher can realistically replicate the study with subjects different in only some of the characteristics. Replication of a single-subject study is, therefore, a process involving many independent researchers at various locations and times.

With future replications in mind, the important task in a single-subject study is not to explain why the subject is selected. Rather, it is important to spell out the characteristics of the selected subject and the selection procedure so that other researchers have sufficient information for replication.

Traditionally, demographic information is reported for a single-subject study. Most frequently, information such as gender, ethnicity, age, classification in school, intelligence measures, diagnostic categories, and prognosis are reported. Homer, Peterson, and Wonderlich (1983) concluded that these particular pieces of demographic information are generally reported as a matter of tradition rather than due to their potential value for future replications. Conceptually, there is an endless list of subject characteristics one can report, ranging from the color of the hair to parents' educational level. The critical task is to report information that may potentially have a bearing on the effectiveness of the treatment. Unfortunately, there is no simple guideline to follow to decide which subject characteristics should be reported. Although it is impossible to report all characteristics of a subject, the experimenter must try not to overlook important characteristics. For a lack of a more formal approach, one should speculate, based on existing theory regarding the intervention strategy and past research, which subject characteristics may have a potential effect on the study outcome and report these characteristics. Traditionally reported demographic information may or may not be relevant.

A possible solution for some studies is to report the criteria used to select the subject, along with other relevant demographic information. In some situations, the single subject is selected based on a set of formal or informal criteria. For example, a subject may be selected because the subject is viewed as susceptible to social stimuli and the intervention strategy involves social rewards (Homer, Peterson, & Wonderlich, 1983). In this case, the social susceptibility is quite important to the effectiveness of the intervention strategy. It should be reported even if the existence of social susceptibility within the subject is only an opinion of the researcher without quantifiable empirical support.

The subject selection process is not always systematic and formal. However, the fact that the researcher uses a particular intervention strategy implies that the researcher had speculated on some relationship between some characteristics of the subject and the intervention strategy. These informal hunches frequently indicate important characteristics. Even when there is no clear systematic subject selection involved, such as when a student is referred to a school psychologist by a teacher, the fact that the school psychologist uses a particular intervention strategy implies that the school psychologist suspected that the strategy will make a difference because of some characteristics of the student. In this case, the school psychologist should report those characteristics in the student's behavioral history that had led the psychologist to the choice of the particular intervention strategy.

The Use of Extreme Cases

Researchers frequently hope to be able to generalize the results of a study without waiting for the uncertain replications to be performed by future researchers. One way to accomplish this is to conduct one's own replications. Unfortunately, conducting a series of replications with different subjects is a time-consuming process for a single researcher or even for a team of researchers. It also places an enormous demand on the resources of the researcher. To expedite the process and to increase the generality of the results of a study beyond its ad hoc nature, some researchers have selected extreme subjects for a single-subject study. For example, a researcher may select the most aggressive, withdrawn, self-injurious, nonsocial, or intellectually retarded subject for observation (Haynes, 1978). The rationale for the selection of the most extreme subjects is that if the treatment is effective with these most severe cases, it should be at least somewhat effective with the less severe cases.

This generalization is inappropriate for at least two reasons. First, the extreme cases may react differently to the treatment than less extreme cases. Second, the observed effectiveness of the treatment with the extreme cases is confounded by the regression effect. A regression effect, also known as regression toward the mean, refers to a statistical tendency of an extreme case to change in the direction of the average. An intuitive explanation of a regression effect is that for an extreme case, there is little room to change to an even more extreme situation, but there is plenty of room to change to a more moderate situation. For example, for a subject selected for a smoking cessation study who smokes 100 cigarettes a day, it is more likely, if the behavior is to change at all, that the subject will reduce the smoking frequency than it is for the subject to smoke even more frequently regardless of the behavior intervention strategy. If for no other reason, the physical limitations themselves (e.g., one cannot smoke in a shower or while asleep) prevent the smoking of even more cigarettes than the already extreme rate of 100 per day, making it more difficult to increase the behavior than it is to decrease it. When a subject with such extreme rates of behavior is chosen for the smoking cessation study and the behavior is reduced in the postintervention period, one cannot ascertain whether the reduction is due to intervention effectiveness or due to a natural regression effect.

In general, the use of an extreme case for a single-subject study is not advisable. It is particularly inappropriate if the reason for the choice is to increase the generality of the outcomes. The use of extreme cases can only be legitimized in situations where the choice is due to ethical or clinical considerations.

CHAPTER 4

Time Sampling

Time is nature's way of keeping everything from happening at once.

—Anonymous

In most scientific investigations, data are drawn from samples across the time dimension as well as across subjects. Data obtained for any investigation represent the quantities of a phenomenon for a particular sample of subjects, which, in turn, represent the population of interest. However, when examined more carefully, the data represent the phenomenon among the sample of subjects only within a specific time period. That is, data are acquired from a slice of time out of the infinite time continuum. For non-behavioral methods of data acquisition, such as self-report questionnaries, tests of skills, and so on, the dimension of time has not been of primary concern. The time dimension, however, is very important to data obtained through direct behavioral observations. Specifically, for behavioral observation, we need to determine not only what to observe and whom to observe but also when to observe and how often.

IMPORTANCE OF THE TIME DIMENSION

There are a number of reasons why the time dimension is important for observational data. Behaviors as expressed through a particular sequence of observable events can often be expected to change rapidly from moment to moment. For example, an individual engaged in a conversation at this moment may or may not be engaged in conversation at the next. Similarly, a fowl engaged in a courting dance this minute may or may not be engaged in the dance in the next minute.

A second reason is that unlike other nonbehavioral data acquisition methods, observational data are frequently gathered over time. For nonbehavioral measures, even when a phenomenon changes rapidly, an aggregate quantity representing the phenomenon over a defined period of time can be obtained directly in a single measure. In behavioral observation, however, an aggregate quantity is obtained through many observations of occurrences over a defined period of time. To illustrate this difference, in a survey questionnaire, one can ask a single question such as, "On the average, how many times did you read a newspaper each week during the last year?" The data collection for an answer to this question is instantaneous. Even though an individual's answer to this question may vary from one moment to the next, the amount of variation is not expected to be substantial. Therefore, problems such as when and how often to gather data for this question are not a serious concern. However, to answer the same question through direct behavioral observation, a researcher would have to observe the behavior of the individual over an entire year. Consequently, the questions of when to observe and how often become important concerns.

A third reason is the need for repeated observations over time for many observational studies to ensure data reliability. In conventional measurement, the answer to a single question is frequently not a reliable indicator of a phenomenon. The solution to this problem is to ask the same question in a variety of ways. A summary of the answers to all these equivalent questions can be considered to be a more reliable indicator than the answer to a single question. Similarly, in behavioral observation, to obtain a stable indicator of a phenomenon, one can observe and record the occurrence or nonoccurrence of a large number of "equivalent" behaviors. This is frequently impractical. Many equivalent behaviors are mutually exclusive because of the physical movements involved. Hence, the occurrence of one behavior would preclude that of another. For example, to measure an individual's "physical agility," observing how the individual jumps would serve as one good indicator. However, it is impossible for the same individual to climb a ladder when engaged in jumping. Therefore, it is not possible to observe two alternate indicators of physical agility at the same time. In order to obtain measures of a series of equivalent behaviors, observations have to be made over a period of time. In other situations, there is simply no equivalent alternative behavior. Individual observations of the same behavior would have to be repeated over time.

Finally, when quantifying a variable, it is highly desirable that the quantity be sufficiently sensitive to minute individual differences. One prerequisite to a sensitive measurement procedure is that the final quantity needs to have a sufficiently wide range of possible scores. This can be accomplished in paper-and-pencil instruments by providing a wide range of possible responses. For example, in a form of Likert-type items, respondents can be asked to express an opinion by responding on a 7-point scale ranging from "strongly agree" to "strongly disagree." In a semantic differential scale, for another example, respondents' feelings regarding some object of measurement can be indicated anywhere along, say, a 9-point scale. In some cases, a theoretical continuum is provided to respondents, and they are asked to mark their relative position on the continuum. The physical distance of the mark from one end of the continuum is used as an indication of respondents' scores. These are various ways through which an item can detect small differences among subjects. When a behavior is being recorded, the behavior either occurs or does not at each specific point in time. To increase the sensitivity of the scores, summaries of data from a number of observations made over time are used. These summaries would provide a wide range of possible scores to differentiate among subjects, across situations, and so on.

DIFFICULTIES OF CONTINUOUS OBSERVATIONS

Because of the unique nature of behavioral observation, the time dimension is as important a consideration as those of the population of subjects and of each subject's behavioral repertoire. The most direct method to account for the time dimension in behavioral observation data is to first define a period of time for which the data are a descriptor. Next, the behavior(s) of interest can be observed on a continuous basis throughout the entire defined period. Data obtained through continuous observations should provide a reasonably accurate description of the behavior(s) of interest. This is analogous to first defining the entire population of subjects and then studying the entire population in subject sampling. In continuous observation, sources of error are limited to human error and data are not contaminated by either random or systematic sampling error.

Attempts have been made to conduct behavioral observations on a continuous basis. Barker and Wright (1955) used a team of observers to continuously record the behavior of a boy throughout an entire day. They also attempted to record parent–child interactions in actual family settings on a continuous basis. In most observation situations, continuous observations over an extended period of time are expensive, intrusive, and impractical.

To gather data on a continuous basis for an extended period of time, a team of observers would have to be employed and rotated frequently. The rotation is necessary to avoid data errors or omissions due to fatigue. It is a very expensive approach in terms of labor cost and observer training. Imagine, for instance, the cost of observing the social interaction of a sample of ten 7-year-old children over a period of one month on a continuous basis in order to gather data regarding the social skills development of 7-year-olds.

In most situations, the continuous presence of an observer or a team of observers is very intrusive to the lives of the subjects. Consider, for example, the extreme intrusiveness of the presence of an observer for two weeks in a family during all waking hours in order to gather data regarding the communication pattern of the family.

In many field research situations, the physical demand placed upon the observer in continuous observation may prove to be impossible. For example, it would require an observer with unusual stamina to keep a group sample of, say, five monkeys in sight continuously in order to record the activities of the monkeys in the wild. The demands of continuous observation on an observer even in a controlled environment are tremendous. When a behavior of interest occurs, an observer using real-time recording must note the time of the onset of the behavior, judge the nature of the behavior, note the time of the termination of the behavior, while recording all these pieces of information on paper and at the same time keeping continuous attention on the subject. In the case of observing a single infrequent behavior emitted by a single subject, it may be possible to accomplish all of these tasks with minimal loss of information. The loss of information in this case would be due to the brief switching of attention away from the subject when recording the time and nature of the behavior on paper. These tasks, however, become impossible when a number of behaviors are observed simultaneously, the behaviors occur very frequently, and/or more than one subject is being observed. For example, imagine the difficulty in continuously and simultaneously observing and recording the incidences of criticism, disagreement, interruption, sarcasm, and excuses emitted by each subject in a heated argument involving four or five subjects.

As discussed in chapter 2, recent electronic event recorders have simplified the recording aspect of continuous observation somewhat. However, the demands of uninterrupted continuous attention to the subject(s), constant decisions, and the recording of all simultaneous behaviors on the observer, as well as the problems of labor cost and intrusiveness, remain persistent obstacles to continuous observations. These problems are compounded astronomically when the period of continuous observation is extensive.

When the subjects involved are competent human adults, an apparent alternative continuous observation strategy is to have the subjects monitor themselves and record their own behaviors. This self-monitor approach, called critical event recording (Haynes, 1978), eliminates the necessity of recording when the behavior of interest is not occurring and hence simplifies the task of continuous observation. Unfortunately, aside from the questionable reliability of this approach, it has been shown to be impractical. For example, Haynes reported a study in which couples were given tape recorders, trained in their use, and asked to record any arguments in their daily lives. It was found that although some couples did record their own arguments, most either did not record at all or recorded infrequently. Additionally, the majority of the couples regarded the recording procedure as disruptive and aversive.

Another apparent solution, as discussed in chapter 2, is to utilize automatic audio- or videotape recorders to record the behavior(s) of subjects continuously. With this procedure, the taped record can be observed later in a more leisurely manner. To transform the streams of a number of different behaviors of a number of subjects to appropriate quantitative data, the tape can be played over and over again, each time concentrating on a single behavior of a single subject. In other words, the use of audio-visual recorders allows an observer to "stretch" the time dimension and "repeat" an event over and over again. This reduces the instantaneous demands on the observer tremendously. However, it is not a panacea to the problems of continuous observation, because the amount of time required for data collection is increased. For example, to collect data on four behaviors of five subjects during 10 one-hour sessions using continuous observation *without* audio-visual equipment requires the employment of an observer for only 10 hours. To collect the same data from 10 one-hour audio-video tapes would require the tapes to be played $4 \times 5 \times 10 = 200$ times and the observer to be employed for 200 hours, instead of the original 10 hours. The trade-off in using audio-visual equipment as an aid to continuous observation is considerably reducing the instantaneous demands on the observer during observation at the expensive of greatly increasing the cost of time and labor. Additionally, the use of automatic audio-visual equipment may prove to be limited to a controlled environment only. In field investigations, the logistics and cost of filming the behaviors of a number of subjects over an extended period of time, compounded by the time and labor cost of later observations of these films, render the audio-visual recording of events impractical for an average field investigator. Thus, continuous observation of behaviors, although ideal, is difficult to attain in most situations.

SAMPLING ALONG THE TIME CONTINUUM

As a practical alternative to continuous observation, time-sampling techniques are frequently employed. In subject sampling, it is important to define the population to which data from a sample of subjects can be generalized. In time sampling, it is important to clearly define the time period to which the sample points of observation can be generalized. Behaviors can be observed at random points within the defined time period to obtain data reflecting a random sample of the behaviors. Just as inferences are made concerning how well data from a random sample of subjects represent the population, they are also made concerning how well data from random observations along the time continuum represent those of the entire time period. A random time-sampling approach has the advantage of being a close parallel to random subject sampling and thus may benefit from all the well-established theories and methods of inferential statistics associated with random subject sampling.

In practice, however, random sampling along the time continuum is not easily accomplished. In a formal random sampling process, the exact points in time at which observations are to be made are determined prior to actual observations through the use of the simple random sampling method described in chapter 3. Achieving randomness of when to observe and when not to observe at points in time places an enormous demand on the observer. Sampling along the time continuum is, therefore, usually either semirandom or systematic.

Time is continuous with no natural discrete "units" of time. To sample along the time continuum, it is necessary to first artificially separate the time continuum into units of time. In time sampling, this is accomplished in two hierarchical levels of sampling. First, time is divided into chunks of time blocks and a sample of these chunks of time blocks is selected. These selected time blocks are called observation sessions. The length of each observation session may be the same or different. Similarly, the amount of time between observation sessions may be equal or unequal. Second, actual observations and recording of behaviors are conducted within each observation session. Sometimes, the "sampling" process within the session may be continuous. At other times, the observation session is further divided into smaller chunks of time units called intervals, and observations are made based upon various systematic sampling schemes within each interval. Figure 4.1 provides a graphic representation of the general manner in which time samples of behaviors are drawn from the time continuum.

In summary, in the time sampling of behaviors, there are two hierarchical levels of representativeness to be considered. First, one needs to consider whether summary descriptors of data for each of the selected observation sessions are an adequate representation of the behavior in the entire time period of interest. Second, when data are gathered at systematic points in time within each observation session, one has to consider whether

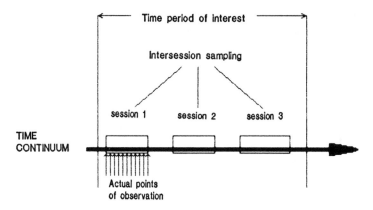

FIGURE 4.1.   Time sampling along the continuum.

these data represent the behavior of the entire observation session. In the discussion following, we first consider intrasession observation (selecting observation points within an observation session).

INTRASESSION OBSERVATION

Within an observation session, data have been gathered in a number of ways. Where it is possible and desired, the data collection process resembles a continuous observation. In other instances, the data gathered represent a systematic sample of the behavior within the observation session. Within the observation session, data for a single behavior or for a number of behaviors can be gathered. Similarly, data reflecting the behaviors of a single subject or a number of subjects can be gathered. In a multiple-subject observation session, continuous observation is much more difficult for the same reasons as it is for an overall continuous observation, cited earlier in this chapter. When observing more than one subject within an observation session, it is extremely difficult, if not impossible, to pay attention to all the subjects at all times. Therefore, sampling techniques are particularly useful for a multiple-subject observation session.

The final outcome of intrasession observation is a set of summary statistics (e.g., prevalence, frequency, etc.) describing the characteristics of the behavior(s) for the entire observation session. Due to evidence from a number of empirical or simulated studies, statistics obtained from continuous intrasession observations have been regarded as more accurate (e.g., Hartmann & Wood, 1982). In fact, results from continuous observation are frequently used as the standard against which the accuracies of results from intrasession sampling are evaluated (e.g., Brulle & Repp, 1984; Powell, 1984). Recent developments in statistical time-sampling theories (e.g., Suen

& Ary, 1986), however, have shown that, when used appropriately, some intrasession sampling results can be as accurate as continuous intrasession observation. In many situations where continuous intrasession observations are not possible, intrasession sampling is an effective alternative.

For intrasession observation, there are three basic approaches to data collection: continuous observation, semicontinuous sampling, and discrete sampling. When used appropriately, any of the three can produce accurate estimates of some descriptive statistics for the session and unbiased estimates of others.

Continuous Intrasession Observation

For data collected through behavior observation methods, there are a number of threats to the quality of the data. One of these threats is sampling adequacy. For continuous intrasession observation, the question of sampling adequacy within the session is eliminated. However, the question remains of the ability of data for the session to represent the behavior in the entire defined period of time. In other words, continuous intrasession observation provides data without intrasession sampling error, but it may contain intersession sampling error. Depending on the desired descriptive statistics for the observation session, continuous observations within a session may be conducted using the frequency recording technique or the real-time recording technique mentioned in chapter 2.

Frequency Recording

With frequency recording (also known as event recording, frequency tally, or trial scoring), one observes the behavior(s) of interest continuously throughout the observation session and notes the number of times each behavior is initiated. This method is most appropriate when the typical occurrence of the behavior(s) of interest occupies a very brief amount of time, when the behavior occurs very frequently, or when frequency is the only behavioral dimension of interest. For example, the observer may record how often a subject gets out of his seat or how often a subject lights a cigarette.

Real-Time Recording

When dimensions of behavior beyond frequency are of interest, real-time recording may be used. In real-time recording, an observer records the exact time of the day at which a behavior of interest is initiated and the exact time at which the behavior is terminated (Sanson-Fisher et al.,

1979). The result of a real-time recording session is a set of clock times (e.g., 10:32:45 a.m.) indicating the initiation and termination of each behavior. From these results, various session descriptive statistics can be derived as follows. For each behavior, the number of initiations is the frequency of behavior occurrence (f_{occ}). If the behavior is occurring at both the start and the end of the observation session, then the frequency of nonoccurrence (f_{non}) is $f_{occ} - 1$. If the behavior is neither occurring at the start nor at the end of the observation session, then $f_{non} = f_{occ} + 1$. In all other situations, $f_{non} = f_{occ}$.

Subtracting the preceding initiation time from each termination time yields the bout duration (B) for that occurrence. Total duration, which is the total amount of time during which the behavior occurs (Powell, 1984), is the sum of all bout durations. Subtracting the preceding termination time from each initiation time yields the interresponse time duration (IRT) for that nonoccurrence. When all bout durations and the length of the observation session (S) are expressed in the same time units (days, hours, minutes, or seconds), prevalence equals the sum of all bout durations divided by the length of the observation session multiplied by 100%. In other words:

$$\text{Prevalence} = \frac{\Sigma\, B}{S} \times 100\%.$$

(4.1)

In chapter 2, we made a distinction between prevalence and rate of occurrence. Prevalence is the proportion of time the occurrence of a behavior occupies within an observation session. Rate of occurrence is how often the behavior occurs per time unit. For the rate of occurrence, a desired standard unit of time needs to be identified (e.g., per day, per hour, or per minute, etc.). The length of the observation session is then converted to the appropriate time unit. For example, if the desired rate is frequency per hour, the length of a 30-minute observation session should be converted to 0.5 hour. Similarly, a 1-hour-and-20-minute observation session is converted to 1.33 hours. On the other hand, if the desired unit is per minute, a 2½ hour session needs to be converted to 150 minutes. Rate of occurrence is computed with the converted observation session length (S_c) through:

$$\text{Rate of occurrence} = \frac{f_{occ}}{S_c}.$$

(4.2)

Mean bout duration is the sum of all bout durations divided by frequency of occurrence:

$$\text{Mean bout duration} = \frac{\Sigma\, B}{f_{occ}}.$$

(4.3)

Mean interresponse time duration is the sum of all interresponse time durations divided by frequency of nonoccurrence:

$$\text{Mean interresponse time duration} = \frac{\Sigma\ IRT}{f_{\text{nonc}}}. \tag{4.4}$$

These statistics and other variations succinctly summarize the nature of behavior occurrences within the real-time observation session. They are also referred to as session scores. They describe quantitatively the different aspects of the behavior that has been expressed in a series of clock times. The use of the real-time intrasession continuous observation approach allows one to obtain data that can be summarized directly into various session scores.

To illustrate the derivation of various session scores from real-time continuous intrasession observation, we use a simple example of observing a single behavior of a single subject. Let us say a real-time continuous intrasession observation procedure is used to observe when a child is reading versus not reading a book within a half-hour observation session between 2:00 p.m. and 2:30 p.m. on a particular day. The resulting data are those presented in Table 4.1. Each bout duration is derived from the difference between each termination time and the immediately preceding initiation time. Each *IRT* duration is derived from the difference between each initiation time and the immediately preceding termination time. In this example, the frequency of occurrence (f_{occ}) is 3 because there are three initiations. The frequency of nonoccurrence (f_{non}) is the same as f_{occ} and is 3. Total duration is the sum of all bout durations and hence:

Total duration = (8 min 30 sec) + (4 min 30 sec) + (3 min 30 sec)
          = 16 min 30 sec.

TABLE 4.1
Data from a Real-Time Recording Session

Behavior Bout Initiation and Termination	Clock Time	Bout Duration (B)	IRT Duration (T)
Session Starts	2:00:00 p.m.		
1st Initiation	2:03:05 p.m.	} 8 min 30 sec	} 3 min 5 sec
1st Termination	2:11:35 p.m.		
2nd Initiation	2:15:45 p.m.	} 4 min 30 sec	} 4 min 10 sec
2nd Termination	2:20:15 p.m.		
3rd Initiation	2:26:30 p.m.	} 3 min 30 sec	} 6 min 15 sec
Session Ends	2:30:00 p.m.		

To compute the prevalence, we convert all bout durations and the length of the observation session to seconds. Hence, prevalence is:

$$\text{Prevalence} = \frac{\Sigma B}{S} \times 100\%.$$

$$= \frac{510 \text{ sec} + 270 \text{ sec} + 210 \text{ sec}}{1,800 \text{ sec}} \times 100\%.$$

$$= 55\%.$$

Let us say we are interested in the rate of occurrence per hour. In this case, the 30-minute observation session is converted to an S_c value of 0.5 hours. Hence, the rate per hour is:

$$\text{Rate of occurrence per hour} = \frac{f_{occ}}{S_c}$$

$$= \frac{3}{0.5}$$

$$= 6.$$

Other session scores can be computed as:

$$\text{Mean bout duration} = \frac{\Sigma B}{f_{occ}}$$

$$= \frac{510 \text{ sec} + 270 \text{ sec} + 210 \text{ sec}}{3}$$

$$= 330 \text{ sec}$$

and $$\text{Mean IRT duration} = \frac{\Sigma IRT}{f_{non}}$$

$$= \frac{185 \text{ sec} + 250 \text{ sec} + 375 \text{ sec}}{3}$$

$$= 270 \text{ sec.}$$

When the occurrence of behavior(s) is infrequent and when only one behavior is observed or when a number of mutually exclusive and exhaustive behaviors of one subject are observed, recording of the initiation and termination time in real-time observation can be accomplished through the use of paper, pencil, and a watch. In some situations, the behaviors of interest in an observation session are mutually exclusive and exhaustive such that when a specific behavior occurs, all the other behaviors do not occur and that one of the behaviors will always be occurring at any point in the observation session. For example, an office worker may sit, stand, or walk but is unlikely to jump, climb, or lie down. Furthermore, sit, stand, and walk are mutually exclusive. In this type of situation, recording only the initiation time of each behavior without recording the termination time is sufficient because the initiation of the next behavior also implies the termination of the current behavior (Sackett, 1978).

With real-time observations of more complicated designs (e.g., multiple subject or multiple behavior), some type of electronic aid such as an electronic real-time event recorder may have to be used. Possible event recorders appropriate for behavioral observation have been identified by, among others, Celhoffer et al. (1977); Crossman, Williams, and Chambers (1978); Fernald and Heinecke (1974); Gass (1977); Repp et al. (1985); Sackett, Stephenson, and Ruppenthal (1973); Sanson-Fisher et al. (1979); Stephenson and Roberts (1977); and Torgerson (1977).

Semicontinuous Sampling

Continuous intrasession observation, whether through frequency recording or real-time observation, is most useful in a single-subject observation session. To observe more than one subject within an observation session, however, continuous observation may not be possible, even with computerized real-time event recorders. This is because of the limited visual scope of an observer. In the continuous observation of a single subject, the view of an observer can be fixed on the subject. Occurrences of one or many behaviors can be seen by the observer. However, when there is more than one subject, the observer's attention has to be divided between the different subjects, making simultaneous continuous observation of all subjects difficult. This is impossible when the subjects are scattered in various locations in such a way that when the vision of the observer is fixed on one subject, other subjects are beyond the scope of the peripheral view of the observer. Therefore, when an observation session involves more than one subject, some type of intrasession sampling scheme is needed.

In many other situations, intrasession sampling may be more practical than continuous intrasession observation. Some examples of these situations are: a real-time event recorder may not be accessible; a real-time event recorder is available but is not portable for a field investigation; a real-time event recorder is determined to be too obtrusive; the observer's time can be more efficiently used for tasks other than watching the subject continuously; and when it is desirable for the observer to make anecdotal notes regarding the behavior to supplement the occurrence/nonoccurrence data. In these and other situations, intrasession sampling methods can be used to produce results that could approximate those of continuous frequency recording or real-time continuous observation.

There are a number of methods for intrasession sampling along the time continuum within the observation session. Of the various methods of intrasession time sampling, two methods use a combination of continuous observation and discrete sampling (dividing the session into discrete units of time) techniques. These are partial-interval sampling and whole-interval sampling. Because of the retention of some form of continuous observation in these two methods, we refer to them as semicontinuous sampling.

Partial-Interval Sampling

First developed by Goodenough (1928) and Olson (1929) to study spontaneous behavior in children, partial-interval sampling has been referred to by a number of names, including "one-zero sampling," "interval sampling," "interval recording," "Hansen frequencies," "modified frequency," "one-zero recording," and "time sampling." The use of the last term to describe this type of intrasession time-sampling method has created some confusion because the term *time sampling* has been used to refer to any one of a large array of intersession or intrasession procedures in which behaviors are sampled along the time continuum.

In partial-interval sampling, the entire length of the observation session is divided into a number of equal time intervals, and observations are made interval by interval. For example, a half-hour observation session may be divided into 30 one-minute intervals or 6 five-minute intervals or 180 ten-second intervals, and so forth. The division of the observation session into equal time intervals serves three purposes. First, it divides the time continuum into discrete units. Discrete sampling is then possible. Second, it permits many behaviors to be observed within a session (Frame, 1979; Hawkins, 1982; Patterson & Maerov, 1978). For example, an observer may concentrate on the observation of Behavior *A* in the first interval, on that of Behavior *B* in the second interval, and Behavior *C* in the third, and so on until all behaviors of interest have been observed for one interval each. The observer can then switch attention back to Behavior *A* and repeat the sequence of observations. Third, the division of the session into discrete intervals allows for a more precise assessment of intrasession data reliability (Bijou et al., 1969). Sample session scores can be used to assess the reliability of session scores obtained from a particular observation system in general. However, session scores cannot be used to assess the reliability of data obtained within a session. For example, one cannot use session frequency scores to assess the reliability of the various initiation and termination times recorded in a real-time continuous intrasession observation. To assess the reliability of intrasession data (such as the initiation and termination times), the time continuum within an observation session needs to be divided into discrete units. This third purpose becomes clear in the next two chapters on reliability.

In partial-interval sampling, an observer observes the behavior of interest interval by interval, and a score is assigned to each interval according to the occurrence or nonoccurrence of the behavior of interest. An interval is assigned a score of 1 if the behavior occurs at any time within the interval, and it is assigned a score of 0 if and only if the behavior never occurs within the interval. In practice, the subject is observed continuously from the start of an interval. As soon as the behavior occurs, the interval is given a score of 1 and observation is no longer necessary for the remainder of the interval. This sampling method allows for efficient use of the observer's time. For instance, if the behavior is occurring at the start of the interval, the interval is scored 1 and the subject can be ignored for the entire interval. The observer can, then, use the interval to perform other tasks, such as making anecdotal notes. In other cases, the subject is observed continuously from the beginning of the interval, and as soon as the behavior is initiated, the interval can be scored 1 and the remainder of the interval can be used for other tasks. If the behavior never occurs within an interval, observation is made continuously throughout the interval, and the interval is scored 0.

The end result of a partial-interval sampling process is a "chain" of 1s and 0s representing the occurrences and nonoccurrences of a behavior within each interval. For example, the end result of a partial-interval sampling process in a 5-minute observation session using 15-second intervals (a total of 20 intervals in 5 minutes) may look like this:

00011001011110011100.

These 1s and 0s are the raw data from which various session scores may be derived.

Partial-interval sampling has been reported as widely used or as the most popular intrasession sampling method (Altmann, 1974; Hartmann & Wood, 1982; Hawkins, 1982; Kelly, 1977). At the same time, however, its ability to produce data that could lead to reliable estimates of session scores is controversial. Numerous studies have been conducted on the use of partial-interval data to derive estimates of session scores. The conclusions of most of these studies are based on recognizable patterns in the analysis of empirical or simulated data. These conclusions have been consistent. It has been found that when prevalence is estimated by dividing the number of intervals scored 1 in partial-interval sampling by the total number of intervals, the result is almost always an overestimate of prevalence (e.g., Dunbar, 1976; Green & Alverson, 1978; Legar, 1977; McDowell, 1973; Milar & Hawkins, 1976; Murphy & Goodall, 1980; Powell et al., 1977; Simpson & Simpson, 1977). When the number of intervals scored 1 that are immediately preceded by an interval scored 0 are used as an estimate of frequency, the result tends to be an underestimate of frequency.

It has also been consistently found that both the true prevalence and the true frequency of an observation session have considerable influence on the number of intervals scored 1 in a partial-interval sampling process (e.g., Bloom & Fischer, 1982; Powell, 1984; Rhine & Linville, 1980). In other words, the number of intervals scored 1 in partial-interval sampling is an omnibus indicator of both prevalence and frequency. This unique characteristic of partial-interval sampling data has led to two diametrically opposite conclusions. On the one hand, some maintain that a composite indicator of both prevalence and frequency, such as the number of intervals scored 1 in partial-interval sampling, is an equally good or better indicator of behavior then either prevalence or frequency alone (e.g., Bloom & Fischer, 1982; Rhine & Flanigon, 1978; Rhine & Linville, 1980). However, others maintain that an omnibus indicator that does not yield either prevalence of frequency per se is an index without contextual reference and is undesirable (e.g., Altmann, 1974; Powell, 1984; Powell et al., 1977; Suen & Ary, 1984b).

Recently, there have been a number of analyses on the theoretical basis and properties of partial-interval sampling and other semicontinuous and discrete intrasession sampling methods (e.g., Ary, 1984; Ary & Suen, 1983; Brown, Solomon, & Stephens, 1977; Griffin & Adams, 1983; Kraemer, 1979; Suen, 1986a; Suen & Ary, 1984b, 1986a, 1986b). Based upon these theoretical deductive analyses, it was found that all session scores (i.e., f_{occ}, f_{non}, prevalence, rate, mean bout duration, and mean IRT duration, etc.) can be estimated either unbiasedly or accurately from the raw data of partial-interval sampling under certain conditions. Furthermore, these statistical conditions can be created or approximated a priori by setting the appropriate length of time for each interval within the observation session. The appropriateness of a selected interval length can also be assessed statistically prior to observation so that adjustments can be made to maximize the reliability and accuracy of session score estimates derived from sampling data. These statistical procedures and their theoretical bases are discussed in detail later in this chapter under Statistical Theory of Intrasession Sampling.

Whole-Interval Sampling

A semicontinuous sampling procedure that is less frequently used is whole-interval sampling (Powell, Martindale, & Kulp, 1975). In whole-interval sampling, an observation session is again divided into a number of discrete intervals. An interval is scored 1 if and only if the behavior occurs throughout the entire interval. Otherwise, the interval is scored 0. In other words, any nonoccurrence of behavior within an interval will lead to a 0 score for the interval. Again, the use of the whole-interval sampling method allows for efficient use of observer time. The subject is observed continuously from the start of each interval. As soon as there is a nonoccurrence of the behavior of interest, the interval is scored 0, and the remainder of the interval can be used by the observer to perform other tasks. The scoring procedure for whole-interval sampling is diametrically opposite to that for partial-interval sampling. Whereas any occurrence of behavior in an interval leads to a score of 1 in partial-interval sampling, in whole-interval sampling, any nonoccurrence of behavior leads to a score of 0 for the interval. Because of these procedural similarities between partial-interval and whole-interval sampling, some (e.g., Hartmann & Wood, 1982; Hawkins, 1982; Powell, Martindale, & Kulp, 1975) considered the latter to be a variant of the former. It is important to point out that although the scoring procedures involved in the two methods are in some respects mirror images, data obtained from the two methods are quite different.

As in the case of partial-interval sampling, session score estimates derived from whole-interval sampling have been found to be biased. It has been shown that dividing the number of intervals scored 1 in whole-interval sampling by the total number of intervals and using the result as an estimate of prevalence will almost always underestimate prevalence. Counting the number of situations in which an interval is scored 1 and is immediately preceded by an interval scored 0 and using the result as an estimate of frequency will almost always underestimate frequency. On the other hand, whole-interval sampling will never overestimate either prevalence or frequency.

Discrete Sampling

Although observations in semicontinuous sampling retain some degree of continuous observation, those in discrete sampling are made at distinct points in time. Theoretically, each point of observation in discrete sampling occupies an infinitesimally brief amount of time, such that the observation is considered instantaneous. Two discrete sampling methods have been commonly used. These are the *ad libitum* method and the *momentary sampling* method.

Ad Libitum Sampling

The ad libitum (ad lib.) sampling method is most commonly used in field investigations, particularly among observers of animal behaviors in natural settings (Altmann, 1974). Behaviors are observed and recorded on a nonsystematic and informal basis. Altmann described ad lib. sampling as "typical field notes." Among the target behaviors of interest, an observer observes whatever is most readily observable and records as much as can be recorded. In a controlled setting, the ad lib. method is used when a behavior is observed at "random" for a specified number of times within in a given observation session (cf. Kubany & Sloggett, 1973). For example, a mentally retarded subject in a residential setting may be observed at random 10 times a day by a nurse and the occurrences or nonoccurrences of particular behaviors of interest are recorded.

In a sense, this approach appears to be a type of passive random sampling procedure in that the time at which a particular behavior is observed and recorded is random. If it is indeed a random sampling process, the array of well-established inferential statistical theories and techniques would be applicable to assess the degree to which the sampled data represent the parameters of the overall observation session. However, upon close examination, this method is far short of a random sampling process. In a random sampling process, a researcher determines when to observe along the time continuum a priori. That is, through the use of a random number table or by other means, a researcher can arrive at a set of random time points at which observations are to be made. Typically, the times of observation of ad lib. sampling, however, are not predetermined randomly but are determined by the activities of the subject(s) and of the observer.

The degree to which summary descriptive statistics derived from an ad lib. sample are unbiased estimates of session scores is further compromised by a number of factors. First, the sampling process may be somewhat systematic because when to observe and what to observe within the observation session are determined by "unconscious sampling decisions" made by the observer (Altmann, 1974). For instance, in the previous example of the nurse observing the mentally retarded subject, it is less likely that the nurse would observe the subject at a time when the workload of the nurse is at a peak than it is at other times. In this case, an external event (workload) determines when observations are most difficult and the nurse would most likely decide not to observe at those times. Second, this sampling process is highly susceptible to observer bias. An observer with a particular preconceived hypothesis of what behaviors can be expected to occur would most likely pay closer attention to the occurrences of those behaviors. Hence, what confirms the hypothesis would be more likely to be recorded. Third, some behaviors tend to attract more attention than others. For instance, it is more likely that an observer would notice and record a fight than a quiet conversation between two subjects. Finally, when a number of subjects are observed, some individual subjects would tend to attract more attention than others. These subjects may tend to emit more inappropriate disruptive behavior, speak louder, be more active, speak more frequently, be different in physical appearance, and so on. Ad lib. time sampling is more analogous to accidental subject sampling than it is to simple random subject sampling.

Various attempts have been made to correct for some of these biases in ad lib. sampling. For example, Chalmers (1968) and Sade (1966) attempted to assess the differential visibility for various subgroups of subjects. This differential visibility could then be used to correct for the fact that some subjects tend to be more visible in an ad lib. sampling session. The assumptions underlying these correction procedures have been severely challenged by Altmann (1974). In general, too little is known about the statistical properties and assumptions of ad lib. sampling today to consider it an adequate intrasession sampling process for rigorous scientific investigations. Hartmann and Wood (1982) suggested that this method does not "deserve formal recognition" because of its nonrigorous nature. However, ad lib. sampling may be useful in an informal observation session to guide the formulation of hypothesis for more rigorous observations at a later date.

Momentary Sampling

Momentary sampling (Bindra & Blond, 1958) has been alternately referred to as "instantaneous time sampling," "scan sampling," "discontinuous probe time sampling," "point sampling," or, simply, "time sampling." In momentary sampling, as in partial-interval and whole-interval sampling, the length of an observation session is divided into a number of time intervals of specified length. Usually the session is divided into equal intervals. The behavior of interest is observed only at the very last moment of each interval. If the behavior is occurring at the exact moment of observation, a score of 1 is assigned to that interval. If the behavior is not occurring at that exact moment, a score of 0 is assigned to that interval.

Alternatively, one may observe and record the occurrence or nonoccurrence of the behavior at the first moment of each interval or consistently at a certain moment within an interval. For example, a common variant of momentary intrasession sampling is to observe and record the behavior in alternate intervals (cf. Haynes, 1978). In a momentary intrasession sampling using 5-second intervals, for instance, the behavior is observed at the last moment of the first 5-second interval. The next 5 seconds are used to record the behavior. The third 5-second interval is used again to observe, and so on. This process is essentially identical to a 10-second momentary intrasession sampling in which the observation is made at the 5th second of every interval. Hawkins, Axelrod, and Hall (1976) likened momentary intrasession time sampling to taking a still photograph at equal intervals of time and then examining each photograph to determine if the behavior has occurred. Figure 4.2 provides a graphic representation of a momentary intrasession sampling process in which observations are made at the last moment of an interval.

Many studies have found that dividing the number of intervals scored 1 by the total number of intervals provides an unbiased estimate of prevalence (e.g., Altmann, 1974; Powell et al., 1977). However, the absolute value of the error in estimating prevalence with momentary sampling can be substantial, especially if the interval size is large (Brulle & Repp, 1984). Momentary sampling scores were found to be either unrelated or only marginally related to frequency (Powell & Rockinson, 1978; Rhine & Linville, 1980). Based upon these inductive analyses, it is generally agreed that the raw chain of 1s and 0s produced by momentary sampling provides no useful information on frequency and that other session summary data involving frequencies—such as rate, mean bout duration, and mean IRT duration—cannot be estimated. Momentary sampling is recommended as the best intrasession sampling method for prevalence estimates (e.g., Altmann, 1974; Powell et al., 1977). Others have recommended against its use on the ground that prevalence alone is not an adequate descriptor of behaviors within a session (e.g., Rhine & Linville, 1980).

Other Intrasession Sampling Methods

Because of the various problems found in empirical or simulated studies

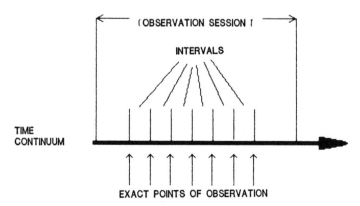

FIGURE 4.2.   A Momentary sampling session in which observations are made at the end of each interval.

associated with partial-interval, whole-interval, and momentary sampling, a number of alternative intrasession sampling methods have been suggested. Most of these alternative methods are variations or combinations of different intrasession sampling methods. For example, Hartmann and Wood (1982) suggested the simultaneous use of momentary sampling and continuous frequency recording. Powell (1984), on the other hand, suggested a combination of momentary sampling and a modified partial-interval sampling process for intrasession sampling. In Powell's system, two scores are assigned to each interval. First, the interval is scored based upon the momentary sampling procedure. Second, the interval is scored 1 if a behavior initiation occurs within the interval. Otherwise, the interval is scored 0. The results are two chains of 1s and 0s. The first chain is used to estimate prevalence; whereas the second chain is used to estimate frequency. In general, these alternative methods have been found or can be expected to produce data with less systematic error than the use of partial-interval, whole-interval, ad lib., or momentary sampling alone.

Most of the findings of the empirical or simulated studies on partial-interval sampling, whole-interval sampling, and momentary sampling can be explained by recently developed statistical theories of intrasession sampling. The application of these theories to partial-interval, whole-interval, or momentary sampling can lead to accurate estimates of session scores with no systematic error. With knowledge of the theoretical basis of intrasession sampling, the demonstrated or expected efficacy of some of the alternative sampling methods, such as the combined method suggested by Powell (1984) and that suggested by Hartmann and Wood (1982), can be explained and predicted, as is elaborated in the next section.

STATISTICAL THEORY
OF INTRASESSION SAMPLING

When intrasession sampling data are used to estimate session scores, there are two possible sources of error, systematic and random sampling errors. Systematic errors are those that cause an estimate to be biased. For instance, when partial-interval sampling data consistently lead to overestimates but not to underestimates of prevalence, the sampling error can be described as systematic. Random intrasession sampling error, on the other hand, may lead to an over- or to an underestimate of an individual session score. In the long run, however, the random errors for a large number of estimates of the session score can be expected to neutralize one another, leading to a total error near 0. Hence, the average across a large number of estimates is an unbiased estimate of the session score in that this average, in theory, contains neither an over- nor an underestimation.

Of the two types of error, systematic error is more serious. Random error can be minimized by increasing the number of observation intervals within an observation session. This, however, will not minimize systematic error. Also, random error affects the reliability of data and can be detected through reliability assessment procedures, as described in the next chapter. Systematic error, however, affects validity but may or may not affect reliability. Hence, systematic error may or may not be detected by reliability assessment procedures.

Using the number of intervals scored 1 that are immediately preceded by an interval scored 0 as an estimate of frequency in partial-interval, momentary, or whole-interval sampling tends to contain both systematic and random errors. Dividing the number of intervals scored 1 by the total number of intervals as an estimate of prevalence in partial-interval and whole-interval sampling also contains both systematic and random errors. Using the same approach in momentary sampling, however, will lead to an estimate of prevalence that contains only random error. Systematic errors in a frequency estimate will also lead to systematic errors in estimates of mean bout duration and mean IRT duration. Systematic errors in prevalence will lead to systematic errors in all other estimates of session scores except for frequency. When both the frequency and the prevalence estimates contain systematic error, all estimates of session scores contain systematic error.

The fact that session score estimates derived from these sampling methods tend to contain systematic error does not imply that only continuous observation methods can be used. When the process used to estimate session scores from the data gathered through these methods is appropriately adjusted, the resulting estimates will contain little or no systematic error under certain conditions. Furthermore, when these statistical conditions are not met, the estimates can be adjusted for the expected systematic error so that the final estimate will be unbiased. These adjustment procedures can be directly deduced from the inherent nature of the three intrasession sampling methods.

Inherent Nature of Intrasession Sampling

Systematic error associated with the prevalence and frequency estimates derived from the three sampling methods are inherent in the definitions of these methods. Specifically, the existence or nonexistence of systematic error is determined by the relationship between the chosen interval length, each bout duration, and each IRT duration. Understanding these relationships can provide a guide to the proper use of intrasession time sampling.

Prevalence Estimates

Within an observation session, there are three types of intervals (Ary, 1984). The first type are those intervals in which the behavior occurs from the beginning until the end of the interval without any IRT. For this type of interval, all three sampling methods will produce a score of 1. The second type of interval are those in which the behavior never occurs. For this type of interval, all three sampling methods will produce a score of 0. The third type of interval is a mixed interval. In this interval, the behavior occurs some but not all of the time. For a mixed interval, the score is different for the three sampling methods. With partial sampling, this interval is scored 1. With whole-interval sampling, this interval is scored 0. With momentary sampling, the interval may be scored 1 or 0, depending on whether the behavior is occurring at the exact moment of observation.

The systematic error in estimating prevalence is due to the different scoring of the mixed intervals. In partial-interval sampling, all mixed intervals in an observation session are scored 1, as if the behavior had occurred during the entire interval in each case. The IRTs within these mixed intervals are ignored. Hence, dividing the number of intervals scored 1 by the total number of intervals would lead to a systematic (consistent) over-estimate of prevalence. In whole-interval sampling, the opposite is the case. That is, all mixed intervals are scored 0, as if the behavior had never occurred in these intervals. Hence, prevalence is systematically underestimated. In momentary sampling, a mixed interval may or may not be scored 1, according to whether the behavior occurred at the exact moment of observation. In the long run, half of the mixed intervals can be expected to be scored 1, whereas the other half would be scored 0. Hence, momentary sampling produces an unbiased estimate of prevalence containing only random error.

Frequency Estimates

When the number of intervals scored 1 that are immediately preceded by an interval scored 0 in the chain of 1s and 0s is used as an estimate of frequency, mixed intervals within the observation session will lead to a systematic underestimation. There are five basic types of mixed intervals (see Figure 4.3). A mixed interval may contain a single behavior initiation (Interval 1 in Figure 4.3). For partial-interval sampling, the behavior initiation is detected only if the preceding interval happens to be scored 0. Otherwise, this behavior initiation is not represented in the frequency estimate. For whole-interval sampling, the behavior initiation is detected only if the next interval (i.e., Interval 2) happens to be scored 1. Other-

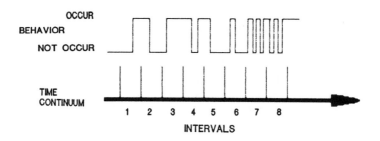

FIGURE 4.3.   Mixed intervals.

wise, this initiation is not represented. For momentary sampling in which observations are made at the last moment of the interval, the initiation is detected.

A second type of mixed interval contains a single behavior termination (Interval 2 in Figure 4.3). This type of mixed interval will have no direct effect on the estimation of frequency for whole-interval and momentary sampling. However, it can have an indirect effect on the detection of behavior initiation in partial-interval sampling. Specifically, if the behavior is initiated again in the next interval, that initiation would not be detected because both intervals are scored 1.

A third type of mixed interval contains first a termination and then an initiation of behavior (Interval 4 in Figure 4.3). For this type of interval, neither partial-interval nor momentary sampling can detect the initiation. The initiation is detected in whole-interval sampling only if both the preceding and the following intervals are scored 1. The fourth type of mixed interval contains first an initiation then a termination within the same interval (Interval 6 in Figure 4.3). Neither whole-interval nor momentary sampling can detect the initiation. The initiation is detected in partial-interval sampling only if both the preceding and the following intervals are scored 0. Finally, the fifth type of interval contains multiple behavior initiations and terminations (Intervals 7 and 8 in Figure 4.3). At best, the sampling methods can detect only one of the many initiations. They may, however, detect none of these initiations.

In summary, the ability to estimate frequency accurately from sampling data depends on the capability of the sampling method to detect behavior initiations. In the presence of mixed intervals, some but not all behavior initiations within these mixed intervals will be detected. However, there is no situation in which a behavior initiation is indicated by an interval scored 1 that is immediately preceded by an interval scored 0 when there is, in fact, no behavior initiation in the actual stream of behavior. Therefore, all three sampling methods will tend to underestimate frequency due to their inability to detect some of the behavior initiations in the mixed intervals. None of the three methods will overestimate frequency.

Conditions Needed
for Intrasession Sampling Accuracy

The three sampling methods will produce accurate or unbiased estimates of session scores if the mixed intervals just described do not exist or exist at a minimum. The existence of these mixed intervals is determined by the relationships among the bout duration, the IRT duration, and the chosen interval length. When these relationships meet certain conditions, the mixed intervals are eliminated or simplified in such a way that accurate or unbiased estimates of session scores are possible. The conditions needed for the three sampling methods are different but symmetrical, with partial-interval and whole-interval sampling forming mirror images and momentary sampling as the center.

Momentary Sampling

With momentary sampling, the data yield an unbiased estimate of prevalence. Frequency, however, is systematically underestimated by momentary sampling data. The underestimation is caused by the existence of the third, fourth, and fifth types of mixed intervals (i.e., Intervals 4, 6, 7, and 8 in Figure 4.3). These mixed intervals can exist only when the interval is longer than either the shortest bout duration or the shortest IRT duration of the observation session. If the interval is shorter than both the shortest bout duration and the shortest IRT duration, these mixed intervals are eliminated. Therefore, for an accurate frequency count within an observation session, the interval must be shorter than both the shortest of all bout durations and the shortest of all IRT durations in that observation session. When these conditions are met, a count of the number of intervals scored 1 that are immediately preceded by an interval scored 0 will produce an accurate frequency count with neither systematic nor random time-sampling error. If the first interval of the chain is scored 1, the frequency count should be adjusted by $+1$.

Dividing the number of intervals scored 1 by the total number of intervals will still produce an unbiased estimate of prevalence. The random error in the prevalence estimate is caused by either overestimating or underestimating the prevalence of behavior in intervals containing either the initiation or termination of a behavior bout. Figure 4.4 shows two examples of over- and underestimating prevalence in momentary sampling. The overestimation is caused by behavior bouts that occupy just over x number of intervals but are scored in $x + 1$ intervals. For example, Bout A in Figure 4.5 occupies just over two intervals but three intervals are scored. Hence, the bout duration is overestimated by almost an entire interval. The underestimation is caused by behavior bouts that occupy almost x

number of intervals but are scored in $x - 1$ intervals. For example, Bout B in Figure 4.4 occupies almost three intervals but is scored in only two intervals. The bout duration is underestimated by almost an entire interval. When the conditions for accurate frequency count are met, all bouts are at most either overestimated by one interval or underestimated by one interval. Since the frequency count is an accurate reflection of the number of behavior bouts, the maximum possible random time-sampling error in the prevalence estimate is $\pm$ (frequency/number of intervals). The expected random error is zero.

Partial-Interval Sampling

In partial-interval sampling, the underestimation of frequency may be caused by any of the five types of mixed intervals described in Figure 4.3. This procedure will fail to detect initiation of behavior if the interval is longer than the bout duration or if the interval is longer than one half of the IRT duration. If the interval is shorter than both bout duration and IRT duration, the third, fourth, and fifth types of mixed intervals are eliminated. However, the remaining first and second types of mixed intervals may still lead to an underestimate of frequency. The first type of interval is problematic for partial-interval sampling if the preceding interval is also scored 1. The second type of mixed interval is problematic if the following interval is also scored 1. These problematic situations will not occur if the interval is shorter than half of the shortest IRT in an observation session because any IRT will always produce at least one score of 0 in the chain. Therefore, for an accurate frequency count within an observation session, the interval must be shorter than the shortest of all bout durations and shorter than one half of the shortest of all IRT durations in that observation session. When these conditions are met, a count of the number of intervals that are scored 1 and that are immediately preceded by an interval scored 0 will produce an accurate frequency count with

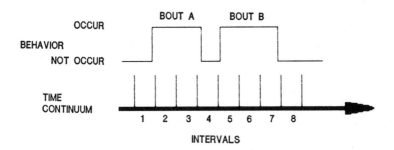

FIGURE 4.4. Over- and underestimation or correction of prevalence.

neither systematic nor random error. Again, if the first interval of the chain is scored 1, the frequency count should be adjusted by +1.

Even when the conditions needed for an accurate frequency count with partial-interval sampling are met, the prevalence estimate derived from dividing the number of intervals scored 1 by the total number of intervals will still be a systematic overestimate. The systematic overestimate is caused, in one extreme, by scoring 1 for both the initiating and terminating intervals of a behavior bout when the behavior barely occupies any time at all in these two intervals. For example, for Bout A in Figure 4.4, four intervals are scored, but the bout occupies only a little over two intervals. In the other extreme, the behavior occupies most of the initiating and terminating intervals. In this case, the bout duration is overestimated by an insignificant amount of time. For example, for Bout B in Figure 4.4, the bout occupies barely under three intervals and three intervals are scored. By and large, over all behavior bouts within an observation session, the average overestimation of bout length can be expected to be one interval length for each bout. Therefore, when the conditions needed for an accurate frequency count are met, the total number of intervals by which the total duration is overestimated corresponds to the frequency of behavior occurrence. Hence, the overestimate of duration can be corrected by subtracting frequency from the number of intervals scored 1. An unbiased estimate of prevalence can be obtained by dividing the adjusted total duration by the total number of intervals. The random error in this adjusted prevalence estimate is caused by either overcorrecting or undercorrecting the total duration. Maximally, either all bouts are overcorrected by one interval each or all bouts are undercorrected by one interval each. Because the frequency count is an accurate reflection of the number of behavior bouts, the maximum possible random error in the prevalence estimate is $\pm$ (frequency/number of intervals). The expected random error of the adjusted prevalence estimate is zero.

Whole-Interval Sampling

In whole-interval sampling, the underestimation of frequency may be caused by any of the first, third, fourth, or fifth type of mixed intervals described in Figure 4.3. These mixed intervals lead to systematic errors if the interval is longer than either the IRT or one half of the bout duration. If the interval is shorter than both bout duration and IRT duration, the third, fourth, and fifth types of mixed intervals are eliminated. However, the first type of mixed intervals leads to error if the following interval is also scored 0. In this case, the behavior initiation is not detected at all. This situation will not occur if the interval is shorter than one half of the shortest bout in an observation session because any behavior bout will always produce at least a score of 1. Therefore, for an accurate frequency count with whole-interval sampling, the interval must be shorter than the shortest of all IRT durations and shorter than one half of the shortest of all bout durations in that observation session. When these conditions are met, a count of the number of intervals scored 1 that are immediately preceded by an interval scored 0 will, again, produce an accurate frequency count with neither systematic nor random error. As it was for the other two sampling methods, if the first interval of the chain is scored 1, the frequency count should be adjusted by +1.

When the conditions needed for an accurate frequency count with whole-interval sampling are met, dividing the number of intervals scored 1 by the total number of intervals will still produce an underestimate of prevalence. This systematic underestimate is caused, in one extreme, by scoring neither the initiating nor the terminating interval of a behavior bout when the behavior barely occupies any time at all in these two intervals. In this case, the amount of underestimation is very small. For example, for Bout A in Figure 4.4, two intervals are scored 1 in whole-interval sampling and the bout occupies only a little over two intervals. In the other extreme, the behavior occupies most of the initiating and terminating intervals. In this case, the bout duration is underestimated by a significant amount of time. For example, for Bout B in Figure 4.4, the bout occupies barely under three intervals, but only one interval is scored 1 in whole-interval sampling. As with partial-interval sampling, over all behavior bouts within an observation session, the average underestimation of bout length can be expected to be one interval length for each bout. Therefore, the overestimate of total duration can be corrected by adding frequency to the number of intervals scored 1. An unbiased estimate of prevalence can be obtained by dividing the adjusted total duration by the total number of intervals. The maximum possible random error in the prevalence estimate is, again, ±(frequency/number of intervals). The expected random error in this prevalence estimate is zero.

Other Methods

Hartmann and Wood (1982) suggested that behavior be observed through a momentary sampling procedure and a continuous frequency recording simultaneously. This approach will produce an accurate frequency with no sampling error because sampling is not involved in the continuous frequency recording. The prevalence estimate derived from the momentary sampling procedure will be unbiased. However, if the conditions outlined earlier for momentary sampling are not met, the range of possible random error in the prevalence estimate will be larger than ±(frequency/number of intervals). If the conditions are met, Hartmann and Wood's approach is redundant because the chain of 1s and 0s alone will produce an accurate frequency.

Powell (1984) suggested that a momentary sampling procedure be supplemented by a simultaneous modified partial-interval sampling procedure. Specifically, two chains of 1s and 0s are recorded. The first chain is the momentary sampling interval scores. The second chain is obtained from the modified partial-interval sampling procedure, in which an interval is scored 1 if a behavior initiation has occurred in the interval and is scored 0 if there is no initiation. When the conditions needed for momentary sampling outlined earlier are not met, the underestimation of frequency from the momentary data is caused by the third, fourth, and fifth types of mixed intervals (i.e., Intervals 4, 6, 7 and 8 in Figure 4.3). The supplemental modified partial-interval sampling procedure in Powell's system will accurately detect the behavior initiations in the third and the fourth types of mixed intervals. However, only one of the many behavior initiations in the fifth type of mixed interval (i.e., Intervals 7 and 8 in Figure 4.3) will be detected. Hence, frequency will still be underestimated. The underestimation of frequency in this system will be less than that derived from the momentary sampling results alone.

Powell further suggested that brief intervals (e.g., 5-second intervals) be used. The use of a brief interval length will minimize the occurrence of the fifth type of mixed intervals. When the fifth type of mixed intervals do not exist in an observation session, Powell's system will produce both accurate frequency and unbiased prevalence. Again, if the conditions for momentary sampling outlined earlier are met, Powell's system is redundant in that the intervals scored 1 in the modified partial-interval chain of 1s and 0s will coincide with the 0–1 pairs of scores in the momentary chain. That is, momentary sampling alone will produce both frequency and prevalence. Hence, the supplemental modified partial-interval sampling procedure will not be needed.

Summary

The three sampling methods are symmetric in many respects. A mixed interval is scored 1 in partial-interval sampling, scored 0 in whole-interval sampling, and may be scored 1 or 0 in momentary sampling. These symmetric differences in the scoring of a mixed interval lead to a symmetric set of conditions for accurate frequency counts. To summarize these symmetrical conditions in symbolic terms: If the interval length is i, the shortest bout in an observation session is b, and the shortest IRT is t, then the conditions needed for accurate frequency counts for the three sampling methods are (Suen & Ary, 1986a):

$$
\left.
\begin{array}{ll}
i < b \text{ and } < .5t & \text{for partial-interval sampling} \\
i < b \text{ and } < t & \text{for momentary sampling} \\
\text{and} \quad i < .5b \text{ and } < t & \text{for whole-interval sampling.}
\end{array}
\right\} \quad (4.5)
$$

When these conditions are met, any of the three sampling methods will produce an accurate frequency count with neither systematic nor random error. To obtain an unbiased estimate of total duration expressed in real-time units instead of intervals (D), the number of intervals scored 1 (S) can be adjusted with the frequency count (F) as needed:

$$
\left.
\begin{array}{ll}
D = i(S - F) & \text{for partial-interval sampling} \\
D = i(S) & \text{for momentary sampling} \\
\text{and} \quad D = i(S + F) & \text{for whole-interval sampling.}
\end{array}
\right\} \quad (4.6)
$$

For example, with a 20-minute session of 120 ten-second intervals, 40 of which are scored 1, having a frequency count of 8, the following duration estimates would be made:

For partial-interval sampling,
$$
\begin{aligned}
D &= i(S - F) \\
&= 10(40 - 8) \\
&= 10(32) \\
&= 320 \text{ seconds.}
\end{aligned}
$$

For momentary sampling,
$$
\begin{aligned}
D &= i(S) \\
&= 10(40) \\
&= 400 \text{ seconds.}
\end{aligned}
$$

For whole-interval sampling,
$$
\begin{aligned}
D &= i(S + F) \\
&= 10(40 + 8 \\
&= 480 \text{ seconds.}
\end{aligned}
$$

If the total number of observation intervals is N, unbiased estimates of prevalence (P) can be obtained by:

$$
\left.
\begin{array}{ll}
P = (S - F)/N & \text{for partial-interval sampling} \\
P = S/N & \text{for momentary sampling} \\
\text{and} \quad P = (S + F)/N & \text{for whole-interval sampling.}
\end{array}
\right\} \quad (4.7)
$$

In our example, the prevalence for partial-interval sampling would be (40 − 8)/120 = .267, for momentary sampling 40/120 = .33, and for whole-interval sampling (40 + 8)/120 = .400. Each of the three P estimates is unbiased. The maximum possible random error for the P estimate is $\pm F/N$. In our example, the maximum possible error is plus or minus .067. The expected random error is zero.

There has in the past been some argument as to whether the total number of intervals (i.e., the number of observations) or the length of each interval is the determinant of the accuracy of session score estimates derived from sampling. Based upon the previous analysis of the relationships among interval length, bout duration, and IRT duration, the conditions in Equation 4.5 are approached only through the shortening of interval lengths. As interval lengths are shortened, the conditions needed to eliminate systematic errors in prevalence and frequency estimates are approached. Increasing the number of observation intervals without shortening each interval length, however, will not reduce systematic error. It will only reduce the amount of random error. This is because the expected random error of zero in prevalence estimate is approximated when there are a large number of behavior bouts. The more observation intervals, the more behavior bouts are likely to be observed.

This difference in the effect of reducing interval length versus increasing the number of intervals is conceptual only. In practice, when changing interval lengths or the number of intervals within an observation session, researchers generally do not change the length of the overall observation session. In this case, an increase in the number of intervals can be accomplished only by decreasing the length of each interval. Conversely, decreasing the length of each interval will always lead to more intervals within the session. Hence, changing either of these parameters without changing the length of the observation session will tend to decrease both systematic and random error.

PROBABILITY OF SYSTEMATIC ERROR IN SINGLE-SUBJECT INTRASESSION SAMPLING

Theoretically, in order for either of the three sampling methods to produce accurate frequency counts and unbiased prevalence estimates, the conditions outlined in Equation 4.5 must be met. In practice, the lengths of the shortest bout (b) and the shortest IRT (t) within a given observation session are unknown. However, the expected b and t values can be estimated based on past knowledge of the behavior. Specifically, knowledge of past b and t values can be used to assess the probability that conditions outlined in Equation 4.5 are violated in an observation session with a certain chosen interval length. If this probability is high, the conditions are most likely violated and the data from the observation session will most likely contain systematic error. In this case, the interval length should be shortened and the probability of systematic error reassessed with the new interval length. If the probability is low, the conditions outlined in Equation 4.5 are approximated. An accurate frequency count can be expected from the sampling data. Furthermore, with the appropriate adjustment outlined in Equations 4.6 and 4.7, unbiased estimates of prevalence and other session scores can be derived from the data.

Suen and Ary (1986a) suggested that the probability of systematic error can be assessed through a Poisson process, as follows: If the average of all past b values is $\bar{b}$ and the average of all past t values is $\bar{t}$, for an observation session with an interval length of i, the probability of systematic error (p_e) can be assessed through:

$$p_e = \sum_{j=0}^{i} \left(\frac{e^{-\bar{b}}\bar{b}^j}{j!} + \frac{e^{-.5\bar{t}}(.5t)^j}{j!} \right) \tag{4.8}$$

for partial-interval sampling,

$$p_e = \sum_{j=0}^{i} \left(\frac{e^{-\bar{b}}\bar{b}^j}{j!} + \frac{e^{-\bar{t}}\bar{t}^j}{j!} \right) \tag{4.9}$$

for momentary sampling, and

$$p_e = \sum_{j=0}^{i} \left(\frac{e^{-.5\bar{b}}(.5\bar{b})^j}{j!} + \frac{e^{-\bar{t}}\bar{t}^j}{j!} \right) \tag{4.10}$$

for whole-interval sampling; where e is a universal mathematical constant approximately equal to 2.718; j is a counter that equals 0, 1, 2, . . . i; and $!$ symbolizes the mathematical factorial process in which a number is multiplied by that number minus 1, and then multiplied by that number minus 2, and so on until 1 is reached.

Central to the application of these equations are the availability of the mean b and mean t values based upon past knowledge of the behavior. Ideally, these two values should be calculated based upon b and t values obtained from previous continuous observations of the behavior. This would lead to the most reliable estimates of $\bar{b}$ and $\bar{t}$. However, prior continuous observations are not always feasible.

A reasonable alternative is to obtain estimates of b and t values by independently interviewing a number of independent caretakers of the subject. It can be expected that a single estimate of b or t provided by a single caretaker will contain errors. However, when the estimate of one caretaker is independent of that of another, the total errors across all caretakers interviewed can be expected to be zero. The average of all b and t estimates are, hence, unbiased estimates of the $\bar{b}$ and $\bar{t}$ values one would have obtained had a number of prior continuous observation sessions been conducted. The larger the number of caretakers interviewed, the more stable is the mean of b and the mean of t and the closer are they to the means of continuous observations. It should be noted that, whenever possible, prior continuous observations should be used to obtain empirical data for the estimation of the two parameters. Within the context of systematic sampling errors, the use of subjective estimates from independent caretakers will pose no threat to the accuracy of the mean b and mean t. However, these mean estimates can be biased if the individual estimates from the caretakers are not truly independent (e.g., prior discussion occurred among caretakers) or if the behavioral definitions used during the caretaker interviews are unclear or biased.

To illustrate the use of the probability method, the following example is used: A researcher wished to observe a particular behavior of a subject with partial-interval sampling procedures. Prior to the observation session, the researcher independently interviewed six caretakers whose interactions with the subject are independent of one another, to assess the possible values of shortest bout (b) and shortest IRT (t). The researcher obtained the following two sets of estimates:

b : (15, 15, 15, 15, 20, 12)
and t : (30, 30, 25, 40, 50, 30).

By computing the mean of all bs and all ts, the researcher determined that $\bar{b}$ = 15.33 and $\bar{t}$ = 34.17. Thus, $.5\bar{t}$ = 17.08.

The researcher wished to use an interval length of 10 seconds. By applying i = 10, and the values of $\bar{b}$ = 15.33 and $.5\bar{t}$ = 17.08 to Equation 4.8, the probability that a partial-interval sampling procedure with an interval of 10 seconds would underestimate frequency, and hence be unable to correct for prevalence overestimation, is approximately 0.15. The researcher might decide that this probability was unacceptable and decide to use an interval length of 5 seconds. The new interval length would reduce the total probability of systematic error to 0.0028 (less than 1%).

Let us assume that the researcher decided to use the 5-second interval because the probability of systematic error of 0.0028 was found to be negligible and proceeded to observe the behavior through partial-interval sampling. Let us also assume that the following chain of scores for each interval in the partial-interval sampling was obtained:

11000111010110110111000000110000011111101000011011

Because the probability of systematic error was low, the conditions outlined in Equation 4.5 for partial-interval sampling was assumed to be met. Hence, frequency could be derived by counting the number of 1s that are immediately preceded by a 0. This frequency is adjusted by +1 for the fact that the first interval was scored 1. The correct frequency is therefore 11, with only 0.0028 probability that the true frequency is less than 11. The unbiased estimate of duration can then be obtained from Equation 4.7. In this case, the number of intervals scored 1 (S) is 26, the frequency (F) is 11, and the number of intervals (N) is 50. Therefore, prevalence (P) is $(26 - 11)/50 = .30$. The maximum random error in the prevalence estimate is $\pm F/N = \pm.22$, with an expected random error of zero.

In the previous example, the exact computational process was not illustrated. This is because the use of some type of electronic computational aid in the application of Equations 4.8 through 4.10 may be needed due to the complicated calculation processes for the natural logarithm and the factorial terms.

Suen and Ary suggested four strategies for the derivation of the probability values in Equations 4.8 through 4.10. First, the metric of i, b, and t can be changed to a larger metric, such as changing from seconds to minutes. This will result in fewer calculation steps. This strategy is applicable when the desired i can be converted into an exact higher unit (e.g., 60 seconds converted into 1 minute). Second, Hays (1973) described a binomial approximation procedure to assess Poisson probabilities, which, in some cases, may be applicable. Third, Pearson and Hartley (1966) provided a detailed table of Poisson cumulative probabilities utilizing chi-square probabilities. This table can be used by setting the chi-square value at $2b$ and $2t$, respectively, with $2i$ degrees of freedom. Further, a microcomputer software for behavioral observation data analysis entitled BOSA (Suen & Yue, forthcoming) contains a routine to compute these probabilities. Appendix B provides a table of probabilities of systematic error in single-subject time sampling for selected intervals, which was constructed through the use of BOSA. To illustrate the use of Appendix B, consider a situation in which the mean b is 20 seconds, the mean t is 30 seconds, and a researcher wishes to employ the partial-interval sampling method with 10-second intervals. For this situation, the table for "interval = 10" would be used. From the table, the probability of systematic error is .1293, or 13%.

Various empirical studies (e.g., Powell et al., 1977; Sanson-Fisher, Poole, & Dunn, 1980) have found that the shorter the interval length, the more accurate the prevalence estimate. This is because the shorter the interval, the more likely that conditions outlined in Equation 4.5 are met. The general recommendation has been to set the interval as short as possible (e.g., 3 or 5 seconds). However, once an interval is at a length appropriate for the b and t values of the behavior, additional reduction of interval length will only slightly increase the reliability of the estimates of session scores. In other words, for every behavior, there is a particular interval length, which is the threshold between reliable and unreliable outcomes. The probability process just described provides a means to identify this threshold. The application of this process would provide the researcher with the flexibility to set longer interval lengths as long as the probability of systematic error is within a tolerable level.

No suggestion has been made as to what may be regarded as a tolerable probability of systematic error. It is important to keep in mind that this probability is the probability that some systematic error is contained within the frequency and/or prevalence estimates derived from the chain of 1s and 0s. It is not an indicator of the amount of systematic error. Hence, it is possible that the probability of the existence of systematic error is high but the actual amount of systematic error is very small. Caution should be taken not to interpret the probability value as a direct indication of the amount of systematic error. For example, if the probability of systematic error for a partial-interval sampling procedure is 0.30, it does not indicate that the prevalence estimate derived from the data will be overestimated by 30%. Theoretically, one can expect that the higher the probability, the more likely it is that the amount of systematic error is large. However, this is not always the case.

PROBABILITY OF SYSTEMATIC ERROR IN MULTIPLE-SUBJECT INTRASESSION SAMPLING

A number of subjects may be observed within an observation session. Thomson, Holmberg, and Baer (1974) described three multiple-subject intrasession sampling methods. These are the contiguous method, the sequential method, and the alternating method. In contiguous sampling, the observation session is divided evenly into segments equal to the number of subjects. Within each segment, a single subject is observed. For instance, to observe five subjects in a 1-hour session, the first subject is observed in the first 12 minutes. The second subject is observed in the next 12 minutes, and so on. In this manner, the multiple-subject sampling session is equivalent to a series of shorter single-subject sampling sessions. Hence, all the previous discussions regarding single-subject sampling would apply to each of the smaller single-subject subsessions.

In sequential sampling, the observation session is divided into intervals, and observations are rotated among the subjects. Hence, the first subject is observed in the first interval. In the next interval, the observer switches attention to the second subject. The third subject is observed in the third interval, and so on until all subjects have been observed. The observer then switches attention back to the first subject and repeats the entire rotation process. The intervals within a sequential sampling process may be scored through one of the three intrasession sampling methods discussed previously. Hence, a sequential sampling session may be scored in a sequential partial-interval, a sequential momentary, or a sequential whole-interval manner.

The alternating method of multiple-subject sampling combines the features of both contiguous and sequential sampling. The observation session is divided into a number of segments and the subjects are divided into an equal number of subgroups. Each subgroup is to be observed within a particular segment only. Within each segment, the subgroup members are observed through a sequential sampling process. In this way, an alternating observation session is equivalent to a series of smaller sequential sampling sessions. Therefore, the following discussion of systematic error in sequential sampling is applicable to both sequential sampling and alternating sampling.

Ary and Suen (1984) demonstrated that the conditions outlined in Equation 4.5 and the equations outlined in 4.6 and 4.7 could be extended to sequential sampling. Specifically, if a sequential partial-interval sampling method is used to observe K subjects using an interval length of i, in order to yield an accurate frequency count and an unbiased prevalence estimate, the value of K times i must be shorter than the shortest $\bar{b}$ among all K subjects and shorter than one half of the shortest $\bar{t}$ among all K subjects. For sequential momentary sampling, K times i must be shorter than both the shortest $\bar{b}$ and the shortest $\bar{t}$ among the K subjects. For sequential whole-interval sampling, K times i must be shorter than one half of the shortest $\bar{b}$ and shorter than the shortest $\bar{t}$ among the K subjects. The probability of systematic error associated with each of the three sequential sampling methods can be assessed by:

$$p_e = \sum_{j=0}^{s} \left(\frac{e^{-B}B^j}{j!} + \frac{e^{-.5T}(.5T)^j}{j!} \right) \quad (4.11)$$

for sequential partial-interval sampling,

$$p_e = \sum_{j=0}^{s} \left(\frac{e^{-B}B^j}{j!} + \frac{e^{-T}T^j}{j!} \right) \quad (4.12)$$

for sequential momentary sampling, and

$$p_e = \sum_{j=0}^{s} \left(\frac{e^{-.5B}(.5B)^j}{j!} + \frac{e^{-T}T^j}{j!} \right) \quad (4.13)$$

for sequential whole-interval sampling; where s is the product of K times i, B is the shortest $\bar{b}$ among the K subjects, and T is the shortest $\bar{t}$ among the K subjects. Note that j in this case is counted from 0 to s instead of from 0 to i.

If the probability of systematic error for sequential sampling with a particular interval length i is high, it does not necessarily imply that the data for all K subjects will contain systematic error. To assess the probability of systematic error for each of the K subjects within a sequential sampling session, the B and T values in Equations 4.11 through 4.13 can be substituted by the $\bar{b}$ and $\bar{t}$ values of each subject. This would result in K probabilities of systematic error, each indicating the systematic error in the frequency and prevalence estimates associated with each subject.

Corrective Procedures

Through the application of the appropriate probability process, it may be found that for a particular behavior, the appropriate interval is so short that interval-by-interval observations would be virtually indistinguishable from continuous observation. For this type of situation, a number of approaches can be taken. If at all possible, the real-time continuous observation method should be used. When this is not possible and when frequency is the only session score of interest, a continuous frequency tally is preferred. If prevalence is the score of interest, momentary sampling with the shortest realistic interval should be employed. If both frequency and prevalence are of interest, a combination of momentary sampling and frequency count, as suggested by Hartmann and Wood (1982), can be employed. Alternatively, the combination of momentary sampling and a modified partial-interval sampling method, as suggested by Powell (1984), can be employed.

If, for whatever practical reason, none of these approaches are appropriate and prevalence is the score of interest, Suen and Ary (1986b) suggested a post hoc correction procedure through which the systematic error associated with partial-interval and whole-interval prevalence estimates can be minimized. Specifically, when the observed frequency, whether or not it is underestimated, is more than five, the post hoc correction procedure will eliminate an average of 70% of the systematic overestimation association with partial-interval prevalence estimates (Suen, 1986a). There is no known post hoc method for correcting the systematic underestimation of frequency.

INTERSESSION SAMPLING

The purpose of intersession sampling is to select chunks of time as observation sessions within the overall period of interest along the infinite time continuum. In other words, one needs to decide how to break the time continuum within the period of interest into chunks of shorter time periods, which of these chunks should be used as observation sessions, and how long each observation session should be. When the period of interest is so short that one can reasonably consider the entire period an observation session of itself, intersession sampling is irrelevant. This is because the behavior can then be observed using one of the intrasession sampling methods discussed previously and the entire period of interest treated as an observation session. The data gathered, however, can only be representative of the observation session and cannot be generalized to other periods of time. In some clinical or applied research situations, the period of interest may well be sufficiently short as to be considered an observation session.

In scientific investigations where theories and hypotheses are tested and the results treated as generalized principles, it is rare that the period of time for inference is sufficiently short to be considered a realistic observation session. When an observation session represents only a segment of the entire period of interest, it is rare that a researcher does not wish to infer beyond the period of time contained within an observation session. For example, in a behavior modification program, a base-line measure is generally established prior to intervention as the basis for determining the effectiveness of the intervention strategy. The data from observation sessions prior to intervention are generalized to the time "prior to intervention." It is rare that one can infer the behavior "prior to intervention" based upon observations made in a single observation session. Hence, a number of observation sessions have to be scheduled, and the overall pattern of or summary statistics for these sessions can be used as an indicator of the behavior "prior to intervention."

When the overall period of interest is not sufficiently short to be considered a single observation session, some smaller observation sessions have to be selected within the period of interest. Where it is practical, the ideal process for the selection of observation sessions should start with the identification of all observation sessions within the defined period of interest. From this pool of possible observation sessions, one can then randomly select a sample of sessions.

Note that earlier in this chapter we discussed the difficulty of randomly observing a behavior along the time continuum. The random sampling discussed here is a random sample of sessions, not points of observation. A random sample of sessions is more practical than a random sample of points of observation. Suppose, for example, we are interested in assessing the proportion of time a nursing home resident spends conversing with others while in a public area. From the daily routines of the residents, we have established that the resident is in a public area (e.g., lobby, dining area, recreation area, etc.) a number of specific hours each day. With consent from the resident and the nursing home administrator, we may observe the resident at any time during those hours. In this situation, to obtain an estimate of the resident's prevalence of conversation, we use all the hours when the resident is in public areas within the overall time period of interest as the pool of possible observation sessions. From this pool, a random sample of 1-hour sessions can be drawn and observations made in the randomly selected observation sessions. This random sampling process, when possible, is important for the assessment of data reliability over the time dimension.

In the next two chapters, reliability is discussed. A number of methods are available today to assess the degree to which data obtained from individual observation sessions can be generalized across the time dimension. Random sampling of observation sessions is a central assumption of these methods. Again, the random sampling of observation sessions is an ideal. In observational studies today, because of various practical considerations, few studies have attained such a statistical ideal for meaningful assessment of reliability across the time dimension.

When a random selection of sessions is not realistic, there are a variety of approaches to selecting the chunks of time along the time continuum as observation sessions. Regardless of the process through which observation sessions are selected, the central issue in their selection is that data gathered in them must be representative of the behavior of interest throughout the period of time to which the data are to be generalized. In the selection of the final set of observation sessions, at least two decisions are made. First, one has to determine the length of each observation session. Second, one has to decide when and how often to schedule these observation sessions.

For some behaviors, natural events offer automatic boundaries for the length of an observation session. For example, if the behavior of interest is a child's in-class behavior, the length of a class session offers a guide for the maximum length of an observation session. One may use the entire class period or part of the period as an observation session. One may also divide the class period into a number of smaller observation sessions. The length of the session may be determined by what is feasible. For example, in order to observe the interaction between a mother and a child at home, the length of each observation session is determined by what is agreeable to the subjects. There is no practical guideline as to what constitutes an adequate length for an observation session. Various logical and practical considerations have to be taken into account. In general, the longer the observation session, the more likely it is that data from the session would represent the behavior over the larger defined period of generalization. However, this is not always true. For example, observing a child's behavior beyond the class session would not yield additional information regarding the child's in-class behavior. On the other hand, observing the mother–child interaction for 2 hours instead of 1 hour would give a more stable indication of the overall mother–child interaction pattern.

The questions of when to schedule an observation session and how often are important questions that may determine the overall quality of the study. Selection of the wrong time and place could lead to a waste of time or data that are not representative of the behavior of interest (Berliner, 1976; Herbert & Attridge, 1975). For example, the chosen observation session may be a period of time during which one does not expect the behavior to occur. Observing the behavior in this session would be a waste of time. For instance, one generally would not schedule a 1-hour observation session to start at 9:00 a.m. in order to observe a child's lunch-time behavior in a school cafeteria. Similarly, one would not select weekend observation sessions to observe the classroom behaviors of schoolchildren. Again, there is no general guideline as to when and how often to schedule observation sessions. The answers to these two questions are dependent upon practical and logical considerations.

Some behaviors occur very rarely in nature. When one wishes to observe these behaviors in their natural environments, observation sessions need to be scheduled at the time when these behaviors are most likely to occur. For example, to observe the behaviors of wild geese during migration, one would have to schedule observation sessions during their annual migration period. In other situations, one may systematically alter the environment in a controlled setting to induce the occurrence of the desired behavior. In these situations, the observation sessions would be determined by when these environmental alterations take place. For instance, in order to observe the "assertiveness" of a shy person, a researcher may make unreasonable requests to the person and observe the response of the person (McFall, 1977). The observation session, in this example, would be determined by when these requests are made and how often. Another example is to ask a couple to discuss an assigned problem between themselves in a clinic and observe their communication behavior (Jacobson, Elwood, & Dallas, 1981). When to observe and how often would be determined by the scheduled visits of the couple to the clinic. In some situations, researchers have "scheduled" observation sessions passively by "observing" only when the behavior of interest occurs. For example, in the critical event-recording approach discussed earlier (Haynes, 1978), subjects are requested to activate a recording device when the behavior of interest occurs. The exact time and frequency of observation sessions are determined by the natural occurrence of events.

For some situations, although the time continuum may be broken into discrete observation sessions, there should not be any time gap between observation sessions. In many chronobiological and neurobiological studies (e.g., Enright, 1981), for instance, the researcher wishes to detect behavioral cycles. The existence of irregular time gaps between observation sessions is detrimental to the identification of cycles (Kendall, 1973). If a behavior cannot be observed through uniform consecutive observation sessions, the best approach is to hypothesize the length of the cycle. The behavior should then be observed in a number of smaller observation sessions at identical and uniformly distributed points within each hypothesized cycle. The cyclicity of the summary descriptive statistics can then be analyzed through estimation techniques that would accommodate this type of data (e.g., Halberg, Tong, & Johnson, 1967).

In summary, the selection of observation sessions within the period of interest along the infinite time continuum is largely governed by the research question and practical limitations. When possible, the ideal process is to identify all possible observation sessions within the period of interest and select a random sample of these sessions. This ideal process will enable meaningful assessments of reliability and elimination of systematic *session* sampling error. When the purpose of an observational study is to identify cycles of behavior, time gap between observation sessions should be avoided.

CHAPTER 5

Reliability:
Conventional Methods

The government are very keen on amassing statistics—they collect them, raise them to the nth power, take the cube root and prepare wonderful diagrams. But what you must never forget is that every one of those figures comes in the first instance from the village watchman, who just puts down what he damn well pleases.

—Comments of an English judge,
quoted in *Some Economic Factors
in Modern Life* by Sir Josiah Stamp (1929)

For any data gathered for the purpose of description or analysis, there are two highly desireable characterisitcs: reliability and validity. Synonyms for reliability include dependability, consistency, predictability, and stability. Validity, on the other hand, refers to the ability of the data to reflect the underlying attribute of interest. Because data are generated through various instruments (questionnaires, tests, scales, etc.), the reliability and validity of data are quite frequently referred to as the reliability and validity of the corresponding instrument. Technically, however, reliability and validity are not properties of an instrument itself (Herbert & Attridge, 1975) because the reliability and validity of a measure depend on many factors besides the instrument. It is therefore more proper to speak of the reliability or validity of an outcome—a test score or an observation score. Reliability or validity of behavioral observation data, then, refers to the reliability or validity of the data as a result of using a particular observer and a particular coding system under a particular set of conditions.

Before data can reflect what they are supposed to reflect, the data must have consistency. Reliability is a necessary but not sufficient condition for validity. Take the example of a courtroom witness. Before the testimony of a witness can be judged as reflecting the truth (validity), the testimony

99

must be consistent (reliability). If a witness contradicts himself or herself or tells different stories at diferrent times or under different cross-examinations (lack of consistency or reliability), we would have to conclude that the tesimony of the witness does not reflect the truth (lack of validity). On the other hand, if the witness consistently tells the same story (reliable), he or she may or may not be telling the truth. This and the next chapter focus on the concept of and methods to assess reliability. Validity is discussed in Chapter 8.

DOES RELIABILITY APPLY
TO DIRECT OBSERVATION?

In earlier years, observational researchers had assumed that direct observation of behavior was by definition bias-free and valid (Cone, 1978). Conventional psychometric issues such as reliability and validity were regarded as irrelevant. We now know that observational data are in fact not exempt from the need to establish evidence of reliability and validity.

Consider for instance that you have observed the vocalization of an infant through momentary time sampling on a 1-hour videotape and have recorded that the infant vocalized 40% of the time. The occurrence/nonoccurrence data are correct as far as you are concerned because they reflect exactly what *you* saw. For your satisfaction, you would conclude that the infant had indeed vocalized 40% of the time. So far so good.

Now comes the difficult part. You reported that the infant had vocalized 40% of the time. We have not observed the videotape and wonder why we should believe you. Perhaps you were distracted at different times within that hour of observation and missed some occurrences. Perhaps you mistook some background noise for the infant's vocalization. Perhaps you made some clerical error in recording and inadvertently recorded an occurrence as nonoccurence, or vice versa.

There are at least two ways you can convince us that what you saw was indeed what was happening. First, you may observe the same videotape over and over again. If you consistently report the same or very similar prevalence of vocalization, we would be more likely to be convinced that the behavior had indeed occurred 40% of the time. Alternatively, you may ask a number of other independent observers with training similar to yours to observe the same videotape. If all independent observers produce similar results, we would also be convinced. In other words, evidence of reliability of behavioral observation data is needed to demonstrate to an external audience that the data reflect reality.

THE IMPORTANCE OF THEORY
OF MEASUREMENT

If you were to observe the same videotape twice and produced consistent results, we would be somewhat convinced. If you were to observe the same videotape 50, 100, 1,000, or 10,000 times, each time producing consistent results, on the other hand, we would become increasingly more convinced. In other words, the more times you observe the same videotape and produce evidence of consistency, the more we trust the reliability of the data. Similarly, the larger the number of independent observers that are used to produce evidence of consistency, the more we would be convinced.

In reality, however, it is impossible to view the same videotape a very large number of times or to employ a very large number of independent observers to observe the same behavior. In fact, unless a videotape recorder were available, it would be impossible to observe a behavior twice, not to mention observing it 50, 100, or 1,000 times. In order to produce the strongest and most convincing evidence possible, theories of measurement have been developed to describe the statistical relationship between the data obtained from a single observer in a single observation session and the data one could obtain should an infinite number of observers be employed or should the same session be observed an infinite number of times. From these theoretical relationships, statistical techniques have been developed to *estimate* the reliability one would obtain should the behavior be observed an infinite number of times or should an infinite number of observers be employed, based on a single session or a small sample of sessions and/or a small sample of independent observers.

Too frequently, applied behavior analysts ask: Do we, as applied researchers, really need to know the abstract theories of measurement? Couldn't we be shown the statistical techniques without the lengthy and boring explanations of where they came from? After all, our business is to apply them, not to improve them. It is the author's hope that we can convince our reader that a *thorough* understanding of these fundamental theories of measurement is essential for all who gather and interpret behavioral observation data.

Theories of measurement and their subsequent psychometric or statistical techniques have been developed primarily by researchers who are interested in paper-and-pencil tests. In many cases, behavioral observation researchers have utilized these statistical techniques without a thorough understanding of the theories from which these techniques have been developed. This type of blind application has not only produced in some cases erroneous interpretations, but, in other instances, behavior analysts have confused themselves.

Consider, for instance, the following mutually contradictory definitions provided by some of the leading applied behavior analysts:

1. Bakeman and Gottman (1986) suggested that *agreement* is the extent to which two observers agree with each other; whereas, *reliability* gauges how accurate a measure is, how close it comes to "truth."

2. Martin and Bateson (1986) maintained that *reliability* is the extent to which measurement is free from random errors; whereas, *accuracy* is concerned with the extent to which measurement is free from systematic errors.

3. Hartmann and Wood (1982) suggested that *agreement* is the degree to which observers assign the same raw score; whereas, *reliability* is the degree to which observers assign the same standard score to an event or person. *Accuracy* measures the degree of consistency between an observer and a criterion and is the preferred measure of *reliability*.

4. Cone (1982) suggested that *accuracy* is a simplistic approach to *validity*. He further suggested that *reliability*, *accuracy*, and *validity* are distinctively different.

Obviously, these mutually contradictory statements cannot all be correct. To determine which are correct, one must understand the theoretical origins of the various statistics.

For now, it suffices to say that evidence of reliability is important to convince an external audience and that an understanding of the theory behind statistical estimates of reliability is crucial in the proper application of these statistical techniques.

UNIT OF ANALYSIS

The first task in assessing reliability is identifying the appropriate unit of analysis (or object of measurement). Unlike conventional paper-and-pencil tests in which the unit of analysis is usually the reliability of the total score of a test, observational data often do not have a clear-cut unit of analysis. Reliability may be assessed for data obtained within a particular observation session (intrasession reliability). It may also be assessed for data obtained across a number of observation sessions (intersession reliability). Furthermore, if the variable of interest for a particular study is a composite behavior consisting of a number of component behaviors (e.g., attending as measured by classroom participation, reading, and writing), reliability can be assessed for each component behavior or for the total composite score. In other situations, the variable of interest may be a score obtained by combining a number of consecutive observations (e.g., a weekly score from combining a number of observations made in a week).

In general, for a confirmatory analysis in which a hypothesis is tested, the unit of analysis for reliability assessment should be directly related to the purpose of the study. For example, if the purpose of the overall study is to investigate a particular composite behavior, reliability assessment should be performed on the composite scores, not the scores for each of

the component behaviors. On the other hand, if each individual component behavior is of interest to the conclusion of the study, reliability estimates for each individual behavior should be analyzed. For exploratory
analyses, reliabilities of individual compnent behavior to identify possible
needs for additional observer training, coding system revision, or improvements in recording procedures (Hartmann, 1977).

INTEROBSERVER AGREEMENT
AND INTRAOBSERVER RELIABILITY

Of various statistical techniques that have been or can be employed to
measure reliability in behavioral observation, a number of them are pure
statistical procedures without a direct relationship to existing theories of
measurement. These are generally employed to produce evidence that the
data are consistent across a number of independent observers and are frequently referred to as *interobserver agreement.*

Other statistical techniques attempt to estimate the consistency of data
should a single observer observe the same behavior over and over again.
These techniques require extensive psychometric theoretical justifications
with considerable limitations and assumptions. We will refer to the results
of these indirect statistical techniques as *intraobserver reliability.*

A group of techniques known alternatively as *observer accuracy*, criterion-
referenced agreement, and transduction accuracy has been suggested as
a third and superior approach to reliability. There is no clear consensus
as to exactly what is being determined by these techniques. We demonstrate in the chapter on validity (i.e., chapter 7) that they are in fact methods
to derive a specific type of validity evidence. Therefore, we do not address issues of observer accuracy in this or the next chapter.

Finally, a group of statistical techniques known as intraclass correlations and a powerful psychometric theoretical framework known as the
Generalizability Theory can accommodate both interobserver agreement
and intraobserver reliability. These are addressed in chapter 6.

INTEROBSERVER AGREEMENT INDICES

Interobserver agreement refers to the extent to which two or more observers agree on the occurrences and nonoccurrences of a behavior. It is
the less complicated of the two pieces of conventional evidence of reliability discussed earlier. In order to assess interobserver agreement, one can
always employ a number of independent observers and assess the degree
to which the observers produce consistent results. The assessment of in-

terobserver agreement is, hence, a direct statistical problem without a need for a psychometric theory. When it is possible to select observers at random from all possible observers, the computed agreement statistic based on a small number of observers will produce a good estimate of the agreement statistic when an infinite number of observers are employed. When random sampling of observers is not possible, the agreement statistic still provides a good description of the agreement among the observers actually employed.

Interobserver agreement indices in behavioral observation are closely akin to a class of reliability indices known as threshold loss functions, generally used in paper-and-pencil criterion-referenced tests (Berk, 1984). A large number of indices have been proposed for the assessment of interobserver agreement. Berk (1979) describes 16 different interobserver agreement indices available to behavior observers. Many of these, however, are overlapping (Fleiss, 1975; Suen, Ary, & Ary, 1986). Of all the available interobserver agreement indices, five have been most popular and/or most frequently recommended for use in observational studies. These are the smaller/larger index, the percentage agreement index, the occurrence agreement index, the nonoccurrence agreement index, and the kappa coefficient.

Smaller/Larger Index

The smaller/larger index (S/L) is perhaps the simplest of all interobserver agreement indices. This index is sometimes referred to as the marginal agreement index (Frick & Semmel, 1978). The use of this index is limited to situations in which only two observers are involved. This index is calculated by simply dividing the smaller of the two values of behavior occurrence (e.g., prevalence, frequency, etc.) reported by two independent observers observing the same event by the larger value. The resulting index ranges in value from 0.00 to 1.00.

To illustrate the application of S/L, picture two observers counting the frequency an infant vocalizes to his mother within the same observation session. The first observer reports that the infant vocalized 9 times, whereas the second observer reports that the infant vocalized 10 times. The S/L agreement is:

$$S/L = \frac{\text{smaller}}{\text{larger}}$$

$$= \frac{9}{10}$$

$$= 0.90.$$

Some (e.g., Lamb, 1978) have suggested that the *S/L* index is one of the more conservative indices and, thus, more desirable. Its usage has been, and continues to be, quite popular, especially among child development researchers and applied behavior analysts (e.g., Eckerman, Whatley, & Kutz, 1975; Gaylord-Ross, et al., 1984; Hart, 1983; Jason & Liotta, 1982; Kelly & Stokes, 1982; Lamb, 1978; Murphy, et al., 1983).

The appropriateness of using *S/L* to assess interobserver agreement however, has been criticized by some (e.g., Flanders, 1967; Hartmann, 1977) and seriously challenged by others (e.g., Suen, Lee, & Prochnow-LaGrow, 1985). It has been shown that *S/L* is not really a measure of interobserver agreement. Even if both Observer *A* and *B* report that a behavior occurs 10 times, we cannot be sure that both reported occurrences in the same 10 cases. Observers could be disagreeing on many specific cases yet have similar or identical totals. The index contains a number of dubious mathematical properties. In addition to its lack of theoretical basis, poor mathematical properties, and problems of interpretation, the index was shown to be an ineffective heuristic substitute for other interobserver agreement indices. Despite its appeal of simplicity, this index should not be used to assess interobserver agreement unless it can be demonstrated to be a meaningful and effective measure of agreement.

Percentage Ageement Index

The percentage agreement index indicates the percentage of times two observers agree that the behavior of interest occurred or agree that it did not occur. The percentage agreement index (*p%*) is computed by:

$$p\% = \frac{\text{No. of agreements}}{\text{No. of agreements} + \text{No. of disagreements}} \times 100\%. \qquad (5.1)$$

Values of *p%* range from 0% to 100%.

Suppose a researcher is interested in the interobserver agreement of data reflecting the agressive behavior of a chimpanzee who has been isolated for a period of time. Two independent observers, after receiving clear behavioral definitions and sufficient training, were assigned to observe the chimpanzee for a given session using a momentary sampling procedure with 10-second intervals. After the observation session, the two observers reported the data shown in Figure 5.1. The two observers agreed on behavior occurrence twice (Intervals 1 and 8); on behavior nonoccurrence five times (Intervals 3, 4, 5, 9, and 10). Therefore, the total number of agreements is (2 + 5) = 7 times. The two observers disagreed three times

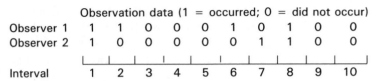

FIGURE 5.1.   Chimpanzee behavior data from two observers.

(Intervals 2, 6, and 7). The percentage agreement index for this observation session computed with Equation 5.1 is:

$$p\% = \frac{7}{7 + 3} \times 100\%$$

$$= 70\%.$$

An alternative way of reporting the same information is the proportion agreement index (p_o). To compute proportion agreement, we can simply remove the 100% from Equation 5.1. The formula for p_o is hence:

$$p_o = \frac{\text{No. of agreements}}{\text{No. of agreements} + \text{No. of disagreements}}. \tag{5.2}$$

In our example, $p_o = .70$.

The proportion agreements and disagreements between two observers recording a dichotomous event are usually organized into a 2 × 2 table (Figure 5.2). Cell b shows the proportion of time both observers reported occurrence, c the proportion of time both observers reported nonoccurrence, a the proportion of time Observer 1 reported occurrence while Observer 2 reported nonoccurrence, and d the proportion of time Observer 1 reported nonoccurrence while Observer 2 reported occurrence. The row sum p_1 is the proportion of occurrence reported by Observer 1, the column sum p_2 is the proportion of occurrence reported by Observer 2, q_1 is the proportion of nonoccurrence reported by Observer 1, and q_2 is

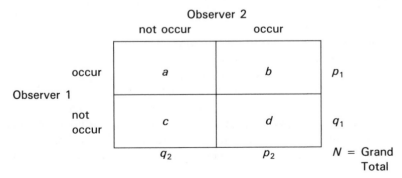

FIGURE 5.2.   2× 2 table of interobserver data.

the proportion of nonoccurrence reported by Observer 2. The values p_1, p_2, q_1, and q_2 are also referred to as the marginal values, or simply marginals. (*Note*: A 2 × 2 table containing actual frequencies instead of proportions and its extension to multinomial data with two observers, such as 3 × 3 table, 4 × 4 table, and so on, are traditionally referred to as square contingency tables. They have also been referred to as agreement matrices or confusion matrices by some behavior analysts.) When viewed from this 2 × 2 organization of the data, p_o can be computed through:

$$p_o = b + c. \tag{5.3}$$

In presenting Equation 5.1 for percentage agreement, many authors have omitted the percent (%) sign. This has generated some confusion as to the exact computational procedure for and the interpretation of percentage agreement (e.g., Araujo & Born, 1985; Bell-Dolan, 1985; Hawkins, 1983). A percentage agreement index should always contain a percent sign indicating the standardization of the agreement in per 100 units.

The percentage agreement index as well as the proportion agreement index have been known by numerous alternative names. Percentage agreement (or its decimal form—proportion agreement) has been alternatively referred to as a percent agreement (Hartmann, 1977), interval-by-interval agreement (Hawkins & Dotson, 1975), exact agreement (Repp et al., 1976), overall reliability (Hopkins & Hermann, 1977), total agreement (House, House, & Campbell, 1981), or point-by-point reliability (Kelly, 1977). These alternative labels all refer to either percentage agreement or proportion agreement.

Of all the interobserver agreement indices, percentage agreement is, by far, the most popular. Kelly (1977) reported that most studies in applied behavior analysis had used percentage agreement as the index of reliability. Mitchell (1979) reported that 49% of observational studies in *Child Development* and 57% of those in *Developmental Psychology* reported only percentage agreement as the indicator of data reliability.

Although it is the most popular interobserver agreement index, percentage agreement is probably also the most controversial. A large number of researchers have pointed out that the percentage agreement index is spuriously inflated by chance agreement. Consider a situation in which two observers are observing a behavior that, in actuality, occurs in 5 of the 100 intervals within a 100-interval observation session. The first observer correctly reports behavior occurrence in 5 of the 100 intervals. The second observer was distracted and did not record any behavior occurrence at all. In this case, both observers agreed that the behavior did not occur in 95% of the 100 intervals, whereas they disagreed on the occurrence/nonoccurrence of the behavior in the remaining 5 intervals. Hence, Equation 5.1 would yield an interobserver agreement index of 95%.

Despite the fact that the second observer completely missed the occurrences of behavior, the two observers appear to have a high level of consistency. This appearance of consistency is due to *chance agreement*. This result erroneously implies a high level of interobserver agreement. In fact, two observers can be observing two totally unrelated events at two different points in time and place and still, through chance, show a spuriously high value of percentage agreement. In general, the more the actual prevalence of behavior occurrence approaches 100% or zero, the more percentage agreement is possibly inflated by chance agreement (Costello, 1973; Hartmann, 1977; Hopkins & Herman, 1977; Johnson & Bolstad, 1973; Mitchell, 1979). Conversely, the closer the prevalence is to 50% the less likely that chance inflation occurs.

One of the questions frequently asked by applied researchers is what magnitude of percentage agreement can be considered a reasonable threshold between acceptable and unacceptable interobserver agreement. Given that the value of percentage agreement is inflated by chance agreement and the degree of chance inflation is dependent upon the actual prevalence of the behavior, it is impossible to provide a meaningful simple rule of thumb. Two identical values of percentage agreement do not indicate the same degrees of chance agreement or the same degrees of genuine agreement. Hence, the magnitudes of percentage agreements between studies are generally not directly comparable.

Many have urged that the use of percentage agreement should be discounted (e.g., Hartmann, 1977; Hartmann & Wood, 1982; Hawkins & Dotson, 1975; Kratochwill & Wetzel, 1977; Suen & Lee, 1985). Others have rigorously defended the use of percentage agreement because it is parsimonious both in concept and in computational procedures (Baer, 1977a; House, Farber, & Nier, 1980). Intuitively, it is appealing because it does not involve relatively sophisticated concepts such as variance, covariance, or probabilities. The simple computational procedures minimize the possibility of computational and rounding errors.

Some have suggested that the inflation of percentage agreement by chance may be negligible in practice. For this latter point, there has been a controversy over the need to correct for chance agreement in the determination of interobserver agreement (e.g., Armitage, Blendis, & Smyllie, 1966; Fleiss, 1975; Goodman & Kruskal, 1954). Some have suggested that observed agreements could be assumed to be in excess of chance, although one must check if the excess was trivial or large. This assumption has been shown to be false. In a reassessment of published data, Suen and Lee (1985) found that observed agreements in applied behavior analysis data were frequently only marginally higher than chance agreement or not in excess of chance agreement at all. This is possibly due to the fact that, in applied behavior analysis, a researcher is frequently interested in increasing a certain desirable behavior that has a low rate of occurrence, or decreasing a certain undesirable behavior that has a high rate of occurrence. Therefore, data in applied behavior analysis would frequently involve extreme rates of occurrence that result in percentage agreement values that are considerably inflated by chance.

At least two approaches have been suggested to "salvage" the percentage agreement index. The first approach is to test for the statistical significance of the percentage agreement index; that is, to determine the probability that a particular percentage agreement value can be obtained by chance, when in reality the two observers are observing different things. Birkimer and Brown (1979) suggested three methods to test for the statistical significance of a given percentage agreement value. Hartmann and Gardner (1979) pointed out that these methods were approximations of the conventional chi-square ($\chi 2$) or the Fisher's Exact Probability test. Although this approach addresses the problem of chance inflation in percentage agreement, its application may be limited. Behavioral data are frequently found to be autocorrelated (*Note*: the extent that behavioral data are autocorrelated is currently controversial. We provide a discussion of the current debate in chapter 8.). When data are autocorrelated, $\chi 2$, Fisher's Exact Probability will give misleading results (cf. Gardner, Hartmann, & Mitchell, 1982).

A second remedy for percentage agreement was suggested by Kelly (1977). He suggested that two conditions be met before a percentage agreement be accepted as indicating sufficient interobserver agreement. First, the prevalence of behavior occurrence should be less than 80% and higher than 20%. Second, the computed percentage agreement value should be at least 90% or higher. Ary and Suen (1985) found that when (a) the two conditions outlined by Kelly are met, (b) the data are not autocorrelated, and (c) there are at least 15 points of observation or intervals in the session, the percentage agreement index is almost always statistically significant. That is, under these conditions, the computed percentage agreement is unlikely to be entirely attributable to chance agreement.

Perhaps the most cogent argument against the continued use of percentage agreement is the evidence presented by Suen and Lee (1985). Reanalyzing a sample of past published data, they found that, had a chance-corrected interobserver agreement index been used in these studies instead of the percentage agreement index, between one fourth to three fourths of the data in prior studies would have been judged as having unacceptably low or negligible reliability.

We suggest that unless the conditions needed for the use of the significance testing and Kelly's guidelines are met, the percentage agreement index should not be used. Even when the conditions are met, other indices should be preferred. Although percentage agreement appears to be easy to interpret, in fact it is not. For example, a 70% agreement with behavior actually occurring 50% of the time really reflects better interobserver agreement than 90% agreement with behavior actually occurring 85% of the time. The meaning of a given percentage agreement differs according to the actual prevalence of behavior occurrence.

Occurrence and Nonoccurrence Agreement Indices

Since the problem of chance inflation is most severe with the percentage agreement index when the prevalence of occurrence is extremely high or extremely low, one solution is to replace percentage agreement with other indices when these situations occur. The occurrence agreement index and the nonoccurrence agreement index are designed to do precisely that (Bijou et al., 1969; Hawkins and Dotson, 1975; Jensen, 1959). The occurrence agreement index is used when the occurrence of behavior is low, and the nonoccurrence agreement index is used when the occurrence of behavior is high. Both the occurrence agreement and the nonoccurrence agreement indices are applicable only to situations involving two observers.

The equation for the computation of occurrence agreement (p_{occ}) is:

$$p_{occ} = \frac{\text{occurrence agreements}}{\text{occurrence agreements} + \text{disagreements}} \times 100\%, \quad (5.4)$$

where "occurrence agreements" is the number of times both observers agree that the behavior has occurred and "disagreements" is the number of times the two observers disagree on the occurrence *and* nonoccurrence of behavior.

Using the data in Figure 5.1, the two observers agreed on the occurrence of aggressive behavior twice and disagreed three times. In the computation of occurrence agreement, the five times in which both observers agreed on the nonoccurrence of behavior are ignored. Applying Equation 5.4, the occurrence agreement for chimpanzee aggressive behavior data is 40%.

As in the case of percentage agreement, occurrence agreement can be expressed in proportional terms by eliminating the term 100% in the equation. In the previous example, the proportion occurrence agreement would be 0.40.

Nonoccurrence agreement is the exact opposite of occurrence agreement. For nonoccurrence agreement, one would consider only the number of times two observers agree that a behavior has not occurred and ignore the number of times both observers agree that the behavior has occurred. Hence, the equation for the nonoccurrence agreement (p_{non}) is:

$$p_{non} = \frac{\text{nonoccurrence agreements}}{\text{nonoccurrence agreements} + \text{disagreements}} \times 100\%, \tag{5.5}$$

where "nonoccurrence agreements" is the number of times both observers agree that the behavior has not occurred. For example, with data in Figure 5.1, the nonoccurrence agreement index is 62.5%.

The occurrence agreement index, for practical purposes, removes most of the chance inflation when the prevalence of behavior is low. Conversely, the nonoccurrence agreement index removes most of the chance inflation when the prevalence is high; that is, a low rate of nonoccurrence. Hence p_{occ} is often recommended when the rate of behavior is low and p_{non} is recommended when the rate of behavior is high (e.g., Bijou et al., 1969).

Kelly (1977) suggested a quite reasonable guideline: When the prevalence of behavior is higher than 80%, the nonoccurrence agreement index is preferred. When the prevalence is between 20 and 80%, the percentage agreement index is preferred. When the prevalence is less than 20%, the occurrence agreement is preferred. However, when the prevalence of behavior changes from time to time within the study, the application of Kelly's guideline would lead to a constant switching of indices, which can be quite confusing.

Even when the conditions for appropriate uses of the occurrence agreement index and the nonoccurrence agreement index are met, they are not totally free from chance inflation. These two indices do minimize chance inflation; but they do not eliminate it completely.

Kappa Coefficient

A frequently recommended interobserver agreement index is the kappa ($\varkappa$) coefficient (Cohen, 1960). Kappa is a flexible index that discounts expected chance agreements and can accommodate dichotomous or multinomial (e.g., verbal communication, nonverbal communication, versus no communication) events involving two or more observers. The generalized equation for kappa coefficient is:

$$\varkappa = \frac{p_o - p_e}{1 - p_e}, \tag{5.6}$$

where p_o is the observed proportion agreement and p_e is the expected proportion agreement by chance. The numerator indicates the difference between the actual observer agreement and the expected chance agreement. The denominator indicates the total possible difference between observer agreement and expected chance agreements. Thus, kappa is the ratio of actual nonchance agreements divided by total possible nonchance agreements.

For a dichotomous event with only two observers involved, the p_o in the numerator in kappa is identical to the p_o in Equations 5.2 and 5.3. The value of the p_e can be derived from the product of the marginals for each cell of interest in the contingency table (the 2×2 table) which represents the agreements and disagreements among observers. In the case of a dichotomous event, the cells of interest are cells b and c (see Figure 5.2), and the marginals are the values p_1, p_2, q_1, and q_2. The corresponding marginals for cell b are p_1 and p_2, and the corresponding marginals for cell c are q_1 and q_2. Hence the expected chance agreement for the 2×2 table is:

$$p_e = p_1 p_2 + q_1 q_2. \tag{5.7}$$

Expressed verbally, if Observer 1 reports that the behavior occurs at a proportion of p_1 of all observations and Observer 2 reports that the behavior occurs at a proportion of p_2 of all observations, we can expect that by chance alone both observers would agree that the behavior occurs at a proportion of $p_1 p_2$ of all observations. Similarly, we can expect that by chance alone both observers will agree that the behavior does not occur at a proportion of $q_1 q_2$ of all observations. Hence, the toal expected chance proportion of observation in which two observers agree that the behavior occurs or does not occur is $p_1 p_2 + q_1 q_2$. Equation 5.6 is hence an equation to remove the expected chance agreement (p_e) from the observed proportion agreement (p_o) and to standardize the statistic by dividing it by $(1 - p_e)$.

Mathematically, a more direct way to express kappa for a dichotomous event involving only two observers, using notations from Figure 5.2, is:

$$\varkappa = \frac{b + c - p_1 p_2 - q_1 q_2}{1 - p_1 p_2 - q_1 q_2}. \tag{5.8}$$

To illustrate, the data from Figure 5.1 can be converted into a 2×2 table as in Figure 5.3. From Figure 5.3, kappa for the chimpanzee data can be computed as:

$$\varkappa = \frac{0.2 + 0.5 - (0.4)(0.3) - (0.6)(0.7)}{1 - (0.4)(0.3) - (0.6)(0.7)}$$

$$= 0.3478.$$

Kappa ranges in value from $+1.00$ to -1.00. A positive kappa indicates that the observers agree more frequently than would be expected by chance. A kappa value of $+1.00$ indicates that the observers agree com-

Observer 2

	not occur	occur	
occur (Observer 1)	0.2	0.2	0.4
not occur	0.5	0.1	0.6
	0.7	0.3	1

FIGURE 5.3. Proportion 2 × 2 table of chimpanzee data.

pletely. A kappa value of 0 indicates that the agreements among the observers are no more than can be expected by chance. A negative kappa indicates that the observers agree less frequently than can be expected by chance. In other words, they disagree more frequently than random expectation. A kappa of − 1.00 indicates total disagreement among the observers. Gelfand and Hartmann (1975) suggested that a kappa of 0.60 be used as the minimallly acceptable level of interobserver agreement. Landis and Koch (1977) suggested that a kappa of 0.80 is an indication of "good" reliability. Hard and fast rules of thumb such as these may oversimplify the interpretation of the values of kappa.

A variation of the kappa coefficient is the weighted kappa (Cohen, 1968). The weighted kappa essentially allows for differential weights to be assigned to individual observed cells and individual marginals. The general purpose of the weighted kappa, however, is to facilitate hypotheses testing. Its use for interobserver agreement or intraobserver reliability has not been common. It is also worthwhile to note that although kappa was developed by Cohen (1960) in the area of psychology and education, another index known as del (∇) was developed by Hildebrand, Laing, and Rosenthal (1974) in sociology. It has been demonstrated (Froman & Llabre, 1984; Hildebrand, Laing, & Rosenthal, 1977) that kappa and del are, in fact, equivalent.

Of the five interobserver agreement indices discussed thus far (i.e., S/L, $p\%$, p_{occ}, p_{non}, and $\varkappa$), kappa is the single least controversial index with the widest application to different types of data and number of observers. Therefore, for behavioral observation research, kappa should be the interobserver agreement index of choice.

Relationship Between Proportion Agreement and Kappa

We should emphasize that kappa is in fact a chance-corrected version of proportion agreement. Although proportion (or percentage) agreement is the most widely used interobserver agreement index, kappa is the most frequently recommended one. This contradiction between theory and practice poses at least two problems of interpretation. First, how do we compare the interobserver agreements between two studies when both reported percentage agreement values with no knowledge of the amount of chance inflation in each? Second, how do we compare the interobserver agreements between two studies when one reported percentage agreement and the other reported kappa? Berk (1979) suggested that to facilitate the comparison of interobserver agreement indices researchers should report the value of the index used and also the original statistics (i.e., the cell frequencies and the marginals). In practice, however, this suggestion is rarely followed.

Another solution is to devise conversion procedures from one index to another. Although the mathematical relationship between proportion agreement and kappa has been demonstrated (Suen, Ary, & Ary, 1986), typically, journal articles do not provide sufficient information to take advantage of these relationships to make direct comparisons. Lee and Suen (1984) suggested a method to calculate the maximum and minimum possible kappa equivalence for a given proportion agreement value when the available information is somewhat limited, the observation session involves only two observers, and the variable is a dichotomous event. This would facilitate comparisons by converting proportion agreements to kappas.

When the available information is severely limited, such as in the case in which a p_1 value is known and only a range of p_o values representing the proportion agreements for various reliability sessions is given, Suen and Lee (1985) described a linear programming method through which the maximum and minimum kappas can be calculated for a given proportion agreement value. This procedure involves complicated fractional and linear programming techniques. Appendix C provides the maximum and minimum values of kappa for given values of p_1 and ranges of p_o values derived through Suen and Lee's linear programming technique. For example, if the range of reported p_o is from .95 to .75 and the p_1 value is .70, from Appendix C, the maximum kappa is .8864 and the minimum kappa is .1781.

Other Interobserver Agreement Indices

Although the interobserver agreement indices just discussed are the most popular or most frequently recommended indices, there are a large number of alternative interobserver agreement indices available to behavioral observers. Table 5.1 summarizes 12 such indices. These indices vary in computational procedures as well as basic statistical orientations. Readers who are interested in these indices should refer to the original authors to gain a proper perspective for each index. The notations used for the formulas in Table 5.1 correspond with those used in Figure 5.2.

INTRAOBSERVER RELIABILITY

We have discussed some of the interobserver agreement indices. They describe the extent to which two or more observers observing the same behavior agree on the occurrence and nonoccurrence of the behavior. Since it is reasonable in practice to employ more than one observer to assess data reliability, the assessment of interobserver agreement is a relatively simple statistical problem. As you can see, the only problem we have to resolve is the problem of chance agreement. Once chance agreement is resolved, the assessment of interobserver agreement is relatively straightforward through kappa.

The assessment of intraobserver reliability, however, is considerably more complicated. With intraobserver reliability, we want to assess the consistency of a single observer should that observer observe the exact same behavior over and over again. Because the exact same behavior will not occur twice, not to mention 50 or 100 times, it is very difficult to assess how much the observer agrees with himself or herself. When it is possible to record the behavior on audio- or videorecorders, we can ask the same observer to listen or view the same tape over and over again and thereby compute the kappa. However, this is frequently not practical, too expensive, or too obtrusive. Furthermore, the observer's fatigue, habit, and boredom will undoubtedly affect the outcomes in such a repetitive task. For the majority of the cases, we have to estimate the intraobserver reliability based on the available information in a single observation session or a single study.

Psychometric Definition of Reliability

In order to estimate intraobserver reliability based on information in a single session or a single study, a simple conceptual definition of reliability as consistency no longer suffices. That is because we have no means of assessing the consistency within a single observer in the sense that we assess the consistency between two or more observers through kappa. A more precise definition that will allow us to "tease out" the within-observer consistency information from limited data is needed.

Let us reconsider the example at the beginning of this chapter of the infant vocalizing to the mother. You reported that the infant had vocalized 40% of the time. In response, we wondered if the prevalence of 40% might contain errors due to your being distracted at different times with-

TABLE 5.1
Some Other Interobserver Agreement Indices

Index	Formula	Source
Crude Agreement A_1	$\dfrac{1}{4}\left(\dfrac{b}{p_1} + \dfrac{b}{p_2} + \dfrac{c}{q_1} + \dfrac{c}{q_2}\right)$	Rogot & Goldberg (1966)
Crude Agreement A_2	$\dfrac{b}{p_1 + p_2} + \dfrac{c}{q_1 + q_2}$	Rogot & Goldberg (1966)
Dice's S_D	$\dfrac{2b}{p_1 + p_2}$	Dice (1945)
Standard Deviation Agreement Index (SDAI)	$\dfrac{n}{n-1}\left(b + c - (b - c)^2\right)$	Armitage, Blendis & Smyllie (1966)
Lambda Coefficient	$\dfrac{2b - (a + d)}{2b + (a + d)}$	Goodman & Kruskal (1954)
Scott's pi	$\dfrac{4(bc - ad) - (a - d)^2}{(p_1 + p_2)(q_1 + q_2)}$	Scott (1955)

Coefficient of Concordance W^a	$\dfrac{s}{(1/12)K^2(n^3 - n)}$	Kendall (1948)
Maxwell & Pilliner's r_{11}	$\dfrac{2(ad - bc)}{(p_1q_1 + p_2q_2)}$	Maxwell & Pilliner (1968)
Agreement Probability	$\displaystyle\sum_{i=an}^{p_2n} \dfrac{(p_2n)!(p_1n)!(n - p_1n)!(n - p_2n)!}{i!n!(p_2n - i)!(p_1n - i)!(n - p_1n - p_2n + i)!}$	Yelton et al. (1977)
Alpha Coefficient^a	$\dfrac{\text{No. of observed agreements}}{\text{Total possible agreements}}$	Cartwright (1956)
Interobserver Agreement	$\dfrac{b}{p_1}(1 - p_1) + \dfrac{d}{q_1}(1 - q_1)$	Clement (1976)
G index	$\dfrac{(b + c) - (a + d)}{N}$	Lienert (1972)

^{a}See original author for explanation of formula.

117

in the session, your mistaking some background noise for the infant's vocalization, or errors in recording occurrences as nonoccurrences, and so on. For a lack of a more descriptive term, psychometricians have called these errors random errors.

Ideally, if you could observe the exact same behavior repeatedly and reported exactly the same prevalence of 40%, then the prevalence would be absolutely reliable with no random error. Realistically, you would most likely report at least slightly different prevalences for the different repeated observation sessions. The mean of all the prevalences from your repeated observations of the *exact* same behavior would provide the best estimate of the actual prevalence. The amount of variations among the reported prevalences, as measured through the variance around the mean, would provide a general indicator of the overall amount of random error in your repeated observations of the same behavior. This variance, referred to as *random error variance*, reflects the expected error associated with any one of the repeated observation sessions. The larger the random error variance, the more the expected error and the less reliable the reported prevalence. Hence, reliability can be more precisely defined as the extent of *absence of random error variance*.

Now, in reality, we cannot observe the *exact* same behavior of the same subject at the same time more than once. As an alternative, we can have the same observer observing the same behavior of *different* subjects (or at different points in time). The variance around the mean of all the reported prevalences in this case is no longer a clear indicator of just the random error variance. This is because the true prevalences for different people may be different. The total variance around the mean of all reported prevalences, in fact, contains both variance due to the true differences among the subjects (or points in time, as appropriate) and random error variance associated with using a particular observer with a particular observation system.

The true variance due to actual differences among subjects is not considered error. To be able to detect differences among subjects is in fact often a major purpose of observation. To assess the reliability of using an observer with an observation system, we should consider only that portion of the total variance that is actually random error variance and not that portion that is true variance. Thus, a good indicator of the *lack* of reliability would be:

Lack of reliability = Toal variance − True variance.

This lack of reliability can be expressed in relative terms as a proportion of the total variance so that the possible values will range from 0 to 1. That is:

$$\text{Index of } \textit{unreliability} \; = \; 1 \; - \; \frac{\text{True variance}}{\text{Total variance}}.$$

If we were to express total variance as σ_x^2 and true variance as σ_t^2, intraobserver reliability (ϱ_{xx}) is then:

$$\text{Reliability} = 1 - \frac{\text{Random error variance}}{\text{Total variance}}$$

$$= \frac{\text{True variance}}{\text{Total variance}}$$

$$= \frac{\sigma_t^2}{\sigma_x^2}. \tag{5.10}$$

This is the conventional definition of reliability that can be found in any classical text on psychometrics. It is important to keep this definition in mind in the assessment of intraobserver reliability. For instance, from this definition, we can see that the psychometric definition of reliability is expressed as a proportion. As such, its value can range only from 0 to 1. Regardless of what statistic is used to estimate this proportion, if the computed value is a negative value, it indicates that the statistic used has failed to estimate reliability. It does not indicate a low reliability. The lowest possible reliability is zero.

Theories of Measurement

If we could tell what the true difference among the subjects (or points in time) are, the task would be simple. Unfortunately, we don't know their true variance. Therefore, we have to estimate the information indirectly through existing statistical techniques based on the available information. In order to justify the use of the existing statistical techniques to estimate the information, we need to have a sound theory to describe the psychometric nature of observed data and the relationship between their psychometric properties and existing statistical techniques.

There are primarily two major theories of measurement today. These are the Random Sampling Theory and the Item Response Theory (Bejar, 1983). The Random Sampling Theory is a general term that includes both the Parallel Tests Model (also described as the Classical Theory) and the Generalizability Theory. Both random sampling approaches begin with the assumption that there is an infinite universe of possible subjects, items, or observation points, depending on the purpose of the measurement procedure. The observed data are comprised of a random sample of such a universe. Item Response Theory, also known as Latent Trait Theory or Item Characteristic Curve Theory, is a descriptor for a large array of alternative models of measurement. Perhaps one of the better known models of Item Response Theory is the one-parameter logistic model commonly known as the Rasch Model. Item Response Theory does not assume the existence of an infinite universe of possible items, subjects, or observation points. Instead, it assumes that the performance of an individual on a particular item in a test is a function of the individual's ability and of random error. If such a function can be estimated through a process known as item calibration, the ability of an individual can be derived from the estimated function.

Currently, there are no known behavioral observations analogs to the various models in Item Response Theory. Therefore, subsequent discussions in this chapter are within the Random Sampling Theory domain only. Readers who are interested in Item Response Theory and its possible but yet unknown potentials for behavioral observation should refer to more specialized texts such as Hambleton and Swaminathan (1985), Lord (1980), Rasch (1980), Warm (1978), or Wright and Stone (1979).

Within Random Sampling Theory, the approaches used in Classical Theory and Generalizability Theory are slightly different. Classical Theory requires some rather restrictive assumptions, whereas the assumptions of Generalizability Theory are less restrictive. Generalizability Theory can be viewed as a "liberalization" of the Classical Theory (Brennan, 1983).

Classical Theory

The basic approach in Classical Theory is that because we do not know the true variance, we would attempt to bypass the variance components and estimate their relative proportion (i.e., reliability) directly from available information. In order to do so, some theoretical assumptions have to be made.

Based on Classical Theory, each single score in a set of data is assumed to contain two components: true score and error score. The various possible causes of error are not differentiated. Rather, we describe error in an omnibus fashion as random error. Hence, a single score (X)—obtained from observation, test item, or otherwise—can be expressed as:

$$X = t + e, \qquad (5.11)$$

where t is the true score and e is the random error. For each score, we further assume that t is not related to e. That is:

$$\text{Cov}(t,e) = 0. \qquad (5.12)$$

or the covariance (or correlation) between true score and random error is zero.

Parallel Tests Assumptions

Based on the assumption that t is not related to e, we may estimate the proportion of true variance directly without estimating the exact amount of true variance. The way to do this is to make a series of assumptions referred to as the Parallel Tests Assumptions.

If we can construct two tests (or identify two observers) so that they are strictly parallel in that they meet the Parallel Tests Assumptions, we can estimate reliability directly. Two tests, say Test A and Test B, are said to meet the Parallel Tests Assumptions if the mean scores on the two tests are equal (i.e., $\mu_A = \mu_B$); the variances are equal (i.e., $\sigma_A^2 = \sigma_B^2$); the relationship between the scores on each test and the true scores is equal (i.e., $r_{tA} = r_{tB}$); and the error in Test A is not related to the error in Test B (i.e., $\text{Cov}(e_A, e_B) = 0$). There are a number of other relatively inconsequential assumptions within the Parallel Tests Assumptions. However, for our purpose, the four assumptions just mentioned will suffice.

If the Parallel Tests Assumptions are met, a computed Pearson's r between the scores in Test A (or Observer A) and those in Test B (or Observer B) will provide a good estimate of the proportion of true variance. Recall from basic statistic that Pearson's r between X and Y (or Tests A and B) is:

$$r = \frac{[\Sigma(X - \bar{X})(Y - \bar{Y})] / N}{\sqrt{\left(\dfrac{\Sigma (X - \bar{X}_2)}{N}\right)\left(\dfrac{\Sigma(Y - \bar{Y})^2}{N}\right)}}$$

$$= \frac{\text{Cov}(X,Y)}{\sigma_X \sigma_Y}$$

When applied to Tests A and B, the Pearson's r between A and B is then:

$$r_{AB} = \frac{\text{Cov}(A,B)}{\sigma_A \sigma_B},$$

where $\text{Cov}(A, B)$ is the covariance between scores from Tests (or observers) A and B, σ_A is the standard deviation of the scores on Test A, and σ_B is the standard deviation of the scores on Test B.

Because under the Classical Theory each score contains two components, t and e, and, further, under the Parallel Tests Assumptions, $\sigma_A^2 = \sigma_B^2$, which indicates that either variance will express the total variance or inconsistency, the Pearson's r between A and B can be expressed as:

$$r_{AB} = \frac{\text{Cov}(t + e_A, t + e_B)}{\sigma_x^2},$$

where σ_x^2 is the total variance of Test A or Test B, e_A is the error of the score for a subject on Test A, and e_B is the error of the score for the same subject on Test B. Mathematically, the numerator can be decomposed through the quadratic algebraic process and r_{AB} becomes:

$$r_{AB} = \frac{\text{Var}(t) + \text{Cov}(t,e_A) + \text{Cov}(t,e_B) + \text{Cov}(e_A,e_B)}{\sigma_x^2}.$$

If the assumptions that t is not related to either e_A or e_B and e_A is not related to e_B are true, the last three terms in the numerator equal zero and drop out of the equation. Hence:

$$r_{AB} = \frac{\sigma_t^2}{\sigma_x^2} = \text{intraobserver reliability.}$$

The important point to remember is that Pearson's r between Tests A and B (or observers A and B) is *not* a reliability estimate per se. When the relationship between Tests A and B does not meet the Parallel Tests Assumptions, r between the two sets of scores is simply a statistical correlation coefficient that describes the relationship between the two sets of scores.

If the Parallel Tests Assumptions are met, on the other hand, the Pearson's r between Observers A and B is a direct estimate of intraobserver reliability. That is, it becomes an estimate of the *proportion* of true variance. Since intraobserver reliability is defined as a proportion, a Pearson's r of less than zero is for all practical purposes uninterpretable.

Strategies to Obtain Parallel Tests

Within the Classical Theory, a major problem is then to identify two tests that will meet the Parallel Tests Assumptions. One way to achieve this is to give an identical test to the same group of subjects twice. Since the same test is given to the same individuals, the scores from the two administrations of the test can be assumed to meet the Parallel Tests Assumptions. The Pearson's r between the two sets of scores obtained through this strategy is referred to as an estimate of *test–retest reliability* or as a coefficient of stability.

As an alternative strategy, one may actively construct two tests so that the items in the two tests are essentially equivalent. This is a common practice with many standardized tests that contain different forms. If one is convinced that the items in two forms of a test (e.g., Nelsen–Denny Reading Test Forms C and D) are really equivalent, then the Parallel Tests Assumptions are approximated. A Pearson's r between the two sets of scores obtained from the two forms would provide a good estimate of reliability. The Pearson's r obtained through this strategy has been referred to as *equivalent-forms reliability* or a *coefficient of equivalence*.

A strategy to avoid constructing two forms of a test is to split a single test into two halves and treat each half as an equivalent form. The two halves can be considered meeting the Parallel Tests Assumptions because all the items in the test have been constructed to measure essentially the same variable or construct. Some approaches include taking odd-numbered items as one half and even-numbered items as another half, or taking the first half as one form and another half as another form. The Pearson's r between the scores in the two forms would provide a good estimate of reliability. This Pearson's reliability is sometimes referred to as the *split-half reliability coefficient* or *internal consistency coefficient*.

A problem with this strategy is that the Pearson's r will tend to underestimate the reliability of the test. The more items there are in a test, the more reliable is the total score of the test because the proportion of error is reduced. The split-half reliability coefficient will indicate only the reliability of half of the test because each "equivalent form" contains only half as many items as the original test. To correct for this underestimation, the Spearman–Brown Prophecy formula is used. The generalized Spearman–Brown formula is:

$$r'_{11} = \frac{Kr_{11}}{1 + (K - 1)r_{11}}, \tag{5.13}$$

where r'_{11} is the corrected reliability, K is the factor by which the length of the instrument has been changed, and r_{11} is the reliability estimated from the shortened instruments. For example, if the instrument is increased threefold, K would be 3. When applied to correct a split-half reliability, K in Equation 5.13 becomes 2. Therefore, the corrected split-half reliability of an instrument is:

$$r'_{11} = \frac{2r}{1 + r}, \tag{5.14}$$

where r'_{11} is the corrected split-half reliability and r is the original Pearson's r between the two halves.

There is no particular reason as to why we should split a test by the odd–even scheme or by the first–second halves scheme or any other scheme, and yet, depending on how the test is split, we will most likely obtain different reliability estimates. The average of the reliabilities from all possible ways to split the test into two halves would provide a better estimate of reliability than any of the reliabilities obtained from a single scheme. Why then shouldn't we split the test into 3, 4, 5, or 10 parts in all possible manners and find the average Pearson's r corrected through Spearman–Brown? The overall average reliability would be even more stable. The most thorough way to split a test is to treat each item in the test as an equivalent form. That is, if a test has N items, we split the test N ways into N equivalent forms so that each form contains only one item. We can find the Pearson's r for each of the $N(N - 1)/2$ possible pairs of items, average them, and apply Spearman–Brown's formula to correct for the shortening of the test into a single item. A method to accomplish precisely this is the Cronbach Alpha (r_α). Cronbach Alpha is defined as:

$$r_\alpha = \frac{N\bar{\varrho}}{1 + (N - 1)\bar{\varrho}},$$

(5.15)

where $\bar{\varrho}$ is the average correlation between all possible pairs of items. Cronbach Alpha is a direct application of the Spearman–Brown formula in Equation 5.13 to the average item reliability. Computationally, it is more convenient to estimate Cronbach Alpha through:

$$r_\alpha = \frac{N}{N - 1} \left(1 - \frac{\Sigma s_n^2}{s_x^2}\right),$$

(5.16)

where s_n^2 is the variance of each item and s_x^2 is the variance of the total score. Eq. 5.16, referred to as Cronbach Alpha, is a conservative estimate of Eq. 5.15, the latter is referred to as standardized item alpha.

Statistically, when a variable is dichotomous (i.e., correct–incorrect, yes–no, occur–not occur, etc.), a proportion p of the subjects is scored positively, and a proportion q (or $1 - p$) of the subjects is scored negatively, the variance can be computed conveniently by pq. Therefore, when the score for each item in a test is dichotomous, the estimation of Cronbach Alpha can be simplified substantially since the variance of each item is p times q. This simplified Cronbach Alpha for dichotomous tests is referred to as the Kuder–Richardson Formula-20 (or KR-20). Specifically, by applying the pq property of dichotomous data to Equation 5.16, KR-20 (r_{20}) is:

$$r_{20} = \frac{N}{N - 1} \left(1 - \frac{\Sigma pq}{s_x^2}\right),$$

(5.17)

where p is the proportion of subjects answering an item correctly and q is the proportion answering incorrectly.

Estimation of Intraobserver Reliability

The key to estimating reliability under the Classical Theory model is to attain two strictly parallel tests such that they meet the Parallel Tests Assumptions. Within this frame of reference, test–retest reliability, equivalent-forms reliability, split-half reliability, Cronbach Alpha, and KR-20 can be viewed as various strategies to approximate such strictly parallel tests. The fundamental objective of obtaining two or more sets of scores that can be considered strictly parallel applies equally to behavioral observation data.

The strategies used with paper-and-pencil tests may be applied to behavior observation data. The behavioral observation analog to the test–retest strategy would be to have the same observer observe the same behavior of the same subject twice in two separate observation sessions. However, the adoption of this strategy is problematic because unlike covert attributes, which are assumed to be relatively stable over time, overt behaviors are frequently volatile. The change in true variance will render data from two observations not parallel.

The behavioral observation analog to the split-half reliability or Cronbach Alpha would be to treat two halves of a single-observer multiple-subject observation session as equivalent forms or to treat each point of observation (or interval) within an observation session as an equivalent form, much as each item is treated as an equivalent form in paper-and-pencil tests. This adaptation is problematic because items in a paper-and-pencil test are deliberately selected so that they are supposed to be equivalent. Each observation point in a session, however, indicates the behavior at the point in time and is ever changing. Therefore, observation points are not really equivalent, and the Parallel Tests Assumptions are most likely to be violated.

Attempts have been made to adapt the test–retest strategy and the internal consistency strategies to behavioral observation (e.g., Haynes, 1978; Heise, 1969). These adaptations are generally not very successful. In general, these two sets of strategies are not commonly used in behavioral observation because of the inherent difficulty in attaining parallel scores in behavioral observation through these strategies.

Although these *strategies* are not commonly used, their associated statistics can be useful under certain conditions. Bakeman and Gottman (1986), for instance, suggested the use of Cronbach Alpha for observational reliability assessment. Although the computational process of Alpha for observational data is different from Equations 5.15 and 5.16 because of the difference in units of analysis, the conceptual definition of Alpha as the average Pearson's r between all possible pairs of units of analysis corrected through the Spearman–Brown formula applies equally to behavioral observation situations. We discuss this further under intraclass correlation in the next chapter.

The equivalent-forms reliability strategy, however, is readily adaptable to behavioral observation. As we can deliberately construct two equivalent forms of a test, we can provide identical training to two observers so that their scores will meet the Parallel Tests Assumptions. When two observers obtain identical training, are given identical sets of behavioral definition, use an identical coding system, and are similar in as many other respects as possible, they are analogous to two equivalent forms of the same test. As such, the two sets of scores obtained from these two observers observing the same behavior in the same session can be considered to have met the Parallel Tests Assumptions. Therefore, intraobserver reliability within the Classical Theory can be most readily estimated through the behavioral observation analog of the equivalent-forms reliability strategy.

Intraobserver Reliability Indices

When it is reasonable to assume that scores from two observers meet the Parallel Tests Assumptions, the intraobserver reliability of a single observer (any one of the two observers) can be estimated directly through the Pearson's r between the two sets of scores. In a multiple-subject observation study, the scores in each set would represent the score for each subject assigned by an observer. In a single-subject study, the scores in each set are the scores assigned to each session by the observer when intersession reliability is of interest or are the scores assigned to each interval or point of observation when intrasession reliability is of interest.

The strategy of estimating intraobserver reliability by treating each observer as an equivalent form and computing the Pearson's r between the two sets of scores has also been referred to as the *interclass correlation* approach (Berk, 1979). Since the strategy used is similar to that used in equivalent-forms reliability and the scores of each observer are not split into parts as with split-half, Cronbach Alpha, or KR-20, correction through Spearman–Brown is not necessary. A high positive Pearson's r indicates that a high proportion of the score variance from a single observer is due to true variance, and hence the scores of a single observer are highly reliable. As the value of the Pearson's r approaches zero, intraobserver reliability becomes lower. A negative r indicates that the two sets of scores from the two observers did not meet the Parallel Tests Assumptions. Hence, the computed Pearson's r, which is an estimate of reliability only when these assumptions are met, does not provide any meaningful information about reliability.

When the observational scores are dichotomous, the computed Pearson's r between the two sets of scores will be identical to a correlation coefficient known as phi (ϕ). Using the notations in Figure 5.2., phi is computed by:

$$\phi = \frac{bc - ad}{\sqrt{p_1 p_2 q_1 q_2}}.$$

(5.19)

Phi is, in fact, Pearson's r for dichotomous variables. It is a simplified method to compute Pearson's r by taking advantage of the fact that when all scores are dichotomous, score variance is pq and covariance is $(bc - ad)$.

When only two "strictly parallel" observers (i.e., two observers with identical training, coding system, observation session, etc.) are employed, the single Pearson's r provides a good estimate of intraobserver reliability. However, this is not the best possible estimate. Any two particular observers selected represent only a sample of two possible observers to receive the same training and so on. Regardless of how the two observers are made to be parallel through identical training, identical coding system, and so on, the two observers will bring with them their own personal experiences and biases. These biases are minimized through rigorous training and clear behavioral definitions. But they are not entirely eliminated. To the extent that these personal biases exist, the two observers are not completely parallel in the sense of the Parallel Tests Assumptions. To the extent that the Parallel Tests Assumptions are violated, the Pearson's r provides an inaccurate estimate of reliability.

A more refined strategy would be to employ more than two observers (let's say K observers). All K observers can then be given identical training, identical behavior definition, and so on to attempt to make their scores as "parallel" as possible. Scores from these observers can then be paired into all combinations that will yield $K (K - 1)/2$ sets of paired scores and the Pearson's r for each pair computed. The average of these $K (K - 1)/2$ Pearson's r would provide a more accurate estimate of reliability because, if we can assume the personal biases among the observers to be random, the random biases are neutralized. This approach to intraobserver reliability has been referred to as the *average intercorrelation approach* (Berk, 1979). It should be noted that, in conventional statistical analysis, in order to obtain an unbiased average Pearson's r, a procedure known as Fisher's zeta transformation is needed. However, when Pearson's r is used to estimate intraobserver reliability based on the Parallel Tests Assumption, Pearson's r becomes a proportion, ranging in values from 0 to 1, instead of -1 to $+1$. Hence, Fisher's zeta transformation is neither necessary nor appropriate for an average intercorrelation approach.

Variance Components
and Standard Error of Measurement

Since reliability is the proportion of the total variance that is true variance, it follows that reliability multiplied by total observed variance would provide a good estimate of true variance. That is:

$$\sigma_t^2 = r_{xx}\sigma_x^2, \qquad (5.20)$$

where r_{xx} is the intraobserver reliability and σ_x^2 is the total variance of a single observer, using the actual variance of either observer as an estimate of total variance.

Since reliability is the proportion of true variance and there are only true and error variances in the Classical Theory, it follows that $(1 - r_{xx})$ is the proportion of error variance. The exact magnitude of error variance (σ_e^2) is then:

$$\sigma_e^2 = \sigma_x^2(1 - r_{xx}). \tag{5.21}$$

A variance expression of error or inconsistency is rather inconvenient for interpretation because a variance is the result of squaring errors. To bring the error variance back down to the level of the original scores, we can take the square root of the error variance. The result of the square root operation is referred to as the standard error of measurement (σ_e). Specifically, the standard error of measurement is:

$$\sigma_e = \sqrt{\sigma_{x2}(1 - r_{xx})}. \tag{5.22}$$

When desired, this standard error of measurement can be used to construct a confidence interval around a score obtained by a single observer in a single observation session. For example, one can be 95% certain that the true prevalence of behavior in a particular observation session with an observed prevalence of X is within the range of $X \pm 1.96\sigma_e$.

Relationship with Interobserver Agreement Indices

Although interobserver agreement indices and intraobserver reliability as measured through Pearson's r under the Classical Theory essentially estimate two different pieces of evidence of reliability, the two approaches utilize the same scores obtained from the same two independent observers. Therefore, knowing the magnitude of interobserver agreement, one should be able to deduce the magnitude of intraobserver reliability and vice versa. Indeed, the exact mathematical relationship between proportion agreement and ϕ (i.e., Pearson's r for dichotomous data) has been shown to be as follows (Lewin & Wakefield, 1979; Suen & Ary, 1984a; Wakefield, 1980):

$$\phi = \frac{p_o + p_1 + p_2 - 2p^1p^2 - 1}{2\sqrt{p_1p_2q_1q_2}}. \tag{5.23}$$

Further, the mathematical relationship betwen $\varkappa$ and ϕ has been shown (Suen, Ary, & Ary, 1986) to be:

$$\phi = \frac{\varkappa(p_1 + p_2 - 2p_1p_2)}{2\sqrt{p_1p_2q_1q_2}}. \tag{5.24}$$

Since published reports of behavioral studies have traditionally reported only interobserver agreement indices such as percentage agreement as the only evidence of reliability (Kelly, 1977; Mitchell, 1979), these equations can be applied to estimate the corresponding ϕ values of these interobserver agreement indices. If the two observers employed in a study can be assumed to have met the Parallel Tests Assumptions, the estimated ϕ would indicate the level of intraobserver reliability of the same study. In other words, when only evidence of the extent of agreements between two observers is provided (i.e., interobserver agreement), one can still estimate the extent that any one of the two observers will produce consistent results in repeated observations of the same session (i.e., intraobserver reliability) based on the interobserver agreement information.

RECENT DEVELOPMENTS

The conceptual approaches and statistical methods discussed in this chapter represent the conventional, and currently prevailing, methods of estimating interobserver and intraobserver reliability. These methods have come under considerable criticism in the past few years because of a number of important conceptual and statistical limitations inherent in these methods. Many behavior analysts as well as psychometricians (e.g., Bakeman & Gottman, 1986; Berk, 1979; Hartmann, 1982; Kazdin, 1977; Mitchell, 1979) have directly or indirectly advocated the use of the Generalizability approach to assess data reliability. In the next chapter, we discuss the specific problems with the conventional methods and the elements of the Generalizability approach as they pertain to behavioral observation.

CHAPTER 6

Reliability:
The Generalizability Approach

Conceptually, the conventional approaches outlined in the previous chapter basically address one question: Are the data reliable? Given that there is only one question, it is difficult to reconcile the fact that one can have two different reliabilities: interobserver and intraobserver. In other words, the simplistic definition of reliability as data consistency is inherently incapable of accommodating the idea that there can be more than one reliability estimate.

The Generalizability approach is a comprehensive model that can conceptually accommodate the coexistence of numerous reliability estimates. This approach departs from the conventional methods in two respects. Statistically, it approaches the task of estimating reliabilities through an alternative technique known as the intraclass correlation. Conceptually, it systematically defines for each reliability assessment situation its unique frame of reference.

THE INTRACLASS CORRELATION
STATISTICAL APPROACH

The intraclass correlation approach is an alternative statistical attempt to estimate the true variance and error variance directly. If these variances can be estimated directly, then the restrictive Parallel Tests Assumptions of the classical approach would not be necessary because the Pearson's *r* would not be needed. An additional "bonus" of the intraclass correlation approach is that it will provide information on both interobserver agreement and intraobserver reliability, as well as other information regarding reliability. The intraclass correlation approach, although not formally introduced until the 1950s and 1960s by individuals such as Ebel (1951), Lindquist (1953), Haggard (1958), and Bartke (1966), had been suggested by various individuals as early as the 1930s and early 1940s (e.g., Burt, 1936; Hoyt, 1941; Jackson & Ferguson, 1941).

Essentially, with the intraclass correlation approach, one attempts to estimate the true variance and error variance components directly through a two-way analysis of variance (two-way ANOVA) procedure. Since the Pearson's *r* is not used, the Parallel Tests Assumptions are not needed. However, in order for the ANOVA procedure to produce reasonable (i.e., unbiased) estimates, the assumptions that subjects (or sessions or points of observation) are randomly selected from a universe of all possible subjects and that observers are randomly selected from a universe of all possible similarly trained observers are still required.

Direct Estimations of Variance Components

When a number of observers record the behaviors of a number of subjects (or sessions or points of observation), the total variance in the scores across all observers can be attributed to three sources: systematic variance across subjects (i.e., true differences among subjects), systematic variance across observers (i.e., systematic biases among observers), and random error variance. Through the usual two-way ANOVA process (*Note*: For a refresher on two-way ANOVA, see for example Hinkle, Wiersma, & Jurs, 1979, or Keppel & Saufley, 1980), the total observed variance can be decomposed into the three corresponding sums of squares: main effect sum of squares for subjects, main effect sum of squares for observers, and error sum of squares. These sums of squares divided by their corresponding degrees of freedom would yield the corresponding mean squares. This is the point at which similarities between the intraclass correlation and the conventional two-way ANOVA ends. With the conventional two-way ANOVA, these mean squares are used to compute *F* ratios for hypothesis testing. With the intraclass correlation approach, however, these mean squares are used to estimate the underlying variance parameters for the three variance components.

For example, in Table 6.1 four observers each observe five subjects, producing a total of 20 scores. When we submit this through a conven-

TABLE 6.1
Intraclass Correlation Example

Subject ($n_s = 5$)	Observer ($n_o = 4$)				Computation by Definition				Simplified Computation
	1	2	3	4	ΣX_o	$\bar{X}_s$	$\bar{X}_s - \bar{X}$	$(\bar{X}_s - \bar{X})^2$	$(\Sigma X_o)^2$
A	5	6	3	5	19	4.75	-.15	.0225	361
B	9	10	7	7	33	8.25	3.35	11.2225	1089
C	6	10	3	7	26	6.25	1.60	2.5600	676
D	1	2	0	1	4	1.00	-3.90	15.2100	16
E	4	5	2	5	16	4.00	-.90	.8100	256

$\Sigma(\bar{X}_s - \bar{X})^2 = 29.8250$

$\Sigma(\Sigma X_o)^2 = 2398$

Computation by Definition

ΣX_s	25	33	15	25
$\bar{X}_o$	5.00	6.60	3.00	5.00
$\bar{X}_o - \bar{X}$	.1	1.7	-1.9	.1
$(\bar{X}_o - \bar{X})^2$	.01	2.89	3.61	.01

$\Sigma(\bar{X}_o - \bar{X})^2 = 6.52$

$\bar{X} = 4.90$
$\Sigma X = 98$

$(\Sigma X)^2 = (98)^2 = 9604$

$(\Sigma X^2) = 644$

Simplified Computation

$(\Sigma X_s)^2$	625	1089	225	625

$\Sigma(\Sigma X_s)^2 = 2564$

tional two-way ANOVA, we obtain the following sums of squares:

$$SS_{total} = \Sigma(X - \bar{X})^2 = 163.8,$$

$$SS_{subject} = n_o\Sigma(\bar{X}_s - \bar{X})^2 = 119.3,$$

$$SS_{observer} = n_s\Sigma(\bar{X}_o - \bar{X})^2 = 32.6,$$

$$SS_{error} = SS_{total} - SS_{subject} - SS_{observer} = 11.9,$$

where $\bar{X}$ is the grand mean of all scores, $\bar{X}_s$ is the mean of the scores assigned to each subject across all observers, X_o is the mean of the scores of each observer across all subjects, n_o is the number of observers (i.e., four) and n_s is the number of subjects (i.e., five). Proceeding with the two-way ANOVA in the usual manner, the mean squares are then:

$$MS_{subject} = SS_{subject}/(n_s - 1) = 29.825,$$

$$MS_{observer} = SS_{observer}/(n_o - 1) = 10.867,$$

and $$MS_{error} = SS_{error}/[(n_o - 1)(n_s - 1)] = 0.992.$$

These mean squares provide a description of the observed variance components found in the given sample of subjects and sample of observers. They are unique to the particular samples used. Recall that under the Random Sampling Theory, the subjects and observers are assumed to be random samples from a universe of possible subjects and a universe of possible observers. To the extent that these assumptions are met and based on the theoretical statistical relationships between population variances and random sample variances in sampling theories, the variance components one would expect had the entire universe of subjects been observed and the entire universe of observers been employed can be estimated through:

$$\sigma_s^2 = (MS_{subject} - MS_{error})/n_o, \tag{6.1}$$

$$\sigma_o^2 = (MS_{observer} - MS_{error})/n_s, \tag{6.2}$$

and $$\sigma_e^2 = MS_{error}, \tag{6.3}$$

where σ_s^2 is the expected subject variance component should the entire universe of subjects been observed, σ_o^2 is the expected observer variance component should the entire universe of observers been employed, and σ_e^2 is the expected error variance for the data in such a comprehensive universe.

For our example,

$$\sigma_s^2 = (29.825 - 0.992)/4 = 7.208$$
$$\sigma_o^2 = (10.867 - 0.992)/5 = 1.975,$$

and $$\sigma_e^2 = MS_{error}, = 0.992.$$

The Interpretation of Variance Components

The estimated variance across subjects (or sessions or points of observation) indicates the actual differences among the subjects. Hence, it is an estimate of true differences or true variance. The error variance σ_e^2 is exactly what it is, and its square root is the standard error of measurement. The variance across observers is indicative of inconsistencies across observers; that is, systematic observer biases.

If the relative magnitude of subject variance is large when compared against the other two variance components, the scores are reliable. If the error variance is relatively large, the scores do not have sufficient intraobserver reliability in that the amount of individual observer random error is large. If the observer variance is relatively large, there is a considerable amount of systematic bias among the observers. In such a manner, the relative contributions of all defined causes to score inconsistency are delineated. Data reliability can be assessed by examining the relative magnitudes of the variance components. Therefore, these variance estimates are the most fundamental information of data reliability and are the building blocks for reliability coefficients.

Reliability Coefficients

For those who are not adept at judging the relative magnitudes of numbers directly, it may be necessary to express these relative magnitudes in ratio terms, such as what proportion of the total variance is subject variance (or true variance). These ratios are then reliability coefficients. With three variance components, one can derive various ratios through various combinations to arrive at different reliability coefficients. Depending on which variance components are included in each ratio, each of these reliability coefficients would provide different reliability information.

For instance, under the Classical Theory, the scores contain a true variance and a random error variance, and intraobserver reliability is the proportion of true variance. Hence, the classical intraobserver reliability would involve only the true variance term (i.e., σ_s^2) and the random error variance term (i.e., σ_e^2). The classical intraobserver reliability coefficient can thus be estimated through the intraclass correlation coefficient (ϱ^2) as (Brennan, 1983):

$$\varrho^2 = \sigma_s^2/(\sigma_s^2 + \sigma_e^2). \quad (6.4)$$

This is identical to what is being estimated under the Classical Theory through Pearson's r, with the exception that the credibility of this estimate is not dependent on meeting the Parallel Tests Assumptions. In our example:

$$\varrho^2 = 7.208/(7.208 + 0.992) = 0.88.$$

If you are interested in the classical intraobserver reliability coefficient only, the processes of estimating the variance components from their corresponding mean squares can be skipped over and the intraclass correlation coefficient ϱ^2 can be estimated directly, as suggested by Hartmann (1982), as follows:

$$\varrho^2 = (MS_s - MS_e)/[MS_s + (n_o - 1)MS_e]. \quad (6.5)$$

This equation is mathematically equivalent to Equation 6.4.

Bakeman and Gottman (1986) suggested the use of an intraclass correlation coefficient equivalence of Cronbach Alpha to estimate reliability across observers. This approach should be used with extreme caution because the resulting intraclass correlation can easily be misinterpreted. Specifically, Bakeman and Gottman suggested using the following intraclass correlation approach to estimate Cronbach Alpha (r_α) (or KR-20 when data are dichotomous), as originally suggested by Wiggins (1973):

$$r_\alpha = (MS_s - MS_e)/(MS_s + MS_e). \quad (6.6)$$

To avoid any misinterpretation of this intraclass correlation coefficient, we must understand how this particular combination of mean squares is related to Cronbach Alpha and what Cronbach Alpha implies in this context. Recall that in the Cronbach Alpha approach in Classical Theory, each item in a test is treated as a parallel test. Cronbach Alpha is the result of adjusting the average Pearson's r for all possible pairs of items through the Spearman–Brown Prophecy formula so that the final reliability coefficient reflects the reliability of the total test rather than that of a single item. If we were to apply the intraclass correlation two-way ANOVA to a set of K items by N subjects data to estimate the variance components and apply Equation 6.4 to estimate the intraclass correlation, the result would indicate the reliability of a single item. That is, the resulting intraclass correlation will be comparable to the average Pearson's r for all possible pairs of items. To estimate the reliability of the total test within the intraclass correlation approach, the Spearman–Brown formula is not necessary. Instead, Cronbach Alpha for the total test can be estimated from the variance components through (Brennan, 1983):

$$r_\alpha = \sigma_s^2/[\sigma_s^2 + (\sigma_e^2/K)]. \tag{6.7}$$

Mathematically, Equations 6.6 and 6.7 are equivalent. Equation 6.6 estimates Cronbach Alpha directly from mean squares without estimating variance components first.

With our example in Table 6.1 and applying Equation 6.7:

$$r_\alpha = 7.208/(7.208 + 0.992/4) = 0.97.$$

When the classical intraclass correlation in Equation 6.4 or 6.5 is applied to a behavioral observation situation, the data are derived from K observer (instead of K items in paper-and-pencil tests) by N subjects (or intervals or sessions). As in the conventional case of K items by N subjects in which the resulting intraclass correlation indicates the reliability of a single item, when applied to a K observers by N subjects situation, the resulting intraclass correlation is the estimated reliability of a single observer. In the case of a paper-and-pencil test with K items, after adjusting item reliability for the test length through Equations 6.6 or 6.7, the resulting Cronbach Alpha indicates the estimated reliability of the total test with K items. Similarly, if we were to apply Equation 6.6 or 6.7 to adjust the reliability of a single observer, the resulting Cronbach Alpha would then indicate the reliability of the *total score across* K *observers*. Since the total score across K observers is essentially meaningless, we can simply divide the total score by K to obtain an average score. Cronbach Alpha then indicates the reliability of this average score.

When interpreting Cronbach Alpha as it applies to behavioral observation data from K observers, it is important to keep in mind that although the traditional intraclass correlation (i.e., Equations 6.4 or 6.5) indicates the reliability of the score from a single observer, Cronbach Alpha (i.e., Equations 6.6 or 6.7) indicates the reliability of the average score across K observers. In other words, the traditional intraclass correlation coefficient indicates the level of intraobserver consistency one can expect should the same behavior be observed through the same coding scheme with an observer with equivalent training in the future. The Cronbach Alpha, on the other hand, indicates the expected consistency of the mean score across K observers should the same behavior be observed through the same coding scheme with K observers with equivalent training in the future. If you intend to *always* use K observers in any future observation of the same behavior with the same coding scheme and the total (or mean) score across the K observers is *always* used as the measure of behavior, Cronbach Alpha is appropriate. However, if you intend to use only a single observer in future observations or the scores of a single observer in subsequent statistical analysis, the traditional intraclass correlation is more appropriate.

Both the traditional intraclass correlation and the Cronbach Alpha ignore the variance component due to observers (i.e, σ_o^2). This is appropriate if observation scores are interpreted within a norm-referenced framework (Brennan & Kane, 1977a). With a norm-referenced interpretation of observation scores, the score for each subject (or session) is interpreted only in terms of its relative position or magnitude to those of other subjects. For example, the frequency of behavior of Subject A is interpreted only in terms of whether it is higher than those of other subjects, about the same as those of other subjects, or lower than those of other subjects. Within this interpretation, systematic inconsistencies across observers is of no consequence because, even if Observer 1 always systematically records a higher behavior frequency than does Observer 2, the rank-orders of the subjects remain the same for both observers. Hence, systematic observer variance will have no consequence on the relative position of each subject. An example of an observation system with a norm-referenced interpretation is the Bayley Scales of Infant Development (Bayley, 1933, 1936, 1969). The final scores on the Bayley Scales are interpreted in terms of group norms.

For many other observational measures, however, a criterion-referenced interpretation is more appropriate. With the criterion-referenced interpretation, a score is interpreted in relation to an absolute criterion rather than the scores of other subjects or sessions. For instance, the frequency of "rocking" of an autistic child may be more meaningfully interpreted in relation to an absolute criterion of zero (never occurred) than in relation to the frequencies of rocking behavior of others in a norm group. Similarly, the prevalence of "attention in class" for a child may be more meaningfully interpreted relative to the absolute prevalences of 100% and 0% rather than the prevalences of other child. For these criterion-referenced interpretations, the systematic variance due to observers becomes a source of error, in addition to random error. This is because although systematic observer variance will have no effect on the relative positions of subject scores, they will distort the absolute position of a score relative to an absolute criterion. Therefore, if scores from an observation session are to be interpreted as an absolute score (i.e., a frequency of 50 means 50 occurrences more than no ocurrence, rather than simply more than, say, 85% of the frequencies of the same behavior emitted by other comparable subjects), the systematic observer variance has to be taken into consideration.

To account for observer variance as a source of error for a criterion-referenced interpretation of scores, the appropriate measure of reliability is (Berk, 1979):

$$\varrho_1^2 = \sigma_s^2/(\sigma_s^2 + \sigma_o^2 + \sigma_e^2). \tag{6.8}$$

With our example, the criterion-referenced intraclass correlation reliability is:

$$\varrho_1^2 = 7.208/(7.208 + 1.975 + 0.992) = 0.71.$$

Since this reliability estimate accounts for both random error and observer error, it can be viewed as an omnibus indicator of interobserver agreement and intraobserver reliability.

GENERALIZABILITY THEORY

As we progressed from interobserver agreement to classical theory to intraclass correlation, it should have become clear that the concept of reliability is becoming more complex than the original simple but relatively unclear idea of consistency versus inconsistency. With interobserver agreement, reliability is simply a matter of whether two independent observers see the same thing, and it is to be estimated through simple 2 × 2 statistics directly. With the classical theory, we attempt to assess the more abstract measure of intraobserver reliability through Pearson's r under the Parallel Tests Assumptions. With the intraclass correlation approach, it becomes clear that, depending on the question asked, we may in fact have different reliability coefficients. If the question is the intraobserver reliability of scores from a single observer that are to be interpreted within a norm-referenced framework, the answer is the conventional intraclass correlation coefficient, ϱ^2. If the question is the reliability of the mean scores across K observers should K observers be always used in the future, the answer is Cronbach Alpha, r_α. If the question is the intraobserver reliability and interobserver agreement of scores from a single observer that is to be interpreted within a criterion-referenced framework, the answer is the criterion-referenced intraclass correlation ϱ_1^2.

Hence, reliability is not an absolute concept without a context. Whether or not a set of scores are reliable depends on what question is being asked. The Classical Theory, which assumes that a score contains only a true score component and a random error component and that reliability is the proportion of true variance relative to the sum of true and random error variances, is incapable of accommodating the idea that for a given set of data there can be more than one reliability coefficient.

In what amounts to a conceptual breakthrough, Cronbach and his associates (Cronbach, Gleser, Nanda, & Rajartnam, 1972) introduced the Generalizability Theory, which takes into consideration the multifaceted nature of reliability. Conceptually, the Generalizability Theory can be viewed as a comprehensive extension of the Classical Theory. In addition, the concept of validity is accommodated within the same conceptual framework as well. We discuss how validity fits in the framework of the Generalizability Theory in the next chapter. The statistical approach used in the Generalizability Theory is a direct multidimensional extension of the ANOVA technique used in the intraclass correlation approach. Since the ANOVA technique is used, as in the case of intraclass correlation, the Parallel Tests Assumptions in Classical Theory is avoided.

The major uniqueness of the Generalizability Theory is in its fundamental idea of reliability and error. Within the Generalizability framework, it is recognized that reliability is not an absolute concept. Rather, depending on the question asked, it is relative to a certain context with a specific set of dimensions (e.g., time, observer, environment, instrumentation, etc.). When a set of observational data is said to be reliable, it implies that the results can be expected to be consistent over a variety of conditions (Nunnally, 1978).

In the Classical Theory, the context for reliability is undefined. When an investigator concludes that a certain set of data is reliable, the question that remains unanswered is, within what context are these data consistent or reliable? It may be the case that the data can be expected to be consistent over time but not across observers, or they can be expected to be consistent across observers but not across different settings. For example, if a set of data has a high level of interobserver agreement, it implies that the results can be expected to be similar should an equivalent observer with the same level of training be employed. On the other hand, if the interobserver agreement between data reported by a human observer using time-sampling techniques and data reported by another observer using an event recorder are high, it implies that the results are consistent over the dimension of instrumentation. If data obtained in a laboratory correlate highly with data obtained in a field experiment, one can conclude that the results are consistent over the dimension of environment.

The interobserver agreement and the intraobserver reliability approaches narrowly define observational data reliability in terms of consistencies between observers and within observers, which are only two of the many aspects of reliability. The Generalizability Theory allows an investigator to assess the quality of data within any chosen unidimensional or multidimensional context. This theoretical approach is particularly suited for behavioral observation data. In behavioral observation, errors can be introduced into the data from a variety of sources. These include scoring method, quality and quantity of observer training, situational variables within the observation session when reliability is assessed, pattern of behavior, and so on (Kazdin, 1977). Instead of considering the portion of variance that is not true variance simply as random error, as in the Classical Theory, the Generalizability approach further decomposes this error variance into specific sources of error. This allows an investigator to isolate sources of error for consideration and for possible correction. Depending on the reliability question asked, some sources of error may be irrelevant. The idea that it is possible that some sources of error may be irrelevant was demonstrated earlier in the intraclass correlation section. Recall that if the question asked is the consistency of scores to be interpreted within a norm-referenced framework, systematic interobserver error variance (i.e., observer biases) is irrelevant.

The Generalizability Theory has been hailed as the most broadly defined psychometric model in existence (Brennan, 1983), a liberalization of the Classical Theory (Brennan, 1984), and a conceptual breakthrough (Bakeman & Gottman, 1986). Berk (1979) suggested that the Generalizability approach offers the precision, comprehensiveness, and flexibility needed for the assessment of behavioral observation data not found in more conventional measures of interobserver agreement and intraobserver reliability. Mitchell (1979) suggested that in behavioral observation the Generalizability approach should be used to identify various sources of error besides observer error. Hartmann (1982) pointed out that a major advantage of a Generalizability approach is its ability to identify sources of error so that an investigator can take steps to improve data. Specifically, a Generalizability study will yield various unbiased estimates of data reliability and provide a comprehensive analysis of possible sources of error. Statistically, a multidimensional Generalizability approach, being a multidimensional extension of the intraclass correlation approach, can provide more specific variance component information than the unidimensional intraclass correlation approach.

Because the statistical techniques used within the Generalizability approach are multidimensional extensions of the ANOVA approach in intraclass correlation, we concentrate, in the following discussion, on the conceptual basis and the processes involved in Generalizability Theory. We note here that for a single-faceted Generalizability analysis, the two-way ANOVA technique in intraclass correlation is appropriate. For a two-faceted Generalizability analysis, the statistical procedure is a three-way ANOVA. It follows that for an N-faceted Generalizability analysis, an $(N + 1)$-way ANOVA is used. More detailed treatment of the statistical techniques of Generalizability assessment of observational data can be found in Suen, Ary, and Greenspan (in press).

THE PROCESS
OF GENERALIZABILITY THEORY

Universe of Admissible Observations

There are three stages in the assessment of data quality under the Generalizability Theory. First, the researcher defines a universe of admissible observations. That is, the researcher defines all the dimensions (facets) of the universe in which observations will take place or, more specifically, the conditions under which future use of the particular observation system should take place. For example, the researcher may be interested in observing a particular behavior in various classroom settings using trained psychology graduate assistants as observers. In this example, the researcher has defined a two-faceted universe of admissible observations. Specifically, the first facet is "observers," which is characterized by "trained psychology graduate assistants," and the second facet is "setting," which is characterized by "classrooms." Subsequent analyses would then be based on observations made under conditions that are samples drawn from these two predefined facets. That is, if subsequent analyses show that the data quality obtained from a particular observation is good, it indicates that the system will yield dependable data in the future when observations are made by trained psychology graduate assistants in classrooms. There is no theoretical limitation on the number of facets to be included in the universe of admissible observations; although the complexity of the subsequent N-way ANOVA may preclude the inclusion of too many facets.

A facet may be either crossed or nested with another facet or with subjects (or sessions or intervals in single-subject studies). If a defined facet in a single-faceted design is crossed with subjects, a score for each subject is obtained for each level of the defined facet. For example, if the defined facet is "observers," each subject is scored by all the observers in the sample. Using the same example, if the observer facet is nested, a different group of observers score a different subset of the sample of subjects. For another example, if a defined facet of classroom is crossed with subjects, all subjects are observed in all classrooms. If it is nested, some subjects are observed in some classrooms; other subjects are observed in other classrooms. Nested-design behavioral observation sessions are not frequently found in reported literature. However, it can take place especially when subjects are observed in natural settings. For example, three teachers may be given the same training and, in order not to interrupt the usual classroom activities, are asked to observe the behaviors of the pupils in their own classrooms, respectively. In this case, subjects (pupils in each classroom) are nested within observers (different teachers for different classrooms).

In a multifaceted design, all of the facets and the subjects may be crossed, all of them may be nested, or one may have a mixed multifaceted design with some of the facets nested and other facets crossed. For example, a child may be observed by a teacher while in school and by a parent while at home. In this case, the environment facet is nested within an observed facet. The possible design is limited only by the complexity of data collection and subsequent statistical analyses. Because of the statistical complexities of the more complicated designs and the relative lack of use of these designs by behavioral observation researchers today, we confine our discussion to the simplest case of single-faceted crossed design. Readers who wish to gain a better understanding of the more complex designs as well as some of the more esoteric theoretical and technical isues related to Generalizability Theory should consult more specialized texts and manuscripts such as Brennan (1983), Cronbach et al. (1972), and Shavelson and Webb (1981). For a more in-depth discussion of some of the more complex multifaceted Generalizability assessment situations in behavioral observation, Suen, Ary, and Greenspan (in press—Appendix) provided some examples and solutions.

G (Generalizability) Study

Once the universe of admissible observation is defined, the second stage of the analysis is conducted. This stage is called the Generalizability study (G study) stage. For the purpose of the G study, a sample of subjects and a sample of each facet are drawn. For example, for a single-faceted observer universe, a sample of subjects and a sample of observers are drawn at random from all possible subjects and observers within the defined universe of admissible observations.

Data gathered within the sample facets (e.g., observational data gathered by the sampled observers in a single-faceted observer universe design) are used for the statistical analyses of the G study. Statistically, the purpose of a G study is to estimate the universe score variance (analogous to true score variance in Classical Theory and intraclass correlation) as well as the variance for each facet and the interaction effect of each combination of facets and subjects. The procedures for the estimation of variance components in the G study for a single-faceted crossed design is identical to the two-way ANOVA process used in the intraclass correlation approach.

For a multifaceted universe, the number of variance components goes beyond that of the unidimensional intraclass correlation ANOVA. For example, for a two-faceted design with the facets of observer and environment, there are seven variance components: subject variance (or universe score variance or true score variance), observer variance, environment variance, observer-by-subject interaction variance, environment-by-subject interaction variance, observer-by-environment interaction variance, and subject-by-observer-by-environment interaction variance. To estimate all these variance components, a multidimensional extension of the intraclass correlation ANOVA procedure is needed. The complexity of the ANOVA process increases exponentially with each additional facet. For instance, increasing the number of crossed facets from 1 to 2 to 3 implies increases in the number of variance components from 3 to 7 to 15. A nested-design involves fewer variance components than its crossed-design counterpart, but the former provides less information.

Once the ANOVA is complete and all variance components estimated, the essential information regarding data quality (i.e., variance components) are attained. At this point, you may do any one of three things. First, for an exploratory analysis, you may examine the relative magnitude of each variance component to identify facets (i.e., sources of error) with large variances. You can then devise strategies to reduce these variances as appropriate (e.g., more observer training, confining future applications of the observation system to classroom settings only, etc.). Second, if you are satisfied with the variance estimates (e.g., the subject variance is considerably larger than all other variances and relative magnitudes of all other variances are negligibly small), you may simply stop here and report these variance components. Third, you may proceed to the next stage of the Generalizability process, known as D (Decision) study considerations, to gain further insights regarding the quality of your data.

D (Decision) Study Considerations

For a given study, you can conduct as many D studies as you desire. The purpose of various D studies is to examine the changes in the variance components should facets be dropped or should the sample size of each facet be changed.

With the various components estimated from a G study, one can take various ratios of the variance components to estimate the reliability of data. For instance, in a single-observer facet crossed-design study, a ratio involving the subject variance and the subject-by-observer interaction variance computed in the fashion of the norm-referenced intraclass correlation coefficient (Equation 6.4) by equating the interaction variance with error variance will yield a reliability coefficient. This reliability (or generalizability) coefficient reflects the degree to which one can generalize the scores, interpreted in a norm-referenced manner, to norm-referenced scores of the same behavior obtained from the same single observer in repeated observations of that identical behavior within the defined universe of observers. In other words, this is equivalent to intraobserver reliability.

Similarly, estimating the criterion-referenced dependability coefficient through Equation 6.8 would provide the criterion-referenced reliability (or dependability) across observers.

However, to stop at these coefficients is to give up the potential to gain additional insight regarding the dependability of the data. For instance, what if the observation system is always used with more than one observer? Consider, for example, a rating scale for a figure-skating contest that is always used by a panel of, say, seven judges and each contestant's score is always based on the average of the scores given by the seven judges. In this case, the average score across the seven judges can be expected to be more consistent than any single score given by any single judge. Using the variance components in the G study to estimate either the norm-referenced or the criterion-referenced reliability coefficients would provide only an estimate of the reliability of the score for a single judge and would provide an underestimate of the reliability of the average score across seven judges. The D study stage allows a researcher to pose different scenarios and then assess the resulting variance components and their corresponding reliability coefficients for each scenario.

In a D study, a researcher first defines a universe of generalization. This universe may consist of a subset or may include all of the facets in the original universe of admissible observations. For example, from an observer cross environment two-faceted universe of admissible observations in the G study, one may define a universe of generalization consisting of only an observer facet, only an environment facet, or both facets. In practice, the universe of generalization for a D study is usually identical to the universe of admissible observations in the G study. Within this defined universe of generalization, the researcher would then specify a tentative sample size for each facet (e.g., number of observers) to be used along with the particular observation system in future applications. The D study variance components are then estimated.

D Study Variance Components

For the purpose of illustration, we will use the data in Table 6.1 as the data for a single-observer facet-crossed-design G study. Through a two-way ANOVA, as performed previously for the intraclass correlation situation, we have estimated the subject variance component, σ_s^2, to be 7.208, the observer variance component, σ_o^2, to be 1.975, and the observer-by-subject interaction variance, σ_{os}^2, which is equivalent to the error variance in a single-faceted crossed-design situation, to be 0.992.

We have, next, defined the universe of generalization as identical to that of the G study; namely, a single-faceted crossed-design universe with an observer facet. (Note: The definition of the universe of generalization from within a single-faceted universe of admissible observations is redundant because the only subset of the latter is an identical universe. It is mentioned here as a reminder that for multifaceted analyses the universe of generalization and the universe of admissible observations need not be identical). Now we examine the change in variance components under different-observer sample-size scenarios. In general, the more observers are employed each time the observation system is used, the more reliable the composite mean scores for the subjects. However, the more observers used, the more practical problems (e.g., identifying sufficient observers, training observers, minimizing obtrusiveness, etc.) can be expected. In D study considerations, one may examine the exact gains in data quality in using different numbers of observers and weigh that information against their corresponding applied problems so that the best decision regarding the number of observers to be used with the observation system can be made.

To simplify discussion, let us consider one of the many possible D study scenarios. In this scenario, five observers are to be used, with the observation system represented by the data in Table 5.2 in all future observation sessions. For this or any other D study scenarios, the universe score variance for the D study is identical to that estimated by the G study (i.e., $\sigma_s^2 = 7.208$). This is because, regardless of how many observers are used, the true differences among the subjects remain unchanged. To denote the other D study variance components, we use the upper case O for observers under the D scenario instead of the lower case o for observers in the G study. Hence, the D study observer variance component is σ_O^2 and the interaction variance component is σ_{Os}^2. These D study variance components are estimated based on their corresponding G study variance components and the defined sample size of the facet in the scenario. For a D study scenario with n_O observers:

$$\sigma_O^2 = \sigma_o^2/n_O \tag{6.9}$$

$$\sigma_{Os}^2 = \sigma_{os}^2/n_O. \tag{6.10}$$

For our D study of the data in Table 6.1 with a scenario of $n_O = 5$, the three variance components are:

$$\sigma_s^2 = 7.208,$$

$$s_O^2 = 1.975 = 0.3950,$$

and

$$\sigma_{Os}^2 = 0.992/5 = 0.1984.$$

From these D study variance components, different types of error variances can be derived. First, an absolute error variance ($\sigma^2(\Delta)$) can be derived. For the single-observer facet-crossed-design universe of generalization, the absolute error variance is:

$$\sigma^2(\Delta) = \sigma_O^2 + \sigma_{Os}^2. \tag{6.11}$$

With our example, the absolute error variance is $(.3950 + .1984) = .5934$. This is the variance of the difference between the observed behavior score and the universe score for the behavior. It is an indicator of the amount of errors associated with the scores relative to the absolute universe score. It is particularly suited for a criterion-referenced interpretation of scores. The absolute error variance of .5934 in our example, when compared against the universe score variance (subject variance) of 7.208, is negligibly small. This indicates that if five observers were used in future administrations of the observation system, the average score across the five observers can be expected to deviate from the universe score of each subject by only a negligible amount.

Another useful error variance estimate is the relative error variance $(\sigma^2(\delta))$. In a single-observer facet universe of generalization:

$$\sigma^2(\delta) = \sigma_{Os}^2. \tag{6.12}$$

With our example, the relative error variance is simply .1984. Had n_O been defined as a number equal to the number of observers in the original G study, this relative error variance would equal the error variance estimated from the same data through the Classical Theory approach, and the square root of this relative error variance would be equal to the classical standard error of measurement. This relationship holds only for a single-faceted universe.

This error variance is an indicator of the amount of error associated with the scores when the scores are used only as indicators of the subjects' positions relative to one another. The square root of this error variance component can be used directly to estimate the confidence interval around the mean score across five observers in a process similar to the classical procedure. Again, when compared against the universe score variance of 7.208, this relative error variance of .1984 is extremely small. This indicates that if the mean across five observers is interpreted within a norm-referenced framework, the expected error is extremely small.

A third error variance that can be derived is the mean error variance $(\sigma^2(\bar{X}))$. This is the error variance in using the observed grand mean across the observers and subjects as an estimate of the grand mean of all possible observers and subjects in the defined universe of generalization. This error variance is estimated based on the original variance components in the G study, the number of subjects (i.e. n_s) in the G study, and the number of observers for the D study (i.e., n_O) as:

$$\sigma^2(\bar{X}) = \sigma_s^2/n_s + \sigma_o^2/n_O + \sigma_{os}^2/n_s n_O. \tag{6.13}$$

With our example:

$$\sigma^2(\bar{X}) = 7.208/5 + 1.975 + .992/(5)(5) = 1.876.$$

This variance component is useful for assessing the amount of error one can expect in using the grand mean of scores for a sample of five subjects using five observers as an estimate of the grand mean of all subjects and all observers in the universe of generalization. This is an indicator of the sampling error associated with the observed grand mean.

Indices of Dependability

From all the variance components estimated for a single D study scenario, a number of supplementary reliability indices can be derived. Classical reliability indices estimate the degree of data consistency within an undefined unidimensional universe. A reliability index estimated within the framework of generalizability, however, has a well-defined and potentially multidimensional context. Further, a different set of reliability indices may be derived for a different D study scenario. Brennan and Kane (1977b) suggested a signal/noise ratio ($\Psi(g)$) as an indicator of the relative precision of the scores interpreted within a norm-referenced framework. It is computed by:

$$\Psi(g) = \sigma_s^2/\sigma^2(\delta). \tag{6.14}$$

In our example, $\Psi(g) = 7.208/.1984 = 36.33$. The higher the value of this index, the more precise is the average score across $n_O = 5$ observers for each subject as an estimate of the relative position of the subject.

A better known index is the Generalizability Coefficient ($E\varrho^2$), which is computed by:

$$E\varrho^2 = \sigma_s^2/[\sigma_s^2 + \sigma^2(\delta)]. \tag{6.15}$$

In our example:

$$E\varrho^2 = 7.208/(7.208 + .1984) = .973.$$

This is a norm-referenced reliability index that indicates the reliability of the mean score across five observers. That is, this Generalizability coefficient of .973 reflects the norm-referenced reliability of the mean score across an n_O of five observers in the D study scenario.

Had the n_O defined for the D study been 1, the Generalizability Coefficient would be identical to the norm-referenced intraclass correlation computed through Equations 6.4 or 6.5 on the same set of data. In other words, the conventional norm-referenced intraclass correlation is a special case of the Generalizability Coefficient when n_O in the D study is defined as 1, in which case the Generalizability Coefficient would indicate the reliability of scores from a single observer.

Had the number of observers defined in the D study (i. e., n_O) been equal to the original number of observers in the G study (i.e., n_o) the resulting Generalizability Coefficient would be equivalent to Cronbach Alpha (or KR-20 for dichotomous data) computed through Equations 6.6 or 6.7 on the original set of data in the G study. Another way to express this is that Cronbach Alpha (or KR-20) is a special case of the Generalizability Coefficient when $n_O = n_o$. In this case, the Generalizability Coefficient would indicate the dependability of the total or average score across n_o observers. Because there is no particular reason to think that the original number of observers used in the G study is superior to a different number of observers, other than the fact that it happens to be the number used in the G study, there is little reason to regard the Generalizability Coefficient for the $n_O = n_o$ D study (or Cronbach Alpha) to be particularly more informative than any other Generalizability Coefficients for different n_O values.

A criterion-referenced Generalizability Coefficient can be assessed through (Brennan, 1983):

$$\Phi = \sigma_s^2/[\sigma_s^2 + \sigma^2(\Delta)]. \tag{6.16}$$

For our example:

$$\Phi = 7.208/(7.208 + .5934) = .924.$$

This indicates the dependability of the average across $n_O = 5$ observers as a measure of the score of each subject relative to an absolute criterion. Had the n_O for the D study been defined as 1, the criterion-referenced Generalizability Coefficient would have been equal to the criterion-referenced intraclass correlation coefficient computed through Equation 6.8 on the original G study data.

Single-Subject Studies

For the sake of simplicity, throughout the previous discussion, a subject-crossed-observer design is used. These variables can be substituted by any other reasonable variables. For instance, the true variance of interest may be that of scores across observation session or across items of a scale. The observer facet may be changed to instrumentation, environment, and so on as appropriate.

In applied behavior research, a single-subject design is frequently used. In these cases, the true variance can no longer be subject variance because there is only one subject. If the behavior of the one subject is observed over a number of observation sessions and the intersession reliability is the appropriate unit of analysis, the true variance would be the variance across sessions. Instead of subject variance, one would estimate session variance and treat this variance as true variance. Similarly, for a single-subject intrasession reliability assessment, the true variance is the variance across intervals or points of observation within the session.

One potential problem with the application of the Generalizability approach to single-subject intersession or intrasession reliability assessment is that within-session as well as between-session scores are sometimes autocorrelated. The Generalizability Theory, being a model within the Random Sampling Theory, assumes independence of data. Applying the Generalizability approach to autocorrelated data will most likely lead to biased estimates of variance components (Maxwell, 1968). For these situations, Suen and Lee (1987a, 1987b) suggested an aggregate–segregate approach. Essentially, the approach involves first aggregating the data from K observers into a single series of observations, each point representing a mean across observers. This series is then modeled through an ARIMA times series process, a technique that is discussed in chapter 9, to remove the autocorrelation from the aggregated data. The aggregated data are then segregated back to reflect K observers. The resulting segregated data would contain no autocorrelation and can be submitted to a Generalizability study. An alternative is to use a single-subject research design known as the randomization test design, which is discussed in chapter 8. Through this design, observational data will contain only a minimal amount of autocorrelation. Preliminary results from ongoing analyses by the first author indicate that the Generalizability approach may be quite robust against autocorrelation. If these results are confirmed, autocorrelation is a negligible problem for Generalizability analyses.

For situations in which a relatively large sample of subjects is used and the sampling process is assumed random, facets of subject characteristics can be ignored without reducing the degree of generalizability of scores to other subjects within the universe of admissible observations. For a single-subject study, however, it would not be reasonable to assume that the scores of a single individual are generalizable to other individuals in the population (Hersen & Barlow, 1976). A question of generalizability for single-subject designs is how dependable will the scores obtained from a particular observation system be should the subject chosen have different characteristics? One approach to answering this question is to restrict generalization to other subjects with similar characteristics only. In this case, a researcher needs only to report all relevant characteristics of the subject so that replications can be performed by others to investigate generalizability (Baer, Wolf, & Risley, 1968; Homer, Peterson, & Wonderlich, 1983; Sidman 1960). This point was made earlier in chapter 3 and is reiterated here as it relates to the concept of generalizability. If one wishes to develop an observation system for a particular single-subject study and to generalize the results across various subject characteristics, these characteristics should be included in the G study and the D study as facets in the universes of admissible observation and generalization, and facet data for the G study should be collected accordingly.

RELIABILITIES OF MACHINE RECORDERS

It is commonly assumed that when behaviors are recorded through a machine such as a computerized event recorder or a videotape, the resulting data are more reliable than those obtained from human observers. There is no clear evidence that indicates that this assumption is true. In a Generalizability analysis using human observers versus audio-recording as one of the facets, Hansen, Tisdelle, and O'Dell (1985) found that the variance component for this facet was very small. In another study, Ary, Van Acker, and Karsh (1986) found that the kappa values for data obtained from human observers using momentary time sampling were slightly higher than those for data obtained through a computerized event recorder.

The explanation of these findings may be as follows: The main sources of error with human observers are random errors in interpreting a behavior, in recording, in tallying, and in transcribing. Machine recording of behaviors is not free from these sources of error. The translation of images on a videotape or sound patterns on an audiotape to quantitative data for analysis involves the same sources of error as in the direct observation of the behavior with human observers. The use of computerized event recorders may reduce the error in tallying. When the event recorder also has the ability to analyze data, error in transcribing is also reduced. However, the use of the event recorder still requires a human observer interpreting a behavior and coding such a behavior into the recorder. The reduction of error in tallying and transcribing may be neutralized by an increase of error in interpreting and coding due to the observer's misplaced confidence in the reliability of the event recorder. The findings in Ary, Van Acker, and Karsh's study may indicate that use of a computerized event recorder may, in fact, lead to an increase of error in interpreting and coding a behavior exceeding the amount of reduction of sampling error and error in tallying and transcribing.

SOFTWARE CONSIDERATIONS

In the simple days when percentage agreement ($p\%$) was commonly accepted as a good indicator of observational data reliability, computation of reliability was relatively simple. For most observation situations, $p\%$ can be calculated with paper and pencil based on a hand tally of scores. As the concepts and techniques for the assessment of reliability become more precise and sophisticated, their computational processes become more complicated. Imagine, for instance, trying to estimate the variance components in a D study by hand with a large amount of interval-level data involving many observers!

Computer software has increasingly become an important consideration in the assessment of behavioral data reliability. Routines to compute Pearson's r are available in all mainframe statistical packages (e.g., SPSSx, SAS, BMDP, MINITAB, etc.), in most of the statistical software for microcomputers, and in many specialized statistical calculators.

The calculation of interobserver agreement indices is relatively simple except for the tallying of scores. This latter task becomes time consuming and error prone when the number of observations is large. We can identify no mainframe computer program that would compute directly any of the five interobserver agreement indices discussed in this chapter. The only microcomputer software available that would compute interobserver agreement indices directly is BOSA (Suen & Yue, forthcoming). Additionally, some computerized event recorders will compute kappa automatically. Another alternative is to tabulate the 2 × 2 table with corresponding expected cell frequencies through the χ^2 routine found in most statistical softwares and extract the cell frequencies, expected frequencies, and marginals as appropriate from the table. These values can then be applied to the desired interobserver agreement index equation. Bakeman and Gottman (1986) also provided a FORTRAN routine for the computation of kappa.

For Generalizability studies and intraclass correlation, which is a special case of Generalizability studies, there is a specialized mainframe program entitled GENOVA (Crick & Brennan, 1982). An alternative is to compute the mean squares (MS) through the ANOVA, General Linear Models (GLM), or regression procedures in most mainframe statistical packages and then apply the appropriate equations to these mean square values to estimate the various G and D study variance components. When the design of a G study or a D study is highly complex (e.g, mixed crossed and nested designs) with a large number of facets, the use of most of these ANOVA, GLM, or regression routines is unsuitable (Bell, 1985). Bell suggested that the VARCOMP routine in SAS may be most appropriate for a complex Generalizability study.

SUMMARY OF RELIABILITY

In these two chapters, we pointed out that when addressing an external audience, behavioral observation data are not exempted from the need for evidence of reliability. Conventionally, the reliability of observational data may be assessed through an interobserver agreement approach or an intraobserver reliability approach. The former indicates the extent to which two or more independent observers observing the same behavior will produce similar results. The latter indicates the extent to which the same observer observing the same behavior over and over again will produce consistent results. The relatively convoluted concept of and the corresponding convoluted theory behind the traditional use of Pearson's r as an estimate of intraobserver reliability has led to considerable confusion in the applied literature regarding the differences among agreement, reliability, accuracy, and validity. The answer lies within a thorough understanding of the Classical Theory of measurement.

The estimation of interobserver agreement is rather straightforward. It is essentially computing the proportion of times two observers agree on the occurrences and nonoccurrences of behavior. The only complication is the statistical problem of chance agreement. Chance agreement can be removed from the proportion agreement statistic, and the result is the kappa coefficient, which is a chance-corrected proportion agreement.

The estimation of intraobserver reliability is considerably more complicated. Because it is often difficult and error prone to have the same observer observing the same behavior over and over again, intraobserver reliability is estimated based on data that can be attained. In order to do so, a more precise psychometric definition is needed. In this psychometric definition, reliability is defined as the proportion of total variance that is true variance. Within the Classical Theory of measurement, the estimation of these variances are bypassed in favor of estimating the proportion of true variance directly. Specifically, if the two sets of scores from two observers can be assumed to have met a set of rather restrictive assumptions, known as the Parallel Tests Assumptions, a Pearson's r between the two sets of data provides a direct estimate of the proportion of true variance, or intraobserver reliability.

The intraclass correlation approach, which is the statistical arm of the

Generalizability Theory, estimates the variance components directly through an ANOVA technique and is based on the random sampling theory. Once these variance components are estimated, the core information for reliability is attained. For convenience of interpretation, ratios of variances can be computed to estimate reliability. However, ratios derived from various combinations of the variance components will produce different reliability estimates, each with its own specific meaning. We demonstrated that by various combinations of the variance components, we can in fact produce a norm-referenced reliability index, a classical reliability index known as Cronbach Alpha, and a criterion-referenced reliability index, which also serves as an omnibus indicator of both intraobserver reliability and interobserver agreement, from within the same set of data in the same ANOVA.

It became clear that reliability is not an absolute concept. Depending on the question asked, different reliability coefficients can be used to provide the answer. The Generalizability Theory is a conceptual breakthrough that recognizes the idea that reliability is relative to the facet of generalization of interest. Further, it recognizes that reliability can be a multifaceted concept. For a given set of data, there can be many possible sources of error. The Generalizability approach allows one to decompose the error portion of scores into various identified sources, instead of simply referring to the portion nebulously as random error. Through an appropriate ANOVA procedure, the relative error due to various sources can be calibrated. With this information, a researcher can identify specific areas for improvement. Various measurement scenarios can be posed, and information from the ANOVA can be analyzed in a process known as Decision Studies to assess the quality of data under these measurement scenarios. Various combinations of the variance components derived within a particular Decision Study scenario will produce various information of error and data reliability.

Both the interobserver agreement approach and the intraobserver reliability approach under the Classical Theory are limited in that each provides only a particular piece of reliability information, which may or may not be relevant to a set of observational data. The intraclass correlation approach is a better alternative to the classical intraobserver reliability approach in three respects: First, it does not require the restrictive Parallel Tests Assumptions; second, it estimates the variance components directly; and third, through various combinations of the variance components, different reliability coefficients for different purposes can be derived. Additionally, the intraclass correlation approach can accommodate both interobserver agreement and intraobserver reliability. The Generalizability approach contains all the advantages of the intraclass correlation. In addition, it can accommodate a multifaceted measurement situation in such a way that errors due to different sources can be estimated. Conceptually, it can accommodate interobserver agreement, intraobserver reliability, validity, as well as other facets of measurement such as the extent to which data can be generalized across environment, setting, recording method, and so on to the extent specified by the researcher with corresponding data collected. Of all the approaches to observational reliability estimations, the Generalizability approach is the most comprehensive and the most informative approach.

We discuss the Generalizability approach further in the next chapter as it relates to validity. For now, it suffices to say that the Generalizability approach should be the approach of choice in assessing behavioral data reliability. All other approaches can be viewed as subsets of the Generalizability approach. The next approach of choice is the intraclass correlation approach. When neither of these two approaches is possible due to applied reasons, both the intraobserver reliability and the interobserver agreement should be assessed, although as a last resort, to estimate the consistency of data.

When the interobserver agreement approach or the intraobserver reliability approach in Classical Theory is used, a single agreement or reliability coefficient will result. However, if the intraclass correlation approach or the Generalizability approach is used, you can have many different possible "reliability" coefficients. If you have to choose a single reliability coefficient within these two approaches, the criterion-referenced dependability coefficient in a Decision Study, Φ, or its special case, the criterion-referenced intraclass correlation coefficient, ϱ_1^2, is probably most appropriate for behavioral observation because it encompasses both information on intraobserver reliability and interobserver agreement.

CHAPTER 7

Validity

Some circumstantial evidence is very strong,
as when you find a trout in the milk.

—Henry David Thoreau

In the previous two chapters, we discussed the various methods available for the estimation of data reliability. Reliability is only a precondition for good data quality. By itself, it does not show that the data are adequate representations of particular behaviors. To accomplish this, validity also needs to be assessed.

Whereas reliability is the degree of data consistency across a defined or undefined dimension, validity is the degree to which a set of data represents what it purports to represent. The degree to which an observation system yields consistent scores (reliability) can be calibrated through statistical techniques, as described in the two previous chapters. The degree to which an observed score represents what it is supposed to represent (validity), however, is an epistemological problem. As such, validity can neither be measured nor be absolutely proven. One can only infer from circumstantial evidence that an observed score is or is not a credible representation of the behavior of interest. This circumstantial evidence may be judgmental in nature or based on analyses of empirical data.

Recall the example of the courtroom witness described in chapter 5. Although it is possible to demonstrate, and even measure, whether a witness is consistent, it is extremely difficult to prove whether the witness is telling the truth. If various other evidence supports the witness's testimony, we infer that the witness is telling the truth. However, we can never be absolutely sure. A case reported recently on the television show *60 Minutes* provides a dramatic illustration of this point. In a criminal case in the early 1970s, more than 30 eyewitnesses consistently and independently identified the same young man (high interobserver agreement) as the robber in a daytime grocery store robbery in Los Angeles. After the man had been in jail for almost 10 years, he was found innocent when the true robber, who was apprehended for an unrelated case, confessed to the crime. Cases like this and many others demonstrate the difficulty of ascertaining validity.

One can never "prove" validity; nor can one describe validity quantitatively. One only accumulates evidence in support of the validity of data obtained through a specific observation system. It is epistemologically reasonable to index the degree of data consistency (reliability) quantitatively. However, it would be unreasonable to index truthfulness (validity). This is because one can theoretically demonstrate that a set of data is absolutely consistent (reliable), but one can never demonstrate that a set of data is *absolutely* true (valid). Although one cannot quantitatively index validity, one can arrive at the *evidence* of validity empirically and describe this evidence quantitatively. When researchers speak of validity coefficients, they are not referring to a direct quantitative measure of validity. Rather, these coefficients are generally statistical descriptions of various pieces of evidence. The fact that validity, unlike reliability, cannot be calibrated directly is an extremely important point. Even if a researcher obtains a perfect "validity coefficient," it is still possible that the measure is not valid. Theories and logic have to be considered. Based on these theories and logical deductions, various pieces of quantitative or qualitative evidence are added on to increase the likelihood that a measure is valid.

In literature concerning psychometrics of behavioral observation, much time and space has been devoted to the issue of reliability. Validity, on the other hand, has not received much attention (cf. Cone, 1982; Herbert & Attridge, 1975; Johnson & Bolstad, 1973; O'Leary, 1979). At least part of this neglect can be attributed to the widespread belief that observational data are inherently valid (e.g., Bakeman, 1978; Goldfried & Linehan, 1977) because of the minimal amount of inferences required on the part of the observers. This belief is justified for some behaviors and not justified for others. The objects of measurement in behavioral observation can range from the very simple to the highly complex and abstract. Dependent upon the complexity and abstractness of the object of measurement, the amount and type of evidence needed to support validity will vary.

OBJECTS OF MEASUREMENT

In behavioral observation, the scores derived from an observation system may represent a variable directly or indirectly. They may also calibrate a simple or a complex behavior. Dependent upon the directness of measurement and the complexity of behavior, the techniques for the gathering of evidence of validity range from the very simple to the highly complex.

The directness of measurement procedures and the complexity of an object of measurement are common characteristics found in everyday measurement of physical objects and are not unique to the measurement of behaviors. For example, when one wishes to measure a simple object such as the height of a building, one may climb the building and use a tape measure to measure the height directly. On the other hand, one may also use a tape measure to measure the length of the shadow and a protractor to measure the angle of the light. From these measurements, one can then deduce the height of the building through trigonometry. In both cases, a simple object (height) is being measured. In one case, the measurement is direct. In the other, the measurement is indirect. The direct measure can be assumed to be more valid because no theoretical inferences are necessary; but the direct measure is also less practical. The indirect measure is more practical but is subject to more possible sources of error (e.g., unclear shadow, competing sources of light, inaccurate protractor, etc.) as well as the correctness of the trigonometric theorem used for deduction.

The object of measurement may also be quite complex, such as the volume of a branch on a tree. In this case, one may cut the branch from the tree and dissect the branch into a number of simpler component shapes. One can then measure and compute the volume of each component shape. The sum of these volumes would be a direct measure of the volume of the branch. On the other hand, if one does not wish to damage the branch, one may make a cast of the branch. From this cast, a model is made. The model can then be placed in a basin of water that has been filled to the top; the water displaced by the model is then gathered. One can then determine the volume of water displaced by placing the water into a measuring cup. The volume of water is then interpreted as a representation of the volume of the branch. The latter method is much more indirect and is subject to more possible measurement and theoretical error than the first method. For example, the exactness in constructing the cast and the model, the amount of water absorbed by the model and hence not displaced, and the correctness of the theory of physics governing the displacement of water, and so on are all threats to the validity of using the volume of water as a representation of the volume of the branch. However, the indirect method is more practical when one does not want to damage the tree.

The principles of measurement and the characteristics of directness and complexity for behavioral observation are not different from those of the measurement of the height of a building or the volume of a branch. The exception is that for behavioral observation, the dimensions of measurement are generally not as tangible as height or volume. Additionally, when an indirect measure is used, the theoretical connection between the object of measurement and the indirect measure is not as clear-cut as the trigonometric theorem that connects the shadow to the height of a building or the law of physics that connects the volume of water displaced to the volume of the branch. In the following discussion, for the sake of conceptual clarity, we polarize the directness of measurement into a dichotomy of direct sample measures versus indirect sign measures. We also categorize the complexity of an observed behavior into molecular versus molar behaviors.

Sample Versus Sign Measures

Observational methods may be used to gather data to reflect the quantity of various objects of measurement. The simplest case is one in which observational data are a direct sample of the object of measurement. For example, in a program designed to increase the frequency of a particular vocalization behavior of an autistic child, the object of measurement is most likely to be the frequency of the particular vocalization behavior. In this case, the observation and recording of the vocalization behavior of the child would yield frequency scores that are a direct sample of the object of measurement. Observational data, however, may also be used as indirect indicators of some underlying and unobservable trait or construct. These data are used as *signs* of the construct (Goodenough, 1949). A construct is a variable that cannot be observed—such as a trait, an attribute, or a quality—but exists in theory and may or may not exist in objective reality. It is literally an abstract entity constructed by scientists based upon theories. Some examples of sign uses of observational data are the frequency of grooming between two monkeys as a sign of a construct called "affection," the prevalence of yelling as a sign of a "hyperactivity" construct, and the prevalence of hitting as a sign of an "aggressiveness" construct.

Prior to the 1970s, when behavioral observation techniques were used, sample measures were frequently considered the only legitimate measure of behavior. During the past 15 years, however, sign measures of "trait-like" dimensions such as assertiveness, social skills, fears, as well as other personality or intellectual constructs have been measured through observational methods more regularly (cf. Ciminero, Calhoun, & Adams, 1977; Eysenck & Eysenck, 1980; Eysenck, Wakefield, & Friedman, 1983; Haynes & Wilson, 1979). There has been some debate recently over the legitimacy of using direct behavioral observation methods to measure signs of an unobservable construct. It has been suggested that for some constructs, self-reports may be more valid than observation (Jacobson, 1985a; 1985b). Others (e.g., Gottman, 1985) contended that many of these high-level abstract constructs are essentially defined by society at large. Hence, an observational code based on the societal definition of the construct is more valid than the subjects' self-reports. Regardless of which argument is correct, no single approach—observation or otherwise— is inherently valid. Empirical as well as judgmental evidence has to be gathered to support any claims of validity. Our purpose here, however, is not to analyze the efficacy of using observational sign measures to calibrate an unobservable construct. Rather, the discussion concentrates on the technique for the validation of observation measures should direct observation be selected as the method for data collection. For readers who are interested in the conceptual issues involved in the use of behavioral observation methods to calibrate an unobservable construct, we suggest their perusal of an excellent debate among Jacobson (1985a, 1985b), Weiss and Frohman (1985), and Gottman (1985).

Molecular Versus Molar Behaviors

The behavior of interest for observation may fall into one of two categories of behaviors: molecular or molar. Molecular behaviors are individually recognizable specific behaviors for which further breakdown into components becomes meaningless for an investigation. For example, in an investigation of the in-seat behavior of students in a classroom, the in-seat versus out-of-seat behavior of a student is a meaningful molecular behavior. Further breakdown of this behavior, through task analyses, for instance, will serve no additional purpose. For another example, in a behavior modification program designed for cigarette-smoking cessation, the only variable of interest may be the molecular behavior of cigarette smoking as measured through the dimension of frequency of cigarette smoking per day. Further breakdown of the behavior of cigarette smoking may not be meaningful for the purpose of the program.

Molecular behaviors, frequently derived through a process of systematic reduction of a phenomenon to a single directly observable overt behavior dimension (cf. Evans, 1985; Eysenck, 1960; Kanfer & Saslow, 1965; Voeltz & Evans, 1983) are widely used as the objects of study (Hoge, 1985), particularly among applied behavior researchers or experimental psychologists with classical as well as operant conditioning orientations. In fact, it was not long ago that the measurement of a single molecular behavior was considered a desirable approach to experimental psychology and behavior therapy (e.g., Ullmann & Krasner, 1965).

In many other situations, however, the variable of interest is more complex and cannot be sufficiently represented by a single molecular behavior. In these situations, the variable is represented by a molar behavior. Molar behaviors are generally a category of behaviors with meaningful component behaviors. For example, "inappropriate disruptive behavior" in a classroom is a molar behavior for which finer behaviors such as "talking out of order," "hitting," "throwing objects," and so forth can be identified as meaningful component molecular behaviors. Each component molecular behavior by itself is an inadequate indicator of the larger and more abstract molar behavior.

In general, molecular behaviors as the measure of interest are used more frequently within studies with an orientation toward behaviorism. It is rare, however, that a researcher will find the measurement of a single molecular behavior sufficient when the purpose of the assessment is outside the realm of behaviorism. On the other hand, molar behaviors as the measure of interest are used widely in various fields of inquiry across different theoretical orientations. For example, in child development, the Brazelton Neonatal Behavioral Assessment Scale (BNBAS) is a molar measure comprised of a number of molecular behaviors (Brazelton, 1973). The purpose of BNBAS is to detect neonatal psychophysiological dysfunction. It has been explicitly pointed out, however, that the individual score for each molecular behavior by itself does not indicate the more abstract and complex phenomenon (molar behavior) of psychophysiological dysfunction (Tronick & Brazelton, 1975). For this scale, the molar behavior is measured by the pattern and organization of responses to individual molecular behavior assessment items. Hence, one can view molecular behaviors as the most fundamental unit of analysis and molar behaviors as the higher level, more abstract, but not directly observable behaviors. Other examples of molar behaviors are "maladaptive behavior," "hyperactivity," "disruptive behavior," "marital discord," and "aversive behavior."

Directness, Complexity, and Validity

Through the interaction of the sample versus sign and the molecular versus molar dichotomies, four types of behavioral measures can be identified: molecular samples, molecular signs, molar samples, and molar signs. Data appropriate for a particular study can be any one or a combination of these four types of measures. For example, if the variable of interest for a study is the prevalence of a child's reading behavior in a study hall (an observable behavior), observation of the prevalence of the child's reading behavior during an observation session would yield the most appropriate molecular sample of the variable. On the other hand, if one is interested in measuring an individual's alcohol dependency (an unobservable trait), the average per day frequency of alcohol consumption over the period of observation is an appropriate molecular sign of alcohol dependency.

Similarly, when a molar behavior is a convenient summary description of its component behaviors and such a molar behavior is the object of measurement, the cumulative score from observation of the component molecular behaviors is a molar sample. For example, when a researcher is only interested in measuring the frequency of "inappropriate disruptive behavior" displayed by a group of pupils in a classroom, the researcher may observe and record the incidents of yelling, talking out of order, hitting, throwing objects, and so on. A composite score obtained by combining scores for these molecular behaviors is a direct molar sample of inappropriate disruptive behavior. This is because the term *inappropriate disruptive behavior* is a convenient summary descriptor of these directly observable molecular behaviors. It is a category of behaviors for which an exhaustive list of component molecular behaviors can theoretically be constructed. It should be pointed out that although an exhaustive list of component molecular behaviors can be constructed, one does not have to include all these molecular behaviors in the system for the observation of the molar behavior. Rather, a sample can be selected based upon clinical considerations (e.g., Mash & Tedral, 1981) so that only those molecular behaviors that are most relevant to the study are included. In these cases, the label assigned to the molar behavior should be selected carefully so as not to mislead others to interpret the score to imply behaviors beyond those selected component molecular behaviors.

If a researcher is, however, interested in measuring a construct called "marital discord," which is an unobservable construct, the researcher may observe the verbal communications between two spouses and record the frequency of criticism, disagreement, interruption, sarcasm, excuses, and so on. The sum of these molecular verbal behaviors can be described as a molar behavior of "aversive communication," which is, in turn, a possible sign of "marital discord." In this case, the sum of the molecular verbal behaviors is a molar sign of marital discord. In the research literature, the term *molar measure* is frequently used to describe molar sign scores (e.g., Hoge, 1985). Molar sample scores, however, have been referred to as composite scores (Hartmann, 1982), molecular-composite measures (Hoge, 1985), or behavior constellation measures (Kazdin, 1985).

In the past, many have contended that behavioral observation data were, by definition, valid (cf. Bakeman, 1978; Cone, 1978; Hartmann & Wood, 1982). To a very limited degree, this assumption is reasonable when the observational data are molecular sample scores. Since a molecular sample score is a direct measure of a behavior at its most explicit manifestation, one can reasonably argue that it is more likely for a molecular sample score to be valid than it is for a molecular sign score, a molar sample score, or a molar sign score. Because of the differences in directness and complexity of these four types of measures, it would take different amounts of evidence to support their validities. Recall the examples of the building and the branch where as the measurement procedure becomes more indirect and the object of measurement becomes more complex, more evidence is needed to support the appropriateness of the final measure.

TYPES OF VALIDITY EVIDENCE

To gather evidence of validity, the existence of a theory or a reasonable conceptual framework surrounding the object of measurement is of utmost importance. Ideally, such a theory should specify the components or underlying dimensions of the object of measurement, alternative means of measuring that object, and relationships between that object and other objects of measurement. Without such a theory, the assessment of validity would be quite difficult or impossible.

With a theory at hand, three main types of evidence of observational data validity can be gathered. These are *content validity*, *criterion-related validity*, and *construct validity*. In the assessment of content validity, one assesses how well all components or underlying dimensions of the object of measurement are represented in the observational system. In criterion-related validity, one assesses how well the system yields results similar to those obtained from alternative means of measuring that object. In construct validity, one assesses whether the extent and the manner in which the measure relates to other objects conforms to those relationships specified in the theory.

For a molar sign measure, it is possible for the score to reflect more than one construct. For this type of situation, the total score as well as some subscores are used. Construct validity for this type of measure is indicated by how well the total and subscores relate to other objects as specified in the theory and how well each subscore forms a distinct subconstruct. It should be pointed out that because the more evidence of validity accumulated around a set of observational data the more one can be certain of its validity, the three types of validity are by no means mutually exclusive. Rather, one should gather as much evidence of each type of validity as possible. These three types of validity are essentially three different strategies of gathering evidence of validity from three different angles.

Content Validity

Content validity is the extent to which a measure reflects the theoretical domain of the variable of interest (i.e., the object of measurement). In conventional paper-and-pencil tests, an instrument consists of a number of items. These items, theoretically, are a sample drawn from the universe of all possible items for a particular construct. This universe of items, or item domain, contains all types of items that represent the content of the construct. An instrument is said to have content validity if the instrument contains representatives of all the different types of items in the item domain for the construct. For example, if one is interested in constructing a test of arithmetic skills, the test would not have content validity if it contained only items of addition and subtraction without any items of multiplication or division. This is because the construct "arithmetic skills" includes all four types of arithmetical operations. The item domain, thus, contains items of all four operations. A test containing only two of the four operations would not be representative of the item domain and, hence, would have limited content validity.

Another example is the measurement of a construct called "alienation," which is an important concept in some sociological and social psychological theories. Based on Dean's (1961) theory, there are three underlying distinct dimensions of alienation. These are normlessness, powerlessness, and social estrangement. An instrument designed to measure alienation has content validity if it contains items reflecting each of the three dimensions of alienation. An instrument that contains items representing, for instance, only the social estrangement item domain would not be a content-valid instrument for alienation. Rather, it could only be used as an instrument for the measurement of social estrangement.

Although it can be supplemented by quantitative information, the establishment of content validity is primarily a judgmental process. It is dependent upon the existence of a well-defined theory that specifies the content of a construct. Based on this theory, the designer of an instrument or an independent panel of experts would judge whether the items in an instrument correspond with the theoretical content of the construct. Analyses of quantitative data, when appropriate, are supplemental.

Content Validity of Behavior Measures

The judgement of content validity is dependent upon the existence of a domain of items. In behavioral observation, the "domains" of items for each of the four different types of measures (i.e., molecular sample, molecular sign, molar sample, and molar sign) are different in size and complexity. Hence, the judgment of their content validity would also have different levels of complexity.

For some molecular sample measures, the measure *is* the domain. As such, these molecular sample measures are, by definition, content valid.

For example, a behavior modification program is designed to stop the object-throwing behavior of a child while the child is in the classroom. The most likely object of measure for this program is the frequency of object-throwing behavior while in the classroom. One then observes the behavior of the child in the classroom and counts the frequency of the object-throwing behavior. Since the molecular sample measure and the object of measurement are identical, it would be absurd to ask if the molecular measure adequately represents the domain of the object of measurement. For this type of molecular sample measure, the object of measurement, the molecular sample measure, and the domain of measurement are the same. Content validity is thus self-evident. It is this axiomatic content validity for some molecular sample measures in behavioral observation that has prompted some in earlier years to overgeneralize and conclude that observational data are, by definition, valid.

Content validity cannot be assumed for all molecular sample measures of behavior. Although, in many cases, the measure is the domain, this is not necessarily the case for all molecular sample measures. Conceptually, a molecular behavior does not contain meaningful finer behaviors to form a domain for a molecular sample measure. However, the domain of the target molecular behavior may be larger than it first appears when variables such as occasion, time, environment, and so on are considered. For example, if the object of measurement is the frequency a child spits food while eating, observing the child's frequency of food spitting at supper time only is not representative of the domain of the object, which also includes food spitting at breakfast, at lunch, and at snack time. Similarly, observing the child at home is not representative of the domain that also includes food spitting in the school cafeteria, in friends' homes, and in restaurants. Hence, observing the child's supper-time behavior at home does not yield a content-valid measure of the child's "food-spitting behavior while eating." This issue of content validity is the often ignored minor difference between the intended object of measurement and what is actually being measured. Observing a child's in-class reading behavior on weekdays only, for instance, would quite likely yield representative and content-valid samples of the child's in-class reading behavior. On the other hand, observing the swimming behavior of an office worker on weekdays probably would not lead to a content-valid measure of the worker's swimming behavior because the worker's swimming behavior would most likely occur on weekends. However, if the intended object of measurement is "weekday swimming behavior," then weekday observations are content valid. This type of problem seems to be quite obvious, yet we often use a molecular sample measure obtained in an interview or role-playing situation, for instance, as if it were a representative and content-valid measure of an individual's behavior.

The key concept here is the idea of a "representative sample of the behavior domain." Theoretically, the domain can be extremely large when different environmental variables are considered. A simple remedy to this ever increasing domain is to explicitly limit the domain of the object of measurement. For example, if the object of measurement is just the "food-spitting behavior of a child at supper time while at a friend's home," it should be specified as such, instead of describing the object as "food spitting while eating." Hartmann and Wood (1982) pointed out that a thorough enumeration of the stimuli, the responses, and other important elements in the domain could promote higher content validity. It could also clearly specify the limits of applicability of an observation system. This is analogous to performing a task analysis and is reminiscent of defining a universe of admissible observations and a universe of generalization in the Generalizability Theory. When an object of measurement has a clear set of specifications and the molecular sample measure adheres to these specifications, content validity can be assumed.

Unlike molecular sample measures, there is no situation in which a molecular sign measure of behavior is by definition content valid. First, molecular sign measures are subject to the problem of the specification of a domain that may include a number of environmental factors such as those previously discussed for molecular sample measures. In addition, two questions have to be considered: (a) Is the chosen molecular behavior a sign of the construct or is it outside the domain of signs for that construct? (b) Is the chosen molecular behavior the only and comprehensive observable sign of the construct? The latter question is analogous to asking whether "sneezing" is an adequate sign of the common cold or "failure to recall events consistently" is an adequate sign of amnesia. The answer to the first question is probably negative. For the second question, "consistent failure to recall events" is a content-valid measure of amnesia. Another more abstract example is observing the amount of time it takes for an individual to climb a tree when confronted by a wild boar. The amount of time may not be a content-valid molecular sign measure of a "fear" construct; rather, it may be a measure of "physical agility," which is outside of the domain of "fear." Nor is it an adequate molecular sign of "fear."

A molar sample measure is a summary descriptor of a category of molecular behaviors. As such, the content validity for each component molecular sample measure as well as the overall molar sample measure need to be assessed. The content validity of each molecular sample measure can be judged, as described before, by considering environmental variables. Judgments are made regarding whether those environmental variables that are important are represented by the molecular sample measure. The content validity of the overall molar sample measure is assessed by judging the exhaustiveness and the representativeness of the component molecular sample measures for the overall molar sample measure. For example, a molar sample measure of "self-care activity" obtained from summing the scores for "eating" and "drinking" behaviors would not be content valid since other self-care activities such as "grooming" and "dressing" are not represented. To go one step further, "grooming" by itself is an intermediate molar sample measure that is comprised of its own set of molecular sample measures. If only "hand washing" is scored but not "tooth brushing," the intermediate molar sample measure of "grooming" would have limited content validity; and, in turn, the overall "self-care activity" molar sample measure would not be content valid.

The question of content validity for a molar sign measure includes all those questions for a molecular sign and a molar sample. In addition, one needs to ask whether the overall molar sign is within the domain and is an adequate representation of the object of measurement. Recall the example of measuring "marital discord." An observation system is constructed to measure the verbal communications between two spouses and to record the frequency of criticism, disagreement, interruption, sarcasm, excuses, and so on. The sum of these molecular verbal behaviors is used as a molar sample measure of "aversive communication," which is, in turn, used as a sign of marital discord. First, one needs to assess the content validity of each molecular sample measure. Next, one needs to assess whether these molecular sample behaviors are exhaustive of all elements in the domain of aversive communication and whether any of the molecular sample measures are actually outside of the domain of aversive communication. Finally, one needs to assess whether aversive communication is an adequate representation of the domain of marital discord.

Much of the eventual judgment of content validity is shaped by the original approach to designing the observational codes. Herbert and Attridge (1975) pointed out that in developing behavioral codes, items comprising the instrument must be exhaustive of the dimensions of behavior under study. Another way to express this is that all molecular behaviors or intermediate molar behaviors must be represented in the overall measurement of a molar behavior. Pragmatically, however, not all behaviors within the domain of a molar behavior can be included. Many molecular behaviors are very difficult to observe, highly prone to observer reactivity, or detectable only through highly complex judgment or inference. Since the exclusion of these molecular behaviors would compromise the content validity of a molar measure, attempts should always be made to tap at least signs of these behaviors. In many cases, imagination and creativity on the part of the researcher are needed.

Systematic, Judgmental, and Quantitative Assessments

The assessment of content validity is primarily a subjective judgmental process. Because of this lack of empirical evidence, some writers (e.g., Messick, 1975) suggested that it should not be considered a type of validity. This radical position is somewhat analogous to throwing the baby out with the bath water. The role of content validity is to provide evidence of validity of the measure. The fact that the evidence does not have a hard empirical basis is not the same as not having any evidence at all. Since the more evidence the more certain we are of the validity of the measure, content validity is as important as other types of validity. A more reasonable position is one of regarding content validity as an important piece of evidence and seeking to improve its objectivity through the development of some quantifiable procedures (Yalow & Popham, 1983).

Attempts or suggestions have been made by various individuals to employ quantitative techniques to derive empirically based circumstantial evidence of content validity or quantitative indices of content validity. For example, Heuer and Wiersma (1977) suggested a systematic rating method in which a number of experts rate each item of a test as a valid item, a reasonably valid item, or an invalid item. A quantitative measure of content validity can then be derived from the proportion of each type of item on the test. Although this approach provides a quantitative indicator of the extent to which all items in a test are judged to be within the domain of the object of measurement, it does not provide any indication of whether all items in the domain are represented. Nunnally (1978) has discussed some potential applications of factor analysis techniques to detect the lack of content validity. Bohrnstedt (1970) suggested the use of cluster analytic techniques, and Nunnally (1978) suggested the use of internal consistency measures of reliability to infer content validity. Henryssen (1971) suggested other data-based methods of arriving at circumstantial evidence of content validity. Because the establishment of content validity is primarily a judgmental process, judgmental quantitative techniques such as those used to arrive at a judgmental prior distribution in the Bayesian inferential process (e.g., Raiffe & Schlaiffer, 1961; Suen & Karabinus, 1986; Winkler, 1968), a weighted-mean method (Suen, 1984), or the Delphi process (Helmer & Rescher, 1959) may be potentially useful in deriving a quantitative indicator of content validity. For example, through one of these quantitative judgmental processes, the proportion of the behavior domain not represented by the observation system and the proportion of behaviors in the system but not within the domain can be estimated. An index may be derived from a combination of the proportion of content not represented and the proportion of behaviors outside of the defined domain.

Although there is no proven empirical or quantitative method of establishing content validity, one can improve the probability that a test is content valid by a systematization of the test construction process. A method to systematize the test construction process in order to improve content validity is through the construction of a table of specifications.

This method is most commonly used in the construction of a classroom test designed to evaluate subject matter learning.

The use of tables of specifications to ensure the content validity of a measure has not been widely used outside of the area of classroom instruction evaluation. The object of measurement in classroom instruction generally has a clear domain that has been specified by the instructor in the list of instructional objectives. To the extent that the instructor adheres to this list of instructional objectives in actual classroom instruction, the objectives form an exhaustive list of the domain for the test. Furthermore, the assignment of weight to each topic area for a classroom test has relatively clear-cut guidance from such factors as the amount of instructional time devoted to the topic area and the general philosophical orientation of the school.

The domain for an object of measurement in areas other than instructional evaluation is not as axiomatic as that of instructional evaluation. Additionally, theories surrounding an object of measurement are generally not that exact as to allow one to assign a meaningful weight to each underlying dimension of the object. For example, it would be very difficult, if not impossible, to assign weights to each of the three dimensions of alienation based on their relative contribution to alienation. For most constructs, there is no convenient guidance for weight assignment, such as instructional time devoted to the topic area in instructional evaluation.

Potentially, the use of tables of specifications to systematize the judgmental process in content validation may be applicable to behavioral observation measures as well as the measurement of other constructs. However, this application is dependent upon the development of more exact theories in behavioral sciences so that meaningful weights can be assigned. Because of the lack of direct application to behavioral observation today, we will not dwell on this any further. For those readers who are interested in the exploration of the use of tables of specifications, Gronlund (1981) provides some excellent instructional examples.

Criterion-Related Validity

The second major type of validity evidence is called criterion-related validity. Literally, criterion-related validity is concerned with how well a set of scores obtained from a particular measurement procedure relates to a chosen criterion. Criterion-related validity is estimated empirically and quantitatively through a statistical correlation between the set of scores obtained from a measurement procedure with those obtained from an alternative method of measuring the criterion.

In the assessment of content validity for a measurement procedure, there is only one theoretically relevant domain. In a sense, this domain is absolute and is the only basis used to judge content validity. The criterion chosen for criterion-related validity, however, is not absolute but is relative to the intended use of the scores from the measurement system. For example, if the intention of a test is to measure academic achievement at a particular point in time, the test scores are said to have criterion-related validity when these scores correlate well with alternative concurrent measures of academic achievement. However, if the intended use of the same test is to predict future academic success, then one seeks a high correlation between scores on the test and future academic success criteria.

This relativity of relevant criterion for criterion-related validity makes it a unique evidence of validity. Because of this unique nature of criterion-related validity, some (e.g., Anastasi, 1976; Hartmann & Wood, 1982) suggested that validity is not an absolute property of an assessment instrument. This statement is true only in reference to criterion-related validity. In some extreme cases, one may even argue that criterion-related validity is the only evidence needed for an assessment instrument. For example, a system of observation codes is devised to record certain behaviors of a client during an intake interview for admission to a mental institution. The intention of the measurement procedure is to predict the probability of the client's violent acting out in the future. In this case, only evidence of criterion-related validity is needed to demonstrate the validity of the system. In other words, if the scores obtained from the observation system correlate highly with observations of violent acting out in the future, the system is valid as a predictor of violent acting out. It is irrelevant whether the behaviors included in the system are a representative sample of the domain of "aggressiveness," "egocentrism," or "communication skills." As long as the system predicts, it is valid from a heuristic point of view.

The important point to consider when determining whether criterion-related validity is sufficient is the interpretation of measurement scores. If scores on the violent acting-out system just discussed are interpreted only as heuristic measures of "institutional violent acting-out propensity," then evidence of criterion-related validity is, by itself, sufficient to support the validity of the scores. On the other hand, the same scores may be interpreted as measures of "aggressiveness" when the molecular behaviors observed in the system are derived from a domain of aggressiveness. In this case, evidence of criterion-related validity would only support the scores as valid predictors of violent acting out. It does not provide evidence to support the validity of interpreting the scores as measures of aggressiveness.

Predictive Validity and Concurrent Validity

A distinction is frequently made between predictive criterion-related validity and concurrent criterion-related validity. The difference between predictive validity and concurrent validity is in the time at which the criterion is being measured. When a test is administered at the same time as the measurement of the criterion, the correlation between the two sets of measures is indicative of concurrent validity. If the measurement of the criterion is administered some time after the test, the correlation is indicative of predictive validity. In fact, one may extend the distinction to a third type of rarely used criterion-related validity, namely, postdictive validity. For example, if statistical data show that the correlation between frequency of class attendance and final course grade is high, then frequency of class attendance is a valid predictor of final course grade. Conversely, final course grade is a valid postdictor of frequency of class attendance.

Some (e.g., Nunnally, 1978) have questioned the usefulness of differentiating among predictive, concurrent, and postdictive validities. The distinctions may serve only to mislead users to interpret them as having different qualities, when in fact all three are conceptually similar. They are different only with respect to the time the alternative measure of the criterion is administered. A more useful approach is to pay closer attention to the intended use of scores obtained from the observation system or test. If the intention of an observation system is, for instance, to measure the current aggressiveness of an individual in order to establish the criterion-related validity of the system, one certainly would not administer an alternative measure of aggressiveness two months after the administration of the system.

Criterion-Related Validity of Behavioral Measures

When the intended use of a molecular sample measure is to reflect the behavior at the time of observation and is not to predict (or postdict) the behavior of other criterion at other times, the criterion-related validity of the molecular sample measure reduces to a measure known as observer accuracy. Observer accuracy, also known as criterion-referenced agreement, is assessed by examining the degree of correspondence (or correlation) between data recorded by an observer and those defined as the criterion. Data recorded by an event recorder, a videotape, a "master" observer, or other means may serve as the criterion.

The alternative means of measuring an object of measurement for the criterion-related validation of a molecular or molar sign measure can be another behavioral measure or some nonbehavioral measure. Assessing "observer accuracy" is an example of using an alternative behavioral measure as the criterion measure. An example of using an alternative nonbehavioral measure as the criterion measure is the validation of a behavioral observation system for the assessment of hyperactivity conducted by Abikoff, Gittlman-Klein, and Klein (1977). In their study, the criterion-related validity of the hyperactivity observation system was assessed by relating scores on the system with scores on the Conners Teacher's Rating Scale for hyperactivity (Conners, 1969). One potentially frustrating aspect of criterion-related validity assessment is that, in some situations, there is simply no relevant behavioral or nonbehavioral criterion measure available.

Validity Coefficient and Sources of Error

Statistical descriptors of criterion-related validity can be derived from a number of different processes. For example, Cone (1977) suggested that statistical evidence of observer accuracy can be derived through the application of the Generalizability Theory. Nunnally (1978), on the other hand, suggested that a factor analysis will also yield evidence of criterion-related validity. A method known as multitrait–multimethod matrix, suggested by Campbell and Fiske (1959), can also be used to assess criterion-related validity. In practice, however, if one wishes only to assess criterion-related validity, the use of these highly sophisticated methods amounts to statistical overkill. These methods are such powerful tools that they are more appropriately used when one wishes to assess reliability, criterion-related validity, and construct validity all at once. Because these tools serve a more general purpose than just criterion-related validity assessment, they are discussed in greater detail later in this chapter under the heading GENERAL PURPOSE STATISTICAL TECHNIQUES.

To assess the criterion-related validity with a single alternative criterion measure, criterion-related validity can be described through an application of an interobserver agreement index (i.e., p_o, κ, etc.). In this application, one replaces the observer variable with the two measures. That is, instead of assessing the agreements between Observer 1 and Observer 2, one assesses the agreements between Measure 1 and Measure 2. The criterion-related validity of a measure can also be described through a Pearson's correlation coefficient between the observation system and the criterion measure. These criterion-related validity descriptors are referred to as validity coefficients.

A validity coefficient is derived empirically from data gathered from a sample of subjects. Before the coefficient can be interpreted as an estimate of the criterion-related validity of the observation system, a number of factors have to be considered. First, the reliabilities of both the observation system and the criterion measure should have been established. The latter is frequently neglected. One should remember that the criterion measure may not be inherently reliable. If the criterion measure is not reliable, the index of agreement or correlation between the scores from the observation system and those from the criterion measure will be substantially underestimated. Second, the validity of the criterion measure should have been established independently. Again, if there is no evidence of validity for the criterion measure, the validity coefficient indicates only the relationship between the two *measures* but not criterion-related validity. Third, the stability of the validity coefficient needs to be assessed. Since the validity coefficient is derived from data obtained from a sample of subjects, it is only a descriptive statistic associated with the particular sample of subjects selected. Should a different sample of subjects be used, the validity coefficient may be quite different. One would logically place more confidence on a validity coefficient that does not change significantly from sample to sample than on one that changes considerably. In other words, a stable validity coefficient is desirable.

If the reliabilities of both the behavioral measure and the criterion measure have been established prior to criterion-related validity assessment, the validity coefficient can be reasonably assumed to be stable. To further ascertain the stability of the criterion-related validity coefficient, and if the validity coefficient is estimated through the Pearson's r procedure, a procedure known as cross-validation may be used. Associated with the Pearson's r is a process known as linear regression, through which one can estimate the value on the criterion measure associated with a given value on the observation system. This is accomplished through a regression equation as follows:

$$Y' = \alpha + \beta X, \tag{7.1}$$

where Y' is the estimated criterion measure value, α is a constant known as the intercept, β is the regression coefficient or beta weight, and X is the actual observation score. Using the data obtained for the estimation of the Pearson's r validity coefficient, the values of α and β can be estimated as follows:

$$\beta = r \frac{S_Y}{S_X}, \tag{7.2}$$

and

$$\alpha = \bar{Y} - b\bar{X}, \tag{7.3}$$

where r is the validity coefficient, s_Y is the standard deviation of the criterion measure scores, s_X is the standard deviation of the observation scores, $\bar{Y}$ is the mean criterion measure score and $\bar{X}$ is the mean observation score.

To conduct a cross-validation, the values of α and β for Equation 7.1 can be derived from Equations 7.2 and 7.3 using the sample data. A second sample of subjects can then be drawn, and scores on both the observation system and the criterion measure are obtained for this second sample. The regression equation derived from the first sample can then be applied to the score on the observation system for each subject on the second sample to estimate the expected criterion measure score for each subject. The Pearson's r between the expected criterion scores and the actual criterion score is then computed. This correlation coefficient is expected to be smaller than the original validity coefficient. If the shrinkage in value is small or negligible, the validity coefficient is stable across samples. However, if the shrinkage is substantial, the validity coefficient is not stable and cannot be generalized to future use of the observation system. An exemplary use of this cross-validation technique to assess the stability of a criterion-related validity coefficient can be found in a technical report by the American College Testing Program (1973).

Reliability and Validity Coefficients

It has been pointed out previously that reliability is a precondition for validity. Reliability and validity are, hence, closely related. This is particularly true between reliabilities estimated through an interclass or intraclass correlation process and a criterion-related validity coefficient estimated through Pearson's r. In fact, the square root of the reliability coefficient in this situation sets the upper limit of the criterion-related validity coefficient. For example, if the reliability of a measure is 0.81, the criterion-related validity of this measure can never exceed 0.90. This close relationship between reliability and criterion-related validity accentuates the fact that a measure has to be reliable before it can be valid.

There are a number of ways to prove the truism of this relationship. For those who are interested in a proof of this relationship, the following is offered: Based on the procedure for the computation of Pearson's r, the theoretical correlation between an observed score and the true score (ϱ_{xt}) can be derived as follows:

$$\varrho_{xt} = \frac{\text{Covariance between true and observed scores}}{(\text{True scores std. dev.}) (\text{Observed scores std. dev.})}. \qquad (7.4)$$

We can theoretically transform all observed and true scores into their standard z score units so that each score is expressed in units of standard deviation from the mean. Let us use a t to represent a standardized true score, an x to represent a standardized observed score, and an e to represent a standardized random error. Recall that $x = t + e$ and t is independent of *e.* The covariance between the true score and the observed score (C_{xt}) is:

$$C_{xt} = (\Sigma xt)/n$$

$$= [\Sigma(t + e)t]/n$$

$$= [\Sigma t^2 + \Sigma te]/n.$$

Because errors are random, the second term in the numerator equals zero. Hence, with *t* expressed in standard *z* units:

$$C_{xt} = \Sigma t^2/n$$

$$= \sigma_t^2.$$

Applying Equation 7.4, the correlation between true score and observed score becomes:

$$\varrho_{xt} = \frac{C_{xt}}{\sigma_x \sigma_t}$$

$$= \frac{\sigma_t^2}{\sigma_x \sigma_t}$$

$$= \frac{\sigma_t}{\sigma_x}.$$

Squaring both sides, we obtain:

$$\varrho_{xt}^2 = \frac{\sigma_t^2}{\sigma_x^2} = \text{reliability}.$$

Therefore,

$$\varrho_{xt} = \sqrt{\text{reliability}}.$$

Thus, the square root of an interclass correlation or an intraclass correlation is the theoretical correlation between the observed score and the true score. However, this is not true with interobserver agreement indices.

The best criterion measure chosen for criterion-related validity can only be one that is absolutely valid. Departure of the criterion measure from absolute validity would introduce spurious error into the criterion-related validity assessment process and, in turn, would lead to a lower correlation between the observed scores and the scores on the criterion measure. Thus, the square root of reliability, which is the correlation between the observed scores and an absolutely valid criterion measure, is the upper limit of criterion-related validity. In practice, a chosen criterion measure is most probably an imperfect indicator of the true scores. Hence, an empirically derived criterion-related validity coefficient is most likely to be less than the square root of reliability.

Construct Validity

Construct validity is concerned with how well a measure reflects a construct. It is an important type of validity evidence when a measurement procedure purports to measure an unobservable construct. Dependent upon the directness of a behavioral measure, construct validity may or may not be relevant. Specifically, for a molecular or molar sample measure, evidence of construct validity is not necessary. This is because both measures are direct descriptors of an observable behavior or a category of observable behaviors. No inference is made to link these measures to any underlying unobservable construct.

For a molecular sign measure or a molar sign measure, however, construct validity is extremely important. Because these measures are used as signs of unobservable constructs, it is important to gather evidence that these signs do indeed reflect those constructs. The central question of validity is whether a score measures what it purports to measure. For a molecular or molar sign measure, neither content validity nor criterion-related validity provides a satisfactory answer to this central question. Content validity only provides evidence of consistency between what the researcher thinks should be included in the measure and what is actually in the measure. Criterion-related validity provides evidence of consistency between the measure and another measure that purports to reflect the same construct. It is possible that neither one reflects the construct in actuality. The establishment of construct validity involves attempts to address the central question of whether a measure reflects what it is supposed to reflect.

Conceptual Process of Construct Validation

The assessment of construct validity is also in part an empirical and quantitative process. However, unlike criterion-related validity, which produces a validity coefficient for a defined criterion, evidence of construct validity is based on the judgment of the statistical results of a series of empirical studies. Since a construct is an unobservable entity, it is not possible to gather direct evidence of construct validity. Instead, circumstantial evidence of construct validity is gathered to support the assumption that the measure reflects the construct. Based on existing theories and conceptual frameworks regarding a construct, a number of internal and external characteristics of the construct can be defined. If a molecular or molar sign measure does indeed reflect this construct, one then would expect the measure to show the same characteristics as those defined for the construct.

The characteristics of the construct are expressed in terms of relationships. First, one defines a number of other variables with which the construct should correlate positively. Next, one defines a number of other variables with which the construct should not correlate. One can also define the exact number of dimensions underlying the construct as well as the subconstruct reflected by each dimension. For each underlying subconstruct, one can also define variables with which the subconstruct should or should not correlate. In this manner, the nature of the construct is defined within the network of internal and external relationships.

To assess the extent to which the scores from an observation system reflect this construct, one would first examine whether the number and nature of the underlying dimensions for an observation system conform with those of the subconstructs in the theory. Then, all external variables within the network of relationships for the overall construct and subconstructs are measured. The statistical correlations among the total observation system score, the subconstruct scores, and the external variables are then computed to examine if their relationships conform with those specified in the network.

Practical and Logical Considerations

All these procedures in theory specification, subconstruct identification, defining the network of relationships, measuring external variables, and examining correlations sound like a rather formidable task; and indeed it would be. The procedures just described are theoretically the ideal process in deriving evidence of construct validity. It is necessitated by the fact that one cannot measure a construct directly; one has to rely totally on circumstantial evidence. By its very nature, circumstantial evidence is not a "proof"; but the more circumstantial evidence that is gathered, the more confidence one has regarding the construct validity of a measure. Therefore, we should strive to attain this ideal process. In practice, however, it is rare that we can identify all external variables. With those external variables that are identified, some may not be measurable. Finally, the total number of measurable external variables identified may be so large that it is impractical to measure them all. Therefore, researchers frequently identify and investigate only a few relationships.

Another practical consideration that necessitates a compromise on the ideal process is the frequent nonexistence of a well-established formal theory from which to derive the relationships. One frequently has to settle for loose propositional statements of relationship. Hence, when a low correlation is found between an observational measure and an external theoretically related variable, we cannot be sure whether it is indicative of a lack of construct validity or that the measure is valid but the hypothe-sized relationship simply does not exist. On the positive side, however, when a high correlation is found, we can be quite certain of the evidence of construct validity.

A major drawback of construct validity is in the frustrating circular na-ture of its logic. In order to assess whether a measure reflects a construct, we examine the empirical relationship between the measure and an exter-nal variable that is supposed to relate to the construct. In order to ascer-tain that the construct does indeed relate to that variable, we need empirical evidence to support such a relationship. To obtain the empirical evidence, we need a valid measure of the construct, which takes us back to the starting point. To further complicate the logic, the measure used to reflect the ex-ternal variable needs to be validated through a similar circular process.

A partial solution to this logical dilemma is offered from a pragmatist's point of view: A construct is not an absolute entity that exists in objective reality. Rather, it is a concept that exists in the mind of a scientist. To the extent that such a concept is useful for theoretical explanations, predic-tions, and manipulations of observed phenomena, we accept such a con-cept as "real." Similarly, the relationship between a construct and an external variable is real if it serves as a useful guide for the understanding and prediction of observed phenomenon. For example, in order to ex-plain the difference in behavior between an individual who is under stress and one who is not, we have created a construct called "anxiety." There-fore, the relatedness between "anxiety" and "behavior under stress" is, by definition, true because anxiety is a useful construct created to explain behavior under stress. Given that the relationship is true, if a measure of anxiety does not correlate well with behavior under stress, it cannot be indicative of a lack of relationship between anxiety and behavior under stress. Hence, it can only be indicative of a lack of construct validity. From this perspective, the logic of construct validity is quite reasonable. However, if one does not accept the idea that anxiety is a real construct only to the extent that it is useful but believes that it exists in objective reality, the assessment of construct validity remains a frustrating process. As Nun-nally (1978) put it, the attempt to establish construct validity for a con-struct that is believed to exist in the objective reality is not a problem of searching for a needle in the haystack but one of searching for a needle that is not in the haystack.

Construct Validity of Behavioral Measures

The assessment of construct validity for behavioral sign measures is not different from the assessment of construct validity for other nonbehavioral measures such as paper-and-pencil tests. The theory surrounding the construct, the defined relationships, and the logic of the process assume central importance. For a molecular sign measure, no internal structure is involved. That is, a molecular sign has only one dimension measured by a single molecular behavior. Hence, the question of internal structure is not involved. Only relationships with external variables have to be defined and analyzed. Therefore, the extensiveness of statistical analyses is greatly reduced. For example, the average frequency that a person drinks alcohol per day is used as a molecular sign of an "alcohol dependency" construct. Let us also assume that it has been specified in the theory surrounding alcohol dependency that the construct is associated with frequency of absence from work, lack of physical activities, level of marital dissatisfaction expressed by spouse, and frequency of illness. To assess the construct validity of the molecular behavior "average frequency a person drinks alcohol per day" as a sign of the construct alcohol dependency, we record the frequency of the alcohol-drinking molecular behavior of a sample of individuals over a month and obtain the average per day frequency of drinking for each individual. For each of these individuals, we also measure each of the four theoretically associated variables. Appropriate statistical methods can then be used to analyze the relationship between the molecular sign measure and the measure for each of the four associated variables. The specific statistical technique used is dependent upon the nature of the data generated by the molecular sign measure and that generated by the measure for each associated variable. In this example, assuming that all data are interval level data, the appropriate method is Pearson's r. If all four Pearson's rs are positive and statistically significant, one would have strong circumstantial evidence of construct validity.

The assessment of the construct validity for a molar sign measure is much more complicated. This is because an internal structure is involved. One must not only define relationships between the overall construct and associated variables, one must also define the internal structure of the overall construct in terms of subconstructs. Additionally, one needs to define relationships between each subconstruct and its own set of associated variables. When these are accomplished, data for the molar sign measure and for a measure of each of the array of associated variables are gathered. With these data, the existence of subscores within the molar measure conforming to the subconstructs of the overall construct is to be verified statistically. Each of the defined relationships among the overall measure, the subscores, and measures of the array of associated variables has to be analyzed and examined. The statistical analysis process is rather tedious and, at times, formidable. Furthermore, the examination and interpretation of the large number of results from these statistical analyses can be rather confusing. Fortunately, with the easy access to computers today and the availability of a number of highly sophisticated statistical techniques, the statistical analysis and interpretation processes can be accomplished efficiently.

For the analysis and interpretation of molar sign measures with a number of underlying dimensions, at least three sophisticated statistical methods are available. These are the Generalizability Theory, factor analysis, and the multitrait–multimethod matrix. Since these methods are general purpose statistical techniques appropriate for reliability, criterion-related validity, and construct validity assessments, we discuss these methods later under the heading GENERAL PURPOSE STATISTICAL TECHNIQUES.

It is important to point out that construct validity is a process rather than an end product. Because construct validity is a cumulation of circumstantial evidence indicating that the characteristics of a molecular or molar sign measure is consistent with the theoretical characteristics of the construct, the more evidence gathered, the more confidence one places in the measure as an indicator of the construct. As new relationships are defined between the construct and other variables, new evidence may be added to the existing body of evidence to further support the validity of the measure. Frequently, the construct validation of a measure is performed over a period of time in a number of independent studies by different investigators.

Other Validity Evidence

Two other sometime-mentioned types of validity evidence are face validity and treatment validity. Face validity refers to the extent to which an observation system "appears" to measure what it purports to measure. It is subjective but may prove to be useful in some applied situations. In interpreting observational scores to clients or consumers of the observation system, a system that has face validity (that "looks good") may be more readily accepted than one that does not. Face validity can also be viewed as a preliminary step toward content validity.

In clinical situations, the measurement process is sometimes an integral part of the overall intervention strategy. For example, measurement results may be provided to clients as feedback to promote maximum treatment effect. This is similar to biofeedback, in which the measurement process plays a major role in the treatment outcome. When a measure serves this additional purpose, an important issue of validity is whether the measure used does in fact contribute to the treatment outcome. Nelson and Hayes (1979) referred to this unique type of validity as treatment validity. This form of validity has not been used widely. However, Cone (1982) suggested that for behavior therapy, due to the expense of comprehensive direct observational assessment, this form of validity is likely to be given increased attention in the future.

GENERAL PURPOSE
STATISTICAL TECHNIQUES

One of the major obstacles to arriving at evidence of construct validity is the potentially large number of internal and external variables and the enormous amount of data one must analyze. After the tedious tasks of statistical computations, one is confronted with the formidable task of making sense out of the intricate network of relationships. There are at least three powerful statistical tools that are important aids in completing the task. These are the Generalizability Theory, factor analysis, and the multitrait–multimethod matrix. The Generalizability Theory and the multitrait–multimethod matrix are techniques applicable to reliability, criterion-related validity, and construct validity assessments. In fact, within the theoretical framework of these two techniques, all three assessment procedures can be conducted simultaneously. Factor analysis is a general multivariate statistical technique applicable to many research situations. It is directly applicable to construct validation. It will also yield information regarding criterion-related validity and content validity.

It should be pointed out that neither of the three statistical methods represents an alternative approach to criterion-related or construct validation. They are simply more efficient methods of organizing, summarizing, and interpreting a complicated network of statistical evidence for criterion-related or construct validity. Just as one would not use a computer to find the answer to 1 + 1, one would not use these methods for the validation of the molecular sign measure involving a simple network of two or three external relations. The network of relationships needed for the reliability and validity assessment of some of the molar sign behavior observation systems, however, can be highly complex. Consider the Behavioral Referenced Rating System (BRRS) of intermediate social skills developed by Farrell et al. (1985). The overall construct of "social skills" consisted of 10 behavioral subconstructs. The overall construct was hypothesized as relating to a global rating of social skills. Each of the 10 behavioral categories was also hypothesized as relating to 14 different external molecular sample measures. In their validation process, Farrell et al. also assessed the validities of the use of the instrument for the subjects and for the confederates separately. In other words, a mind-boggling total of 2,802 individual relationships had to be computed, analyzed, summarized, and interpreted! For this type of situation, powerful and efficient statistical tools would have to be used to make sense out of the complex network of relationships. In their extreme case, Farrell et al. employed the highly sophisticated mutlivariate technique known as canonical correlation analysis (Timm, 1975) to facilitate the summarization and interpretation of results. In most situations, however, fewer relationships are involved and the three methods discussed following will be sufficiently efficient.

Generalizability Theory

The general conceptual and statistical process of the Generalizability Theory was discussed extensively in chapter 6. We will not repeat the discussion here. Instead, we discuss the application of the Generalizability approach to validity. Cone (1977) suggested that the Generalizability approach could be applied to assess the criterion-related validity known as observer accuracy. This can be accomplished through replacing the observer facet with an instrumentation facet consisting of observer and criterion measures. For an elaborated example, suppose a researcher is interested in the criterion-related validity of data recorded by an observer. The behavior of interest is recorded simultaneously by the observer, a "master" observer, another observer using an electronic real-time event recorder, and another observer scoring the videotape of the behavior. The four sets of data can be interpreted as the data for four levels of a facet called "instrumentation." Examination of the variance components estimated through a G study within the Generalizability framework would provide evidence of criterion-related validity. Specifically, if the variance component associated with the facet of instrumentation is negligible relative to other variance components, using the observer as the instrument of behavioral observation has criterion-related validity.

The estimates of variance components in Generalizability are meaningful only if the scales of measurement for all levels of a facet are identical. For criterion-related and construct validation, it is highly probable that the scale in the criterion measure or for the external variables is different. This can be remedied by standardizing all scores to z scores. Subsequently, all levels of the "instrumentation" or "theoretical correlates" facet are expressed in a uniform scale of z scores. At this point, it is not clear if the Generalizability approach is directly applicable to the investigation of the internal structure of a molar sign measure.

When a facet contains very few levels, the estimated variance component for the facet is unstable and may even be a nonsensical negative value. For this reason, if the number of criterion measures for criterion-related validity is small, the use of interobserver agreements or interclass correlations may be more effective. For instance, for the criterion-related validity of a molecular sample measure not intended for predictive use, a Pearson's r may be more effective when only a single criterion measure is used. Similarly, for a molecular sign measure with hypothesized relationships with only one or two external dichotomous variables, Pearson's correlations (i.e., ϕ) may be more effective.

Factor Analysis

Factor analysis is a category of multivariate statistical methods. The purpose of a factor analysis is to reduce a set of variables or measures to a smaller number of hypothetical variables or higher level constructs. Nunnally (1978) suggested that factor analysis is a method that would produce evidence of content, criterion-related, as well as construct validity. However, its application is most effective when used for construct validation. Hence, factor analysis is most frequently associated with construct validation only (e.g., Wiersma & Jurs, 1985).

For the purpose of construct validation, factor analysis can facilitate the examination of internal and external structures or relationships simultaneously. Internally, if a construct contains a number of theoretical subconstructs, a valid molar sign measure of this construct should also contain the same number of intermediate-level molar sign measures reflecting the subconstructs. Therefore, if a factor analysis of a large array of behaviors observed in a molar sign observation system effectively reduces the array to a small number of intermediate-level constructs (factors) and an examination of the behaviors within each factor shows that the factors correspond with the conceptual descriptions of the theoretical subconstructs, the internal structure of the overall molar sign measure is construct validated. Externally, if a number of external variables are identified as relating to each theoretical subconstruct, a factor analysis of all the behaviors in the molar sign system and all the external variables together should show a number of factors corresponding to the number of theoretical subconstructs. Furthermore, all the external variables associated with each subconstruct should also be found within the factor corresponding to the subconstruct. For a molecular sign measure, the purpose of a factor analysis is to examine the external structure only. For a molar sign measure, a factor analysis would examine both internal and external structures.

For the factor analysis of a molecular sign measure, let us consider the earlier example of "alcohol dependency." It was hypothesized that alcohol dependency was related to frequency of absence from work, lack of physical activities, level of marital dissatisfaction expressed by spouse, and frequency of illness. A factor analysis of the molecular sign measure "frequency of drinking alcohol" and measures of the four external variables should reduce all five measures to a single construct (factor). If this is the case, the molecular measure as a sign of "alcohol dependency" is construct validated. However, if results of the factor analysis show that the molecular sign and two external variables form one factor whereas the two remaining external variables form another factor, the molecular measure as a sign of alcohol dependency is only partially construct validated.

To illustrate the validation of both internal and external structures, let us consider the example of an "alienation" construct. According to one theory, alienation should contain three subconstructs known as "normlessness," "powerlessness," and "social estrangement." A large number of behaviors are observed with the composite score as a molar sign of alienation. A number of external measures are also hypothesized as relating to the three subconstructs, respectively. A factor analysis of all component behaviors and all external measures should reduce all measures to three factors only. Furthermore, the external measures associated with each subconstruct should also fall within the factor that reflects that subconstruct. When results of a factor analysis depart from this pattern, the circumstantial evidence of construct validity is compromised.

The mathematical process involved in factor analysis is complex. Furthermore, there are many different mathematical approaches to the task of factor analysis, leading to slightly different results. We do not attempt to explain the statistical basis of various approaches to factor analysis. Instead, we do provide an overview of the conceptual process involved in the more commonly used approaches to factor analysis. Readers who are interested in the statistical processes of factor analysis are requested to consult the numerous reference books available on multiple regression, multivariate analysis, or factor analysis.

Factor analysis may be used to find the underlying structure within a group of measures. One approach is referred to as exploratory factor analysis. In this approach, a researcher has no preconceived idea of what may be found.

On the other hand, the nature of the structure may be hypothesized in advance and factor analysis used to test these hypotheses. This approach is referred to as confirmatory factor analysis. Because of the matrix algebra involved, the definitiveness of the final results is greatly influenced by the number of subjects (sample size) used in the factor analysis. In general, the larger the sample size, the more stable the results. Hence, for a confirmatory factor analysis, a large sample of subjects is necessary. Nunnally (1978) suggested that, as a rule of thumb, one should have at least 10 times as many subjects as variables.

Factor analysis is not a single statistical procedure but is a category of procedures. The following is an oversimplified explanation of the general conceptual process of a factor analysis: Based on the intercorrelations among all measures, the measures are substituted initially by an equal but not corresponding number of factors. These factorial substitutions are derived from first creating a factor that accounts for the most variance in all the measures. Next, another factor is created to account for most of the remaining variance. This is continued until all variances are accounted for. In this manner, the early factors are most powerful substitutes of the measures, and the later ones are trivial because they account for very little variance. Using different criteria, a final small number of factors out of all the factors is retained. Two common criteria used are the Kaiser criterion and the Scree Test. These criteria are generally based on the proportion of variance accounted for by each factor. Those that account for large proportions of variance are more likely to be retained than those that account for trivial amounts. Regardless of which criterion is being used, as a general rule of thumb, the final set of factors together should account for at least 60% of the total variance of all measures. This is because if the factors together account for only a small portion of the variance, these factors cannot be considered useful substitutes of the original measures.

Although these initial factors are the most powerful ones, they are nonsensical because the first of this set of factors takes up the lion's share of the variance, making it the best factor without a meaningful contextual reference. That is, the first factor would correlate with a large portion of the measures when these measures may not form a meaningful subconstruct. To arrive at more meaningful factors, the initial set of factors are "rotated" so that the accounted for variance is distributed more evenly among the factors. Dependent upon the theoretical relationships among the subconstructs to be represented by these factors, the factors are rotated in an orthogonal or an oblique manner. An orthogonal rotation is used when the subconstructs are theoretically independent of one another. An oblique rotation is used when they are mutually related. Again, there are many methods of rotation. The most common method is an orthogonal rotation technique called Varimax rotation.

After the rotation process, a final set of factors is extracted. The correlation between each factor and each of the original measures is indicated by factor loading. One can then examine the matrix of all factor loadings to identify those measures that "belong together." Specifically, all the measures with high loadings within the same factor are components of the factor. One then examines the component measures within a factor to determine what these measures have in common conceptually and assigns a label to reflect this commonality. When used for construct validation, the number of final factors should correspond with the hypothesized number of subconstructs. The labels assigned to these factors should also reflect the nature of these subconstructs. When these criteria are met, the overall molar measure is construct validated.

Again, factor analysis is a sophisticated category of techniques designed to reduce a large amount of variables or measures to a small number of constructs. It is an efficient means of examining an otherwise unmanageable network of relationships. However, there are many different methods of conducting factor analysis. Different criteria are available to extract the initial factors. There are many different methods of factor rotations. Additionally, the final reduction of the original measures into a few quantities reflecting a subject's scores on the subconstruct measures may be accomplished by a judgmental method or a factor-scoring method. In other words, the use of factor analysis involves a series of decisions regarding the choice of the appropriate technique. The preceding discussion is an oversimplified explanation of the fundamental process. Readers who wish to employ this technique should gain a better understanding of the method by consulting more specialized reference books.

Multitrait–Multimethod Matrix

The multitrait–multimethod matrix, suggested by Campbell and Fiske (1959), is not a statistical technique per se. Rather, it is a sensible way of organizing the complex network of reliability coefficients, criterion-related validity coefficients, and construct validity relationships into a parsimonious matrix. The organization of the matrix is presented in such a way that interpretation of the relationships for evidence of reliability and validity becomes relatively simple. For a multitrait–multimethod matrix, the difference between criterion-related validity and construct validity is ignored. Rather, this is substituted by the concepts of convergent and discriminant validities. Convergent validity is evidenced when two measures that are supposed to correlate highly do indeed correlate highly with each other. Convergent validity is needed for criterion-related validity and for those relationships between the measure and those external variables that are supposed to correlate with the measure in construct validity. Discriminant validity is needed for those relationships between a measure and those internal and external variables that are not supposed to correlate with the measure in construct validity. For example, within the three dimensions of alienation, normlessness should not correlate highly with social estrangement. If they do correlate highly, then they are not two distinct dimensions. In this case, the internal structure of the alienation measure is suspect. Additionally, social estrangement should not correlate highly with external variables associated with normlessness. If they do correlate highly, the submeasure of social estrangement is mislabeled.

Perhaps the best approach to illustrate the use of the multitrait–multimethod matrix is to start from the simple cases of monotrait–multimethod matrix and multitrait–monomethod matrix. Consider the case in which a single construct is measured by three alternative measurement methods (Methods 1, 2, and 3). Each method has its own reliability coefficient and each pair of measures has its own validity coefficient. The validity coefficients should be indicative of convergent validity because the three methods are supposed to measure the same trait or construct. For the three methods (let us say, the measurement of "fear" through a behavioral observation system, a self-report questionnaire, and a global rating by experts), there is a total of six reliability and validity coefficients. These can be organized into a matrix, as in Table 7.1. In this configuration, the diagonal values (designated as rs) indicate the reliabilities of the three methods and the off-diagonal values (designated by cvs) are convergent validities. In this manner, one can examine reliabilities and validities at one glance. In general, one would expect the diagonal values to be higher than those of the off diagonal. Additionally, all values should be sufficiently high to warrant a conclusion of validity.

One may also measure three distinct constructs or subconstructs with a single method, as in the case of measuring normlessness, powerlessness, and social estrangement with a single system designed to measure the overall molar sign of alienation. In this case, designating the three traits as X, Y, and Z, the reliability and validity values can be organized into a multitrait–monomethod matrix, as in Table 7.2. Again, the diagonal values represent reliabilities. These values should be reasonably high. The off-diagonal values (designated by dvs), however, are indicative of discriminant validities, and they should not be high.

As can be expected, the more traits measured and the more methods used, the more complex the matrix. Let us consider the case of measuring Traits X, Y, and Z, using Methods 1, 2, and 3. For this problem, there is a total of 36 reliability and validity coefficients. These coefficients can be organized into a multitrait–multimethod matrix, as in Figure 7.3. This matrix differs from those of Figure 7.1 and 7.2 in that two symbols, $dv1$ and $dv2$, are introduced. All the other symbols are consistent in meaning, as those in Figures 7.1 and 7.2. The values of $dv1$s are the discriminant validity coefficients when all traits are measured by the same method. The values of $dv2$s are those when the traits are measured by different methods.

TABLE 7.1
Monotrait–Multimethod Matrix

	Method		
Method	1	2	3
1	r		
2	cv	r	
3	cv	cv	r

TABLE 7.2
Multitrait–Monomethod Matrix

Trait	Trait X	Y	Z
	X		
X	*r*		
Y	*dv*	*r*	
Z	*dv*	*dv*	*r*

To derive evidence of validity, the matrix is examined for a number of characteristics. First, all *r* values should be high. This is because reliability is a prerequisite to validity. Second, all *cv* values should be significantly different from zero and have reasonably high values for evidence of convergent validity. Third, the *cv* values should be higher than the *dv*2 values for evidence of discriminant validity. Similarly, the *cv* values should also be higher than the *dv*1 values for additional evidence of discriminant validity. The pattern of *dv*1 and *dv*2 values within each triangle should be similar. When these conditions are met, either Method 1, 2, or 3 is a reliable and valid method for the measurement of Traits *X*, *Y*, and *Z*.

THREATS TO VALIDITY

For behavioral observation, there are a number of factors that can potentially reduce the validity of an observation system. These include ambiguous behavioral codes, systematic sampling error, subject reactivity, observer bias, and observer drift. These factors can introduce systematic (nonrandom) error into an observation system. Hence the resulting measure becomes an indicator of both the object of measurement and some

TABLE 7.3
Multitrait–Multimethod Matrix

	Trait	Method 1			Method 2			Method 3		
		X	Y	Z	X	Y	Z	X	Y	Z
	X	*r*								
Method 1	*Y*	*dv*1	*r*							
	Z	*dv*1	*dv*1	*r*						
	X	*cv*			*r*					
Method 2	*Y*	*dv*2	*cv*		*dv*1	*r*				
	Z	*dv*2	*dv*2	*cv*	*dv*1	*dv*1	*r*			
	X	*cv*			*cv*			*r*		
Method 3	*Y*	*dv*2	*cv*		*dv*2	*cv*		*dv*1	*r*	
	Z	*dv*2	*dv*2	*cv*	*dv*2	*dv*2	*cv*	*dv*1	*dv*1	*r*

unknown extraneous variable. Most of these threats can be minimized through systematic observer training prior to data collection, pilot observations, occasional reliability and validity checks, and careful logistic arrangements.

An ambiguous behavioral code or definition may cause an observer to record a behavior that is not the intended object of measurement. Similarly, the ambiguous behavioral code may be interpreted in such a way that the intended object of measurement is not being recorded by the observer. This problem can be minimized by careful development of the behavioral code. Generally, when defining the behavior for observation, inferential language such as "intends to," "is happy," or "is excited" should be avoided. The definition should be expressed in clear and precise language so that a user of the observation system will have no difficulty distinguishing the target behavior from other behaviors. There are at least two approaches from which one can provide a reasonably clear behavioral definition. A behavior can be described functionally or topographically (Johnston & Pennypacker, 1980; Lehner, 1979; Rosenblum, 1978). A topographical description is one in which the behavior is described in terms of precise physical movements. A functional description is one in which the behavior is described in terms of the overall effect of the physical movements. Lehner (1979) provided the example of a dove's "rapid alternate contraction and relaxation of the pectoralis muscles" as a topographical description, whereas "wing flapping," or "flying" is a functional description of the same behavior. Generally, a topographical description is more precise and unambiguous. However, a functional description may be more practical in some observation situations.

The systematic error associated with certain time-sampling methods was discussed extensively in chapter 4. To reiterate, when certain statistical conditions are not met, partial-interval sampling will overestimate prevalence and underestimate frequency, whole-interval sampling will underestimate both prevalence and frequency, and momentary sampling will underestimate frequency. These systematic errors may be minimized through a number of methods. The use of a real-time event recorder would eliminate the need for interval sampling. Continuous observation, when practical, may also be used when the number of subjects observed is small. The probabilistic approach suggested by Suen and Ary (1986a), as described in chapter 4, can be used a priori to set the interval length that would lead to a negligible amount of systematic error. The systematic error associated with a particular sampling method can also be minimized statistically through the post hoc correction procedure (Suen, 1986a; Suen & Ary, 1986b) described in chapter 4. If prevalence is the only dimension of interest, momentary sampling procedures can be used.

Subject reactivity refers to the tendency of a subject to behave differently in the presence of an observer. Subject reactivity is, to a large extent, dependent upon the obtrusiveness of the method of observation. There are a number of ways to minimize this threat to validity. The apparent approach is to reduce the obtrusiveness of the observation process. This has been accomplished through a variety of tactics: observe behavior through a one-way mirror, record the behavior through audio- or videorecorders for later observation, minimize interaction between observer and subject(s), minimize eye contact between the observer and the subject by having the observer wear reflective sunglasses so that the subject would not know when he or she is being observed, and so on. There has also been some evidence that reactivity is transient (Haynes, 1978; Kazdin, 1974) in that subject reactivity is greatly reduced once the subject(s) is accustomed to the presence of the observer. Hence, one way to reduce reactivity is to place the observer in the observation setting for a period of time prior to actual observation.

Observer bias refers to the tendency of an observer to "see" what the observer wants to see. This threat to validity can, again, be minimized through a number of tactics. Clear behavioral codes will reduce the amount of inferences needed from the observer and would, hence, reduce the possibilities of "misreading" behaviors on the part of the observer. If the observer is not informed of the research hypothesis, it would be less likely for the observer to have an expectation of what will occur. Results of a study by O'Leary, Kent, and Kanowitz (1975) suggested that positive social feedback from the researcher to the observer when the data collected are consistent with the hypothesis will increase observer bias in future observations.

Observer drift is the gradual and systematic change of cues or criteria used by the observer to score a behavior. Although the scores recorded at the beginning of an observation session may reflect the behavior of interest, those at the end of the session may no longer be indicators of the behavior but may have "drifted" to a slightly or significantly different behavior. Observer drift may also occur from one observation session to the next. Observer drift is particularly problematic when the observation tasks are relatively uncomplicated and repetitive and when the observation session is lengthy. Observer drift in a single observer can be detected through occasional interobserver agreement/reliability assessment. It is also possible, however, that two observers maintain a high interobserver agreement/reliability but have both drifted together. This type of observer drift, referred to as consensual observer drift (Johnson & Bolstad, 1973), is more difficult to detect. When possible, occasional criterion-related validity assessment may be conducted to detect the presence of consensual observer drift. A number of tactics have also been suggested to prevent observer drift. Reid (1982) suggested that, if possible, observers should be separated completely to avoid consensual drift. Paul and Lentz (1977) suggested that review sessions with the observers be conducted regularly and the observers be quizzed on the behavioral definitions. Haynes (1978) suggested that teams of observers be rotated. Licht et al. (1980) found that intentional overtraining of observers could minimize or eliminate observer drift. Reid (1982) also suggested that providing incentives or scientific stimulation to the observers could maintain their level of interest and minimize observer drift.

CHAPTER 8

Time Series Analysis: Introduction

Yet to calculate is not in itself to analyze.

— Edgar Allen Poe
The Murders in the Rue Morgue

An important, and somewhat troublesome, dimension in the analysis of behavioral observation data is the dimension of time. In chapters, 4, 5, and 6, we discussed extensively the relative importance of the time dimension for behavioral observation sampling and reliability assessment. The inclusion of the time dimension not only necessitates the consideration of sampling schemes and reliability assessment in terms of time, it also represents a troublesome dimension for statistical analysis. The consideration of time is particularly important in single-subject behavioral studies, for which the time dimension is frequently the only source of data variation.

A major problem with analyzing data when they are colleted along the time continuum is the inability of conventional inferential statistics, such as those discussed in Appendix A, to yield reliable results. The crux of the problem is that at least a portion of human or animal behaviors are serially dependent along the time continuum. A behavior is said to be serially dependent when the level of behavior at a particular point in time is related to those in previous points in time. The cause of serial dependence—be it inertia, habit, instinct, or whatever—is not our primary concern. Rather, the fact that it exists is troublesome for statistical analysis.

Numerous researchers (e.g., Gardner, Hartmann, & Mitchell, 1982; Glass, Willson, & Gottman, 1975; Hartmann et al., 1980; Jones, Vaught,

& Weinrott, 1977; Jones, Weinrott, & Vaught, 1978) have demonstrated or suggested that serial dependency is a common phenomenon in studies in which behavioral observation data are used. Recently, Huitema (1985) contended that data in applied behavior analysis are essentially not serially dependent. His conclusion, however, has been challenged by others (e.g., Sharpley & Alavosius, in press; Suen, 1987; Suen & Ary, 1987). Common sense would indicate that when behaviors occur in time, at least some of the behaviors would be serially dependent—what you are doing now may well be determined by what you did a moment ago. For the statistical analysis of behavioral observation data, it is therefore important for us to consider statistical techniques appropriate for serially dependent data.

A large body of knowledge has been accumulated over the past two decades regarding the statistical analysis of serially dependent data. Many of these techniques were developed in the areas of engineering, business, economics, and biology. Their application to behavioral observation studies have been shown to be appropriate and important in many cases. These techniques are generally referred to as time series analysis techniques.

PROBLEMS OF SERIAL DEPENDENCY

When the purpose of an analysis is to describe a behavior, as in an *ex post facto* study, or to assess the effects of a particular behavioral intervention method, as in a quasi-experimental design, the existence of serial dependency renders most of the conventional statistical methods inappropriate. The problem is more severe when the purpose of the study is to assess intervention effectiveness.

For an *ex post facto* description of a behavior of either a single subject or a group of similar subjects, conventional descriptive statistics such as mean, median, and variance are good descriptors of the behavior, even in the presence of serial dependency. The problem in this situation is that the description is incomplete. With these conventional statistics, the possible existence and the nature of serial dependency in the data remain unknown. An important characteristic of the data is missing from the description. For example, given that the mean of a number of observations is 5.5 and the standard deviation is 2.87, one would have no way of knowing whether the observations resemble a series of random events along the time continuum, such as 3, 1, 7, 2, 9, 6, 10, 8, 5, 4, or if the data have a certain serially dependent temporal order, such as 1, 2, 3, 4, 5, 6, 7, 8, 9, 10. For both cases, the mean is 5.5 and the standard deviation is 2.87.

If the *ex post facto* study involves finding some relationship between the behaviors of two or more subjects, the existence of serial dependency poses another problem in addition to the problem of incomplete description. Specifically, in such a study, we test the observed relationship against a null hypothesis of no relationship. In general , the higher the value of an inferential statistic, the smaller the probability of committing a Type I error when one rejects the null hypothesis. When the data for each of the subjects are serially dependent, the value of the inferential statistic used may be inflated, which will in turn lead to an erroneously small estimated probability of Type I error. Hence, the probability of error when one concludes an existence of the relationship is, in fact, much higher than revealed by the inferential statistic. Gardner, Hartmann, and Mitchell (1982), for instance, reported that in the presence of serial dependency, a χ_2 probability value may be underestimated by as much as 1,700%. McDowall et al. (1980) suggested that with serially dependent data, a t value may be inflated by 300%–400%. Sharpley and Alavosius (in press) showed that with a level of serial dependency commonly considered negligible, the probability associated with a t value can be underestimated substantially.

In a single-subject quasi-experimental study in which the effectiveness of an intervention strategy is evaluated, the existence of serial dependency in the underlying behavior poses yet a third problem in addition to the two just mentioned. Generally, to assess the effectiveness of an intervention strategy, we compare the level of behavior in the preintervention phase (or base line) with that of the postintervention phase. If the two levels of behavior are different in the hypothesized direction, we conclude that the intervention is effective. With serially dependent data, not only is the null hypothesis a competing explanation for the observed difference, serial dependence presents another competing hypothesis.

With the conventional null hypothesis, we postulate that the observed difference is due to random sampling fluctuation. With the additional serial dependency hypothesis, we postulate that the observed difference is the consequence of serial dependency. For example, the behavior may follow a natural upward trend prior to intervention. A higher postintervention behavior level may be due to the continuation of this upward trend, not intervention. For another example, suppose a behavior follows a cyclical pattern and the preintervention phase happens to correspond with the trough of the cycle, whereas the postintervention phase happens to coincide with the peak of the cycle. In this case, the difference in behavior before and after intervention is entirely due to a natural cycle of behavior.

INDICATORS OF SERIAL DEPENDENCY

Before we can deal with the problem of serial dependency, we need to have a way to detect its existence. We present two statistical indicators of serial dependency: the autocorrelation function and Young's (1941) C statistic. The former is the most commonly used indicator of serial dependency. The latter has been shown to be an elegant alternative (Tryon, 1982).

We should emphasize that both statistics are omnibus indicators of serial dependency, in that both will indicate whether serial dependency exists in a set of data and to what extent. However, the nature of the serial dependency (linear trend, curvilinear trend, cycles, etc.) is not discernible from either of these two statistics. For example, Tryon's (1982) suggestion of using a combination of the C statistic and regression technique to determine the nature of and to assess intervention effectiveness may in fact overextend the ability of the C statistic. The C statistic does not provide any information beyond the existence or nonexistence of serial dependency.

The Autocorrelation Function

The autocorrelation function (ACF) is fundamentally a set of Pearson's product-moment correlation coefficients. With the ACF, instead of finding the correlation between two variables, the correlation between two different observations of the same variable made at two different points in time is assessed. The temporal distance between the two observational points in time is referred to as the *lag*. If the ACF computes the correlation between two observations made at consecutive points in time, the ACF is called a lag-1 ACF. Another way to express this is that a lag-1 ACF is the Pearson's r between an observation at time t and one at time $t + 1$. Similarly, a lag-2 ACF is the correlation between observations made at time t and time $t + 2$. Theoretically, we can compute the correlation between any two observations made along the time continuum. Hence, we can have a lag-k ACF in which the two observations are made k points in time apart.

The generalized formula for the computation of a lag-k ACF is:

$$\text{Lag-}k \ \text{ACF} = \frac{\Sigma \ (X_t - \bar{X})(X_{t+k} - \bar{X})}{\Sigma \ (X_t - \bar{X})^2}, \qquad (8.1)$$

where X_t is the observation made at time t, $\bar{X}$ is the mean of all observations, X_{t+k} is the observation made at time $t + k$, and k is the lag width. For example, for a lag-2 ACF, Equation 8.1 becomes:

$$\text{Lag-2 ACF} = \frac{\Sigma \ (X_t - \bar{X})(X_{t+2} - \bar{X})}{\Sigma \ (X_t - \bar{X})^2},$$

Figure 8.1 provides an example of the computation of a lag-1 ACF. The previous autocorrelation formula is the raw score formula and is appropriate when there is a single mean in the time series, which is generally the case. However, if the time series data are from a study consisting of more than one phase, it is quite likely that the mean of each phase is different. In this case, the mean $\bar{X}$ for Equation 8.1 should change according to the phase in which X_t and X_{t+1} are members. For example, if a time series represents data gathered in a base-line phase and a postintervention phase, the mean base-line X should be used for those X_t and X_{t+1} values in the baseline phase and the mean postintervention X should be used for the other observations. Thus, a more general form of Equation 8.1 is:

$$\text{Lag-}k \text{ ACF} = \frac{\Sigma \ (e_t)(e_{t+k})}{\Sigma \ (e_t)^2}, \tag{8.2}$$

where e_t is the deviation of X_t and e_{t+k} is the deviation of X_{t+k} from the corresponding phase mean, respectively. In other situations, e_t and e_{t+k} may be the deviation scores from a predicted or mean value. Because of this flexibility, and ACF is frequently viewed as the correlation between *error* terms at times t and $t + k$ (e.g., Huitema, 1985). This follows if one defines the difference between a score and the mean, $X - \bar{X}$, as error. With this definition, all Pearson's *r*s are correlations between error terms. For our purpose, it suffices to view a lag-k ACF as the correlation between two observations that are k observations apart.

Statistical Significance Tests

There are a number of methods to test for the statistical significance of an autocorrelation. The most common method is the Bartlett test (Bartlett, 1946). With the Bartlett test, the standard deviation of the theoretical sampling distribution (i.e., the standard error) of a lag-k ACF is given by:

$$se_{\text{lag}-k\,\text{ACF}} = \sqrt{1/N(1 + 2 \sum_{i=1}^{k} \text{ACF}_i^2)}, \tag{8.3}$$

where $se_{\text{lag}-k\,\text{ACF}}$ is the standard error of a lag-k ACF, N is the number of pairs of observations for the ACF, and ACF_i is the lag-i ACF. Therefore, for an approximately .05 level of significance, one can compare the observed value of the lag-k ACF against ± 2 (se). If the observed ACF is greater in absolute value, then the null hypothesis of ACF = 0 can be rejected. If the observed ACF is within the range of ± 2 (se), one fails to reject the null hypothesis of no autocorrelation.

Time	1	2	3	4	5	6	7	8	9	10	11	
Time Series data	14	27	29	35	21	12	25	36	33	28	26	$\Sigma X = 286$ $\bar{X} = 286/11$ $= 26$
X_t	14	27	29	35	21	12	25	36	33	28		
X_{t+1}	27	29	35	21	12	25	36	33	28	26		
$X_t - \bar{X}$	−12	1	3	9	−5	−14	−1	10	7	2		
$X_{t+1} - \bar{X}$	1	3	9	−5	−14	−1	10	7	2	0		
$(X_t - \bar{X})(X_{t+1} - \bar{X})$	−12	3	27	−45	70	14	−10	70	14	0		$\Sigma (X_t - \bar{X})(X_{t+1} - \bar{X})$ $= 131$
$(X_t - \bar{X})^2$	144	1	9	81	25	196	1	100	49	4		$\Sigma(X_t - \bar{X})^2$ $= 610$

$$\text{Lag-1 ACF} = \frac{\Sigma (X_t - \bar{X})(X_{t+1} - \bar{X})}{\Sigma (X_t - \bar{X})^2}$$

$$= \frac{131}{610}$$

$$= .215$$

FIGURE 8.1. Computation of a lag-1 ACF.

For example, with the data in Figure 8.1, the standard error can be computed as:

$$se_{\text{lag} - 1 \text{ ACF}} = \sqrt{1/N(1 + 2 \Sigma \text{ ACF}_1{}^2)}$$

$$= \sqrt{1/10[1 + 2(.225)^2]}$$

$$= \sqrt{.110}$$

$$= .332.$$

With this standard error, the critical values for the rejection of the null hypothesis of zero autocorrelation is $\pm 2(se) = \pm 2 (.332)$ or $\pm .664$. Since the observed ACF is .215, which is neither greater than $+.664$ nor smaller than $-.664$, it is not significantly different from a zero ACF. Hence, in this case, we fail to reject the null ACF hypothesis.

We should note that the previous significance-testing approach is not appropriate for a special branch of time series analysis, known as time series regression, that assesses the relationship between two time series variables. For this type of analysis, the autocorrelation is computed on the error from a regression prediction. Two other statistical tests of significance may be used when the ACF is computed based on deviation scores from predicted scores through a regression analysis. The Geary test is a nonparametric test based on a count of sign changes in the deviation from the regression prediction score. The alternative is the Durbin–Watson d statistic, which is a parametric statistic. We do not cover time series regression analysis in this text. Readers interested in these two statistics or time series regression in general may consult Durbin and Watson (1950, 1951), Geary (1970), Habibagahi and Pratschke (1972), or Ostrom (1978).

Correlogram

We may calculate the lag-1 through lag-k ACFs for any given set of time series data. It is also possible that a set of time series data shows no significant ACF at lag-1 but has a significant ACF at higher lags. To ensure that significant ACFs at higher lags are detected, we may compute ACFs for a large number of lags and then assess the statistical significance of each. The computational process and the judgments of statistical significance of ACFs for a large number of lags can be tedious and confusing. As an aid for the assessment of a series of lag-1 through lag-k ACFs, and ACF correlogram can be constructed through the time series programming routine in most computer statistical packages (e.g., SPSSx, SAS, BMDP, MINITAB). An ACF correlogram is a graphic representation of the ACFs for a single set of time series data at different lags and their cor-

AUTOCORRELATION FUNCTION FOR VARIABLE X
AUTOCORRELATIONS *
TWO STANDARD ERROR LIMITS .
AUTO. STAND.

LAG	CORR.	ERR.	-1	-.75	-.5	-.25	0	.25	.5	.75	1
1	0.154	0.098									
2	-0.060	0.098									
3	-0.059	0.097									
4	0.026	0.097									
5	-0.097	0.096									
6	-0.110	0.095									
7	-0.083	0.095									
8	-0.115	0.094									
9	-0.060	0.094									
10	0.053	0.093									
11	-0.024	0.093									
12	0.009	0.092									
13	0.104	0.092									
14	0.134	0.091									
15	-0.053	0.091									
16	-0.152	0.090									
17	-0.035	0.090									
18	-0.137	0.089									
19	-0.024	0.089									
20	0.155	0.088									
21	-0.060	0.087									
22	-0.110	0.087									
23	0.023	0.086									
24	0.012	0.086									
25	-0.069	0.085									

FIGURE 8.2. An ACF correlogram.

responding critical values for a .05 level of statistical significance. Figure 8.2 provides an example of an ACF correlogram constucted through the Box–Jenkins routine in SPSSx. In this Figure, the lag-1 through lag-25 ACFs are represented by asterisks (*), and their corresponding critical values are represented by single dots (.). With this ACF correlogram, the lag-1 through lag-k ACFs can be visually assessed at one glance for possibly significant higher lag ACFs. In Figure 8.2, none of the ACFSs are statistically significant.

An ACF correlogram is not only a convenient tool for the judgment of the existence of serial dependency. As shown in the next chapter in the discussion of a technique known as ARIMA, and ACF correlogram is an invaluable tool in the assessment of the nature of the underlying serial dependency.

Young's C Statistic

An infrequently used alternative to the ACF is the Young's C statistic (Young, 1931). Like the ACF, the C statistic is an omnibus indicator of serial dependency. Unlike the ACF, however, the C statistic will indicate only the existence of a lag-1 serial dependency. The C statistic is computed by:

$$C = 1 - \left(\frac{\displaystyle\sum_{t = 1}^{N - 1} (X_t - X_{t + 1})^2}{2 \displaystyle\sum_{t = 1}^{N} (X_t - \bar{X})^2} \right)$$

(8.4)

The numerator is the sum of square successive differences. Figure 8.3 provides an example for the computation of the C statistic for the set of time series data given in Figure 7.1.

The standard deviation of the theoretical sampling distribution of this statistic (i.e., standard error) is dependent entirely on the total number of observations and can be estimated by:

$$se_C = \frac{1}{N - 1} \sqrt{N - 2.}$$

(8.5)

The ratio of the C statistic and its standard error approximates a z score in the unit normal z distribution for a time series with 25 observations or more. That is:

$$z = \frac{C}{se_C}$$

(8.6)

Time	1	2	3	4	5	6	7	8	9	10	11	
Time Series data	14	27	29	35	21	12	25	36	33	28	26	$\Sigma X = 286$
												$\bar{X} = 286/11$
												$= 26$
$X_t - \bar{X}$	−12	1	3	9	−5	−14	−1	10	7	2	0	
$(X_t - \bar{X})^2$	144	1	9	81	25	196	1	100	49	4	0	$\Sigma(X_t - \bar{X})^2$
												$= 610$
X_t	14	27	29	35	21	12	25	36	33	28		
X_{t+1}	27	29	35	21	12	25	36	33	28	26		
$X_t - X_{t+1}$	−13	−2	−6	14	9	−13	−11	3	5	2		
$(X_t - X_{t+1})^2$	169	4	36	196	81	169	121	9	25	4		$\Sigma(X_t - X_{t+1})^2$ $= 814$

$$C = 1 - \frac{\Sigma(X_t - X_{t+1})^2}{2\Sigma(X_t - \bar{X})^2}$$

$$= 1 - \frac{814}{2(610)}$$

$$= .333$$

FIGURE 8.3. Computation of the C statistic.

when N is greater than or equal to 25. Tryon (1982) showed that this ratio does not depart markedly from the z score when the number of observations is as few as eight. For the data in Figure 8.3, for instance, the standard error is:

$$se_C = \frac{1}{N-1} \sqrt{N-2}$$

$$= \frac{1}{11-1} \sqrt{11-2}$$

$$= .300.$$

The estimated z score is hence:

$$z = \frac{C}{se_C}$$

$$= \frac{.333}{.300}$$

$$= 1.110.$$

The critical value for statistical significance at the one-tailed .05 level in a z distribution is 1.645. Therefore, the observed serial dependency of C = .326 is not significant. This lack of a statistically significant serial dependency based on the C statistic for this set of data, incidentally, agrees with the finding of nonsignificance when the ACF is used for the same set of data. The C statistic and the ACF are simply two alternative means of assessing the serial dependency of the time series data. The significance of the two results should be quite similar.

The C statistic has been enthusiastically endorsed by some (e.g., Tryon, 1982) as an excellent alternative to other methods of time series data analysis. It should be pointed out that the C statistic is only an omnibus indicator of serial dependency. It does not assess the nature of the serial dependency and is, hence, not a substitute for other more powerful time series techniques, such as those discussed later in this chapter and in the next two chapters. Like the ACF, the C statistic is a good tool for the preliminary investigation of the existence of serial dependency. When serial dependency is evidenced, other appropriate time series techniques are needed for data analysis.

ANALYSIS OF SERIALLY DEPENDENT DATA

Visual Inspection of Graphic Display

Before we proceed with the discussion of the statistical approaches to time series analysis, an ongoing debate regarding the simple approach of visually inspecting graphic displays of time series data should be presented. If the purpose of a study is to evaluate the effects of an intervention strategy on the level of behavior of subjects, the time series data can be plotted on a graph in which the x-axis represents the points of observation along the time continuum and the y-axis represents the level of behavior. With such a graph, we can visually inspect the general trend of the behavior before intervention. If after the intervention the level of behavior changes markedly from the preintervention level, we can conclude that the intervention strategy has made a difference.

When the intervention makes a clear difference that can be detected visually in such a graph, a statistical analysis of the same data will most likely confirm the visual conclusion. However, if the data show a considerable amount of fluctuation before and after intervention and/or if the apparent difference made by the intervention is not drastic, the effectiveness of the intervention may not be discernible from a visual inspection of the graph. Because of this lack of sensitivity and precision in visual inspections of graphs, many (e.g., Glass, Willson, & Gottman, 1975; Gottman & Glass, 1978, Hartmann et al., 1980) have suggested that visual inspections of graphs may not be adequate in the assessment of the effectiveness of intervention.

Others (e.g., Baer, 1977b; Michael, 1974; Parsonson & Baer, 1978) have defended the sole use of visual graphic inspection without statistical analysis rigorously. The basic argument is that variables (or intervention strategies) that are basic to a science are resilient and unambiguous. With these variables, the effects are drastic and are clearly discernible from a graph. Variables that lead to only trivial effects that can be detected only through sensitive statistical techniques are unlikely to be basic variables. The effects created by these weak variables are quite likely limited to the specific set of environmental or laboratory conditions of the study. At best, the contribution of these variables is trivial. At worst, they may mislead investigators away from the more important basic variables.

Proponents of statistical techniques have argued that a visual inspection of graphic displays is a judgmental process. The same graph inspected by different judges may lead to a variety of conclusions. Additionally, concluding that a trivial effect is not important to the science is not the same as not being able to detect that effect. The detection of trivial effects may provide clues to other resilient basic variables. It was also pointed out that in the presence of serial dependency, visual inspections of graphs agree less frequently with statistical analysis results than when serial dependency is absent (Hartmann et al., 1980; Jones, Weinrott, & Vaught, 1978). Because of the presence of serial dependency, the effects of intervention may be obscured by the apparent trend. Hence, visual inspections will produce less valid conclusions. Unlike the study of animal behavior in a laboratory where many variables can be controlled and manipulated, studies of human behavior generally do not have the type of rigorous laboratory controls that help to produce large and dramatic effects. With a few isolated exceptions, empirical scientific progress is generally not made through dramatic discoveries. Rather, progress is frequently made through the accumulation of "trivial" findings, much in the same way the banking and insurance industries build their fortunes from small interest rates (Gilbert, Light, & Mosteller, 1975). Therefore, trivial effects are just as important as drastic effects.

The important point is that visual inspections of graphic displays and statistical techniques are not mutually exclusive. One helps the other in achieving the overall goal of evaluating the effectiveness of an intervention. It would be prudent for us to start a time series analysis with a visual inspection of the graph to detect possible effects and to help determine the appropriate statistical approach (e.g., ARIMA vs. Fourier analysis). Statistical analyses of time series data are primarily procedures to test hypothesized parameters. A visual inspection of the graph of the raw data would provide important clues for the formulation of hypothesized parameters to be tested. A statistical analysis of the data would supplement the otherwise less reliable visual inspection.

Randomization Tests

An alternative approach to either the visual inspection of graphic displays or sophisticated statistical analysis is to minimize the amount of serial dependency in the data through manipulations of the research design. The associated statistical techniques in this general approach to assessing the effectiveness of intervention when the underlying behavior is serially dependent is known as nonparametric randomization tests. They are not so much statistical techniques specifically designed to analyze serially dependent data; rather, they are techniques to analyze the resulting data after the effects of serial dependency of the behavior on the data have been removed through particular experimental design schemes. Strong advocates for these techniques include Edgington (1967, 1975, 1982) and Levin, Marascuilo, and Hubert (1978).

Specifically, to assess the effectiveness of one or more intervention strategies, the entire duration of the experiment can be divided into a number of blocks of time. Each block is assigned to be a treatment phase or a no-treatment (base-line) phase at random. Alternatively, in a multiple-treatment comparison, various treatments can be assigned to different blocks at random.

Instead of analyzing a number of observations within each block or phase, only a summary measure (e.g., mean of all observations) for each phase is used for analysis. In other words, the most basic unit of analysis in a randomization test is not an observation point. Rather, it is the summary measure for each phase. Proponents of this approach have suggested that even if the underlying behavior has a high level of serial dependency, summary measures for the various phases are essentially not serially dependent. Even in the rare situations in which they are serially dependent, the degree of serial dependency is trivial.

When the phases of the experiment are randomly assigned and the summary measure of each phase is used as the basic unit of analysis, the data (i.e., the summary measures) are open to a large array of nonparametric statistics for analyses. The application of these techniques are, however, dependent on whether the treatment and/or base-line phases have been appropriately randomized.

The first phase of most experiments is the base-line phase. Such a predetermined no-treatment phase would destroy the randomization design. Hence, for a randomization test, if the first phase is a base-line phase, it is generally excluded from analysis. Another limitation of the randomization test approach is that the number of time blocks for phases has to be quite large for the randomization process to be effective (Edgington, 1982).

We do not discuss each of the multitude of possible nonparametric statistics for this type of experimental design. Marascuilo and McSweeney (1977) discussed the use of the Kruskal–Wallis test for this purpose. Levin, Marascuilo, and Hubert (1978) discussed the use of Mann–Whitley's U and Spearman's rho. Edgington (1982) demonstrated the uses of the Wilcoxon matched-pairs signed-rank test, the Mann–Whitley U test, the sign test, and the Fisher's exact test. Furthermore, Levin, Marascuilo, and Hubert discussed the use of computers as an aid to generate probability distributions to assist decision making. Readers are referred to these publications for more detailed discussions of this approach.

Linear Regression

Another method for the analysis of time series data is linear regression (cf. Johnston, 1966; Kaestener & Ross, 1974; Kmenta, 1971). When applied to time series data, linear regression is a technique in which the level of behavior is predicted based on the time of observation. First, the underlying serial dependency is assumed to be a monotonic and linear trend. Next, based on the observed relationship between the time of observation and the level of behavior, the best linear trend is fitted to the data. After a number of statistical tests, this trend is assumed to be the best model to summarize the underlying trend.

When applied to time series data, it is assumed that the mathematical model that best describes the underlying linear trend is:

$$X_t = \alpha + \beta_t + e_t, \qquad (8.7)$$

where X_t is the observed level of behavior at time t; α is called the intercept and equals the level of behavior at time 0; β is the regression coefficient or the slope of the linear trend; t is the discrete time unit t (e.g., 0, 1, 2, 3, . . . , t) corresponding to the observation X_t; and e_t is the random error associated with the observation at time t. The expected sum of the e_t values is zero. The objective of linear regression is to estimate the best-fitting model in the form of Equation 8.7, based on the observed baseline data to describe the underlying linear trend. Once the best-fitting model is determined, the expected level of behavior in the postintervention phase can be projected by setting the time t value at those in the intervention phase. For example, if the base line consists of 10 observations (i.e., $t = 0, 1, 2, . . . , 9$) and the linear model derived from the base-line data has an estimated α of 20 and an estimated β of 30, then the best predicted value of X_t at time t is:

$$X_t' = 20 + 30t + e_t,$$

where X_t' is the expected level of behavior at time t. Because e_t is expected to be zero, it drops out of the model. To project into the postintervention phase, the time t values for the postintervention phase (i.e., 10, 11, 12, ...) are applied to the model. Hence, for time 10 (1st point in the postintervention phase), the expected level of behavior is:

$$X_{10}' = 20 + 30(10) = 320.$$

In a similar fashion, the expected level of behavior at times 11, 12, 13, ... are 350, 380, 410, ... To assess the effectiveness of the intervention strategy, one can compare these expected values with the actual observed values in the postintervention phase through an appropriate test such as a t test. If there is a significant amount of difference, one would conclude that the intervention is effective.

Estimation of α and β

To identify the appropriate linear model to describe the underlying trend one uses the observed data in the base line to estimate the values of α and β in the model. The most common method used to estimate the values of α and β for the linear model in Equation 8.7 is a method known as the least squares method. In this method, the set of α and β values for which the sum of the squared differences between the predicted and the actual levels of behavior is minimized are estimated. Based on this least squares criterion, the best estimate of β is given by:

$$\beta' = \frac{\Sigma\,(t - \bar{t})(X_t - \bar{X})}{\Sigma\,(t - \bar{t})^2}, \tag{8.8}$$

where β' is the estimated β, $\bar{t}$ is the mean of all time values in the base line, and $\bar{X}$ is the mean of all X_ts in the base line. From this estimated β, the value of α is estimated by:

$$\alpha' = \bar{X} - \beta'\bar{t}, \tag{8.9}$$

where α' is the estimated α. Figure 8.4 provides an example of the estimation of the linear model to fit the data in Figure 8.1. As shown in Figure 8.4, under the least square criterion, the best-fitting model to describe the data is $X_t' = 19.365 + 1.327(X_t)$.

The value of β' is closely related to the value of the Pearson's r for the same set of data. Note that unlike a lag-k ACF in which the Pearson's r describes the relationship between observations at time t and time $t + k$, this Pearson's r is the relationship between "time" and "level of behavior." Specifically,

$$\beta' = r\,\frac{S_x}{S_t}, \tag{8.9}$$

where r is the observed Pearson's r, S_X is the standard deviation of the levels of behavior, and S_t is the standard deviation of the time values. Equation 8.9 is, hence, an alternative approach to the estimation of β'.

Standard Error of Estimate

When an X_t is predicted based on the estimated linear regression model, the predicted X_t' is unlikely to be exactly equal to the actual X_t. This difference between the actual X_t and the predicted X_t' is the e_t term in Equation 8.7. The expected error in prediction can be expressed indirectly through the standard error of estimate (S_e), which is the standard deviation of the $X_t - X_t'$ differences and is estimated by:

$$S_e = \sqrt{\frac{\Sigma(X_t - X_t')}{N - 2}}, \tag{8.10}$$

where X_t is the observed level of behavior at time t, X_t' is the expected level of behavior at time t, and N is the total number of observation points. Imagine if a large number of observations of the same behavior are made simultaneously at time t, the expected standard deviation of the distribution of observed scores for time t is represented by S_e. In other words,

Time	0	1	2	3	4	5	6	7	8	9	10	
												$\Sigma t = 55$
												$\bar{t} = 55/11$
												$= 5$
Time Series Data	14	27	29	35	21	12	25	36	33	28	26	$\Sigma X = 286$
												$\bar{X} = 286/11$
												$= 26$
$X_t - \bar{X}$	−12	1	3	9	−5	−14	−1	10	7	2	0	
$t - \bar{t}$	−5	−4	−3	−2	−1	0	1	2	3	4	5	
$(t - \bar{t})(X_t - \bar{X})$	60	4	9	18	5	0	1	20	21	8	0	$\Sigma(t - \bar{t})(X_t - \bar{X})$
												$= 146$
$(t - \bar{t})^2$	25	16	9	4	1	0	1	4	9	16	25	$\Sigma(t - \bar{t})^2$
												$= 110$

$$\beta' = \frac{\Sigma(t - \bar{t})(X_t - \bar{X})}{\Sigma(t - \bar{t})^2}$$

$$= \frac{146}{110}$$

$$= 1.327.$$

$$\alpha' = \bar{X} - \beta'\bar{t}$$

$$= 26 - 1.327(5)$$

$$= 19.365$$

FIGURE 8.4. Estimation of linear regression parameters.

S_e is an indicator of the amount of error associated with the regression model or equation. To gain a better conceptual picture of what a particular S_e value implies, sometimes we establish a confidence interval around a predicted X_t. For example, we can be 95% certain that the actual level of behavior is within the range of $X_t' \pm 1.645(S_e)$.

Significance of β'

The value of β' and, subsequently, the value of α' are estimated from the observed values of X_t in the base line. These actual observations represent a sample of the underlying behavior. The estimated values of β' and α' are, thus, subject to sampling error. For instance, the underlying behavior may not have a linear trend at all (i.e., $\beta = 0$) but the model estimated from the sample may show a trend (i.e., $\beta' > 0$). In this case, the estimated trend is an artifact of the sampling process. To safeguard against this situation, we can test for the statistical significance of the estimated β'.

When testing for the significance of β', we assess the probability that, by random sampling alone, a β' as high or higher than the estimated value can be obtained from a sample of an underlying behavior in which $\beta' = 0$. To accomplish this, we first assess the standard error of β' (i.e., the standard deviation of the sampling distribution of β') through:

$$S_{\beta'} = \frac{S_e}{\sqrt{\Sigma(t - \bar{t})^2/N}}.$$

(8.11)

A Student's t statistic (not to be confused with the t in Equation 8.11, which represents the time variable) can then be obtained by:

$$t = \frac{\beta' - \beta}{S_{\beta'}},$$

(8.12)

where β is the hypothesized value of β. In the case of testing against the null hypothesis, the hypothesized value of β is zero. The significance of β' can then be assessed by comparing the Student's t value against the critical value of t with $N - 2$ degrees of freedom at the appropriate alpha level.

Linear Regression of Curvilinear Trends

The linear regression approach just described assumes that the underlying behavior follows a linear trend. However, the actual behavior may follow a curvilinear rather than a linear trend. There are many possible forms of curvilinear trends. For example, a cyclical trend is a curvilinear trend. Of the various curvilinear trends, three monotonic curvilinear trends can be modeled with linear regression techniques after the data have been appropriately transformed. These include the power curve, the exponential curve, and the logarithmic curve. If, after a careful visual inspection of the graph, we find that the trend is unlikely to be linear but appears to resemble one of these three types of curvilinear trends, we may then apply these techniques to describe the trend. The standard error of estimates resulting from these curvilinear trends can then be compared against that of a linear trend. The one with the smallest standard error would be the best model to describe the trend.

For an underlying time series behavioral pattern, a power curve trend can be represented by the following mathematical model:

$$X_t = \alpha t^\beta + e_t, \tag{8.13}$$

where, again, X_t is the observed level of behavior at time t, α and β are two unknown constants to be estimated, t is the time at which X_t is observed, and e_t is the random error associated with the observation X_t. Figure 8.5 shows the general form of a power curve. To estimate the values of α and β for a power curve, the data can be transformed through a log (base 10) transformation process. Specifically, if X_t and t are transformed,

FIGURE 8.5.   A power curve.

the model in Equation 8.13 can be alternatively expressed as:

$$\log X_t = \log \alpha + \beta \log t + e_t. \tag{8.14}$$

This is a linear regression model. The values of $\log \alpha$ and β in Equation 8.14 can be estimated through the previously discussed linear regression procedure using $\log X_t$ and $\log t$ as the observed data. Once the value of $\log \alpha$ is estimated, it can be transformed back to α through an antilog procedure. With the estimated α and β values, the model described in Equation 8.13 is identified.

An exponential curve model can be expressed as:

$$X_t = \alpha 10^{\beta t} + e_t. \tag{8.15}$$

Figure 8.6 provides the general form of an exponential curve. This trend can be modeled through the following linear regression:

$$\log X_t = \log \alpha + \beta t + e_t. \tag{8.16}$$

The logarithmic curve model can be expressed as follows:

$$X_t = \alpha + \beta \log t + e_t. \tag{8.18}$$

FIGURE 8.6.   An exponential curve.

Figure 8.7 shows the general form of a logarithmic curve. The logarithmic curve can be modeled directly as a linear regression problem by transforming all t values to log t.

Limitation of Linear Regression

The appropriateness of the use of linear regression techniques to model time series data has been severely challenged. The most cogent argument against the use of linear regression is that linear regression assumes that the observations of the underlying behavior are mutually independent. However, this assumption is violated when data are serially dependent. When data are serially dependent, the standard error of β' can be underestimated by as much as 456%, and the t statistic used to test for the significance of β' can be inflated by as much as 200% (Gottman & Glass, 1978). Hence, an unreliable estimate of β may result. This unreliable β' can be erroneously interpreted as a reliable representation of the underlying β due to the small apparent standard error and the apparent significance of the t statistic. When the model is not an accurate representation of the underlying behavior, the postintervention projections are not reliable. Hence, the comparison between the projected and the actual postintervention level of behavior cannot be reliable.

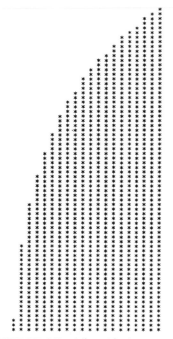

FIGURE 8.7.   A logarithmic curve.

However, linear regression as well as curvilinear regression have been suggested as appropriate under certain conditions (Huitema, 1985). Specifically, once the best linear regression model is determined for a set of time series data, the residuals can be computed. The residuals (or errors in prediction) are the individual differences between each observation at each point in time and the predicted value for that point in time (i.e., residual $= X_t - X_t'$). The ACF of the set of residual values can be assessed. If there is no evidence of a significant ACF among the residuals, the linear regression model is appropriate and reliable.

The appropriateness of linear regression for the analysis of time series data depends on a lack of serial dependency among the residuals and the correctness of the assumption that the underlying behavioral trend can be described with a linear model (e.g., not cyclical). Another limitation of a linear regression modeling of time series data is that the standard error of β' at the begining and the end of sample time series can be significantly larger than that at the midpoint of the series. This violates another assumption of linear regression known as homoscadasticity. Gottman and Glass (1978) provided a discussion of this and other limitations of the application of linear regression to time series data. Because of these limitations of linear regression, a number of alternative techniques have been developed specifically for time series analysis. In the next chapter, we review a frequently recommended technique for behavior analysis known as ARIMA. In chapter 10, we discuss two other techniques, known as Markov chain and Fourier analysis.

CHAPTER 9

Time Series Analysis: ARIMA

The Auto Regressive Integrated Moving Average (ARIMA) approach is a set of powerful statistical techniques through which the exact nature of the serial dependency of a set of observations made over a period of time can be assessed. This allows for forecasting. It can also be used to assess the exact short-term and long-term effects of a behavioral intervention introduced at a particular time in the time series. In general, an underlying assumption of ARIMA is that the observations made along the time continuum are measured minimally through an interval scale. In other words, ARIMA cannot be applied for nominal or ordinal data. For nominal data, a technique known as the Markov Chain, which is discussed in the next chapter, should be used instead.

The ARIMA approach consists of a large array of highly complex mathematical techniques for time series analysis. It is impossible to provide a comprehensive discussion of the techniques either in breadth or in depth within this chapter. We do, however, provide readers with an elementary introduction to the concepts and some of the basic techniques in an ARIMA analysis. For a more in-depth understanding of these techniques, more specialized texts such as Cryer (1986), Gottman (1981), McDowall et al. (1980), and Vandaele (1983) should be consulted. For a succinct explanation of the specific application of these techniques to data analysis of a single-subject study, the article by Gottman and Glass (1978) is suggested. For a conceptual explanation of the basic orientation of the ARIMA, we suggest Hartmann et al. (1980) and Jones, Vaught, and Weinrott (1977). The development of ARIMA techniques is largely due to the work of Box and Jenkins (1976). Glass, Willson, and Gottman (1975) first introduced its potential application to the behavioral sciences. These two latter texts represent the two most authoritative sources of reference for behavioral scientists.

ARIMA methods can be used to analyze data in a simple time series that contains no behavioral intervention. In this case, the objective of the ARIMA analysis is to describe the nature of the serial dependency of the time series in exact mathematical terms. Frequently, a simple time series analysis is conducted for the purpose of forecasting some future event. By identifying the exact nature of the serial dependency in the past, one can project the event into the future, assuming that the serial dependency will continue in the same fashion.

ARIMA methods can also be used to analyze data in an interrupted time series that contains an intervention at a particular time within that series. The objectives of an ARIMA analysis of an interrupted time series are to identify the sources and nature of serial dependency in the data and to assess the impact or effectiveness of the intervention after the serial dependency has been accounted for.

The most basic ARIMA approach is to identify the existence and the nature of serial dependency in the underlying "population" based on the observed data. However, in some situations, the serial dependency may be cyclical. A time series containing a cyclical serial dependency is said to contain an element of seasonality. The identification of seasonal serial dependency requires an extension of the basic ARIMA approach. The extended method is sometimes referred to as SARIMA (Seasonal *A*uto*R*egressive *I*ntegrated *M*oving *A*verage) models. (Other methods for the analysis of seasonality include Fourier analysis and spectral analysis, which is discussed later in the next chapter.) For our purpose, we concentrate on only an ARIMA analysis of an interrupted time series without accounting for seasonality. Readers who are interested in a SARIMA analysis of an interrupted time series should consult the specialized texts referenced earlier.

There are two primary steps in the ARIMA analysis of an interrupted time series. First, one attempts to find the best statistical description or model that will fit the observed data as a postulated model of the nature of the underlying serial dependency. When the model is identified and its appropriateness tested, the final step is to assess the impact of the behavioral intervention. This is accomplished by first removing the effects of the identified serial dependency model from the data and then identifying the best statistical model that describes the extent and nature of the impact of the intervention in the remainder of the data.

We describe the basic elements in each of the two steps. However, we first discuss some of the fundamental statistical principles that form the theoretical basis for ARIMA.

THE STATISTICAL PRINCIPLES

Recall that with conventional statistical analyses, the fundamental assumptions are that data are drawn randomly from a population and that the score of one subject is independent of that of another. These two assumptions form the pillars of conventional inferential statistics. Most inferential statistical techniques are derived based on these two premises.

With serially dependent time series data, regardless of whether or not the first assumption of conventional statistics (i.e., random sampling) is violated, the second assumption is clearly not met. That is, when data are serially dependent, no observation is totally independent. Rather, each observation is influenced to some extent by the values of previous observations.

One approach to resolving the problem of serial dependnecy is to develop statistical techniques to analyze serially dependent data such that the techniques are robust even when the assumption of independence is violated. Another approach is to depart completely from conventional statistics and develop a set of statistical techniques that do not require the assumption of independence of observations. Furthermore, these techniques would deal with the existence of serial dependency head on. Of these two approaches, the second is more direct. ARIMA represents such an approach.

Since the basic assumptions of conventional statistics are no longer appropriate, ARIMA requires a fundamental set of statistical principles from which statistical techniques can be derived. For an interrupted time series analysis, the value of each observation in the time series can be decomposed into two basic components: a *deterministic* component and a *stochastic* component. The deterministic component in an interrupted time series analysis refers to that part of an observation score that is the result of an intervention treatment. This component is, thus, alternatively referred to as the intervention component. The stochastic component is also known as the noise component. It is analogous but not equal to the error component in conventional statistics. Symbolically, an observation score X_t obtained from an observation made at time t in the time series can be decomposed as:

$$X_t = I_t + N_t, \qquad (9.1)$$

where I_t is the deterministic (or intervention) component and N_t is the stochastic (or noise) component for the observation at time t.

For a better understanding of the model presented in Equation 9.1, an oversimplified analogy can be made with the Classical Theory of measurement discussed in chapter 5. Recall that in the Classical Theory of measurement, the observed score for subject i can be decomposed into a true score component for subject i and an error component for subject i. If, instead of subject i, we consider observation at time t, we obtain a rough analogy. The deterministic component I_t is the component of interest in an interrupted time series analysis because it describes the effectiveness of the intervention; much as the true score is the component of interest in the Classical Theory of measurement. Of course, they are not strictly equivalent, because in one situation we are interested in a treatment effect, whereas in the other we are interested in a score only.

The time series model departs from the Classical Theory of measurement model when the stochastic component is considered. In the Classical Theory of measurement, the error component consists of only random error. In the time series model, however, the stochastic component contains noise from three possible sources. These include trend, seasonality, and random error. We tentatively define a trend as a natural tendency of the observed value of the behavior (prevalence, frequency, etc.) to increase or decrease in value systematically as time progresses without any intervention. We show later that this definition is inadequate or even inappropriate. However, for the time being, this definition suffices. Seasonality refers to a natural tendency of the observed behavior to fluctuate in a systematic manner without any intervention. The observed behavior first increases, then decreases, then increases again, and so on in a regular and cyclical manner. Random error is also called *random shock* or *white noise* and is equivalent to the random error term in the Classical Theory of measurement. The following discussion concentrates on only two of the three sources of error in the stochastic component, namely, trend and random shock. The techniques for modeling seasonalities (SARIMA) are an extension of those used to model trends.

The primary objective of an ARIMA analysis for an interrupted time series study is to assess the impact of the intervention. In other words, the component I_t is of interest. However, since a direct assessment of the intervention effect is most likely affected by the stochastic or noise component (N_t), this effect should be removed before I_t can be assessed meaningfully. To accomplish this, we first assume that noise accounts for all the variations in the observed scores. That is, we assume that:

$$X_t = N_t. \tag{9.2}$$

This is a null hypothesis directly parallel to the null hypotheses in conventional inferential statistics, in which random error is assumed to account for all observed differences. With this null assumption, we postulate that the stochastic component accounts for all the variations in the observed data.

For a nonseasonal ARIMA, the first task is to identify a statistical description or model of the stochastic component through a series of model identification procedures. The final model identified through these procedures accounts for the nature of the serial dependency. Based on the identified model, the effects of serial dependency can be removed from the data statistically. After the effects of serial dependency are properly removed from the data and if the null hypothesis is true, the remainder of each score, or the residual score, may be accounted for by random shock only. In other words, through proper model identification, the systematic portion of the stochastic component (N_t) is accounted for. Under the null hypothesis, the remaining unaccounted for score is due the random portion of N_t only.

Once the appropriate model is identified, the deterministic (or intervention) component, I_t, is added to the residuals of the model. This new model, then, represents the research hypothesis of intervention effectiveness. If the addition of the deterministic component leads to a statistically significant amount of additional explanation power, the intervention is deemed to be effective, and the null hypothesis that the residuals of serial dependency contain only white noise (or random shock) is rejected. Various intervention models can also be fitted to the residual data to identify the best model that describes the characteristics of the effectiveness of the intervention (e.g., an abrupt change of behavior that sustains throughout the posttreatment phase or a gradual change of behavior that becomes extinct gradually, etc.).

Null models for the stochastic component can only be identified based on available observed data in a time series. Since the observed data contains both a deterministic and a stochastic component, the deterministic component will confound any null model specified for the stochastic component. Hence, to identify a null model in order to describe the stochastic component, it is important that any possible deterministic component should be removed prior to model identification.

For an interrupted time series analysis, we can first assume that the stochastic component is not related to the deterministic component (intervention effect). If this is true, then the stochastic component should be similar in nature before and after the intervention. Based on this assumption, only the preintervention data are used for the model identification process. When only the preintervention data are used, the effects of the deterministic component (i.e., intervention effect) are not present in the data. Once the null stochastic model is identified, the preintervention and the postintervention data can be combined and the intervention effect is assessed based on the combined series.

A second approach to minimizing the possibility of a misidentification of the null model due to intervention effect was suggested by Glass, Willson, and Gottman (1975). In this approach, the similarity of the stochastic component before and after intervention is not assumed. A separate model identification process is performed for the preintervention and the postintervention data. The final model is estimated by a weighted average of the two sets of results.

A third approach was suggested by McSweeney (1977). In this approach, a separate model is identified for the preintervention data, the postintervention data, and the combined data. If the three sets of results are inconsistent, the most conservative model is used. Others (e.g., Stoline, Huitema, & Mitchell, 1980) have suggested other alternative approaches through analyses of variance to isolate the stochastic model from intervention effects.

To simplify our subsequent discussion, we assume that the first approach of using only the preintervention phase data is chosen. To use the Glass et al. approach or the McSweeney approach, one can simply repeat the procedures for the preintervention data using the postintervention data or the combined data, as appropriate.

STOCHASTIC PARAMETERS

Although rarely expressed as such, null hypothesis testing in conventional inferential statistics is essentially a model testing process. Specifically, we postulate a null model that states that there is no relationship among the variables under investigation and that all observed variations are due to sampling fluctuations caused by drawing a random sample from the population. Next, we test how well the observed data fit this model. If the probability of obtaining the observed results from the postulated model is very low (i.e., $p < \alpha$), we conclude that the model is inappropriate and reject this null model. The basic principle used in the identification and fitting of null models in ARIMA is fundamentally similar to that of conventional statistics.

The Stochastic Process and Its Realization

Before we proceed any further, it is worthwhile to point out a language and conceptual difference in the sampling processess used in conventional and ARIMA null model identification. With the conventional null model, the observed variation in scores is due to drawing a *sample* from a *population*. The term *sample* implies a random process, whereas the term *population* implies an independence of scores. With ARIMA, the scores in the population do not need to be mutually independent. Additionally, the actual observations are made consecutively within a certain chunk of time along the time continuum. This does not resemble a random sample.

Another major difference between sampling in ARIMA and conventional sampling is the possible existence of *moving average* in the former. When different random samples are drawn from the same population, the mean (average) of each sample is expected to approximate the mean of the population, with the sampling fluctuation of the mean governed by its standard error. In other words, the mean of a random sample from an independent population can be expected to cluster around a constant value. This is not necessarily the case with time series data. Sample means may in fact change systematically from one sample to another. For example, if the underlying behavior (population) follows an upward trend, observing a behavior at a number of sample points in time on Day 2 will most likely yield a sample mean higher than that of sample points on Day 1. Depending on when the sample observations are taken, the sample mean becomes systematically higher as time progresses. This systematic change in sample mean is referred to as a moving average.

Hence, different terms are used to express the sampling process in a time series situation. Specifically, the underlying null population, which is the set of *potential* observations one makes along the time continuum, is called the *stochastic process*. As the term *process* implies, the potential observations are not in a static state, as in the case of a population; rather, the stochastic process may lead to many possible sets of observations. The actual sample of observations is called a *realization of the process*. In conventional statistics, we attempt to infer from the sample to the population. Similarly, in ARIMA, we attempt to build a model to describe the underlying stochastic process based on the data gathered through the realization of the process.

Model Parameters

A nonseasonal stochastic process can be described by various combinations of three basic characteristics known as model parameters. These three parameters are an *autoregressive* (AR) function, a *differencing* (I) function, and a *moving average* (MA) function. They describe three possible characteristics of the serial dependency in the stochastic process.

Before we proceed to explain each of the parameters, we first consider the simplest null model in which the stochastic process can be entirely explained by random shock. This is the case in which serial dependency does not exist in the process. Using a_t to symbolize the random shock at time t and θ_0 to symbolize the grand mean value of the entire underlying process (analogous to the population μ in conventional statistics), the observed score at time t can be expressed as:

$$X_t = \theta_0 + a_t. \tag{9.3}$$

With this model, the observed variations in scores can be entirely explained by random shocks. This is the model identical to the null model in conventional statistics. To simplify discussion, we assume that θ_0 is zero. (We can theoretically transform all observed scores by subtracting θ_0 from each score so that the mean score is zero). Thus, the model becomes:

$$X_t = a_t. \tag{9.4}$$

Although this may be the simplest model, it may not be the most appropriate one, in that it may not agree with evidence obtained from the observed data in the realization of the stochastic process. Specifically, this model cannot account for any observed serial dependency. Data with serial dependency may suggest that an autoregressive function, a differencing function, and/or a moving average function may provide a model that agrees with the observed data more closely.

Autoregressive Parameter

An autoregressive function describes the extent to which an observed value at time t is influenced by a function of *previous observed values* at time $t - 1, t - 2, t - 3, \ldots, t - p$. The *order* of the autoregressive process describes which preceding observed values have effects on the present observation. In a first-order autoregressive process, an observation is influenced by a function of the immediately preceding observed value only. That is, X_t is influenced only by X_{t-1}. In a second-order autoregressive process, X_t is influenced by a function of X_{t-1} and a function of X_{t-2}. In a pth order autoregressive process, X_t is influenced by functions of $X_{t-1}, X_{t-2}, X_{t-3}, \ldots, X_{t-p}$. The relationship between an observed value and a previous observed value in the series is expressed in the form of a coefficient ϕ. This coefficient specifies what function of the previous observed value influences the current observation directly. This is called the parameter of the autoregressive process. We use the term *coefficient* instead of *parameter* to distinguish ϕ from the three ARIMA model parameters. This ϕ is a coefficient analogous to a regression coefficient and should not be confused with the special Pearson's correlation coefficient for dichotomous variables, also known as ϕ (see Appendix A).

Symbolically, a first-order autoregressive process can be expressed as:

$$X_t = a_t + \phi_1(X_{t-1}) \tag{9.5}$$

Note that in a first-order autoregressive process, an observed score at time t is composed of a random shock (a_t) (see Equation 9.4) and a first-order autoregressive function (ϕ times X_{t-1}). Note also that the subscript "1" for ϕ is used to designate that ϕ_1 is associated with the observed value at time $t-1$. The coefficient associated with the observed value at time $t-2$ is hence ϕ_2, at time $t-3$ is ϕ_3, and so on.

A pth order autoregressive process is the direct extension of Equation 9.5. Hence, the model for a second-order autoregressive process is:

$$X_t = a_t + \phi_1 (X_{t-1}) + \phi_2 (X_{t-2}),$$

the model for a third order autoregressive process is:

$$X_t = a_t + \phi_1 (X_{t-1}) + \phi_2 (X_{t-2}) + \phi_3 (X_{t-3}),$$

and the model for the pth-order autoregressive process is:

$$X_t = a_t + \phi_1 (X_{t-1}) + \phi_2 (X_{t-2}) \ldots \ldots + \phi_p (X_{t-p}). \tag{9.6}$$

Through various model identification procedures, the most appropriate model can be identified and the values of the associated ϕ coefficients can be estimated. To express that a process can be described by a first-order autoregressive process, the symbol AR(1) is used. Hence, a second-order autoregressive model is AR(2) and a pth-order autoregressive model is AR(p).

Differencing Parameter

The stochastic process may also be described by a differencing parameter. In a differencing model, an observed score is the sum of the immediately preceding score and a random shock. Hence, for a first-order differencing model, an observed score at time t can be expressed as:

$$X_t = a_t + X_{t-1}. \tag{9.7}$$

The order of a differencing model does not indicate how many previous observations to consider. Rather, it refers to the number of times the time series should be transformed through a differencing prodedure.

When a stochastic process can be described with a differencing parameter, the time series is said to be *nonstationary*. Within a nonstationary time series, the autoregressive and the moving average parameters change with time. This is an undesirable property because it would be difficult to identify a model to fit an ever-changing set of data. Hence, a fundamental assumption in ARIMA is the *weak stationarity assumption*, which postulates that the ARIMA parameters do not change with time. When nonstationarity is evidenced, the time series should be transformed through differencing. In differencing, one subtracts the immediately preceding observation from each observation. This transformation process reduces the nonstationarity of the series. If the transformed data still show evidence of nonstationarity, the differencing is repeated until the series is stationary. The order of a differencing model refers to the number of times the differencing transformation operation is needed.

Although Equation 9.7 succinctly expresses the model for a first-order differencing process, to express the model for a dth-order differencing is considerably more difficult. This is because a dth-order differencing model is the first-order differencing model compounded d times. To illustrate, a second-order differencing model is:

$$X_t = a_t + 2X_{t-1} - X_{t-2} \qquad (9.8)$$

and a third-order differencing model is:

$$X_t = a_t + 3X_{t-1} + X_{t-3}. \qquad (9.9)$$

Because nonstationarity poses a serious problem for the estimation of other ARIMA parameters, it is important to remove the nonstationarity prior to modeling the process with autoregressive or moving average parameters. Hence, when nonstationarity is suspected, the proper differencing parameter should be identified first. The process for the detection of nonstationarity is discussed later. Once the appropriate differencing parameter is identified, the data can be transformed appropriately to a set of stationary data.

Moving Average Parameter

We may also postulate a moving average model to describe the underlying stochastic process. A moving average function describes the extent to which an observed score X_t at time t is influenced by portions of the *random shocks* at times $t - 1, t - 2, t - 3, \ldots, t - q$. Note that in an autoregressive model, each observation is influenced by functions of the previous *observed scores*. In a differencing model, each observation is *totally* dependent on previous observed scores. In a moving average model, however, the observation is influenced by portions of previous random shocks only.

As with autoregressive and differencing processes, moving average persons can be described in terms of their orders. A first-order moving average model, symbolized by MA(1), postulates that an observed score at time t is a function (a portion) of the random shock at time $t - 1$ only. The relationship between the observed score at time t and the random shock at time $t - 1$ is expressed by a coefficient θ_1. Hence, the decomposition of an observed score in MA(1) is:

$$X_t = a_t + \theta_t(a_{t-1}). \qquad (9.10)$$

Through a direct extension, an observed score in an MA(q) model can be decomposed as:

$$X_t = a_t + \theta_1(a_{t-1}) + \theta_2(a_{t-2}) \ldots + \theta_p(a_{t-q}). \tag{9.11}$$

ARIMA Models

The three parameters just described are not mutually exclusive. One may find that the best model for a particular set of data is a combination of parameters. To accommodate all three parameters for a generalized model, ARIMA models are generally expressed as ARIMA(p, d, q). The three terms within the parentheses represent the three parameters. Hence, p represents an autoregressive parameter, d a differencing parameter, and q a moving average parameter. The values of p, d, and q correspond to the order of each of the three parameters.

Thus, the random shock model in which $X_t = a_t$ is expressed as ARIMA(0,0,0) because neither of the three parameters are involved. For a first-order autoregressive model, the symbolic representation is ARIMA(1,0,0). For a second-order autoregressive model, it is ARIMA(2,0,0). A first-order differencing model is ARIMA(0,1,0), and a first-order moving average model is ARIMA(0,0,1). Models involving more than one parameter are direct extensions of the previous symbolism. For example, a model involving a first-order differencing and a second-order moving average would be ARIMA(0,1,2).

A Conceptual Explanation

Now that we have discussed the mathematical definitions of the three parameters, we return to the starting point and discuss their conceptual natures. The purpose of an ARIMA analysis is to model the stochastic component of a time series. The stochastic component of a nonseasonal time series contains trend and white noise. The final result of an ARIMA is a set of statistical descriptors for the systematic portion of the stochastic component, which is trend.

A brief review of the literature shows that, although it has been defined mathematically in various manners, the term *trend* is not well defined conceptually. Additionally, there is a considerable amount of discrepancy in the use of this term. A major source of confusion is the frequent use of the word *trend* synonymously with the term *nonstationarity*. Recall that the existence of nonstationarity confounds the estimation of the autoregressive and the moving average parameters. Thus, nonstationarity should be removed through an appropriate differencing parameter prior to the estimation of the autoregressive and the moving average parameters. There is an apparent contradiction here. If the purpose of an ARIMA analysis is to model the "trend" and yet the trend (nonstationarity) can be removed through differencing, then the differencing parameter alone should be able to describe the trend without the other two parameters. Additionally, if the only systematic stochastic component in a time series is trend and differencing describes this trend, then what do the autoregressive and the moving average parameters describe?

Conventionally, a time series is frequently explained conceptually in terms of *signal* and *noise*. We, instead, explain time series by borrowing concepts from another branch of physics. A score at a particular time in a null time series can be viewed as the resultant of three counteracting "forces": random shock, inertia, and momentum. Random shock is a convenient term to describe all the unknown forces that cause a score to be at a particular level. Inertia is the tendency of a score to stay at the level of the previous point in time. This is a force to maintain a score in a static state over time. Momentum is the tendency of a score to continue the systematic process of change of score in previous points in time. This is the dynamic force to maintain the systematic *change* of score over time. The existence of either one or both of the latter two forces will lead to serial dependency in a time series, because in both cases a current score is influenced by previous scores. The scores of a time series may be the results of pure random shocks, a combination of random shocks and the static force, a combination of random shocks and the dynamic force, or a combination of all three forces.

From this view, a more useful definition of the word *trend* is that a trend is a systematic tendency over time independent of intervention. The results of the static force is hence a static trend or a systematic tendency to maintain the previous score. The result of the dynamic force or momentum is a dynamic trend or a systematic tendency to continue the previous process of change of scores. Nonstationarity is then the existence of a dynamic trend. The differencing parameter is used to describe the dynamic force that has led to the dynamic trend or nonstationarity. The autoregressive and the moving average parameters are used to describe the static force or inertia, which causes the time series scores not to fluctuate extremely from one point in time to the next. At any point, the score in a time series is a result of a tug-of-war among an unknown combination of inertia, momentum, and random shock. Perhaps a seemingly paradoxical statement made by Jean Paul Sartre can effectively sum up the possible coexistence of inertia and momentum: "I have changed as everyone changes: within a permanency."

Because the systematic portion of a score may be accounted for by either inertia, momentum, or both, one would not be able to describe these forces unless it is known for certain whether both forces are at work or only one is responsible. If only one is responsible, it is necessary to determine whether the force is inertia or momentum. A solution is to look for signs of one of the two forces. In ARIMA, the existence of nonstationarity (or dynamic trend or momentum) is the simpler one to detect. When this dynamic force is evidenced from the data, we can derive a mathematical model to describe this dynamic force. With the exact description, we can then remove the effects of this dynamic force from the data through the appropriate differencing parameter. When this dynamic force is removed, the remaining time series is said to be stationary; which, in our analogy, would contain either random shocks only or both random shocks and inertia (or static force). We can then assess if a static force exists in the remaining data; and, if so, derive a mathematical model through the autoregressive and/or moving average parameters to describe this static force.

MODEL IDENTIFICATION

The identification of the proper model to describe the stochastic component of a time series involves three reiterative steps. First, based on preliminary information, a model is tentatively identified. Next, based on the tentative model, the corresponding coefficients or parameters (i.e., ϕ and θ) are estimated. Third, using the estimated coefficients, the goodness-of-fit of the model is assessed. If the fit is found to be satisfactory, the model identification process is complete. However, if the fit is unsatisfactory, we return to the first step and identify another tentative model. The first step is referred to as the initial identification or model specification stage. The second step is the estimation stage, and the last step in the cycle is the diagnostic stage.

Model Specification

By changing the values of p, d, and q, there is an extremely large number of possible models for any given set of time series data. Speculating on the most appropriate model would be an impossible task. Fortunately, each ARIMA model has its distinct statistical "signature." By examining these statistical signatures, we have a general guide for initial speculation of the most appropriate ARIMA model. These statistical signatures are embedded within the autocorrelation function (ACF) and another indicator known as the partial autocorrelation function (PACF) of the time series.

ACF and PACF

The ACF is simply the general lag-k autocorrelation for a time series, discussed in the previous chapter. A lag-k PACF is a correlation between an observation at time t (i.e., X_t) and one at time $t - k$ (i.e., X_{t-k}) after the effects of the intermediate observations (i.e., $X_{t-1}, X_{t-2} \ldots X_{t-k+1}$) have been removed. The value of a PACF is hence a conditional correlation in that the value of the coefficient between two observations is conditional to the values of the intermediate observations. As such, PACF cannot be computed in a clear manner through the application of a single equation, as in the case of an ACF. To begin with, the terms and forms of the equation will necessarily change as the lag is increased because more intermediate observations are involved. The exact process used to derive the equation for the computation of the PACF for each lag involves the estimation of two multiple linear regression equations. Specifically, in the first equation, the values of all the intermediate observations are used to predict X_{t-k}. The PACF is then the correlation between the errors of prediction in the two equations.

Because the estimation of the PACF for each lag requires two separate multiple linear regressions, the assessment of the prediction error for each observation for each regression, and the calculation of the correlation between the two sets of errors, it is a rather formidable task to estimate the lag-1 through lag-k PACF for a time series. With the easy access to computers today, PACFs are generally estimated through a computer. We discuss some of the computer software available for ARIMA analyses later.

Multiple linear regression is beyond the intended scope of this text. A proper treatment of the technique would require a substantial increase in the length of this chapter. Readers who wish to gain a more in-depth understanding of how PACFs are derived should consult more specialized texts on multiple linear regression, such as Cohen and Cohen (1983) or Pedhazur (1982). Basically, the mathematics of the three steps involved in estimating a lag-k PACF can be summarized as follows: First, the values of the intermediate observations X_{t-1} through X_{t-k+1} are used as predictors to derive two regression equations to predict X_t and X_{t-k}, respectively. If all scores are transformed to their respective z scores, the two resulting regression equations would have the forms:

$$z'_t = \beta_1 z_{t-1} + \beta_2 z_{t-2} + \cdots \cdots \beta_{k-1} z_{t-k+1} \qquad (9.11)$$

and

$$z'_{t-k} = \beta_1 z_{t-k+1} + \beta_2 z_{t-k+2} + \cdots \cdots \beta_{k-1} z_{t-1}, \qquad (9.12)$$

where z'_t and z'_{t-k} are the predicted or expected z values of the scores at time t and time $t - k$; z_{t-1}, z_{t-2}, and so on are the observed z scores for $t - 1$ through the point before $t - k$ (i.e., $t - k + 1$); the βs are the weights or regression coefficients associated with the predictors, analogous but not similar to the β in a simple linear regression discussed in the previous chapter. Note that the sequence of predictors is different between the two equations and the β estimates are necessarily different. From these two equations, the values of each pair of observations at times t and $t - k$ are predicted. These expected values are subtracted from the actual observed values, z_t and z_{t-k}, to obtain the errors in prediction. Thus, the prediction errors (e_t and e_{t-k}) are:

$$e_t = z_t - z'_t \tag{9.13}$$

and

$$e_{t-k} = z_{t-k} - z'_{t-k}. \tag{9.14}$$

The correlation coefficient for the two resulting sets of error estimates is the lag-k PACF.

An alternative approach to the computation of PACFs, which will yield results identical to those computed through the multiple linear regression procedures, is to derive PACFs from ACFs. Mathematically, using r_1 for a lag-1 ACF, r_2 for a lag-2 ACF, and r_3 for a lag-3 ACF, it can be shown that:

$$\text{Lag-1 PACF} = r_1, \tag{9.15}$$

$$\text{Lag-2 PACF} = \frac{r_2 - r_1^2}{1 - r_1^2}, \tag{9.16}$$

and

$$\text{Lag-3 PACF} = \frac{r_3 + r_1 r_2^2 + r_1^3 - 2r_1 r_2 - r_1^2 r_3}{1 + 2r_1^2 r_2 - r_2^2 - 2r_1^2}. \tag{9.17}$$

As can be seen, the derived equation for the estimation of PACF increases in complexity as the lag length increases. Therefore, although it is relatively simple to estimate the lag-1 through lag-k ACF for a time series, the estimation of lag-1 through lag-k PACF is an extremely tedious and time-consuming exercise.

ACF and PACF Correlograms

Recall that lag-1 through lag-k ACF can be graphically displayed as an ACF correlogram. Similarly, lag-1 through lag-k PACF can be displayed as a PACF correlogram. Together, the ACF and the PACF correlograms are useful tools to perform the initial identification of ARIMA models. Specifically, the distinct "signature" associated with each model manifests itself in distinct patterns in the ACF and the PACF correlograms. These patterns are inherent mathematical properties associated with each model and can be proven to be uniquely associated with that model. Box and Jenkins (1976), McDowall et al. (1980), and Vandaele (1983) provided the proofs for the patterns associated with some of the more commonly encountered models.

Standard Errors of ACF and PACF

Examination of the correlogram for the initial tentative model specification is by and large a judgmental process. This judgment, however, can be aided by knowledge of the significance of each ACF and PACF. In principle, the assessment of the statistical significance of an ACF and PACF is not different from that of most conventional inferential statistics. Specifically, based on the null assumption of a zero ACF, if the observed ACF is more than two (more exactly, 1.96) standard error units from a zero value in either direction (positive or negative), the ACF is said to be statistically significant with a less than 5% two-tailed probability of committing a Type I error. Similarly, if the observed PACF is more than two PACF standard error units from the null PACF, the observed PACF is significant at the .05 level.

As discussed in Chapter 8, the standard error of a lag-k ACF is estimated based on the values of lag-1 through lag-k ACF by (Bartlett, 1946):

$$se_k = \sqrt{\frac{1}{N} \left(1 + 2 \sum_{i=1}^{k} r_i^2\right)}$$

$$(9.18)$$

The standard error of a lag-k PACF is estimated by (Quenouille, 1949):

$$se_{kk} = 1/\sqrt{N}, \qquad (9.19)$$

where se_{kk} is the standard error of a lag-k PACF and N is the number of pairs of observations used to estimate the PACF.

Correlogram Patterns for Specific Models

The first step in model specification is to calculate the lag-1 through lag-k ACFs and PACFs of an observed set of time series data (i.e., a realization of the underlying stochastic process). The value of k is determined by the number of observations in the time series. As a general rule of thumb, if there are N observations in the series, k should not be higher than $N/4$ (Hartmann et al., 1980). The reason for this rule is that the higher the lag, the more unstable the estimated values of ACFs and PACFs. Consider for example the ACFs and PACFs for a time series with 72 observations. The lag-1 ACF and PACF are estimated based on 71 pairs of observations. This is because the 72nd observation in the series has no following observation to form a pair. Following the rule of thumb, the highest lag for which an ACF and a PACF are estimated is $N/4$ or lag-18. The estimation of the lag-18 ACF and PACF is not based on 71 pairs of observations, as in the case of the lag-1 ACF and PACF. Rather, there are only 54 pairs of observations. This is because after the first 54 observations in the series, the observations in the remainder of the series have no corresponding observation 18 points away to form a lag-18 pair. Thus, for this example, a lag-20 ACF (or PACF) is based on 52 pairs of observations, a lag-30 ACF is based on 42 pairs of observations, and a lag-50 ACF is based on 22 pairs of observations. The higher the lag order, the smaller the portion of the series is used, and hence the higher the sampling error. In most computer programs, the highest lag is defaulted to about 25 (based on the assumption that the series has at least 100 observations), unless a user specifies a higher order. For the convenience of discussion, the examples that follow show only lag-1 through lag-25 ACFs and PACFs.

After the ACFs and PACFs are computed, their respective patterns are examined. Each ARIMA model has its own unique ACF and PACF pattern. Based on the patterns of these autocorrelation functions, we can speculate a possible model for the data.

The White Noise Model ARIMA(0,0,0)

The simplest model is the white noise or random shock model expressed by ARIMA(0,0,0). The lag-1 through lag-k ACFs and PACFs are all very small, fluctuating around zero, and all are well within two standard errors of their respective null distributions. Because assessing the patterns of 25 ACF values and 25 PACF values (as well as their corresponding standard errors) can be quite confusing, the correlograms for the ACFs and the PACFs are generally drawn for an efficient visual inspection of the patterns.

For the purpose of illustration, we have simulated observational data through a computer based on an ARIMA (0,0,0) model. Figure 9.1a shows the ACF correlogram and Figure 9.1b, the PACF correlogram printout of this simulated time series using the Box–Jenkins routine in the computer package SPSSx. With these correlograms, the asteriks (*) indicate the magnitudes of the ACFs and PACFs. The dots (.) indicate the boundaries of ± 2 standard errors. As can be seen, all ACFs and PACFs are well within their corresponding standard error boundaries, showing that none of the ACFs and PACFs are statistically significant.

The nonexistence of significant ACF or PACF is a "signature" of an ARIMA(0,0,0) model. This implies that each observation point deviates

```
AUTOCORRELATION FUNCTION FOR VARIABLE X
AUTOCORRELATIONS *
TWO STANDARD ERROR LIMITS
     AUTO. STAND.
LAG  CORR.   ERR.  -1  -.75  -.5 -.25   0   .25  .5   .75    1
                   :----:----:----:----:----:----:----:----:
  1   0.154  0.098                    .    :   *.
  2  -0.060  0.098                    .   *:   .
  3  -0.059  0.097                    .   *:   .
  4   0.026  0.097                    .    :*  .
  5  -0.097  0.096                    . * :   .
  6  -0.110  0.095                    . * :   .
  7  -0.083  0.095                    . * :   .
  8  -0.115  0.094                    . * :   .
  9  -0.060  0.094                    .  *:   .
 10   0.053  0.093                    .   :*  .
 11  -0.024  0.093                    .   *   .
 12   0.009  0.092                    .   *   .
 13   0.104  0.092                    .   : * .
 14   0.134  0.091                    .   :  *.
 15  -0.053  0.091                    . *:    .
 16  -0.152  0.090                    .* :    .
 17  -0.035  0.090                    . *:    .
 18  -0.137  0.089                    .* :    .
 19  -0.024  0.089                    .   *   .
 20   0.155  0.088                    .   :  *.
 21  -0.060  0.087                    . *:    .
 22  -0.110  0.087                    .* :    .
 23   0.023  0.086                    .   *   .
 24   0.012  0.086                    .   *   .
 25  -0.069  0.085                    . *:    .
```

FIGURE 9.1a. ACF correlogram of simulated white noise series, ARIMA(0,0,0).

```
PARTIAL AUTOCORRELATION FUNCTION FOR VARIABLE X
PARTIAL AUTOCORRELATIONS *
TWO STANDARD ERROR LIMITS
     PR-AUT STAND.
LAG  CORR.   ERR.  -1  -.75  -.5 -.25   0   .25  .5   .75    1
                   :----:----:----:----:----:----:----:----:
  1   0.154  0.100                    .    :   *.
  2  -0.086  0.100                    . * :   .
  3  -0.037  0.100                    .  *:   .
  4   0.037  0.100                    .   :*  .
  5  -0.118  0.100                    . * :   .
  6  -0.077  0.100                    . * :   .
  7  -0.066  0.100                    . * :   .
  8  -0.125  0.100                    .* :    .
  9  -0.041  0.100                    .  *:   .
 10   0.040  0.100                    .   :*  .
 11  -0.081  0.100                    . * :   .
 12   0.011  0.100                    .   *   .
 13   0.074  0.100                    .   :*  .
 14   0.066  0.100                    .   :*  .
 15  -0.085  0.100                    . *:    .
 16  -0.137  0.100                    .* :    .
 17  -0.014  0.100                    .   *   .
 18  -0.167  0.100                    .* :    .
 19   0.029  0.100                    .   :*  .
 20   0.172  0.100                    .   :  *.
 21  -0.151  0.100                    .* :    .
 22  -0.069  0.100                    . *:    .
 23   0.011  0.100                    .   *   .
 24  -0.134  0.100                    .* :    .
 25  -0.068  0.100                    . *:    .
```

FIGURE 9.1b. PACF correlogram of simulated white noise series, ARIMA(0,0,0).

from the mean at random. Figure 9.2 shows the actual simulated time series. As shown, the observations fluctuate widely around the mean and there is no discernible pattern.

Differencing Model ARIMA(0,d,0)

For an ARIMA(0,1,0) model, the lag-1 ACF and the lag-1 PACF are both expected to be very high in magnitude (near $+1.00$ or -1.00). The higher lag ACFs are expected to remain high for a considerable number of lags as the lag order increases. In other words, the ACFs for an ARIMA(0,1,0) are unlikely to become insignificant within a few lags. Starting from lag-2, higher lag PACFs for an ARIMA(0,1,0) model, however, are expected to be insignificant. In other words, the expected pattern of PACFs is one in which the lag-1 PACF is very high and immediately becomes insignificant at lag-2 and beyond. Figures 9.3a and 9.3b show the ACF and PACF correlograms, respectively, for a set of computer-simulated ARIMA(0,1,0) data.

An ARIMA(0,1,0) model indicates the existence of nonstationarity within the time series. Using our earlier analogy, the time series contains effects of a "dynamic trend" or "momentum." With a dynamic trend of unknown magnitude, it is difficult to assess if a static trend also exists; and, if so, what would be the best model to describe the static trend (i.e., autoregressive or moving average parameters). Figure 9.4 shows the raw simulated time series. A dynamic trend is clearly evidenced. The forms of the ACF and PACF correlograms indicate that the observed trend is at least partially due to a dynamic force.

Because the appropriateness of subsequent estimates of autoregressive and moving average parameters will be confounded by the existence of nonstationarity (or dynamic trend) when the pattern in Figures 9.3a and Figure 9.3b is found, the data should be transformed through a differencing procedure prior to further analyses. Recall that a differencing procedure involves subtracting X_{t-1} from X_t. The ACF and PACF correlograms for the transformed series is then examined. If the patterns still resemble those of Figures 9.3a and 9.3b, a need for a higher order differencing is indicated. We can repeat the differencing procedure until the ACF correlogram no longer shows a slow decaying pattern. We then inspect the ACF and PACF correlograms of the final differenced series to identify possible autoregressive or moving average patterns as evidence of a static trend as well. If the ACF and PACF correlograms of the final differenced series indicate that the transformed series is a random shock model, ARIMA(0,0,0), the only parameter involved in the series is then the differencing parameter. That is, the only 'forces" at work are random shocks and a dynamic trend. The appropriate model is thus ARIMA(0,d,0), where d is the number of times the differencing operation is repeated.

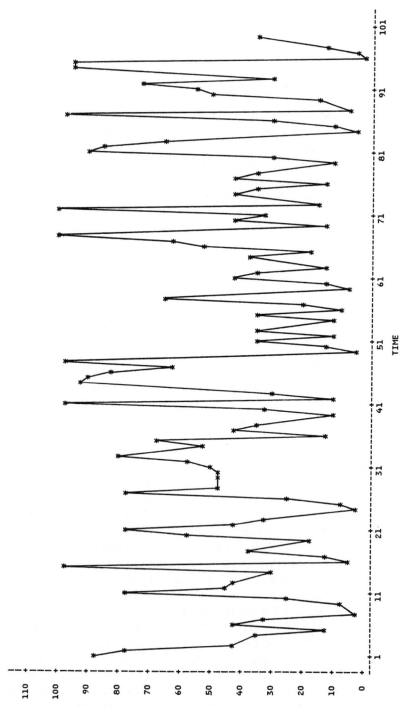

FIGURE 9.2.   Raw data of simulated ARIMA(0,0,0) series.

```
AUTOCORRELATION FUNCTION FOR VARIABLE X
AUTOCORRELATIONS *
TWO STANDARD ERROR LIMITS
     AUTO. STAND.
LAG  CORR.  ERR.  -1  -.75  -.5 -.25    0    .25  .5   .75   1
                  :----:----:----:----:----:----:----:----:
  1  0.969  0.098                  .    :    .                   *
  2  0.939  0.098                  .    :    .                  *
  3  0.907  0.097                  .    :    .                *
  4  0.877  0.097                  .    :    .               *
  5  0.846  0.096                  .    :    .              *
  6  0.817  0.095                  .    :    .            *
  7  0.788  0.095                  .    :    .           *
  8  0.759  0.094                  .    :    .          *
  9  0.731  0.094                  .    :    .         *
 10  0.703  0.093                  .    :    .        *
 11  0.674  0.093                  .    :    .       *
 12  0.645  0.092                  .    :    .       *
 13  0.616  0.092                  .    :    .      *
 14  0.588  0.091                  .    :    .     *
 15  0.560  0.091                  .    :    .    *
 16  0.531  0.090                  .    :    .    *
 17  0.503  0.090                  .    :    .   *
 18  0.475  0.089                  .    :    .   *
 19  0.448  0.089                  .    :    .  *
 20  0.420  0.088                  .    :    . *
 21  0.393  0.087                 .    :    . *
 22  0.365  0.087                 .    :    .*
 23  0.338  0.086                 .    :    .*
 24  0.311  0.086                 .    :   .*
 25  0.284  0.085                 .    :   .*
```

FIGURE 9.3a. ACF correlogram of simulated ARIMA(0,1,0) series.

```
PARTIAL AUTOCORRELATION FUNCTION FOR VARIABLE X
PARTIAL AUTOCORRELATIONS *
TWO STANDARD ERROR LIMITS
     PR-AUT STAND.
LAG  CORR.  ERR.  -1  -.75  -.5 -.25    0    .25  .5   .75   1
                  :----:----:----:----:----:----:----:----:
  1  0.969  0.100                  .    :    .                   *
  2 -0.013  0.100                  .    *    .
  3 -0.025  0.100                  .    *    .
  4 -0.007  0.100                  .    *    .
  5 -0.015  0.100                  .    *    .
  6 -0.000  0.100                  .    *    .
  7 -0.009  0.100                  .    *    .
  8 -0.014  0.100                  .    *    .
  9  0.002  0.100                  .    *    .
 10 -0.017  0.100                  .    *    .
 11 -0.029  0.100                  .   *:    .
 12 -0.024  0.100                  .    *    .
 13 -0.011  0.100                  .    *    .
 14 -0.014  0.100                  .    *    .
 15 -0.012  0.100                  .    *    .
 16 -0.022  0.100                  .    *    .
 17 -0.013  0.100                  .    *    .
 18 -0.015  0.100                  .    *    .
 19 -0.014  0.100                  .    *    .
 20 -0.024  0.100                  .    *    .
 21 -0.005  0.100                  .    *    .
 22 -0.022  0.100                  .    *    .
 23 -0.029  0.100                  .   *:    .
 24 -0.002  0.100                  .    *    .
 25 -0.023  0.100                  .    *    .
```

FIGURE 9.3b. PACF correlgoram of simulated ARIMA(0,1,0) series.

235

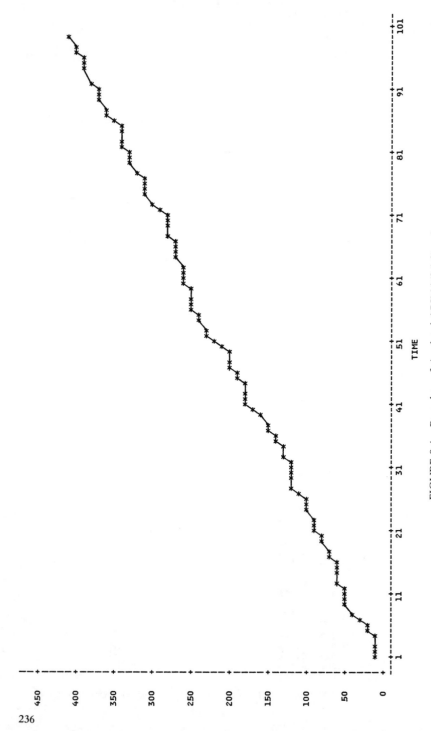

FIGURE 9.4. Raw data of simulated ARIMA(0,1,0) series.

Note that when a static trend also exists, the PACF correlogram may not change even if the series has been sufficiently differenced. Therefore, the need for additional differencing should depend on the form of the ACF correlogram of the transformed series only. Figure 9.5 shows the ACF correlogram of the same simulated ARIMA(0,1,0) series after the data have been transformed through one differencing. Note that all ACFs have become insignificant, indicating that the transformed series consists of only random shocks. This is further supported by an examination of the transformed series. Figure 9.6 shows the same simulated data for the ARIMA(0,1,0) model after they have been transformed through one differencing. All observations fluctuate randomly and widely around the mean. Hence, there is sufficient evidence to specify tentatively the original series as an ARIMA(0,1,0) model with no other parameters involved.

To illustrate an ARIMA(0,2,0) model, another set of data is simulated. At first glance, an ARIMA(0,2,0) or any ARIMA(0,d,0) series is indistinguishable from an ARIMA(0,1,0) series. The patterns of the ACF and PACF correlograms are similar to those of an ARIMA(0,1,0) series, and the raw data appear to be similar. Figures 9.7a and 9.7b show the ACF and PACF correlograms of the simulated ARIMA(0,2,0) series. Note that

```
AUTOCORRELATION FUNCTION FOR VARIABLE X
AUTOCORRELATIONS *
TWO STANDARD ERROR LIMITS
        AUTO.  STAND.
LAG    CORR.   ERR.  -1  -.75  -.5 -.25   0   .25  .5   .75    1
                            :----:----:----:----:----:----:----:----:
  1   0.149   0.098                       .    * .
  2  -0.011   0.098                       .    *
  3  -0.075   0.097                       . *:   .
  4  -0.006   0.097                       .    *
  5  -0.116   0.096                       . * .   .
  6  -0.071   0.096                       . *:   .
  7  -0.071   0.095                       . *:   .
  8  -0.181   0.095                       *    :   .
  9  -0.051   0.094                       . *:   .
 10   0.082   0.094                       .   : * .
 11   0.032   0.093                       .   :*  .
 12  -0.025   0.093                       . *:   .
 13   0.100   0.092                       .   : * .
 14   0.107   0.092                       .   : * .
 15   0.010   0.091                       .    *
 16  -0.148   0.091                       .* :   .
 17  -0.035   0.090                       . *:   .
 18  -0.159   0.089                       .* :   .
 19  -0.030   0.089                       . *:   .
 20   0.182   0.088                       .   :  .    *
 21  -0.055   0.088                       . *:   .
 22  -0.104   0.087                       .* :   .
 23  -0.030   0.087                       . *:   .
 24  -0.016   0.086                       .    *  .
 25  -0.092   0.085                       .* :   .
```

FIGURE 9.5.   ACF correlogram of simulated ARIMA(0,1,0) series after one-degree differencing transformation.

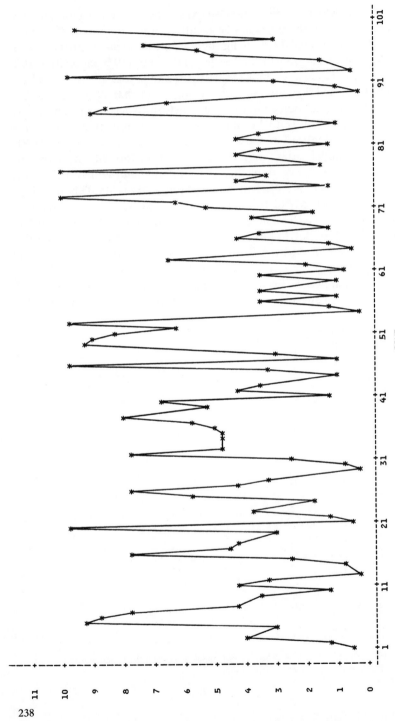

FIGURE 9.6. Transformed data of simulated ARIMA(0,1,0) series after one-degree differencing transformation.

```
AUTOCORRELATION FUNCTION FOR VARIABLE X
AUTOCORRELATIONS *
TWO STANDARD ERROR LIMITS
      AUTO. STAND.
LAG   CORR.  ERR.  -1   -.75  -.5  -.25   0   .25   .5   .75   1
                   :----:----:----:----:----:----:----:----:
  1   0.967  0.098                    .   :    .                *
  2   0.934  0.098                    .   :    .                *
  3   0.901  0.097                    .   :    .              *
  4   0.869  0.097                    .   :    .             *
  5   0.836  0.096                    .   :    .            *
  6   0.804  0.095                    .   :    .           *
  7   0.772  0.095                    .   :    .          *
  8   0.740  0.094                    .   :    .         *
  9   0.708  0.094                    .   :    .        *
 10   0.677  0.093                    .   :    .       *
 11   0.645  0.093                    .   :    .      *
 12   0.614  0.092                    .   :    .     *
 13   0.584  0.092                    .   :    .     *
 14   0.553  0.091                    .   :    .    *
 15   0.523  0.091                    .   :    .   *
 16   0.493  0.090                    .   :    .   *
 17   0.464  0.090                    .   :    .  *
 18   0.435  0.089                    .   :    .  *
 19   0.406  0.089                    .   :    . *
 20   0.378  0.088                    .   :    .*
 21   0.350  0.087                  .   :    . *
 22   0.323  0.087                  .   :    .*
 23   0.296  0.086                  .   :   .*
 24   0.270  0.086                  .   :   . *
 25   0.244  0.085                  .   :   . *
```

FIGURE 9.7a.   ACF correlogram of simulated ARIMA(0,2,0) series.

```
PARTIAL AUTOCORRELATION FUNCTION FOR VARIABLE X
PARTIAL AUTOCORRELATIONS *
TWO STANDARD ERROR LIMITS
      PR-AUT STAND.
LAG   CORR.   ERR.  -1   -.75  -.5  -.25   0   .25   .5   .75   1
                    :----:----:----:----:----:----:----:----:
  1   0.967   0.100                   .   :    .                *
  2  -0.015   0.100                   .   *    .
  3  -0.015   0.100                   .   *    .
  4  -0.015   0.100                   .   *    .
  5  -0.015   0.100                   .   *    .
  6  -0.015   0.100                   .   *    .
  7  -0.015   0.100                   .   *    .
  8  -0.015   0.100                   .   *    .
  9  -0.015   0.100                   .   *    .
 10  -0.015   0.100                   .   *    .
 11  -0.015   0.100                   .   *    .
 12  -0.015   0.100                   .   *    .
 13  -0.015   0.100                   .   *    .
 14  -0.015   0.100                   .   *    .
 15  -0.015   0.100                   .   *    .
 16  -0.014   0.100                   .   *    .
 17  -0.014   0.100                   .   *    .
 18  -0.014   0.100                   .   *    .
 19  -0.014   0.100                   .   *    .
 20  -0.014   0.100                   .   *    .
 21  -0.014   0.100                   .   *    .
 22  -0.014   0.100                   .   *    .
 23  -0.014   0.100                   .   *    .
 24  -0.014   0.100                   .   *    .
 25  -0.014   0.100                   .   *    .
```

FIGURE 9.7b.   PACF correlogram of simulated ARIMA(0,2,0) series.

239

the ACFs show the same high initial ACF value with a very slow decaying pattern for higher lag ACFs, as those of an ARIMA(0,1,0) series.

Similarly, an inspection of the raw ARIMA(0,2,0) series reveals the same general dynamic trend as that of the ARIMA(0,1,0) series. Figure 9.8 shows the raw ARIMA(0,2,0) series. Note that it is quite similar to the ARIMA(0,1,0) series in Figure 9.4.

The detection of a higher than first-order ARIMA(0,d,0) series is dependent on the evidence after differencing. With a higher order ARIMA(0,d,0) series, the pattern of the ACF correlogram persists until the proper number of differencing transformations has been completed. Then the ACF correlogram changes into either a random shock model, an autoregressive model, a moving average model, or a combination of the latter two models. Figure 9.9 shows the ACF correlogram of the simulated ARIMA(0,2,0) after one differencing transformation. Note that the correlogram shows the same slow decaying pattern. Figure 9.10 shows the corresponding transformed series data. Again, it shows a dynamic trend similar to the original raw series. Therefore, the need for additional differencing transformations is evidenced.

Figure 9.11 shows the correlogram of the ARIMA(0,2,0) series after a second differencing transformation is made. Note that all ACFs have become insignificant, indicating that the transformed series is a random shock or white noise model. Figure 9.12 shows the series data after two differencing transformations. All transformed observations fluctuate randomly and widely around the mean, giving additional evidence that the transformed series consists of only white noise.

Autoregressive Model ARIMA(p,0,0)

Theoretically, with an ARIMA(p,0,0) model, the lag-1 ACF is expected to be nonzero and the magnitude of this ACF is a function of the ϕ coefficients of the actual model. The higher the value of the ϕ coefficients, the higher the lag-1 ACF. The ACFs of subsequent lags are expected to decay at a moderate rate and become insignificant after a few lags. The PACFs of an ARIMA(p,0,0) model should show only a nonzero PACF at a number of lags corresponding to the order of the model (i.e., the value of p). After the lag corresponding to p, the PACFs become zero. For example, for an ARIMA(1,0,0) model, the lag-1 ACF should be nonzero and the magnitudes of ACFs for subsequent lags should decay gradually at a moderate rate and become zero after a few lags. For the same model, however, only lag-1 PACF should be nonzero. The PACFs for all other lags should be zero. For an ARIMA(2,0,0) model, the pattern of ACFs is not too different from that for an ARIMA(1,0,0) model. The PACFs should show nonzero PACFs at the first two lags and become zero from lag-3 on.

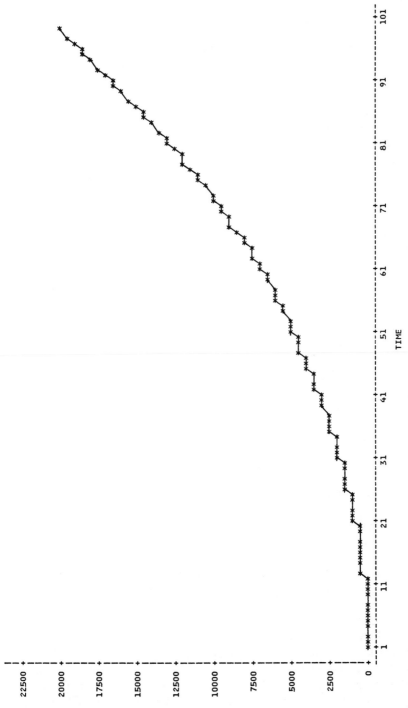

FIGURE 9.8. Raw data of simulated ARIMA(0,2,0) series.

```
AUTOCORRELATION FUNCTION FOR VARIABLE X
AUTOCORRELATIONS *
TWO STANDARD ERROR LIMITS
     AUTO. STAND.
LAG  CORR.   ERR. -1  -.75  -.5 -.25   0   .25  .5   .75   1
                  :----:----:----:----:----:----:----:----:
  1  0.970  0.098                 .    :   .              *
  2  0.939  0.098                 .    :   .              *
  3  0.907  0.097                 .    :   .             *
  4  0.876  0.097                 .    :   .             *
  5  0.846  0.096                 .    :   .            *
  6  0.816  0.096                 .    :   .           *
  7  0.786  0.095                 .    :   .           *
  8  0.755  0.095                 .    :   .          *
  9  0.725  0.094                 .    :   .        *
 10  0.695  0.094                 .    :   .        *
 11  0.665  0.093                 .    :   .       *
 12  0.635  0.093                 .    :   .       *
 13  0.605  0.092                 .    :   .      *
 14  0.575  0.092                 .    :   .     *
 15  0.545  0.091                 .    :   .     *
 16  0.515  0.091                 .    :   .    *
 17  0.485  0.090                 .    :   .    *
 18  0.457  0.089                 .    :   .   *
 19  0.429  0.089                 .    :   .   *
 20  0.401  0.088                 .    :   .  *
 21  0.373  0.088                 .    :   . *
 22  0.346  0.087                 .    :   . *
 23  0.319  0.087                 .    :  . *
 24  0.292  0.086                 .    :  .*
 25  0.266  0.085                 .    :  .*
```

FIGURE 9.9.   ACF correlogram of simulated ARIMA(0,2,0) series after one-degree differencing transformation.

These are the theoretical "signatures." In practice, because of white noise, the signatures of different-order autoregressive models are not always clearly discernible from empirical data. This is because the single tell-tale indicator of the order of a model is the number of lags with non-zero PACFs. The magnitudes of those PACFs beyond lag-1, although non-zero, are typically very small. Frequently, these small observed magnitudes render them indistinguishable from zero, or are, at least, judged as statistically insignificant. Nevertheless, the general signatures for an ARIMA(p,0,0) model are distinct. The area of uncertainty is whether the correct order is identified.

Figures 9.13a and 9.13b show the ACF and PACF correlogram patterns for a simulated ARIMA(1,0,0) series with a ϕ_1 value of .9. Note that in Figures 9.13a and 9.13b the ACFs remain significant for some time, but the PACFs become insignificant immediately at lag-2. This shows a clear signature of an ARIMA(1,0,0) series.

An ARIMA(2,0,0) series was also simulated using a ϕ_1 of .9 and a ϕ_2 of .01. Figures 9.14a and 9.14b show the correlograms of this simulated series. The ACFs show the same gradually decaying pattern. For the PACF correlogram, however, only lag-1 PACF is clearly significant. The lag-2 PACF is right at the point of two standard errors, giving hint of a possible second-order autoregressive series. The lag-2 PACF of an

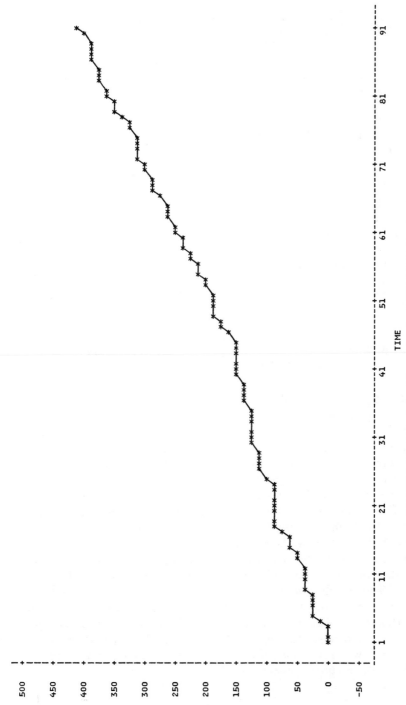

FIGURE 9.10. Transformed data of simulated ARIMA(0,2,0) series after one-degree differencing transformation.

```
AUTOCORRELATION FUNCTION FOR VARIABLE X
AUTOCORRELATIONS *
TWO STANDARD ERROR LIMITS
        AUTO. STAND.
LAG   CORR.    ERR.  -1   -.75  -.5 -.25   0   .25  .5   .75   1
                     :----:----:----:----:----:----:----:----:
  1   0.145   0.099                       .    :  *.
  2  -0.077   0.098                       . *  :    .
  3  -0.079   0.098                       . *  :    .
  4   0.168   0.097                       .    :  *.
  5   0.047   0.097                       .    :*   .
  6   0.021   0.096                       .    *    .
  7  -0.064   0.096                       .  *: .
  8   0.023   0.095                       .    *    .
  9   0.070   0.095                       .    :*   .
 10   0.093   0.094                       .    : *  .
 11   0.070   0.094                       .    :*   .
 12   0.129   0.093                       .    :  *.
 13   0.164   0.093                       .    :  *.
 14   0.119   0.092                       .    : *  .
 15  -0.171   0.091                       .*   :    .
 16  -0.022   0.091                       .    *    .
 17  -0.002   0.090                       .    *    .
 18   0.064   0.090                       .    :*   .
 19   0.013   0.089                       .    *    .
 20   0.052   0.089                       .    :*   .
 21   0.042   0.088                       .    :*   .
 22  -0.095   0.087                       .*   :    .
 23   0.036   0.087                       .    :*   .
 24  -0.039   0.086                       .  *: .
 25  -0.048   0.086                       .  *: .
```

FIGURE 9.11.   ACF correlogram of simulated ARIMA(0,2,0) series after two-degree differencing transformation.

ARIMA(2,0,0) is expected to be small in magnitude and, for a given ϕ_1, is a function of the value of ϕ_2.

A visual inspection of a raw ARIMA(p,0,0) series will not reveal any dynamic trend. Nor will the series resemble a random shock series. Figure 9.15 shows the raw data of the simulated ARIMA(2,0,0) series. Except for the first few observations, the remainder of the series shows no clearly discernible trend. Nor does the series resemble that of a white noise model (i.e., Figure 9.2). With a white noise model, the observations fluctuate widely from one extreme to the other along the time dimension. With an ARIMA(p,0,0) series, the points do not fluctuate extremely. This is because each point is influenced by its preceding points. Consequently, the preceding points would tend to have a moderating effect on each observation. The overall series is hence "smoothed" because of this moderating effect or inertia. This lack of exteme fluctuations is a sign of the underlying static force and is indicative of either an autoregressive model, a moving average model, or a combined model. This smoothed pattern of raw data when combined with the ACF and PACF signatures provide evidence of an autoregressive model.

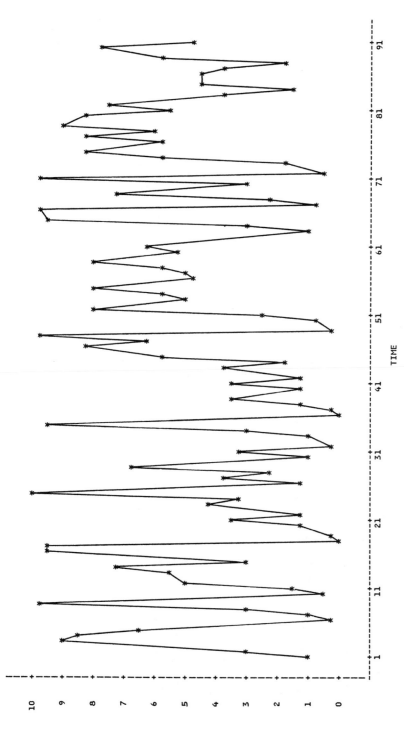

FIGURE 9.12. Transformed data of simulated ARIMA(0,2,0) series after two-degree differencing transformation.

```
AUTOCORRELATION FUNCTION FOR VARIABLE X
AUTOCORRELATIONS *
TWO STANDARD ERROR LIMITS
        AUTO. STAND.
LAG  CORR.    ERR.  -1  -.75  -.5 -.25   0   .25  .5   .75   1
                     :----:----:----:----:----:----:----:----:
  1   0.886   0.098               .    :   .                *
  2   0.782   0.098               .    :   .            *
  3   0.695   0.097               .    :   .         *
  4   0.621   0.097               .    :   .       *
  5   0.537   0.096               .    :   .     *
  6   0.473   0.095               .    :   .   *
  7   0.422   0.095               .    :   .  *
  8   0.368   0.094               .    :   . *
  9   0.315   0.094               .    :   .*
 10   0.266   0.093               .    :   .*
 11   0.231   0.093               .    :   .*
 12   0.204   0.092               .    :  *
 13   0.178   0.092               .    :  *
 14   0.137   0.091               .    :  *.
 15   0.108   0.091               .    : * .
 16   0.069   0.090               .    :*  .
 17   0.036   0.090               .    :*  .
 18   0.007   0.089               .    *   .
 19  -0.017   0.089               .    *   .
 20  -0.032   0.088               .   *:   .
 21  -0.048   0.087               .  *:    .
 22  -0.056   0.087               .  *:    .
 23  -0.054   0.086               .  *:    .
 24  -0.074   0.086               .  *:    .
 25  -0.112   0.085               . *  :   .
```

FIGURE 9.13a.   ACF correlogram of simulated ARIMA(1,0,0) series with $\phi_1 = .9$.

```
PARTIAL AUTOCORRELATION FUNCTION FOR VARIABLE X
PARTIAL AUTOCORRELATIONS *
TWO STANDARD ERROR LIMITS
        PR-AUT STAND.
LAG  CORR.    ERR.  -1  -.75  -.5 -.25   0   .25  .5   .75   1
                     :----:----:----:----:----:----:----:----:
  1   0.886   0.100               .    :   .                *
  2  -0.018   0.100               .    *   .
  3   0.025   0.100               .    *   .
  4   0.015   0.100               .    *   .
  5  -0.079   0.100               . *  :   .
  6   0.039   0.100               .    :*  .
  7   0.025   0.100               .    :*  .
  8  -0.046   0.100               .   *:   .
  9  -0.011   0.100               .    *   .
 10  -0.027   0.100               .   *:   .
 11   0.030   0.100               .    :*  .
 12   0.021   0.100               .    *   .
 13  -0.007   0.100               .    *   .
 14  -0.086   0.100               . *  :   .
 15   0.021   0.100               .    *   .
 16  -0.074   0.100               .   *:   .
 17   0.000   0.100               .    *   .
 18  -0.007   0.100               .    *   .
 19  -0.020   0.100               .    *   .
 20   0.028   0.100               .    :*  .
 21  -0.024   0.100               .    *   .
 22   0.019   0.100               .    *   .
 23   0.041   0.100               .    :*  .
 24  -0.119   0.100               . *  :   .
 25  -0.100   0.100               . *  :   .
```

FIGURE 9.13b.   PACF correlogram of simulated ARIMA(1,0,0) series with $\phi_1 = .9$.

```
AUTOCORRELATION FUNCTION FOR VARIABLE X
AUTOCORRELATIONS *
TWO STANDARD ERROR LIMITS
     AUTO. STAND.
LAG  CORR.   ERR.  -1  -.75  -.5 -.25   0   .25  .5   .75   1
                   :----:----:----:----:----:----:----:----:
 1   0.896  0.098                    .   :   .               *
 2   0.763  0.098                    .   :   .           *
 3   0.645  0.097                    .   :   .        *
 4   0.540  0.097                    .   :   .     *
 5   0.420  0.096                    .   :   .  *
 6   0.320  0.095                    .   :   . *
 7   0.244  0.095                    .   :  .*
 8   0.160  0.094                    .   : *.
 9   0.078  0.094                    .   : * .
10   0.030  0.093                    .   :* .
11  -0.003  0.093                    .   *  .
12  -0.009  0.092                    .   *  .
13   0.003  0.092                    .   *  .
14   0.023  0.091                    .   *  .
15   0.032  0.091                    .   :* .
16   0.046  0.090                    .   :* .
17   0.074  0.090                    .   :* .
18   0.097  0.089                    .   : *.
19   0.128  0.089                    .   : *.
20   0.152  0.088                    .   : *.
21   0.158  0.087                    .  :   *
22   0.147  0.087                    .  :   *
23   0.139  0.086                    .  :   *
24   0.132  0.086                    .  :   *
25   0.112  0.085                    .  : *.
```

FIGURE 9.14a.   ACF correlogram of simulated ARIMA(2,0,0) series with $\phi_1 = .9$ and $\phi_2 = .01$.

```
PARTIAL AUTOCORRELATION FUNCTION FOR VARIABLE X
PARTIAL AUTOCORRELATIONS *
TWO STANDARD ERROR LIMITS
     PR-AUT STAND.
LAG  CORR.   ERR.  -1  -.75  -.5 -.25   0   .25  .5   .75   1
                   :----:----:----:----:----:----:----:----:
 1   0.896  0.100                    .   :   .               *
 2  -0.198  0.100                  * :   .
 3   0.019  0.100                    . *    .
 4  -0.025  0.100                    . *:   .
 5  -0.158  0.100                    .*  :   .
 6   0.056  0.100                    .   :*  .
 7   0.006  0.100                    .   *   .
 8  -0.131  0.100                    .*  :   .
 9  -0.013  0.100                    .   *   .
10   0.082  0.100                    .   : * .
11  -0.037  0.100                    . *:   .
12   0.130  0.100                    .   : *.
13   0.038  0.100                    .   :* .
14  -0.011  0.100                    .   *  .
15  -0.030  0.100                    . *:   .
16   0.047  0.100                    .   :* .
17   0.050  0.100                    .   :* .
18  -0.016  0.100                    .   *  .
19   0.108  0.100                    .   : * .
20  -0.055  0.100                    . *:   .
21  -0.046  0.100                    . *:   .
22   0.003  0.100                    .   *  .
23   0.033  0.100                    .   :* .
24  -0.008  0.100                    .   *  .
25  -0.023  0.100                    .   *  .
```

FIGURE 9.14b.   PACF correlogram of simulated ARIMA(2,0,0) series with $\phi_1 = .9$ and $\phi_2 = .01$.

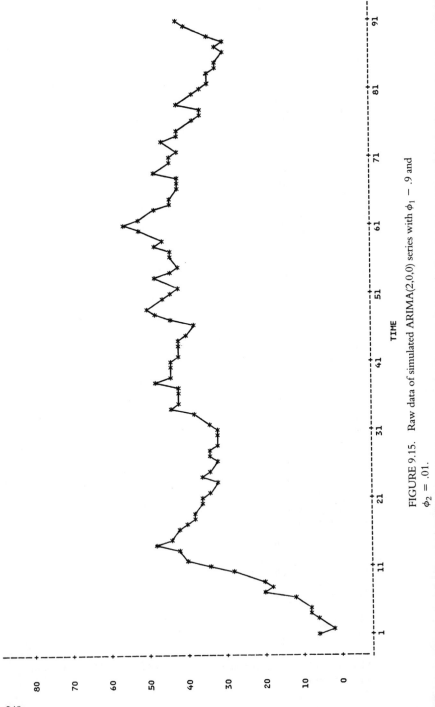

FIGURE 9.15. Raw data of simulated ARIMA(2,0,0) series with $\phi_1 - .9$ and $\phi_2 = .01$.

Moving Average Model ARIMA(0,0,q)

The theoretical ACF and PACF signatures of an ARIMA(0,0,q) series are opposite to those of an ARIMA(p,0,0) series. Specifically, the ACFs are expected to decay rapidly, and the number of significant lags corresponds to the order of the moving average parameter. Hence, for an ARIMA(0,0,1) series, only the lag-1 ACF is expected to be significantly different from zero. For an ARIMA(0,0,2) series, only the lag-1 and lag-2 ACFs are expected to be significant. The PACFs of an ARIMA(0,0,q) series are expected to have a moderate lag-1 PACF, and the PACFs of subsequent lags are expected to decay gradually. Unlike the ARIMA(p,0,0) model, the order of an ARIMA(0,0,q) model is easier to detect. This is because the ACFs are expected to be zero only at lags larger than q. All ACFs with lags less than or equal to q are expected to be significantly different from zero. Hence, the number of significant lags in the ACF would serve as a good indicator of the order of the moving average parameter, q.

Figures 9.16a and 9.16b show the correlograms of a simulated ARIMA(0,1,0) series with a θ_1 value of $-.9$. As can be seen, the lag-1 ACF is significant, and the ACFs after lag-2 are all insignificant, except for the 15th and 16th lags. These two latter significant lags are called spikes.

```
AUTOCORRELATION FUNCTION FOR VARIABLE X
AUTOCORRELATIONS *
TWO STANDARD ERROR LIMITS
      AUTO. STAND.
LAG   CORR.   ERR.  -1  -.75  -.5 -.25   0  .25  .5  .75   1
                     :----:----:----:----:----:----:----:----:
  1   0.516  0.098              .    :    .    *
  2  -0.023  0.098              .    *    .
  3  -0.051  0.097              .   *:    .
  4  -0.003  0.097              .    *    .
  5  -0.055  0.096              .   *:    .
  6  -0.076  0.095              .  * :    .
  7  -0.093  0.095              .  * :    .
  8  -0.116  0.094              .  * :    .
  9  -0.029  0.094              .   *:    .
 10   0.037  0.093              .    :*   .
 11  -0.002  0.093              .    *    .
 12   0.006  0.092              .    *    .
 13   0.070  0.092              .    :*   .
 14  -0.047  0.091              .   *:    .
 15  -0.236  0.091           *. .    :    .
 16  -0.247  0.090           *. .    :    .
 17  -0.172  0.090             .* :    .
 18  -0.125  0.089              . * :    .
 19  -0.006  0.089              .    *    .
 20   0.107  0.088              .    : *  .
 21   0.068  0.087              .    :*  .
 22   0.060  0.087              .    :*  .
 23   0.086  0.086              .    : *.
 24  -0.016  0.086              .    *   .
 25  -0.059  0.085              . *:    .
```

FIGURE 9.16a.   ACF correlogram of simulated ARIMA(0,0,1) series with $\theta_1 = -.9$.

```
PARTIAL AUTOCORRELATION FUNCTION FOR VARIABLE X
PARTIAL AUTOCORRELATIONS *
TWO STANDARD ERROR LIMITS
    PR-AUT STAND.
LAG  CORR.    ERR.  -1  -.75  -.5 -.25   0   .25  .5  .75   1
                       :----:----:----:----:----:----:----:----:
  1  0.516   0.100                  .    :   .        *
  2 -0.394   0.100           *      .    :   .
  3  0.272   0.100                  .    :   .*
  4 -0.201   0.100                  *    :   .
  5  0.046   0.100                  .    :*  .
  6 -0.065   0.100                  .   *:   .
  7 -0.078   0.100                  .  * :   .
  8 -0.041   0.100                  .   *:   .
  9  0.087   0.100                  .    : * .
 10 -0.073   0.100                  .   *:   .
 11  0.017   0.100                  .    *   .
 12  0.039   0.100                  .    :*  .
 13  0.024   0.100                  .    *   .
 14 -0.211   0.100                  *    :   .
 15 -0.098   0.100                  . *  :   .
 16 -0.108   0.100                  . *  :   .
 17 -0.087   0.100                  . *  :   .
 18 -0.042   0.100                  .   *:   .
 19  0.098   0.100                  .    : * .
 20  0.004   0.100                  .    *   .
 21 -0.026   0.100                  .   *:   .
 22  0.066   0.100                  .    :*  .
 23 -0.085   0.100                  . *  :   .
 24 -0.102   0.100                  . *  :   .
 25  0.063   0.100                  .    :*  .
```

FIGURE 9.16b.   PACF correlogram of simulated ARIMA(0,0,1) series with $\theta_1 = -.9$.

Spikes may be due to seasonality or chance. In this example, since the data were simulated without a seasonality component, we know that the spikes are due to chance. However, in practice, we cannot be certain. In this case, we may tentatively specify the model as an ARIMA(0,0,1) model and assess the goodness-of-fit later in the diagnostic stage of the analysis. In Figure 9.16b, the PACFs decay gradually and become insignificant after lag-4. This serves as additional evidence of an ARIMA(0,0,1) model.

Figures 9.17a and 9.17b show the correlograms of a simulated ARIMA(0,0,2) series with a θ_1 of $-.9$ and a θ_2 of $-.5$. The moderate decaying pattern of the PACFs combined with the rapid decay of ACFs suggest an ARIMA(0,0,q) model. The two significant ACFs at lag-1 and lag-2 suggest a second-order moving average series.

A raw ARIMA(0,0,q) series is not as clearly distinguishable from a white noise series as an ARIMA(p,0,0) series. This is because the moderating effects of the preceding observations are not as strong as those of an autoregressive series. Figure 9.18 shows the raw data of the simulated ARIMA(0,0,2) series. The observations fluctuate more extremely than those of an ARIMA(p,0,0) series but not as extremely as those of a white noise series.

```
AUTOCORRELATION FUNCTION FOR VARIABLE X
AUTOCORRELATIONS *
TWO STANDARD ERROR LIMITS
      AUTO. STAND.
LAG   CORR.   ERR.  -1  -.75  -.5 -.25   0   .25  .5   .75   1
                      :----:----:----:----:----:----:----:----:
  1   0.709  0.098                      .    :    .              *
  2   0.233  0.098                      .    :    .*
  3  -0.036  0.097                      .   *:    .
  4  -0.068  0.097                      .   *:    .
  5  -0.034  0.096                      .   *:    .
  6  -0.023  0.095                      .    *    .
  7  -0.016  0.095                      .    *    .
  8   0.020  0.094                      .    *    .
  9   0.102  0.094                      .    :  * .
 10   0.156  0.093                      .    :   *.
 11   0.111  0.093                      .    :  * .
 12   0.009  0.092                      .    *    .
 13  -0.061  0.092                      .   *:    .
 14  -0.101  0.091                      .  * :    .
 15  -0.173  0.091                      . *  :    .
 16  -0.208  0.090                      *    :    .
 17  -0.112  0.090                      .  * :    .
 18  -0.007  0.089                      .    *    .
 19  -0.045  0.089                      .   *:    .
 20  -0.185  0.088                      *    :    .
 21  -0.268  0.087                    * .    :    .
 22  -0.232  0.087                    * .    :    .
 23  -0.135  0.086                      *    :    .
 24  -0.072  0.086                      .   *:    .
 25  -0.090  0.085                      .  * :    .
```

FIGURE 9.17a. ACF correlogram of simulated ARIMA(0,0,2) series with $\theta_1 = -.9$ and $\theta_2 = -.5$.

```
PARTIAL AUTOCORRELATION FUNCTION FOR VARIABLE X
PARTIAL AUTOCORRELATIONS *
TWO STANDARD ERROR LIMITS
      PR-AUT STAND.
LAG   CORR.   ERR.  -1  -.75  -.5 -.25   0   .25  .5   .75   1
                      :----:----:----:----:----:----:----:----:
  1   0.709  0.100                      .    :    .              *
  2  -0.543  0.100            *         .    :    .
  3   0.270  0.100                      .    :    .*
  4  -0.059  0.100                      .   *:    .
  5  -0.058  0.100                      .   *:    .
  6   0.029  0.100                      .    :*   .
  7   0.016  0.100                      .    *    .
  8   0.048  0.100                      .    :*   .
  9   0.133  0.100                      .    :  * .
 10  -0.049  0.100                      .   *:    .
 11  -0.044  0.100                      .   *:    .
 12   0.003  0.100                      .    *    .
 13  -0.018  0.100                      .    *    .
 14  -0.120  0.100                      .  * :    .
 15  -0.141  0.100                      . *  :    .
 16   0.080  0.100                      .    :  * .
 17   0.102  0.100                      .    :  * .
 18  -0.196  0.100                      *    :    .
 19  -0.149  0.100                      . *  :    .
 20  -0.083  0.100                      .  * :    .
 21  -0.025  0.100                      .   *:    .
 22  -0.037  0.100                      .   *:    .
 23  -0.021  0.100                      .    *    .
 24  -0.047  0.100                      .   *:    .
 25  -0.045  0.100                      .   *:    .
```

FIGURE 9.17b. PACF correlogram of simulated ARIMA(0,0,2) series with $\theta_1 = -.9$ and $\theta_2 = -.5$.

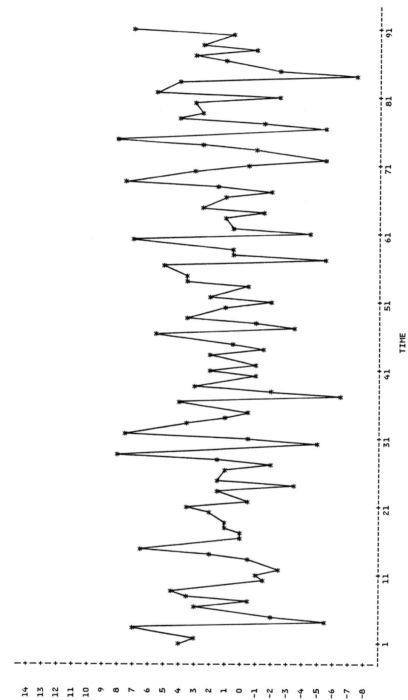

FIGURE 9.18. Raw data of simulated ARIMA(0,0,2) series with $\theta_1 = -.9$ and $\theta_2 = -.5$.

Summary

By examining the patterns of the ACF and PACF correlograms, a researcher can gain some evidence of the possible model that may best describe the underlying stochastic process. The possible models are not limited to the simple one-parameter models just discussed. The actual process for a particular set of data may be any combination of these models: ARIMA(0,1,1), ARIMA(2,1,0), ARIMA(3,0,2), and so on. In practice, however, complex models beyond the one-parameter models just described are rare. For example, Glass et al. (1975) found that only 2% of a sample of time series in behavioral sciences required a second- or higher order autoregressive parameter, and few required higher order moving average parameters. McCain and McCleary (1979) reported that a mixed process was rare in behavioral observation studies. Hence, the one-parameter models just discussed should suffice in the majority of situations in behavioral observation.

Parameter Estimation

In the parameter estimation stage of an ARIMA analysis, one estimates the values of the ϕ and θ coefficients of the specified model. If the model specified, based on the correlogram patterns, is either an ARIMA(0,0,0) or an ARIMA(0,d,0) series, parameter estimation is not necessary because no coefficient is involved. In other words, parameter estimation is necessary only if either the autoregressive, the moving average, or both parameters are involved in the specified model.

The parameters (coefficients) can be estimated only from a stationary process (i.e., a process containing only inertia). Therefore, if the model specified is a mixed model involving a differencing parameter—for example, ARIMA(0,1,1)—the coefficients are estimated using the transformed data after the appropriate number of differencings. For an ARIMA(0,1,1) model, parameter estimation is performed on the series after one differencing.

Methods of Estimation

The coefficients may be estimated through one of three methods: the method of moments, the least squares method, or the maximum likelihood method. The method of moments is the simplest method for the estimation of ϕ coefficients but can be extremely complicated in estimating θ coefficients. Additionally, it may result in multiple solutions for a set of θ values. This problem with estimating the coefficients for the moving average series arises from a mathematical condition for θ known as the *invertibility* condition. The invertibility condition restricts the possible values of various θ coefficients. This restriction is necessary because, mathematically, if the invertibility condition is not met, one may derive a solution in which the farther back an observation is, the more effect the observation has on the present observation. That is, for example, X_{t-10} would have more effect on X_t than would X_{t-1}. This situation is conceptually unacceptable. Hence the invertibility restriction is imposed.

The least squares method does not have problems with the estimation of θ coefficients. However, it has two limitations. First, it cannot use all the available information for a more accurate estimation. Second, it cannot adequately minimize a mathematical function, known as the unconditional sum-of-squares function. Minimizing this function is an important process in arriving at the most accurate estimates, particularly when the series is of moderate length or when seasonality is involved.

With the maximum likelihood method, all valuable information is used, and the problem of minimizing the unconditional sum-of-squares function is dealt with head-on. Unfortunately, this method also involves the extremely complex mathematics of solving joint probability density functions. Potentially, the maximum likelihood method is the most powerful one in that it is applicable to large series as well as to complicated ARIMA models.

Even with the simplest method of moments, the estimation of coefficients is tedious without the aid of a computer. The only exception is a model involving only a first- or second-order autoregressive parameter. In this case, the method of moments can efficiently estimate the values of the ϕ coefficients. We discuss only the method of moments. For an explanation of the least squares method and the maximum likelihood method, the text by Cryer (1986) is recommended.

Estimating ϕ Through the Method of Moments

With the method of moments, the values of the ϕ coefficients for an ARIMA(p,0,0) model can be obtained through the solution of a series of simultaneous equations called the Yule–Walker equations (Yule, 1927). using $r_1, r_2, \ldots r_p$ to represent the lag-1, lag-2, $\ldots$, lag-p ACF values of the model, the generalized Yule–Walker equations can be expressed as:

$$r_1 = \phi_1 + \phi_2 r_1 + \ldots\ldots + \phi_p r_{p-1}$$
$$r_2 = \phi_1 r_1 + \phi_2 + \ldots\ldots + \phi_p r_{p-2}$$
$$.$$
$$.$$
$$.$$
$$r_p = \phi_1 r_1 + \phi_2 r_2 \ldots\ldots + \phi_p. \tag{9.20}$$

For an ARIMA(1,0,0) model, the Yule–Walker equations are reduced to:

$$r_1 = \phi_1. \tag{9.21}$$

Thus, the lag-1 ACF is the estimate of ϕ_1 for an ARIMA(1,0,0) model. For the simulated example presented by Figures 9.13a and 9.13b, the estimated ϕ_1 coefficient (parameter) is:

$$\phi_1 = r_1$$
$$= .886$$

In other words, the underlying process of this simulated set of data can best be described by the model:

$$X_t = \phi_1 X_{t-1} + a_t$$
$$= .886 \, (X_{t-1}) + a_t.$$

For an ARIMA(2,0,0) model, the Yule–Walker equations reduce to two simultaneous equations with two unknowns, ϕ_1 and ϕ_2:

$$r_1 = \phi_1 + \phi_2 r_1 \tag{9.22}$$

and
$$r_2 = \phi_1 r_1 + \phi_2. \tag{9.23}$$

Solving these two equations for ϕ_1 and ϕ_2, we obtain:

$$\phi_1 = \frac{r_1 \, (1 - r_2)}{1 - r_1^2} \tag{9.24}$$

and
$$\phi_2 = \frac{r_2 - r_1^2}{1 - r_1^2}. \tag{9.25}$$

For the simulated example represented by Figures 9.14a and 9.14b, $r_1 = .986$ and $r_2 = .763$. Thus, the coefficients can be estimated as:

$$\phi_1 = \frac{r_1(1 - r_2)}{1 - r_1^2}$$

$$= \frac{.896(1 - .763)}{1 - (.896)^2}$$

$$= 1.077$$

and
$$\phi_2 = \frac{r_2 - r_1^2}{1 - r_1^2}$$

$$= \frac{.763 - (.896)^2}{1 - (.896)^2}$$

$$= -.202.$$

Hence, the estimated mathematical model to describe the underlying process is:

$$X_t = a_t + \phi_1 X_{t-1} + \phi_2 X_{t-2}$$
$$= a_t + 1.077(X_{t-1}) - .202(X_{t-2}).$$

Estimating θ Through the Method of Moments

For an ARIMA(0,0,q) model, the estimation of θ coefficients through the method of moments is much more complicated. It is also possible that there is no solution for the θ coefficients, which implies that the invertibility condition may be violated. In which case, the appropriateness of the specification of the ARIMA(0,0,q) is suspect. With the method of moments, the estimation of the θ values for an ARIMA(0,0,q) model is accomplished through the solution of the following generalized equation for the lag-1 through lag-k autocorrelations of a moving average model:

$$r_k = \frac{-\theta_k + \theta_1\theta_{k+1} + \theta_2\theta_{k+2} + \ldots + \theta_{q-k}\theta_q}{1 + \theta_1^2 + \theta_2^2 + \ldots + \theta_q^2} \tag{9.26}$$

where $k = 1, 2, 3, \ldots, q$. For an ARIMA(0,0,1) model, the above equation reduces to:

$$r_1 = \frac{-\theta}{1 + \theta^2}. \tag{9.27}$$

Solving for θ, we obtain:

$$\theta = \frac{-1 + \sqrt{1 - 4r_1^2}}{2r_1}. \tag{9.28}$$

The square root operation in this equation would lead to two possible solutions for θ. According to the invertibility condition for an ARIMA(0,0,1) model, the absolute value of the θ in the model has to be smaller than 1. One of the two possible solutions for the above equation is 1 and is hence not acceptable. Thus, the solution that is smaller than 1 is the estimated value of θ.

The estimations of θ coefficients for higher order moving average models become progressively more complicated. For an ARIMA(0,0,2) model, for example, Equation 9.26 reduces to:

$$r_1 = \frac{-\theta_1(1 - \theta_2)}{1 + \theta_1^2 + \theta_2^2} \tag{9.29}$$

and

$$r_2 = \frac{-\theta_2}{1 + \theta_1^2 + \theta_2^2} \tag{9.30}$$

Again, there is more than one solution for each of the θ values. For an ARIMA(0,0,2) model, the condition of invertibility is more complicated and can be expressed by:

$$\left.\begin{array}{c} \theta_2 + \theta_1 < 1, \\ \theta_2 - \theta_1 < 1, \\ |\theta_2| < 1. \end{array}\right\} \quad (9.31)$$

and

The solutions that satisfy these conditions are the best estimates of θ_1 and θ_2. As can be seen, the estimation of higher order moving average models quickly becomes very complicated.

Fortunately, with the easy access to computers today, these estimation procedures can be performed efficiently with computers. Once the model has been specified and the values of the associated coefficients estimated, a diagnostic check is performed to assess the appropriateness of the model. If the model is found to be appropriate, the impact of the intervention can be assessed. However, if the model is not appropriate, one returns to the model specification stage and respecifies the model.

Diagnostic Check

The first step in the diagnosis of the goodness-of-fit of the model specified and the parameters estimated is to compute the residuals of the data under the specified model. In other words, the portion of each observation that cannot be accounted for by the model is computed from the observed data. If the model is appropriate, the residuals should consist of only white noise.

Recall that the generalized model for an ARIMA(p,0,0) series is:

$$X_t = a_t + \phi_1 X_{t-1} + \phi_2 X_{t-2} \ldots \ldots \phi_p X_{t-p}.$$

In this model, the residual or white noise component is expressed by a_t. With the specified model and the estimated coefficients, the value of the residual for each observation can be derived from this equation. Hence, for example, for a specified ARIMA(1,0,0) model with an estimated ϕ of .7, the residual for each observation can be derived by:

$$a_t = X_t - .7X_{t-1}.$$

For an ARIMA(2,0,0) model with $\phi_1 = .7$ and $\phi_2 = .2$, the residuals can be derived by:

$$a_t = X_t - .7X_{t-1} - .2X_{t-2}.$$

In this fashion, the residuals of the specified models are derived. The ACFs and PACFs of the residuals (i.e., the time series consisting of a_t values) can be calculated. If the model is correct, the time series as well as the correlograms should resemble those of a white noise model, ARIMA(0,0,0). A visual inspection of the series and the correlograms should provide evidence as to whether the model is appropriate.

To safeguard against misjudgment of the residual series and correlograms, a Q statistic proposed by Box and Pierce (1970) can be used to test for the statistical significance of the ACFs for k lags as a whole. The Q statistic is given as:

$$Q = N \sum_{i=1}^{k} r_i^2, \tag{9.32}$$

where N is the number of observations in the series and k is the highest lag of the correlogram being assessed. When N is large, the value of Q approximates that of a χ^2 with $k - p - q$ degrees of freedom for a model with a pth-order autoregressive term and a qth-order moving average term. If the Q value exceeds the corresponding critical value of χ^2, the model is misspecified, and the researcher should return to the model specification state.

The Q statistic approximates a χ^2 only when the number of observations, N, is very large. Ljung and Box (1978) found that even with an N of 100, the Q approximation of χ^2 is not satisfactory. Hence, they recommend a modified Q statistic. The modified statistic is known as the Ljung–Box–Pierce statistic and is symbolized by Q^*:

$$Q^* = N(N + 2) \sum_{i=1}^{k} \frac{r_i^2}{n - i}. \tag{9.33}$$

The Q^* statistic more closely approximates the χ^2 for more moderate sample sizes (e.g., 50–100).

INTERVENTION IMPACT ASSESSMENT

Once the appropriate model is identified for the preintervention time series, the entire series can be combined for the analysis of the impact of the intervention. When the entire series is combined and the model is identified, one can remove the stochastic component from each observation. The residual should then contain the white noise and a possible intervention effect. If the residuals for both the preintervention and postinvervention phases combined contain only white noise, the intervention is judged to be not effective. In the intervention assessment stage of the analysis, one is interested in determining if the residuals of the identified model contain only white noise or if an intervention effect is evidenced.

The impact of an intervention may have a number of different forms. An intervention may produce no impact at all. It may produce an abrupt change in behavior and the change may be permanent in that the effect of the change does not become extinct with time. It may also produce an abrupt change and the change may be only temporary. Conversely, an intervention may have a gradual but permanent impact or a gradual and temporary impact. Figures 9.19a through 9.19e provide the graphic representations of these five forms of intervention impact. We, however, confine our discussion to the simple cases of no impact and an abrupt permanent impact. More comprehensive treatment of the more complex impact models can be found in McDowall et al. (1980).

To facilitate discussion, we use Y_t to represent the raw observation score at time t in the pre- and postintervention combined series and y_t to represent the residual of Y_t after the effects of the stochastic model have been removed from Y_t. (Note that we use y_t instead of e_t. The latter symbol was used to represent error in prediction or deviation from the prediction line in linear regression, which contains only random error. The former, however, may contain only the random portion of the stochastic component or may contain a random error and a deterministic component.) The value of y_t can be derived based on the specified model in the same manner for the derivation of a_t values in the diagnostic check stage of model identification. Thus, for an ARIMA(1,0,0) model, y_t is derived from:

$$y_t = Y_t - \phi_1 Y_{t-1} \qquad (9.34)$$

and for an ARIMA(2,0,0) model:

$$y_t = Y_t - \phi_1 Y_{t-1} - \phi_2 Y_{t-2}. \qquad (9.35)$$

The null hypothesis for the set of y_t observations is that the intervention has no impact at all. Because under the null hypothesis all observations are random, the effectiveness of the intervention can be assessed through any appropriate conventional statistical procedure. For example, the intervention effectiveness can be assessed through a one-sample de-

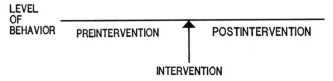

FIGURE 9.19a.   No intervention impact.

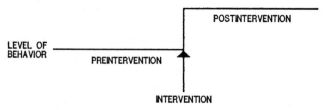

FIGURE 9.19b.   An abrupt and permanent. impact.

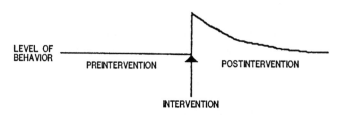

FIGURE 9.19c.   An abrupt and temporary impact.

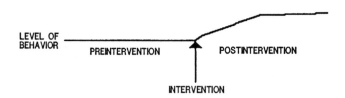

FIGURE 9.19d.   A gradual and permanent impact.

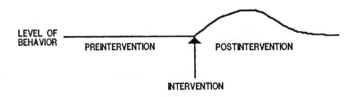

FIGURE 9.19e.   A gradual and temporary impact.

pendent *t*-test using the observations in the preintervention phase as one sample and those in the postintervention phase as another sample. If the difference between the pre- and postintervention means is found to be statistically insignificant, one concludes that there is insufficient evidence of intervention effectiveness.

If the intervention has no effect, the ACF correlogram of the y_t time series will resemble that of a white noise model. Additionally, a simple Pearson's *r* between *t* and y_t should be zero. Hence, this information provides additional evidence for a lack of intervention impact.

If a statistically significant impact is found, the magnitude of the impact of the intervention can be assessed. The simplest method for an abrupt and permanent change model is to subtract the mean of y_ts in the preintervention phase from that of the y_ts in the postintervention phase. The difference is the impact of the intervention. This method assumes that an abrupt and permanent change is the correct model.

An alternative approach is to use a regression model. The advantage of the regression model is that it can accommodate more complex impact models through simple extensions of the model. The first step is to set up an intervention variable, *I*. This variable equals 0 for all observations prior to intervention and equals 1 for the observations at the time of intervention and thereafter. For example, if the intervention is introduced at time t = 100, I equals 0 for $t < 100$ and equals 1 for $t \geq 100$. For an abrupt and permanent intervention impact, using ω to represent the magnitude of the impact, the model can be expressed as:

$$y_t = \omega I_t + a_t, \qquad (9.36)$$

where a_t is the white noise component of y_t. This is the model for a conventional linear regression. The coefficient ω is directly comparable to the β coefficient in conventional linear regression. Hence, ω can be estimated through the conventional linear regression process.

For more complex models such as an abrupt but temporary impact, a gradual and permanent impact, or a gradual and temporary impact, additional terms are added to the above regression equation to assess the rate of change, magnitude of change, as well as form of change.

SOFTWARE

ARIMA analysis, as shown in the previous discussion of its elementary components, consists of a series of complex mathematical operations. It is rare that one can perform an ARIMA analysis with a calculator. The use of computers is inevitable. Currently, there are a number of softwares available to assist a researcher in the computation and estimation of various statistics in ARIMA.

Popular statistical packages such as BMDP, SAS, SPSSx, and MINITAB all contain time series analysis routines. Most of these packages are available for both mainframe and microcomputers. Additionally, there are programs written specifically to perform ARIMA analysis. These include PACK (Pack, 1977) and TMS (Bower et al. 1974). These programs generally produce similar results. The appropriateness of each program is determined by accessibility and desired features.

CHAPTER 10

Time Series Analysis: Other Methods

We saw in chapter 9 that ARIMA is a powerful statistical approach to the analysis of serial dependency and behavioral intervention effectiveness in the presence of serial dependency; however, it is a parametric technique. When the variable of interest forms only a nominal scale, ARIMA is not applicable. Also, ARIMA is primarily a within-subject analytic technique and does not lend itself directly to an analysis of a cross-subject design. In these situations, an effective nonparametric alternative to ARIMA is the Markov Chain process.

THE MARKOV CHAIN METHOD

Through the Markov Chain process, one can meet a number of diversified analytic objectives. One may forecast the extent that a particular behavior will increase, decrease, or remain constant in frequency in the future. One may assess whether the level (e.g., frequency) of behavior will eventually stabilize and how long it will take before this stability will occur. One may also assess whether a number of different behaviors will form a cyclical pattern, reach a state of equilibrium, or eventually converge into a single behavior. Additionally, one may also analyze the effectiveness of a behavioral intervention strategy or assess the interaction between two or more subjects.

In principle, a Markov Chain analysis is not too different from an ARIMA analysis. In both cases, one first attempts to identify a model to describe the underlying serial dependency or stochastic process. This model serves as an aid for the understanding of the nature of the behavior. With this model as the null hypothesis, one can then assess the effectiveness of an intervention strategy by examining whether the postintervention data depart significantly from the null model.

TYPES OF MARKOV CHAINS

A Markov Chain is a stochastic process expressed in probabilistic terms. In this stochastic process, the probability of occurrence of a particular event at time t is determined by what occurred in the immediately preceding time, $t - 1$. Mathematically, there can be a number of different types of Markov Chains. A Markov Chain may be finite or infinite. In a finite Markov Chain, the number of exhaustive and mutually exclusive categories of events is finite and the occurrence of each event is assumed to be influenced only by the immediately preceding event (e.g., occur vs. not occur). Each of the finite categories need not describe a single distinct event. For example, one may have the categories *sit*, *stand*, *walk*, and *other*. In this example, "other" is not a single distinct behavior but is identifiable due to the absence of the other categories of behavior.

The assumption that an event at time t is influenced only by the immediately preceding event at time $t - 1$ does not imply that other preceding events at times $t - 2, t - 3, \ldots, t - k$ have absolutely no effect on the event at time t. Rather, the assumption is that the cumulative effects of all the events at previous times are embedded in the event at $t - 1$.

For a Markov Chain analysis, the time continuum may be divided into discrete time units or may remain a continuum. In the overwhelming majority of Markov Chain analyses in behavioral observation, discrete time units are used and the Markov Chain is finite. We will, hence, discuss the techniques involved in a finite, discrete-time Markov Chain process. For other types of Markov Chains, readers may consult more specialized texts such as Isaacson and Madsen (1976) or Kemeny and Snell (1960).

The Transition Matrix

Rather than describing the underlying stochastic process through an autoregressive moving average equation, as in the case of ARIMA, a Markov Chain analysis describes the process in terms of probabilities. Specifically, instead of being expressed in the form of a linear equation as in ARIMA, the model in Markov Chain is expressed in the form of a conditional probability matrix known as a transition matrix. A matrix is any data organized in the form of rows and columns. The contingency table in a χ^2 analysis or the 2 × 2 table for the assessment of percentage agreement are examples of matrices. A transition matrix is a special type of matrix in that the rows represent the events at time $t - 1$ and the columns represent the events at time t. The cells represent the probability that a particular event will occur at time t given that the event occurred at time $t - 1$. It is "transitional" because the matrix represents the "transition" of events from time $t - 1$ to t.

Figure 10.1 provides the generalized form of a transition matrix. In this matrix, the variable has k possible categories (or events). These mutually exclusive categories are generally referred to as *states* in a Markov Chain analysis. Thus, S_1 represents the occurrence of a unique state that is different from the states $S_2, S_3, \ldots, S_k$. The rows represent the occurrence of each of the k states at time $t - 1$. The columns represent the occurrence of the states at time t. Each cell represents the probability of the corresponding state at time t's occurring, given that the corresponding state at time $t - 1$ has occurred. Thus, p_{11} is the probability that S_1 will occur at time t given that S_1 has occurred at time $t - 1$; p_{13} is the probability that S_3 will occur at time t given that S_1 has occurred at time $t - 1$; and p_{kk} is the probability that state k will occur at time t given that state k has occurred at time $t - 1$.

Note that for each row, the sum of all probabilities across all columns is 1.00. A conceptual explanation of this unique characteristic is that each of the probabilities in the cells is a conditional probability. It is a probability that the column state will occur at time t *given* that the row state *has occurred* at time $t - 1$. Because the occurrence of the raw state is a given, it is a certainty. Hence, the probability of each row state's occurring at time $t - 1$ is 1.00. Symbolically, a conditional probability is generally

		Time t					
	States	S_1	S_2	S_3	......	S_k	Total
	S_1	P_{11}	P_{12}	P_{13}	......	P_{1k}	1.00
	S_2	P_{21}	P_{22}	P_{23}	......	P_{2k}	1.00
Time	S_3	P_{31}	P_{32}	P_{33}	......	P_{3k}	1.00
$t - 1$	.	.					.
	.	.					
	.	.					.
	S_k	P_{k1}	P_{k2}	P_{k3}	......	P_{kk}	1.00

FIGURE 10.1.   A generalized transition matrix.

represented by $Pr(Y|X)$, which reads "the probability that Y will occur given that X has occurred," which is different from an unconditional probability, symbolized by $Pr(Y)$, which reads "the probability that Y will occur." Hence, the cell probabilities in Figure 10.1 can also be expressed in conditional probability forms. For example, p_{23} could be written as $Pr(S_3|S_2)$.

To construct a transition matrix model of the underlying process, we start from the construction of a frequency matrix summary of the observed chain or raw scores. For example, the behaviors of a subject are observed once every 3 minutes for an hour. At each observation, the behaviors of the subject are coded by either an X, a Y, or a Z, representing three exhaustive and mutually exclusive categories of a particular type of behavior of interest. After 1 hour of observation, the following chain of raw data is obtained:

$$X\ X\ Y\ X\ Y\ Z\ Z\ Z\ X\ Z\ X\ Y\ Z\ X\ X\ Z\ Y\ Y\ Z\ X$$

A 3 × 3 frequency matrix, as shown in Figure 10.2, can then be constructed based on this chain of data. It is a 3 × 3 matrix because there are 3 possible behaviors at both time $t - 1$ (or 3 minutes prior to t) and time t. By examining the chain of raw scores, it can be seen that the number of times an X is followed by another X is 2. Thus, the first cell in the matrix, which represents the number of times a State X at time $t - 1$ is followed by a State X at time t, is 2. Again, by examining the chain, it can be seen that the number of times a Y is followed by an X is 1. Hence, the cell corresponding to this combination is 1. In this fashion, the values (or frequencies) of the remaining cells in the matrix are obtained.

This frequency matrix can then be transformed into a transition matrix by dividing each cell by the row total. Hence, the conditional probability $Pr(S_1|S_1)$ is the frequency of occurrence of State 1 at time $t - 1$ followed by an occurrence of State 1 at time t divided by the total frequency that State 1 occurs at time $t - 1$. The conditional probability $Pr(S_2|S_3)$ is the result of dividing the frequency of a State 3 at time $t - 1$ followed by a State 2 at time t combination by the total frequency of State 3 at time $t - 1$. In our example, $Pr(X|X)$ is $2/7 = .286$, $Pr(Y|X)$ is $3/7 = .428$, and $Pr(Z|X)$ is $2/7 = .286$. Similarly, $Pr(X|Y)$ is $1/5 = .200$, and so on. Figure 10.3 is the resulting transition matrix.

		State	Time t			
			X	Y	Z	Total
Time $t - 1$		X	2	3	2	7
		Y	1	1	3	5
		Z	4	1	2	7
		Total	7	5	7	19

FIGURE 10.2.   The frequency matrix of the sample data.

| | Time t | | | |
State	X	Y	Z	Total
X	.286	.428	.286	1.00
Y	.200	.200	.600	1.00
Z	.571	.143	.286	1.00

Time $t - 1$

FIGURE 10.3.   The probability transition matrix of the sample data.

This transition matrix is a summary description of the Markov Chain lag-1 stochastic process of the behavior expressed in the form of a matrix. Each cell represents the probability that a particular state will occur at time t given the state at time $t - 1$. This matrix forms the basis for all subsequent analyses.

Lag-k Transition Matrix

The initial transition matrix only provides the probabilities of the occurrences of various states based on the immediately preceding event. If this matrix is used to represent the underlying stochastic process, a lag-1 stochastic process is assumed. If this lag-1 transition matrix is indeed the appropriate model for the underlying stochastic process, it can be applied directly for prediction. The first step is to assess the unconditional probability of occurrence for each event at time 0 (the starting point of prediction). Based on the raw data for Figure 10.2, X occurred 8 out of 20 times. Thus, the unconditional probability that X will occur at time 0 $(Pr(X_0))$ is 8/20 = .40. Through the same process, the unconditional probability of occurrence for Y $(Pr(Y_0))$ and Z $(Pr(Z_0))$ at time 0 is 5/20 = .25 and 7/20 = .35.

To assess the probability that a particular event will occur at time 1, the unconditional probability of each state at time 0 is multiplied by the conditional probability that represents the transition from that state to the predicted state. The sum of these products is the projected probability. Hence with our example, the probability that X will occur at time 1 $(Pr(X_1))$ is given by:

$$Pr(X_1) = Pr(X_0)Pr(X|X) + Pr(Y_0)Pr(X|Y) + Pr(Z_0)Pr(X|Z)$$

$$= .40(.286) + .25(.200) + .35(.571)$$

$$= .364.$$

Similarly, $Pr(Y_1)$ and $Pr(Z_1)$ are given by:

$$Pr(Y_1) = Pr(X_0)Pr(Y|X) + Pr(Y_0)Pr(Y|Y) + Pr(Z_0)Pr(Y|Z)$$

$$= .40(.428) + .25(.200) + .35(.143)$$

$$= .271$$

and

$$Pr(Z_1) = Pr(X_0)Pr(Z|X) + Pr(Y_0)Pr(Z|Y) + Pr(Z_0)Pr(Z|Z)$$

$$= .40(.286) + .25(.600) + .35(.286)$$

$$= .365.$$

To predict the events at time t, the above process is repeated using the new unconditional probabilities for each step, until t is reached. For example, the probability of X occurring at time 2 $Pr(X_2)$ would be:

$$Pr(X_2) = Pr(X_1)Pr(X|X) + Pr(Y_1)Pr(X|Y) + Pr(Z_1)Pr(X|Z)$$

$$= .364(.286) + .271(.200) + .365(.571)$$

$$= .367.$$

These predictions are meaningful only if the assumption is that the underlying process is a lag-1 process. This assumption is rather limited in that the underlying process may in fact be higher than lag-1. The lag-k conditional probabilities for the lag-k transition matrix can be derived directly and efficiently from information in the initial lag-1 transition matrix. However, for a better understanding of the method, we first present the intuitive approach one would take to derive such a probability.

Let us first examine the possible sequence of events. Given that X occurs at time t, either X, Y, or Z may occur at time $t + 1$. Hence, for Y to occur at time $t + 2$, there are three possible "paths" of behavior through the three time units t, $t + 1$, and $t + 2$. These paths can be represented by the sequences XXY, XYY, and XZY. The probability that Y will occur at time $t + 2$ given that X has occurred at time t is the probability that either of these three sequences will occur.

The probability of each two-event sequence is contained in the transition matrix. A three-event sequence is the extension of the two-event sequence. The probability of a three-event sequence is the product of the probabilities of the two two-event sequences. Consider, for example, if the probability of XY is .5 and the probability of YZ is .5, the probability of XYZ is .5 × .5, or .25. This is because if it is given that Y occurs at time $t + 1$, there is a 50% chance that Z will occur at time $t + 2$. However, Y at time $t + 1$ is not a given certainty. X at time t is however given. With this given X at time t, there is only a 50% chance of Y occurring at time $t + 1$. The probability of Z occurring at time $t + 2$ is thus only 50% of this 50% probability. Hence, the probability of the XYZ sequence is 25%.

Extending this logic, the probability of Y occurring at time $t + 2$ given that X has occurred at time t is the total probability of the occurrences of the XXY, XYY, and XZY sequences. For our example, the probability of Y occurring at time $t + 2$ given that X has occurred at time t is:

$$Pr(Y_{t+2} \mid X_t) = Pr(X|X)Pr(Y|X) + Pr(Y|X)Pr(Y|Y) + Pr(Z|X)Pr(Y|Z).$$
(10.1)

Using the information in the lag-1 transition matrix in Figure 7.29, this probability is:

$$Pr(Y_{t+2}|X_t) = Pr(X|X)Pr(Y|X) + Pr(Y|X)Pr(Y|Y) + Pr(Z|X)Pr(Y|Z)$$

$$= (.286)(.428) + (.428)(.200) + (.286)(.143)$$

$$= .249.$$

The previous computation of the probability of Y at time $t + 2$ given X at time t indicates a few characteristics of prediction in a Markov Chain. First, the probability of a particular state may change as the time lag progresses from 1 to k. Note that, given X at time t, the lag-1 probability of Y at time $t + 1$ is .428. The corresponding lag-2 probability is changed to .249 and may change further at lags 3, 4, 5, and so on. Second, the computation of additional lags will become progressively more complicated. For example, consider the case in which X at time t is given and one wishes to assess the probability that Y will occur at time $t + 3$. In this case, the probability is the sum of the probabilities of the occurrences of the sequences $XXXY, XXYY, XXZY, XYXY, XYYY, XYZY, XZXY,$ $XZYY,$ and $XZZY$. With a $t + 4$ time lag, there are 27 possible paths or sequences. Hence, the assessment of probabilities becomes complicated very rapidly. Third, note that the probability of Y occurring at time $t + 2$ given that X occurs at time t is the sum of the products of each cell in row X multiplied by its counterpart in column Y of the transition matrix. That is, the fist cell in row X is multiplied by the first cell in column Y, the second cell in row X by the second cell in column Y, and the third cell in row X by the third cell in column Y.

Matrix Algebra

Given the previous characteristics, the assessment of the lag-k conditional probability of the occurrence of a particular state can be much more efficiently accomplished through techniques of a branch of mathematics known as matrix algebra. Additionally, to apply the model to actual prediction, the multiplications of the unconditional probabilities by the conditional probabilities can be accomplished more efficiently with matrix algebra. In matrix algebra, which is essentially a form of mathematical shorthand, mathematical computations are performed on entire matrices rather than individual numbers. The techniques that are of particular relevance to a Markov Chain analysis include the multiplication of matrices and the multiplication of a vector by a matrix.

In matrix algebra, a matrix is symbolized by an upper-cased boldfaced letter, such as **A** or **B**. When **A** is multiplied by **B**, a matrix **C** is obtained such that each cell in **C** is the sum of the product of each cell in the corresponding row of **A** and each cell in the corresponding column of **B**. Consider the following two 3×3 matrices **A** and **B** with cells (elements) represented by the letters in lower cases:

$$\mathbf{A} = \begin{bmatrix} a & b & c \\ d & e & f \\ g & h & i \end{bmatrix} \quad \mathbf{B} = \begin{bmatrix} r & s & t \\ u & v & w \\ x & y & z \end{bmatrix}$$

The product of these two matrices can be represented by a matrix **C** with elements as follows:

$$\mathbf{C} = \begin{bmatrix} ar+bu+cx & as+bv+cy & at+bw+cz \\ dr+eu+fx & ds+ev+fy & dt+ew+fz \\ gr+hu+ix & gs+hv+iy & gt+hw+iz \end{bmatrix}$$

With this multiplication of matrices (note that in matrix algebra, **AB** $\neq$ **BA**), the prediction of events beyond lag-1 can be expressed more efficiently. Specifically, if $\mathbf{P}_1$ is the initial lag-1 transition matrix, the probability of occurrence for each state at time $t + 2$ can be expressed by a lag-2 transition matrix $\mathbf{P}_2$ such that:

$$\mathbf{P}_2 = \mathbf{P}_1^2. \tag{10.2}$$

To illustrate, we will use a 2×2 transition matrix $\mathbf{P}_1$. If the $\mathbf{P}_1$ for the lag-1 transitions of occurrences and nonoccurrences of a behavior between time t and $t + 1$ is:

$$\mathbf{P}_1 = \begin{array}{c} \\ \text{occur} \\ \text{not occur} \end{array} \begin{array}{cc} \text{occur} & \text{not occur} \\ \begin{bmatrix} .60 & .40 \\ .20 & .80 \end{bmatrix} \end{array}$$

then the lag-2 transition matrix $\mathbf{P}_2$ of occurrences and nonoccurrences at time $t + 2$ given the occurrences and nonoccurrences at time t is:

$$\mathbf{P}_2 = \mathbf{P}_1^2$$

$$= \begin{array}{c} \\ \text{occur} \\ \text{not occur} \end{array} \begin{array}{cc} \text{occur} & \text{not occur} \\ \begin{bmatrix} (.6)(.6)+(.4)(.2) & (.6)(.4)+(.4)(.8) \\ (.2)(.6)+(.8)(.2) & (.2)(.4)+(.8)(.8) \end{bmatrix} \end{array}$$

$$= \begin{array}{c} \\ \text{occur} \\ \text{not occur} \end{array} \begin{array}{cc} \text{occur} & \text{not occur} \\ \begin{bmatrix} .44 & .56 \\ .28 & .72 \end{bmatrix} \end{array}$$

$\mathbf{P}_2$ succinctly summarizes the lag-2 probability for each state at time t + 2 given the state at time t. In the same fashion, the lag-k probabilities of each state can be projected for any time lag into the future. The lag-k transition matrix $\mathbf{P}_k$ is simply:

$$\mathbf{P}_k = \mathbf{P}_1{}^k. \qquad (10.3)$$

Thus, $\mathbf{P}_3$ is:

$$\mathbf{P}_3 = \mathbf{P}_1{}^3$$
$$= \mathbf{P}_2\,\mathbf{P}_1.$$

$$= \begin{array}{cc} & \begin{array}{cc} \text{occur} & \text{not occur} \end{array} \\ \begin{array}{c} \text{occur} \\ \text{not occur} \end{array} & \left[\begin{array}{cc} .44(.6)+.56(.2) & .44(.4)+.56(.8) \\ .28(.6)+.72(.2) & .28(.4)+.72(.8) \end{array}\right] \end{array}$$

$$= \begin{array}{cc} & \begin{array}{cc} \text{occur} & \text{not occur} \end{array} \\ \begin{array}{c} \text{occur} \\ \text{not occur} \end{array} & \left[\begin{array}{cc} .38 & .62 \\ .31 & .69 \end{array}\right] \end{array}$$

As one projects a transition matrix into higher lags, the matrix may eventually take on a number of different forms. These forms provide important information for an understanding of the nature of the behavior over time as well as for other analytic processes such as hypothesis testing.

A special kind of matrix, useful in Markov Chain analyses to express unconditional probabilities, is a vector. A vector is a matrix that has only one row or one column. It is symbolized by a lower-cased, bold-faced letter (e.g., $\mathbf{a}$). When a matrix is premultiplied by a row vector, the result is another vector. Each element in the new vector is the sum of the cross products of each element in the initial vector and those in the corresponding column of the matrix. For example, if we were to multiply the following vector $\mathbf{a}$ by the matrix $\mathbf{B}$:

$$\mathbf{a} = [\,a\ b\ c\,] \qquad \mathbf{B} = \left[\begin{array}{ccc} r & s & t \\ u & v & w \\ x & y & z \end{array}\right]$$

the result would be a vector $\mathbf{c}$ such that:

$$\mathbf{c} = [\,ar + bu + cx \quad as + bv + cy \quad at + bw + cz\,].$$

To illustrate, let us say that for the occurrence/nonoccurrence example, we have obtained the unconditional probabilities at time 0 of .30 for occurrence and .70 for nonoccurrence. This can be written in the form of a vector $\mathbf{a}$ as follows:

$$\mathbf{a} = \begin{array}{cc} \text{occur} & \text{not occur} \\ [\ .30 & .70\ ]. \end{array}$$

To obtain the vector **c** that contains the unconditional probabilities of occurrence and nonoccurrence at time 1, we can simply multiply **a** by $\mathbf{P}_1$ as follows:

$$
\begin{aligned}
\mathbf{c} &= \mathbf{aP}_1 \\
&= [\ .30 \quad .70\ ] \ \times \ \begin{bmatrix} .60 & .40 \\ .20 & .80 \end{bmatrix} \\
&= [\ .3(.6) + .7(.2) \quad\quad .3(.4) + .7(.8)\ ] \\
&= [\ .32 \quad .68\ ].
\end{aligned}
$$

Forms (Models) of Markov Chain

An initial lag-1 transition matrix projected to k lags may show specific patterns. These patterns reflect the nature of the underlying Markov Chain stochastic process. We may use the pattern or model resulting from projecting a set of base-line data to the intervention phase as the expected pattern without intervention. By comparing the actual intervention data with the expected pattern, we may discern if the intervention is effective. For the purpose of analyzing behavioral observation data, three forms of Markov Chain processes are particularly informative. These are the steady state process (or regular chain), the absorbing chain, and the clyclical chain.

The Steady State Process. A steady state process is one in which the probability of occurrence of each category of behavior ultimately reaches a point of equilibrium, which is also known as the fixed vector point. Once the point of equilibrium is reached, the probabilities remain constant for all future lags. Take our occurrence/nonoccurrence example just discussed. If we were to project into time $t + 6$, the resulting lag-6 transition matrix ($\mathbf{P}_6$) would become:

$$
\mathbf{P}_6 \ = \ \begin{matrix} \\ \\ \text{occur} \\ \text{not occur} \end{matrix} \begin{matrix} \text{occur} \quad \text{not occur} \\ \begin{bmatrix} .33 & .67 \\ .33 & .67. \end{bmatrix} \end{matrix}
$$

Further projections into lags beyond lag-6 will show an indentical matrix. In other words, the probabilities of occurrences and nonoccurrences reach a state of equilibrium by lag-6 and will not change beyond that lag. Based on this constant matrix, one can project that, in the long run, it is twice as likely (67%) that the behavior will *not* occur than that it will occur (33%) at any given time, regardless of what happens prior to that time. These equilibrium probabilities are useful for a number of reasons. They serve as the model in the description of the underlying stochastic process. They form a useful basis for forecasting or prediction. And they can be used as the expected probabilities for hypotheses testing.

With a steady state matrix, no matter what the actual initial unconditional probabilities are, the unconditional probability vector will eventually "settle" at the values of the rows of the steady state matrix. The number of steps it takes for the unconditional probabilities to reach the steady state is the same number of steps it takes for the conditional probabilities to reach equilibrium.

To illustrate, let us assume that the initial unconditional probabilities for our occurrence/nonoccurrence example at time 0 is $\mathbf{a}_0$ such that:

$$\begin{array}{cc} & \text{occur} \quad \text{not occur} \\ \mathbf{a}_0 \;=\; & [\,.90 \quad .10\,\,]. \end{array}$$

Given that the lag-1 transition matrix is $\mathbf{P}_1$:

$$\mathbf{P}_1 \;=\; \begin{array}{c} \\ \text{occur} \\ \\ \text{not occur} \end{array} \begin{array}{c} \text{occur} \quad \text{not occur} \\ \begin{bmatrix} .60 & .40 \\ .20 & .80 \end{bmatrix} \end{array}$$

The expected unconditional probability vectors at time 1, 2, 3, . . . , 6 are as follows:

$$
\begin{array}{llll}
 & & & \text{occur} \quad \text{not occur} \\
\mathbf{a}_1 & = & \mathbf{a}_0 \mathbf{P}_1 & = \quad [\;.56 \quad .44\;] \\
\mathbf{a}_2 & = & \mathbf{a}_0 \mathbf{P}_1^2 & = \quad [\;.42 \quad .58\;] \\
\mathbf{a}_3 & = & \mathbf{a}_0 \mathbf{P}_1^3 & = \quad [\;.37 \quad .63\;] \\
\mathbf{a}_4 & = & \mathbf{a}_0 \mathbf{P}_1^4 & = \quad [\;.35 \quad .65\;] \\
\mathbf{a}_5 & = & \mathbf{a}_0 \mathbf{P}_1^5 & = \quad [\;.34 \quad .66\;] \\
\mathbf{a}_6 & = & \mathbf{a}_0 \mathbf{P}_1^6 & = \quad [\;.33 \quad .67\;].
\end{array}
$$

From time 6 on, the unconditional probability vector remains a constant, and the unconditional probabilities in the vector are identical to the conditional probabilities in each row of the steady state matrix $\mathbf{P}_6$.

The steady state matrix is the theoretical expected matrix of the behavior in the long run. It may be the case that a lag-1 matrix is a steady state matrix; in which case, the lag-1 model is the best model to describe the underlying stochastic process. In general, if a lag-1 model is found to be adequate, it is the model of choice because of its conceptual parsimony. However, a lag-1 model may not be adequate. Jaffe and Feldstein (1970) demonstrated a method through which the adequacy of the lag-1 model can be tested indirectly. Essentially, the method involves comparing the actual lag-k conditional probabilities obtained by examining the raw data with the theoretical lag-k conditional probabilities obtained through $\mathbf{P}_1{}^k$.

The Absorbing Chain.   The absorbing chain, also known as an ergodic process, is a unique type of steady state process. This occurs when one of the categories of behavior has the characteristic that, once it occurs, it will continue to occur thereafter. In an absorbing chain, all events will ultimately change to that single absorbing event. For example, based on past observations of a client at 15-minute intervals between 10:00 p.m. and 2:00 a.m., the following lag-1 transition matrix is derived:

$$\mathbf{P}_1 \quad = \quad \begin{array}{c} \\ \text{asleep} \\ \text{read} \\ \text{other} \end{array} \begin{array}{ccc} \text{asleep} & \text{read} & \text{other} \\ \left[\begin{array}{ccc} 1.0 & 0.0 & 0.0 \\ 0.8 & 0.1 & 0.1 \\ 0.7 & 0.2 & 0.1. \end{array}\right] \end{array}$$

In this process, once the client is asleep at time t, the client will continue to be asleep at time $t + 1$. However, if the client is engaged in reading or other activities at time t, the behavior may change at time $t + 1$. Thus, the "asleep" state is an absorbing state in that once this state is "entered," there is no "exit." If this matrix is extended to lag-4 through $\mathbf{P}_1{}^4$, a steady state will be attained, and $\mathbf{P}_4$ will have the following pattern:

$$\mathbf{P}_4 \quad = \quad \begin{array}{c} \\ \text{asleep} \\ \text{read} \\ \text{other} \end{array} \begin{array}{ccc} \text{asleep} & \text{read} & \text{other} \\ \left[\begin{array}{ccc} 1.0 & 0.0 & 0.0 \\ 1.0 & 0.0 & 0.0 \\ 1.0 & 0.0 & 0.0 \end{array}\right] \end{array}$$

This indicates that, given the initial lag-1 transition matrix, it is certain that the client will be asleep by the fourth observation interval. Once asleep, it is certain that the client will stay asleep for the duration of the observation session. In an absorbing chain, all events are inevitably drawn to that single absorbing event.

For the purpose of illustration, let us assume the extreme case that the initial unconditional probability of the behavior at time 0 can be represented by a vector $\mathbf{a}_0$ in which the reading behavior is a certainty:

$$\mathbf{a}_0 \quad = \quad \begin{array}{ccc} \text{asleep} & \text{read} & \text{other} \\ [\ 0.00 & 1.00 & 0.00\ ]. \end{array}$$

The unconditional probabilities at time 1 (15 min later) is then $\mathbf{a}_0\mathbf{P}_1$, which results in a vector $\mathbf{a}_1$ of:

$$\begin{array}{rl} \mathbf{a}_1 \quad = & \mathbf{a}_0\mathbf{P}_1 \\ & \begin{array}{ccc} \text{asleep} & \text{read} & \text{other} \end{array} \\ = & [\ 0.80 \quad 0.10 \quad 0.10\ ]. \end{array}$$

If we were to project this vector to time 4 (1 hr later) through $\mathbf{a}_0\mathbf{P}_1^4$, we would obtain the vector $\mathbf{a}_4$ as follows:

$$\mathbf{a}_4 \;=\; \mathbf{a}_0\mathbf{P}_1^4$$

$$\begin{array}{ccc} \text{asleep} & \text{read} & \text{other} \\ =\quad [\; 1.00 & 0.00 & 0.00 \;]. \end{array}$$

Had the initial unconditional probability of reading been less than 1 and the unconditional probability of asleep been higher than 0, the absorbing state of asleep could have been reached before time 4. The length of time prior to the attainment of the inevitable outcome (asleep) is a function of the initial unconditional probabilities.

Cyclical Chain. Another possible Markov Chain process is that of a cyclical chain. Unlike an absorbing chain, it is possible to go from every state to every other state in a cyclical chain. However, each state occurs only at particular predictable intervals. Consider the following $\mathbf{P}_1$, for example:

$$\mathbf{P}_1 \;=\; \begin{array}{c} \\ W \\ X \\ Y \\ Z \end{array} \begin{array}{cccc} W & X & Y & Z \\ \begin{bmatrix} 0 & 1 & 0 & 0 \\ 0 & 0 & 1 & 0 \\ 0 & 0 & 0 & 1 \\ 1 & 0 & 0 & 0 \end{bmatrix} \end{array}$$

In this transition matrix, if W occurs at time t, it is certain that X will occur at time $t + 1$. If X occurs at time t, it is certain that Y will occur at $t + 1$. Similarly, Y will always lead to Z, and Z will always lead to W. Hence, the events will always follow a totally predictable pattern. If W occurs at time t, X will occur at time $t + 1$, Y will occur at $t + 2$, Z will occur at $t + 3$, and the behavior will return to W at $t + 4$, and so on. The cyclical pattern can be represented by W-X-Y-Z-W-X-Y-Z-W-X . . . . .

A cyclical chain is said to be *irreducible*. An irreducible chain is one that does not have a state of equilibrium. A cyclical chain cannot reach a steady state. Using the aforesaid cyclical matrix, the lag-2 through lag-5 transition matrices are:

$$\mathbf{P}_2 \;=\; \mathbf{P}_1^2 \;=\; \begin{bmatrix} 0 & 0 & 1 & 0 \\ 0 & 0 & 0 & 1 \\ 1 & 0 & 0 & 0 \\ 0 & 1 & 0 & 0 \end{bmatrix}$$

$$\mathbf{P}_3 \;=\; \mathbf{P}_1^3 \;=\; \begin{bmatrix} 0 & 0 & 0 & 1 \\ 1 & 0 & 0 & 0 \\ 0 & 1 & 0 & 0 \\ 0 & 0 & 1 & 0 \end{bmatrix}$$

$$\mathbf{P}_4 = \mathbf{P}_1{}^4 = \begin{bmatrix} 1 & 0 & 0 & 0 \\ 0 & 1 & 0 & 0 \\ 0 & 0 & 1 & 0 \\ 0 & 0 & 0 & 1 \end{bmatrix}$$

$$\mathbf{P}_5 = \mathbf{P}_1{}^5 = \begin{bmatrix} 0 & 1 & 0 & 0 \\ 0 & 0 & 1 & 0 \\ 0 & 0 & 0 & 1 \\ 1 & 0 & 0 & 0 \end{bmatrix}$$

As can be seen, $\mathbf{P}_1$ through $\mathbf{P}_4$ complete a cycle and $\mathbf{P}_5$ returns to the pattern of $\mathbf{P}_1$. This cyclical process will continue, and the transition matrix at any lag will always be different from that at the next lag. The cyclical pattern is also evidenced in the unconditional probability vector. Let us say that the unconditional probability vector at time 0 is:

$$\mathbf{a}_0 = [\ .3\quad .5\quad .1\quad .1\ ].$$

Then, the unconditional probability vector at subsequent points of time will show the same cyclical pattern:

$$\begin{aligned}
\mathbf{a}_1 &= \mathbf{a}_0 \mathbf{P}_1 &= [\ .1\quad .3\quad .5\quad .1\ ] \\
\mathbf{a}_2 &= \mathbf{a}_0 \mathbf{P}_1{}^2 &= [\ .1\quad .1\quad .3\quad .5\ ] \\
\mathbf{a}_3 &= \mathbf{a}_0 \mathbf{P}_1{}^3 &= [\ .5\quad .1\quad .1\quad .3\ ] \\
\mathbf{a}_4 &= \mathbf{a}_0 \mathbf{P}_1{}^4 &= [\ .3\quad .5\quad .1\quad .1\ ]
\end{aligned}$$

At time 4, the unconditional probabilities return to those of time 0.

The previous example shows a simple cyclical process. It is possible that the underlying process contains a more complex cycle. Furthermore, there may be more than one cycle, each with a different periodicity (the amount of time to return to the initial state). For example, consider the following lag–1 transition matrix:

$$\mathbf{P}_1 = \begin{array}{c} \\ U \\ V \\ W \\ X \\ Y \\ Z \end{array} \begin{array}{c} \begin{array}{cccccc} U & V & W & X & Y & Z \end{array} \\ \begin{bmatrix} 0 & .5 & 0 & 0 & .5 & 0 \\ 0 & 0 & 1 & 0 & 0 & 0 \\ 0 & 0 & 0 & 1 & 0 & 0 \\ 1 & 0 & 0 & 0 & 0 & 0 \\ 0 & 0 & 0 & 0 & 0 & 1 \\ 1 & 0 & 0 & 0 & 0 & 0 \end{bmatrix} \end{array}$$

The process for this matrix contains two cycles. The first cycle can be represented by the sequence $U\text{-}V\text{-}W\text{-}X\text{-}U\text{-}V$ . . . and the second cycle can be represented by $U\text{-}Y\text{-}Z\text{-}U\text{-}Y\text{-}Z\text{-}U$ . . . . The periodicity of the first cycle is 4 steps and that of the second cycle is 3 steps.

A more efficient method to detect these cycles is through a *state transition diagram*. A state transition diagram is a graphic representation of the

Markov Chain, in which the relationship between each pair of states, is described by a path with the associated conditional probability. The previous two-cycle matrix can be represented by the state transition diagram in Figure 10.4. The two cycles are immediately apparent in the diagram.

Other Processes

We have introduced a few simple Markov Chain processes. These processes or models are not necessarily mutually exclusive. In a more complex matrix involving many categories of states, it is possible that these processes appear in various combinations. For example, in a large transition matrix, it is possible that part of the matrix contains a steady state process, another part an absorbing chain, and another part a clyclical chain.

A fourth type of Markov Chain not commonly considered in behavioral studies is one known as a *random walk process*. It has been suggested that a theoretical random walk process can be posed as a null hypothesis to test against the steady state process. Gottman and Notarius (1978) provided a discussion of the nature of a random walk process and a method to use the random walk process for hypothesis testing in behavioral analyses.

The Markov Chain processes discussed in this chapter involve only a single transition matrix. They involve only a single subject, a single set of behavior categories, and each row and column of the transition matrices represents a single event. Additionally, in the illustrations used, there are only a few states or categories of behavior. In practice, however, the processes may involve much more complex matrices. For example, in Altmann's (1965) study of monkeys, the transition matrix was a 120 × 120 matrix. In other words, there were a total of 14,400 conditional probabilities. Fortunately, the size of the transition matrix need not be a major problem today. Many statistical softwares (e.g., SAS) contain routines for matrix algebra.

The process may also involve more than one subject, as in the case of analyzing the sequential interaction between two subjects. Analyses involving more than one subject are referred to as dyadic, triadic, quartic,

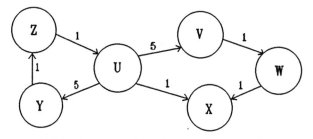

FIGURE 10.4.   A state transition diagram of a two-cycle process.

. . . interaction analyses. An interaction analysis is, as expected, more complex than a single-subject analysis. A major consideration in an interaction analysis is the possibility that the occurrence of a behavior is a result of a serial dependency between subjects as well as within subjects (Gardner, Hartmann, & Mitchell, 1982). For example, Subject A exhibits behavior X and Subject B exhibits behavior Y at time t. At time $t + 1$, Subject B exhibits behavior Z. There are three possible hypothetical interpretations of this pattern. First, Z is totally unrelated to either X or Y. Second, the behavior Z of Subject B is the result of a serial dependency on the behavior Y of the same subject, which is the within-subject serial dependency hypothesis. Third, the behavior Z of Subject B is the result of a serial dependency with the X behavior of Subject A.

TESTING OF MODEL ADEQUACY

Once the transition matrix model is constructed for the stochastic process, the model can be tested to assess if the identified model is a good description of the underlying process. The most common approach is to test whether the model is significantly different from a null model of no serial dependency.

One common inferential statistic application for this purpose is the χ^2 test of independence. The χ^2 test can be applied directly to the *frequency* transition matrix (see Figure 10.2) in the usual fashion for the test of independence. The null hypothesis being tested is that the behavior at time $t - 1$ is not related to the behavior at time t. For example, using the information in Figure 10.2, the χ^2 value is 3.48 with 4 degrees of freedom. The associated probability of obtaining a χ^2 value this high or higher from a no serial dependency sampling distribution is a little less than 50%. Hence, the Markov Chain model is rejected.

A potential pitfall of the use of the χ^2 test of independence is found in its application in analyzing dyadic interactions. This is because the χ^2 test does not account for the potential serial dependency within each of the two subjects. When within-subject serial dependence exists, the cross-subject χ^2 can be inflated considerably. For example, Gardner, Hartmann, and Mitchell (1982) showed that, for some situations, the inflated χ^2 can lead to an estimate of Type I error probability as much as 1,600% less than the actual probability.

A method suggested by Bakeman (1978) was designed for the analysis of dyadic interaction sequence. In this method, a z approximation technique of the binomial test is used. Instead of testing the entire transition matrix, each cell is tested individually. The null hypothesis is that behavior X of Subject A at time t is not related to behavior Y of Subject B at time

$t + 1$. The z index is computed by:

$$z = \frac{x - NP}{\sqrt{NPQ}} \qquad (10.4)$$

where x is the joint frequency of behavior X of Subject A and behavior Y of Subject B (i.e., the number of times behavior X of Subject A is followed by behavior Y of Subject B), N is the number of times behavior X of Subject A occurs, P is the unconditional probability that behavior Y of Subject B will occur, and Q is $1 - P$. For example, the behavior X of Subject A is followed by the behavior Y of Subject B 100 times ($x = 100$) in an observation session. Subject A exhibits behavior X a total of 200 times ($N = 200$). Subject B exhibits behavior Y 30% of the time ($P = .30$) regardless of what Subject A was doing prior to behavior Y. Then, the z index is:

$$z = \frac{x - NP}{\sqrt{NPQ}}$$

$$= \frac{100 - (200)(.3)}{\sqrt{(200)(.3)(1 - .3)}}$$

$$= 6.17.$$

Because of the possible existence of within-subject serial dependency, Bakeman suggested that the z index should be interpreted only as an index and not a z statistic. In other words, the z value should not be converted to a Type I error probability from a z distribution. Bakeman further suggested that, as a decision rule, one accepts the existence of a sequential relationship between the two subjects on the two behaviors when z is larger than 2. Hence, for the previous example, since the z is larger than 2, one would conclude that behavior Y of Subject B is dependent upon behavior X of Subject A.

Bakeman's z approach has been challenged by Allison and Liker (1982). For dichotomous events or 2×2 tables, a z-score is essentially the square root of χ^2. Therefore, Bakeman's z approach is in fact not an alternative to the chi-square approach but the same approach under disguise. As serial dependency affects chi-square probabilities, so it does with z probabilities.

Other methods for the statistical test of the adequacy of a Markov Chain model can be found in Allison and Liker (1982), Budescu (1984), Crow (1979), Jaffe and Feldstein (1970), Lemon and Chatfield (1971). Additionally, various methods have been developed to derive an autocorrelation coefficient for a Markov process. These can be found in Allison and Liker

(1982), Devore (1976), Kim and Bai (1980), Klotz (1973), and Lindqvist (1978).

Intervention Assessment

Once the appropriate model is identified, the testing of the effectiveness of a behavioral intervention strategy is rather straightforward. One can use the long-run expected conditional probabilities as the null hypothesis and compare these to actual conditional probabilities obtained after behavioral intervention. If the actual conditional probabilities after intervention is significantly different from the expected probabilities, one may conclude that the intervention is effective.

For example, a preintervention transition matrix attains a steady state as follows:

$$\mathbf{P}_{pre} = \begin{array}{c} \\ occur \\ \\ not\ occur \end{array} \begin{array}{cc} occur & not\ occur \\ \begin{bmatrix} .3 & .7 \\ .3 & .7 \end{bmatrix} \end{array}$$

This steady state matrix contains the long-term expected conditional probabilities of the behavior occurrence/nonoccurrence without intervention. Let us say an intervention strategy designed to increase the occurrence of the behavior has been implemented. If the intervention strategy is not effective, the postintervention transition matrix is expected to be the same as the long-run steady state preintervention matrix. Thus, the preintervention steady state transition matrix can serve as the null hypothesis. Data gathered after the intervention show that the actual transition matrix is:

$$\mathbf{P}_{post} = \begin{array}{c} \\ occur \\ \\ not\ occur \end{array} \begin{array}{cc} occur & not\ occur \\ \begin{bmatrix} .6 & .4 \\ .8 & .2 \end{bmatrix} \end{array}$$

The steady state preintervention matrix can be compared to the postintervention matrix through a χ^2 test of goodness-of-fit. First, the elements in $\mathbf{P}_{pre}$ and $\mathbf{P}_{post}$ can be converted to frequencies by removing the decimals. The χ^2 value is then computed in the usual fashion by using the frequencies in $\mathbf{P}_{pre}$ as the expected frequencies (E) and the frequencies in $\mathbf{P}_{post}$ as the observed frequencies (O):

$$\chi^2 = \Sigma \frac{(O - E)^2}{E}$$

$$= \frac{(6 - 3)^2}{3} + \frac{(4 - 7)^2}{7} + \frac{(8 - 3)^2}{3} + \frac{(2 - 7)^2}{7}$$

$$= 16.19.$$

With 1 degree of freedom, this χ^2 value is significant with less than .01 probability of Type I error. Thus, one can conclude that the intervention is effective in increasing the occurrence of the behavior. Additional examples of the use of the Markov Chain to assess the effectiveness of behavioral intervention can be found in Raush (1972) and Stuart (1971).

AN ALTERNATIVE TO MARKOV CHAIN

A method developed by Sackett (1974) has been enthusiastically endorsed and refined by some behavior analysts (Bakeman & Gottman, 1986; Gottman, 1979; Gottman & Notarius, 1978). The Sackett method is also known as the lag-sequential analysis. There are two types of lag-sequential analysis: autolags and cross lags. In an autolag analysis, one tests the observed conditional probability that a behavior follows itself within a subject against the null hypothesis expressed by the unconditional probability of occurrence of the behavior. In a cross-lag analysis, one behavior is chosen as the criterion behavior. The conditional probabilities of a second behavior following the criterion behavior at various lags are assessed and plotted on a probability profile. The extent to which the conditional probabilities depart from the overall expected unconditional probability can be inspected visually to detect possible serial dependence and the lag at which serial dependence occurs.

Figure 10.5 shows a probability profile of a criterion behavior A followed by a behavior B at various lags. A peak in the probability profile indicates the lag at which behavior B is most likely to occur, and a trough indicates the lag at which it is least likely to occur. Hence, in Figure 10.5, behavior B is most likely to occur two lags after the occurrence of the criterion behavior A and least likely to occur five lags after the criterion.

With both the autolag and the cross-lag method, the goodness-of-fit of the identified model can be tested against a null of no serial dependence through Bakeman's z index, discussed earlier. Since the lag-sequential method hinges on the z index, it contains the same pitfalls of the z approach to test for the significance of Markov Chain. Additionally, when the lag-sequential analysis involves the analysis of a dyadic interaction, the z score, as suggested by Gottman (1979), fails to account for sampling error (Allison & Liker, 1982). Allison and Liker (1982) have subsequently suggested methods to improve the statistical analyses of a lag-sequential analysis. For a more comprehensive discussion of Sackett's method and its problems, the works of Sackett (1974, 1979), Bakeman (1978), Bakeman and Dabbs (1976), Gottman, Markman, and Notarius (1977) Gottman (1979), Allison and Liker (1982), Bakeman and Gottman (1986) are suggested.

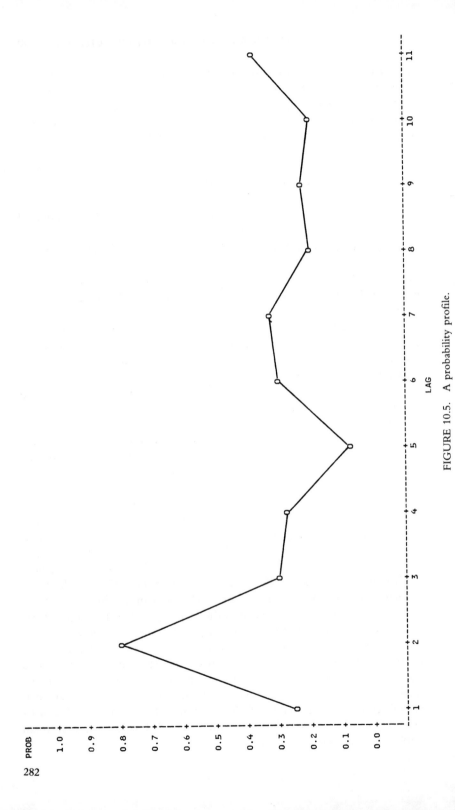

FIGURE 10.5. A probability profile.

ANALYSES OF RHYTHM

Another general area of investigation with sequential data is the study of natural rhythms. Techniques for the study of rhythms have been of primary interest to investigators in chronobiology, neurobiology, and physiology. Exemplary use of these techniques can be found in such journals as the *Journal of Interdisciplinary Cycle Research*, *Chronobiologia*, the *International Journal of Chronobiology*, and *Neuropadiatrie*. These techniques have also been used in behavioral observation studies in psychology and special education, particularly in the investigation of stereotypic behaviors (e.g., Meier-Koll & Pohl, 1981; Meier-Koll et al., 1977; Pohl, 1977). We provide a very brief introductory review of some of the basic concepts and two of the most commonly used techniques in the study of rhythms. For a more in-depth treatment of the study of rhythm, specialized texts such as Aschoff (1981), Bloomfield (1976), Colquhoun (1971), Jenkins and Watts (1969), Kendall (1973), and Koopmans (1974) may be consulted.

In a study of rhythm, a researcher hypothesizes that the behavior observed contains a particular *periodicity*. At regular and predictable intervals, the behavior repeats itself. For example, the asleep/awake behavior of a human being tends to repeat itself between every 23 to 25 hours. Another example is the rapid eye movements (REM) of a human being while sleeping, which appear at regular and predictable intervals. Studies have also found that some stereotypic behavior (e.g., hand waving) among mentally retarded patients tends to repeat itself in frequency every 90 minutes (Sorosky et al., 1968).

These rhythms of behaviors may be caused by an internal organic function within the subject or a regular fluctuation in the external environment. When the periodicity is caused by an internal biological function, it is said to be an *endogenous* rhythm. When it is caused by an external environmental fluctuation, it is called an *exogenous* rhythm. In behavioral studies, it is very likely that a rhythm has both endogenous and exogenous components.

The rhythm of a behavior may take on one of two major forms. It may contain repetitive linear trends that move upward and downward at regular intervals. This type of rhythm is referred to as a *saw-tooth* rhythm. Alternatively, the rhythm may be curvilinear, with the level of behavior oscillating up and down in a harmonic manner. This type of rhythm is referred to as a *sinusoid* because of its resemblance to a trigonometric sine wave or cosine wave. Figure 10.6 shows a saw-tooth rhythm and Figure 10.7 shows a sinusoidal rhythm.

The objective of a study of rhythm is to identify a mathematical model that can describe the nature of the periodicity. This model may be identified through a number of means. One approach is to use the Seasonal Au-

FIGURE 10.6.   A saw-toothed rhythm.

toRegressive Integrated Moving Average (SARIMA) approach. This approach basically attempts to identify a repetitive ARIMA model. The assumption of this approach is that the change of behavior within each cycle is linear and that these linear trends repeat themselves. Hence, it is a useful approach if the rhythm can be assumed to form a saw-tooth rhythm. We have discussed the basic ARIMA extensively earlier. SARIMA is an extension of ARIMA.

The more common methods used to study rhythm assume that the underlying rhythm is sinusoidal. These methods fall under a general category of techniques known as the *Fourier Analysis*. A third method, which is much simpler than either SARIMA or Fourier analyses, is the method of autocorrelation. The method of autocorrelation does not require an assumption of either a saw-tooth rhythm or a sinusoid. However, it will yield only limited information.

Fourier Analysis

In a Fourier analysis, based on the sinusoidal assumption, a rhythm can be totally described by four indicators or parameters (see Figure 10.7). The first parameter is *period*, which is the length of time it takes for the behavior to repeat itself.

The second parameter of interest is *phase*. It refers to where the behavior is within the period. A convenient reference point is the *acrophase*, which is the phase at which the behavior is at the maximum level or the peak. One may also describe a phase in terms of the time of the phase relative to the period. For example, one may describe a particular phase as being at the 4th hour of a 12-hour cycle or period. Since a Fourier analysis of rhythm is based on trigonometric functions, a phase is frequently described in terms of its angle within the period. For example, if a behavior has a cycle of 12 hours, the end of the 12th hour is $360°$ (or $0°$ or 2π radian). The end of the 3rd hour is then $90°$ (or $.5\pi$ radian), the end of the 6th hour is $180°$, and the end of the 9th hour is $270°$. Extending this description, the end of the 2nd hour is $60°$, or $.34\pi$ radian, and the end of the 18th hour is $180°$, or π radian.

The third parameter of interest is the *mesor*, which is the center line of

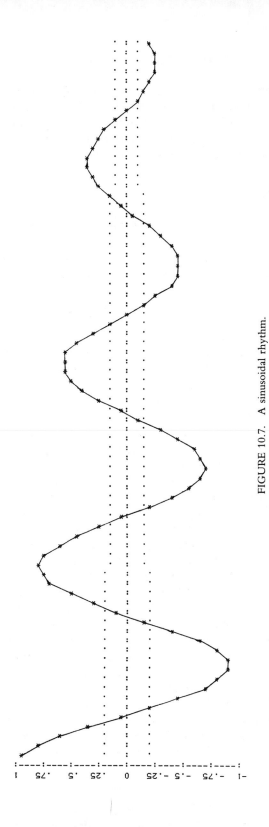

FIGURE 10.7.   A sinusoidal rhythm.

the cycles. This is similar, but not necessarily equal, to the mean level of behavior. In the sinusoid represented by Figure 10.7, for instance, the mesor is slightly higher than the mean. The fourth parameter of interest is *amplitude*. This is the height from the mesor to the acrophase. It is equal to half of the distance between the peak and the trough.

Statistical Model Estimation

There are a number of different statistical approaches to a Fourier analysis. They all have the same objective of identifying the values of the four basic parameters to describe the underlying sinusoidal stochastic process governing the observed data. In the most basic form of Fourier analysis, the mathematical model used to describe the sinusoid is:

$$X_t = M = A \cos(\text{ft}) + B \sin(\text{ft}) + e_t, \qquad (10.5)$$

where X_t is the observed score at time t, M is the mesor, and e_t is the random error (or random shock or white noise) at time t. The remainder of the equation can be explained as follows: If P is the phase at time t and R is the amplitude of the sinusoid, the A coefficient in Equation 10.5 is R times the cosine of P, or $(R \cos P)$. (Cosine is a trigonometric function defining the ratio between two lines of a triangle based on the observed angle). The coefficient B is the negative of amplitude (R) times the sine of P or $(-R \sin P)$. The value t is the time at which X_t is observed. A convenient way to determine the value of t is to set the time of the first observation at zero. From there on, the times of the subsequent equally spaced observations are 1, 2, 3, and so on. The value of f is referred to as the *angular velocity* or *frequency* of the sinusoid. The angular velocity is the rate of change of behavior for a given increment in time t. In other words, it is how much change in behavior level is expected from time t to time $t + 1$. It is directly related to the period of the rhythm.

In general, the value of f in the Fourier model cannot be estimated from the observed data. One speculates the value of f on the basis of a hypothesized period. For example, if a 24-hour period is hypothesized, the behavior would complete a cycle in 24 hours. The rhythm would complete 360 degrees in that time period. Hence, if observations are made every hour, one would expect the change of angle per observation, or angular velocity, to be 360°/24, or 15°. (Mathematically, it is more convenient to express the angle and angular velocity in radian terms. Thus, the hypothesized value of f, in this case, is about .08π, or .25 radian.)

With the hypothesized value of f, one can then estimate the values of the remainder of Equation 10.5 based on the observed data. The mesor (M) is estimated from the mean of all observations:

$$M^\star = \bar{X} = \Sigma \, X_t/N, \qquad (10.6)$$

where $M^\star$ is the estimated mesor and N is the total number of observations. The coefficients A and B can be estimated as follows:

$$A^\star = (2/N) \ \Sigma \ [(X_t - M^\star) \cos ft] \qquad (10.7)$$

and $$B^\star = (2/N) \ \Sigma \ [(X_t - M^\star) \sin ft], \qquad (10.8)$$

where $A^\star$ is the estimated A and $B^\star$ is the estimated B. Given the estimated values of A and B and given that A is $(R \cos P)$ and B is $-(R \sin P)$, the estimated values of R^* and P^* can be obtained by solving the two simultaneous equations.

Once the model is estimated based on the hypothesized f, it can be tested against the null hypothesis that the actual underlying model is that of a series of random shocks. In other words, under the null hypothesis, the elaborated sinusoid model does not describe the underlying stochastic process better than using the simple mean of the data. To test against this null hypothesis, an F ratio can be used. Since the hypothesized errors are serially dependent, the conventional mean square error term in the F ratio does not apply. Instead, the F ratio is computed by:

$$F = \frac{\Sigma[(X_t - M^\star)2/(N - 1)]}{\Sigma\{[X_t - M^\star - R^\star \cos(ft + P^\star)]/(N - 3)\}}. \qquad (10.9)$$

The statistical significance of this F ratio is assessed with $(N - 1)$ and $(N - 3)$ degress of freedom. If the F is found to be significant, the sinusoid model is a good description of the underlying process.

A variation of the Fourier method is one known as the *Minnesota cosinor analysis*, or simply *cosinor analysis* (Halberg et al., 1977; Halberg, Tong, & Johnson, 1967). This technique involves the creation of a number of short time series, fitting a sinusoid model to each series and assessing the goodness-of-fit of the phase and amplitude. Interested readers should refer to the original publications of Halberg and associates. A critical evaluation of the technique was given by Van Cauter and Huyberechts (1973).

Spectrum Analysis

Through the F ratio just described, one can only be relatively certain that a sinusoid model is a better description of the underlying process than a random shock model. It does not indicate that the specific set of estimated amplitude (R^*), mesor (M^*), and phase (P^*) parameters do indeed provide the best model to describe the process. Recall that these parameters are estimated based on a hypothesized angular velocity parameter (f). This hypothesized value of f determines the estimated values of the coefficients A^* and B^*, which, in turn, determine the estimated values of R^* and P^*. When f is misspecified, although the resulting model is a better description of the underlying process than a random shock model, it is not the best possible model. The actual goodness-of-fit of the model is, hence, determined by the subjectively specified f value.

Theoretically, one can specify many possible angular velocities. These different angular velocities will lead to different models (i.e., different values of A^* and B^*). Only one of these is the best-fitting model. Hence, there is a need for a method to identify the f value that would lead to the best model. A technique known as *power spectrum analysis*, or simply *spectrum analysis*, was developed by Bingham, Godfrey, and Tukey (1967) to meet this need. With this technique, numerous models are constructed based on a large number of possible angular velocities (or frequencies). The angular velocity (f) and the estimated amplitude (R^*) of each of the many estimated models are used to plot a *raw spectrogram* or a *periodogram*. In this periodogram, the angular velocity of each model is plotted on the x-axis against the corresponding amplitude on the y-axis. This diagram is examined to identify the peak of the plot. The angular velocity with the highest amplitude is the best angular velocity. Hence, the estimated model corresponding to that angular velocity is the best-fitting model.

Visual inspection of the periodogram to identify the peak can be troublesome and unreliable, especially when the periodogram shows a great deal of random fluctuation. Various methods have been developed to "smooth" the periodogram for easier inspection. There are two approaches to smoothing the periodogram. The first approach is to *filter* the raw data prior to model estimations through various means (Orr & Naitoh, 1975; Tukey, 1967). The filtering of raw data is also known as *prewhitening*, based on the analogy that the spectrum of white light is relatively flat (Thrall & Engelman, 1981). The effect of filtering the raw data prior to analysis generally reduces the fluctuation of the data and leads to a smoother periodogram. A second approach is to smooth the periodogram by adjusting the values on the periodogram itself (Blackman & Tukey, 1958). This process is also known as *recoloring*.

The computational process involved in estimating the numerous models for a spectrum analysis is overwhelming, even with the aid of a computer. Cooley and Tukey (1965) developed a computer algorithm known as fast Fourier transform (FFT) to improve the efficiency of model estimations through a computer. This technique is generally used in Fourier computer programs such as the BMDP1T.

With a spectrum analysis, one can theoretically estimate a model each for an infinite number of possible angular velocities. The question is which angular velocities should be used. The angular velocities to be used may be determined by the time interval between successive observations and the length of the time series. Mathematically, the highest meaningful angular velocity that can be used for a spectrum analysis is known as the *Nyquist frequency* and is determined by $1/2d$ where d is the width of an observation interval. The number of angular velocities to be used for a spectrum analysis can be determined by $N/2$ where the N is the total number of observation points. In a special class of Fourier analysis known as *harmonic analysis*, the angular velocities to be used are predetermined to be $2\pi/N$, $4\pi/N$, $6\pi/N$, $8\pi/N$, and so on.

Autocorrelation Method

The autocorrelation method is an effective method in the study of rhythm if one is concerned only with the period parameter. This method makes no assumption about the form of the rhythm and is equally applicable to a saw-tooth process as well as to a sinusoidal process. Since one can estimate only the period parameter of the rhythm, one cannot actually describe the process itself, as in SARIMA and Fourier analysis.

The method is relatively simple and straightforward. One simply calculates the lag-1 through lag-k autocorrelation functions (ACFs) from the raw data. If periodicity exists in the data, the ACF correlogram will also resemble harmonic waves. Since the longer lag ACFs are generally smaller in magnitude, one can expect that the amplitudes of the waves become smaller as the lag increases. Figure 10.8 shows the ACF correlogram of a set of sinusoidal data. When the raw data contain periodicity, the ACF correlogram will resemble this figure. To estimate the period of the underlying rhythm, one can simply calculate the average distance between two successive recurrences of the same phase. For example, one may take the average distance between two successive peaks as the estimated period of the underlying cycle.

The ACF correlogram in Figure 10.8 is one in which the underlying process contains no white noise. In practice, the pattern of the ACF correlogram is not as clear, and hence the distance between two successive recurring phases is not as easily discernible. However, the ACF correlogram is generally smoother than the raw data, and hence the cycles are easier to detect. To further improve the ACF correlogram, some of the prewhitening procedures can be used to prefilter the raw data prior to the construction of the correlogram. One common prewhitening procedure is to take a weighted average of the adjacent observations to replace an observation. For example, the "filtered" value of the observation at time t can be obtained from giving a weight of 1 each to the observations at time $t - 1$, t, and $t + 1$, and giving a weight of .5 to the observations at times $t - 2$ and $t + 2$. Hence, the filtered observation at time t is $(.5X_{t-2} + X_{t-1} + X_t + X_{t+1} + .5X_{t+2})/4$. With the filtered data, the cycles in the ACF correlogram can be expected to be more discernible.

The autocorrelation method can be used in and of itself to estimate the period of the rhythm. It can also be used as a preliminary investigation

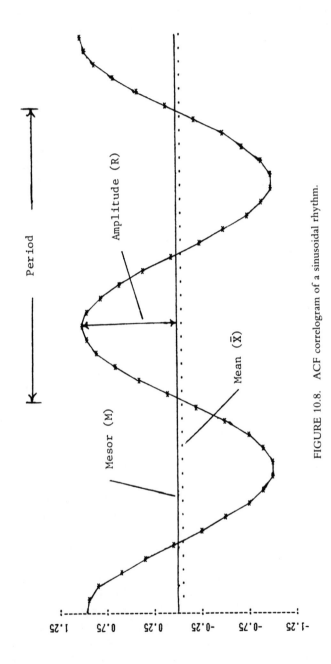

FIGURE 10.8.   ACF correlogram of a sinusoidal rhythm.

prior to a formal Fourier analysis. An interesting application of the autocorrelation method is in the identification of periodic serial dependency between two time series (e.g., from two subjects). Orr and Naitoh (1975) and Walter (1963) provided some discussion on the use of the autocorrelation method for this latter purpose.

SAMPLE SIZE CONSIDERATIONS

In this and the two preceding chapters, we discussed a number of statistical techniques for the analysis of time series data. Some of these methods are highly sophisticated and powerful. The usefulness of these methods, however, may be somewhat limited by an investigator's ability to obtain a relatively large number of observations. In principle, at least, ARIMA, Fourier analysis, and the autocorrelation method of identifying rhythm periods will not be able to yield stable results unless a large number of observations are made over a period of time. The main reason being that in these methods, statistical techniques are used to estimate unknown underlying parameters. Hence, for these techniques, sample size (number of observations, not the number of subjects) is an important consideration.

For a stable ARIMA analysis, it has been recommended that the minimum number of observations be 100 (Hartmann et al., 1980). It has been argued (Sharpley & Alavosius, in press), however, that when one is interested only in intervention impact assessment but not in long-term forecasting, as few as 20 observations can lead to stable results. For a Fourier analysis, the minimum recommended number of observations is 200 (Orr & Naitoh, 1975). Additionally, the data should contain at least five cycles for a meaningful estimation of the parameters in Fourier analysis. With the autocorrelation method for the analysis of rhythm, the stability of the average period length is determined by how many complete cycles are revealed by the ACF correlogram. The more cycles, the better the estimated period. Recall, however, that ACFs for lags beyond $N/4$ are generally unreliable. Following this rule, a meaningful ACF correlogram for a time series with 200 observations is one that stops at lag-50. Dependent upon the actual underlying cycle of the behavior, a correlogram containing only 50 lags may show so few complete cycles (e.g., 2 or 3 cycles) that the average period length estimated is not reliable at all. Hence, it is quite possible that even a time series with 200 observations is insufficient for the application of the autocorrelation method.

Readers are reminded that the need for relatively large sample sizes is not unique to time series analysis. When the number of observations is extremely small, not only are the sophisticated techniques such as ARIMA and Fourier analysis not useful, simpler methods as well as conventional statistical estimates of points and intervals can be equally unreliable. For example, the simple assessment of serial dependency through autocorrelation can be unreliable when the number of observations is extremely small. Based on the Bartlett (1946) estimation of standard error for an ACF, discussed earlier, if the number of observations is less than 12, the observed ACF has to be perfect (i.e., ACF = 1.00) before it can be judged as statistically significant. When there are as many as 30 observations, the minimal ACF to be judged as significant is still as high as .43. Even with the relatively simple Young's statistic, when there are only four observations, the observed C has to be .92 (almost perfect serial dependency) before it can be judged as statistically significant.

There are two aspects at the crux of the problem of small numbers of observations. If the only purpose of an analysis is to test against a null hypothesis, a very small sample size would render the test powerless in that the probability of a Type II error is high. For example, if there is a true underlying autocorrelation of .99 but only 12 observations are made to assess this autocorrelation, even if one can accurately obtain the .99 ACF with the sample, one would still fail to reject the null hypothesis of 0 ACF. A second aspect is in model fitting. With model fitting, one not only tests against a null hypothesis, one attempts to estimate the actual value of the parameter based on the sample statistic. If an ACF of .9 is found to be statistically significant, for instance, one is not content with simply concluding that there is an autocorrelation. One would like to conclude further that the observed .9 value or some adjusted value derived from the sample is an accurate estimate of the true underlying ACF. For this second purpose of analysis, sample representativeness is much more crucial than it is for a null hypothesis testing situation. Hence, all model-fitting techniques, ranging from linear regression to Fourier analysis, require that the sample size be relatively large.

CHAPTER 11
Summary

Solutions to problems are easy to find:
the problem's a great contribution.
What is truly an art is to wring from your mind
a problem to fit a solution.

—Anonymous

Our intention in writing this book was to put together a large array of heretofore fragmented theoretical information and recent advances in behavioral observation measurement and statistics. In doing so, it was our hope that many of the existing confusions and contradictions, especially in the applied literature, could be clarified. We hope we have done so effectively.

To summarize the discussions in this book, we would like to point out that from the perspectives of sampling, measurement, and statistics, data aquired through the direct observation of behavior are not fundamentally different from data acquired through other means, in that they are governed by the same set of psychometric and statistical principles. Two of the most important differences are that observational data are frequently acquired over time, and that an observer is used in data acquisition in place of a questionnaire, test, or other paper-and-pencil instrument. A third difference that may be important in some situations is that many observational studies use a single-subject design.

With regard to sampling issues in an observational study, a researcher needs to determine which behaviors to observe, which subjects to observe, and when to observe. If a study is one of basic research, the question of which behaviors to observe is largely governed by the research question.

sible, either partial-interval, whole-interval, or momentary time sampling will produce reliable duration and frequency information (and subsequently prevalence, rate, and other measures) under specific conditions. In general, the conditions needed for reliable data are more likely met for momentary time sampling than for the other two time-sampling methods.

Observational data reliability had been an area of controversy and confusion. The most basic question was whether we needed to assess observational data reliability to begin with. Additionally, a large array of techniques had been suggested as methods to assess observational data reliability. In this book, we demonstrated first that observational data are not exempted from the fundamental question of reliability. Next, we showed that most of the popular techniques could best be described as measures of interobserver agreement. Interobserver agreement, by itself, is important but not sufficient evidence of data reliability. Another piece of important evidence is that of intraobserver reliability. The proper interpretation of intraobserver reliability measures lies within an understanding of the fundamental theory of measurement.

Next, we discussed the intraclass correlation approach to observational data reliability, which has been advocated by some as an alternative to other measures of interobserver agreement or intraobserver reliability. However, we demonstrated that the intraclass correlation approach is not just an alternative but a superior one to conventional intraobserver reliability approaches. Additionally, the intraclass correlation approach can accommodate both interobserver agreement and intraobserver reliability simultaneously. Finally, we introduced the enormous potential for the application of Generalizability Theory, which is a multidimensional intraclass correlation approach to observational data reliability assessment.

The assessment of observational data validity is not different in principle from that of any other data. The amount of validity evidence needed is determined by whether the data are behavioral signs or samples of a variable and whether the data consist of a molar behavior or a molecular behavior. In some limited situations, accuracy is by itself adequate evidence of validity.

When data are not serially dependent, the statistical analysis of observational data is rather straightforward, with "classical" or nonparametric statistical techniques as appropriate. Whether the existence of serial dependency in observational data is the rule or the exception is currently quite controversial, and the situation is unlikely to be cleared up in a short time. Common sense would indicate that some observational data are serially dependent whereas others are not. In this book, we showed two techniques through which serial dependency in the data can be detected.

In the presence of serial dependency, classical and nonparametric statistics provide biased results. We provided an extensive survey and conceptual explanations of some of the more common time series analysis techniques for the analysis of serially dependent data. In summary, three of the techniques—visual inspection of graphs, linear regression, and curvilinear regression—have been criticized by many as inadequate, biased, or inappropriate. The randomization test approach is essentially not a statistical solution. Rather, it is a research design solution. With the randomization test approach, the issue of serial dependency is made irrelevant through an experimental treatment scheme that minimizes the probability of serial dependency.

When data are already collected and they are determined to contain serial dependency, it is unrealistic to start from scratch through the randomization approach to minimize serial dependency. In such a situation, interval level data can be analyzed through a Box–Jenkins ARIMA approach and nomimal data can be analyzed through the Markov Chain method. If the research question is to detect cycles of behavior, the Fourier analysis, spectrum analysis, SARIMA, or the correlogram method may be employed as appropriate.

APPENDIX A:
Introductory Statistics

In this book, we assume that readers have a working knowledge of introductory descriptive and inferential statistics. For those who have not used statistics for an extensive period of time, the following is a brief refresher on these techniques. Because introductory statistics embodies a large array of fundamental theories and techniques, we include only techniques that are most pertinent to the analysis of direct behavioral observation data. For a more complete treatment of these and other statistical techniques, readers should consult more comprehensive texts such as Ary and Jacobs (1976), Glass and Hopkins (1984), Hays (1973), Hinkle, Wiersma, and Jurs (1979), or one of numerous other introductory statistical texts.

DESCRIPTIVE STATISTICS

Descriptive statistics summarize a large amount of data through a small number of quantitative descriptors. Dependent on the type of data being gathered for a study, different descriptive statistics are appropriate.

For a single variable or a *univariate* situation, the distribution of the data can be summarized in four statistics. A *central tendency statistic* describes the most representative value in the distribution. A *dispersion statistic* describes how the data differ in value from the central tendency. A *skewedness statistic* describes whether the majority of the data tend to cluster at one end of the distribution, and a *kurtosis statistic* describes whether the data are evenly distributed among the possible values.

For a two-variable, or *bivariate*, situation, the relationship between two variables can be summarized by a *coefficient of correlation*. For measures of the simultaneous relationships among more than two variables, multiple regression or multivariate analysis techniques, which are extensions of the bivariate situation with some adjustments, are used.

Central Tendency Statistics

For nominal data, the value that best represents all the data is the value that occurs most frequently, the *mode*. For ordinal, interval, and ratio data, the distribution can be summarized by the *median*. If all cases are ordered from the lowest value to the highest value, the median is the midpoint, above and below which half of the cases occur. To compute the median, first divide all possible values of the variable into intervals of equal width, then apply the equation:

$$\text{Median} = l + \left(\frac{.5n - cf_b}{f_w}\right)i, \qquad (A.1)$$

where l is the lower limit of the interval in which the median falls, n is the number of cases in the data set, cf_b is the total number of cases below the interval in which the median falls, f_w is the number of cases within the interval containing the median, and i is the width of the interval.

The third measure of central tendency is the average of all values, referred to as the arithmetic mean, or simply the *mean*. It is an appropriate measure of central tendency for interval- or ratio-level continuous variables. The mean is computed by:

$$\bar{X} = (\Sigma X)/N, \qquad (A.2)$$

where $\bar{X}$ is the mean, ΣX is the summation of all X values, and N is the number of cases. (For a dichotomous variable in which the cases are scored as either 1 or 0, the mean equals the proportion of cases scored 1 [i.e., p].)

Of the three common measures of central tendency just described, the mean is most informative, and hence most desirable. This is because methods that qualify how well the mean summarizes the distribution in terms of dispersion, skewedness, and kurtosis are available.

Dispersion Statistics

For nominal data, a dispersion statistic is not meaningful because the numbers are mere labels. For ordinal, interval, and ratio data, the simplest method is to describe the dispersion in terms of the *range* of values, which is the distance between the highest and the lowest value. That is:

$$\text{Range} = X_h - X_l, \tag{A.3}$$

where X_h is the highest value and X_l is the lowest value. Range is based on the two highly unstable extreme values in the distribution. Since the two extreme values are influenced by sampling fluctuation, the range is inherently unstable. A way to obtain a more stable measure is to discard the extreme cases and find the range for some predetermined middle portion of the distribution. A statistic that does this is the *interquartile range*, which is the distance between the highest and the lowest values in the middle 50% of the distribution. The lowest value of this range is the point below which 25% of the cases in the distribution fall. It is referred to as the 1st quartile (Q_1). The highest value is the point below which 75% of the cases fall, referred to as the 3rd quartile (Q_3). The calculations of Q_1 and Q_3 are:

$$Q_1 = l + (\frac{.25n - cf_b}{f_w})i \tag{A.4}$$

$$Q_3 = l + (\frac{.75n - cf_b}{f_w})i, \tag{A.5}$$

where l is the lower limit of the interval containing Q_1 for Equation A.4 and that containing Q_3 in Equation A.5; cf_b is the cumulative frequency below the interval containing Q_1 or Q_3, as appropriate; f_w is the frequency within the interval containing Q_1 or Q_3; and i is the interval width. Thus:

$$\text{Interquartile range} = Q_3 - Q_1. \tag{A.6}$$

The most frequently used method of capturing the dispersion characteristics of a distribution of interval or ratio data is to assess the total amount of squared error that results from using the mean to represent the entire distribution. This sum of squared errors is called the *sum of squared deviation* or simply *sum of squares*. The sum of squares (SS) is computed by:

$$SS_x = \text{sum of squares of } X = \Sigma (X - \bar{X})^2. \tag{A.7}$$

The average squared deviation is referred to as the *variance* and indicates the amount of squared error for a typical case in the distribution. Conventionally, the symbol S^2 refers to the variance of a sample distribution and σ^2 refers to the variance of the population distribution. The variance of the population (σ^2) is computed by:

$$\sigma^2 = (\Sigma (X - \bar{X})^2)/N. \tag{A.8}$$

The variance of a sample (S^2) is an estimate of the population variance (σ^2). However, applying Equation A.8 directly to sample data tends to yield an S^2 value that is an underestimate of the population σ^2. If $N - 1$ is substituted for N in Equation A.8 and we apply the new equation to sample data, the resulting S^2 is a better estimate of σ^2. Therefore:

$$S^2 = (\Sigma (X - \bar{X})^2)/(N - 1). \tag{A.9}$$

The square root of a variance is called a *standard deviation*. In the special case of a dichotomous variable, the variance equals pq, where q is the proportion of cases scoring zero.

Skewedness and Kurtosis

Skewedness refers to the symmetry, and kurtosis to the "peakedness" of a distribution. Since skewedness and kurtosis statistics are rarely used in behavioral observation, we do not discuss their computation procedures. Readers may consult other introductory statistical texts for their computation.

Effect Size

To assess the difference between two distributions, comparing their means may provide an incomplete picture. Only when the variance, skewedness, and kurtosis of the two distributions are identical will the difference between the two means be a truthful indicator of the difference between the two distributions. To supplement the inadequacy of the difference between two means when the variances of the two distributions are different, we can use the standard deviation of one of the distributions as the basis for comparision. The result is the *effect size* statistic. For a comparison of a control and an experimental group mean, the difference between two means can be expressed in units of control group standard deviation. Thus:

$$ES = \frac{\bar{X}_E - \bar{X}_C}{S_C}, \tag{A.10}$$

where $\bar{X}_E$ is the experimental group mean, $\bar{X}_C$ is the control group mean, and S_C is the control group standard deviation. A more precise effect size is one that takes into account the standard deviations of both groups as follows (Hedges, 1981):

$$ES = \frac{\bar{X}_E - \bar{X}_C}{\sqrt{\dfrac{(N_E - 1)S_E^2 + (N_C - 1)S_C^2}{N_E + N_C - 2}}}, \tag{A.11}$$

where N_E and S_E^2 are the sample size and sample variance of the experimental group and N_C and S_C^2 are those of the control group.

Bivariate Statistics

When we have paired scores on two variables, correlation procedures allow us to assess the direction and the strength of the relationship between the two variables. One way to summarize the relationship between two interval variables X and Y is through their *covariance*, which is:

$$Cov(X,Y) = \frac{\Sigma (X - \bar{X})(Y - \bar{Y})}{N}. \qquad \text{(A.12)}$$

A negative covariance indicates a negative relationship. A positive covariance indicates a positive relationship. When the covariance is zero, the two variables are not related. In order to interpret its magnitude, the covariance can be standardized through the standard deviations of the X and Y variables. The result is a statistic known as *Pearson's product-moment correlation coefficient* or simply Pearson's r:

$$r = \frac{Cov(X,Y)}{S_X S_Y}, \qquad \text{(A.13)}$$

where S_X is the standard deviation of X and S_Y is the standard deviation of Y. The Pearson's r is based on the assumption that the relationship is linear. If the relationship is not linear, other indexes, such as eta squared (E^2) (Kerlinger, 1973) or omega squared (ω^2) (Hays, 1973) should be used.

For ordinal data, correlational procedures are available to compute statistics based on the ranks of the data rather than the raw data. For instance, the following set of scores can be ranked from the lowest to the highest as shown:

Score	3	8	8	11	14	19	19	19	20	32
Rank	1	2.5	2.5	4	5	7	7	7	9	10

The best known of the correlation procedures for ranked data is the Spearman Rho (ϱ_s), which is:

$$\varrho_s = 1 - \frac{6 \Sigma d^2}{N(N^2 - 1)}, \qquad \text{(A.14)}$$

where d is the difference in ranks between the two variables for each subject. Had we used the paired ranks to calculate a Pearson's r, we would have arrived at the same result. The Spearman Rho is the Pearson's r with rank data.

An alternative method for assessing the association for paired ranked data was known as tau. Tau is the ratio between the observed number of appropriate ranks minus the number of inappropriate ranks (designated s) and the maximum possible appropriate pairs:

$$t = \frac{s}{\text{maximum possible appropriate ranks}} \qquad (A.15)$$

$$= \frac{s}{N(N - 1)/2}.$$

To assess the extent of agreement among rankings of three or more observers, Kendall Coefficient of Concordance W can be used. If we designate the sum of the ranks assigned to each subject as R, the sum of squared ranks (S) is:

$$S = \frac{\Sigma R^2 - \dfrac{(\Sigma R)^2}{N}}{N}. \qquad (A.16)$$

The highest possible sum of squares of Rs is:

$$\frac{1}{12} K^2 (N^3 - N), \qquad (A.17)$$

where K is the number of observers. Then:

$$W = \frac{S}{\dfrac{1}{12} K^2 (N^3 - N)}. \qquad (A.18)$$

It has been shown that the average of all the possible Spearman Rhos for paired observers can be calculated as follows:

$$\text{Average } \varrho_s = \frac{KW - 1}{K - 1}. \qquad (A.19)$$

For nominal data, one of the most widely used correlation coefficients in behavioral observation is the phi coefficient (ϕ). Phi is a special case of the Pearson's r where all X and Y scores are zeros or ones.

Pearson's contingency coefficient (C) is a measure of association between two nominal variables. The computation of C is based on a chi-square (χ^2) statistic, which is most conveniently computed when the data are organized into a contingency table, such as in Table A.1. In Table A.1, each entry in the table, referred to as cell frequency, represents the num-

TABLE A.1
Pre- and Post-intervention 2 × 2 Contingency Table

After Intervention

			Total
	A	B	$A + B$
Before Intervention	C	D	$C + D$
	$A + C$	$B + D$	N

ber of children with the particular combination of characteristics. The total for each row and each column is referred to as the marginal. The χ^2 statistic is the total squared difference between the observed frequency and the expected frequency among the cells in the contingency table. The expected frequency for each cell equals the product of the corresponding marginals for the cell divided by the grand total number of cases. Chi-square is computed by:

$$\chi^2 = \Sigma \frac{(f_o - f_e)^2}{f_e},$$

(A.20)

where f_o is the observed cell frequency and f_e is the expected cell frequency. Pearson's C coefficient is computed by:

$$C = \sqrt{\frac{\chi^2}{\chi^2 + N}}.$$

(A.21)

The lowest possible value of C is 0.00, indicating no relationship. The maximum possible value depends upon the number of rows and columns and will never exceed 1.00. For a square contingency table where the number of rows equals the number of columns, the maximum possible value of C is:

$$\text{Maximum } C = \sqrt{\frac{k - 1}{k}},$$

(A.22)

where k is the number of rows (or columns) in a square table. When both variables are artificial dichotomies (e.g., pass–fail), the tetrachoric correlation may be used (see Ary & Jacobs, 1976).

Correlation indices are available for mixed cases where one variable is measured at one level and the other at a different level. When one variable is nominal and dichotomous and the other variable is ratio or interval, the point biserial correlation is used. If the dichotomous variable is X and the interval or ratio variable is Y, the point-biserial correlation coefficient is:

$$r_{pb} = \frac{\bar{Y}_1 - \bar{Y}_0}{S_Y} \sqrt{pq},$$

(A.23)

where $\bar{Y}_1$ is the mean of Y values for those cases with X equal to 1, $\bar{Y}_0$ is the mean of Y values for those cases with X equal to 0, p is the proportion of cases in the total sample with X values of 1, q is the proportion of cases with X values of 0, and S_Y is the sample standard deviation of all Y values for both groups combined. As in the case of ϕ, r_{pb} is a simplified computational procedure of Pearson's r when one variable is dichotomous and the other is at either an interval or a ratio level by taking advantage of the p and $\sqrt{pq}$ properties of a dichotomous variable. Together, ϕ, r_{pb}, ϱ_s, and Pearson's r are sometimes referred to as members of the Pearson product-moment correlation coefficient family.

INFERENTIAL STATISTICS

Inferential statistical techniques are methods to assess how well descriptive statistics that are derived from a random sample actually represent the parameters of the population. There are two mutually complementary approaches to inferential statistics: significance testing and parameter estimation. The significance-testing approach attempts to ascertain that the descriptive statistic is not a result of sampling artifacts from a population with a zero parameter. The parameter estimation approach attempts to estimate the magnitude of the actual population parameter based on the sample descriptive statistic.

Statistical Significance Testing

When a difference (or relationship) is indicated by the sample statistic, there are at least two competing explanations. The sample difference may reflect a true population difference or it may be due to sampling fluctuation. Significance-testing methods are designed to assess the plausibility of the latter explanation. A "straw man" hypothesis called the *null hypothesis*, under which it is postulated that the population parameter (or difference) is zero and that any nonzero sample statistic is due to sampling fluctuation, is first set up.

If the null hypothesis is true, repeated random samples drawn from the population will produce different sample statistics, forming a *sampling distribution*. If the magnitude of the sample statistic is placed within the context of the theoretical sampling distribution, we can assess mathematically the probability that a random sample drawn from the null population could produce a statistic (or a difference) with that particular or a larger magnitude. If the probability is low, we can conclude that the null scenario is not a strong competing explanation.

Since the decision to retain or reject the null hypothesis hinges on the judgment as to whether the probability is high or low, it is important that such a judgment is impartial. To ensure impartiality, the cutoff between high and low probabilities, called *alpha*, is determined prior to tests of significance. Conventional alpha values commonly used are .05, .01, and .001.

Even with these low alpha values, errors can occur. The error of rejecting the null hypothesis when it is in fact true is a *Type I* error. A *Type II* error is the error of accepting the null hypothesis when in fact a true difference exists in the population. When the significance-testing probability is smaller than alpha, the chance of committing a Type I error is low. The sample descriptive statistic is then said to be *statistically significant*. When the probability is larger than alpha, the chance of committing a Type I error is relatively high. The sample descriptive statistic is then said to be *statistically nonsignificant*.

There are two categories of statistical techniques used to test for statistical significance. Parametric statistics, or classical inferential statistics (e.g., Bradley, 1968), are used for testing the significance of descriptive statistics for which arithmetic operations are meaningful (e.g., means, variance, Pearson's *r*). For descriptive statistics on which arithmetic operations cannot be performed meaningfully (e.g., mode, median, interquartile range), *nonparametric* statistical techniques, or *distribution-free statistics*, are appropriate. In this appendix, we review only a few of the significance tests commonly encountered in behavioral observation studies.

PARAMETRIC STATISTICS

The Normal Distribution

The techniques in parametric statistics are based on a particular form of probability distribution known as the *normal* distribution. The graph of a normal distribution is symmetrical with a shape resembling that of a bell; thus, it is also referred to as a bell-shaped curve. Figure A.1 shows the general form of a normal distribution. A normal curve has a number of specific properties that make it very useful for probability assessments. The most useful property of the normal curve is the known proportions of cases within regions of the distribution. For instance, about 34% of the cases are within one standard deviation below the mean, and 34% of the cases are within one standard deviation above the mean.

A special form of the normal distribution is the *unit normal distribution*, which is also called the *z*-distribution. A *z*-distribution results when each of the scores in a normal distribution has been transformed so that it is expressed in units of standard deviation. Each score X is transformed to a z score through:

$$z = (X - \mu)/\sigma. \tag{A.24}$$

The *z*-distribution is very useful because of two reasons: (a) the population distributions of many natural events resemble the normal distribution closely and (b) the distribution of the means of samples drawn from most populations resembles a normal distribution. The latter characteristic is known as the *central limit theorem*. If a sample of N cases is repeatedly drawn from the same population, each sample has a sample mean and all the sample means form a distribution by themselves. The shape of this distribution of means, referred to as the *sampling distribution of the mean*, approaches that of the normal distribution as the sample size N increases. As N increases, the standard deviation of the sampling distribution of the mean, referred to as the *standard error of the mean*, approaches $\sigma/\sqrt{N}$.

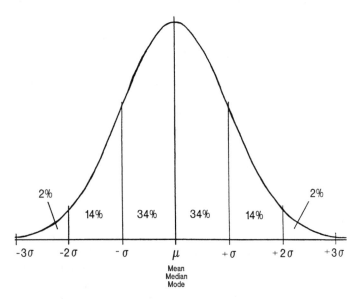

FIGURE A.1.   The normal curve.

Tests Based on the z-Distribution

When the variance of the population, σ^2, is known, all the sample means in the sampling distribution of the mean can be converted to z-scores through Equation A.24. In the resulting z-distribution, the mean is zero and the standard deviation is $1/\sqrt{N}$. The location of the mean from a particular sample can be expressed as a z-score in this z-distribution through:

$$z = (\bar{X} - \mu)/\sigma_{\bar{X}}, \tag{A.25}$$

where $\bar{X}$ is the mean of a sample, μ is the hypothesized population mean (or 0), and $\sigma_{\bar{X}}$ is the standard error of the mean, which equals $\sigma/\sqrt{N}$. The probability values associated with various z scores in a z-distribution are generally presented in the form of a z table and can be found in most introductory statistical texts.

A research hypothesis that has a definite direction calls for a *one-tailed* test of significance, which assesses the probability of obtaining a particular or more extreme z score on one side of the mean. If one simply hypothesizes that the population mean is *different* from the null mean, a *two-tailed* test is called for. In this case, the actual probability is twice that of the smaller portion associated with a z score.

Another useful application of the z-distribution is testing the significance of a sample Pearson's r. If all rs in the sampling distribution of a given ϱ are transformed to a statistic known as Fisher's Zeta, Z_r, through:

$$Z_r = .5 \log_e (1 + r) - .5 \log_e (1 - r), \tag{A.26}$$

the resulting Z_r values will have an approximately normal distribution and the standard error of the Z_r sampling distribution will be:

$$S_{Zr} = \sqrt{1/(N - 3)}. \tag{A.27}$$

A z score can then be derived through:

$$z = \frac{Z_r - Z_\varrho}{\sqrt{1/(N - 3)}}. \tag{A.28}$$

For a ϕ coefficient, statistical significance can be tested directly through:

$$z = \phi \sqrt{N}. \tag{A.29}$$

Tests Based on the t-Distribution

The z-test is appropriate only when the population σ is known. In most research situations, σ is unknown. Recall that the best estimate of σ based on sample data is through S. To the extent that S is an accurate estimate of σ, the central limit theorem applies to the sampling distribution of the mean. Hence, the standard error of the sampling distribution can be estimated through $S_X = S/\sqrt{N}$. If S_X is indeed identical to σ_X, the distribution of the scores standardized through $(X - \mu)/S_X$ would be a z distribution. To the extent that S_X is different from σ_X, the distribution of the standardized scores departs from a z distribution. The standardized score based on the estimate of σ_X through S_X is called a t-score. Specifically,

$$t = \frac{\bar{X} - \mu}{S_X}.$$
(A.30)

The distribution of t scores differs in various degrees from a z-distribution in kurtosis. As the sample size approaches infinity, a t-distribution approaches a z-distribution. The assessment of probabilities associated with different t values requires different probability tables with different degrees of freedom. The degree of freedom is a statistical characteristic associated with a distribution. Conceptually, it indicates how many of the values in a distribution are "free" to change.

To simplify these tables, the critical values for different alpha levels for different degrees of freedom are generally given in statistical tables. To test for the significance of a t value, one compares the obtained t value from the study against the critical value at the chosen alpha level. If the observed t is larger than the critical value, the actual probability is less than alpha and the t is statistically significant.

In its most generalized form, the t value for a statistic is computed through:

$$t = \frac{\text{statistic} - \text{parameter}}{\text{estimated standard error}},$$
(A.31)

where statistic is the sample statistic, parameter is that of the population under the null hypothesis (i.e., 0), and estimated standard error is the standard error of the sampling distribution.

To compare a sample mean with a hypothetical population mean of zero, the statistic is the sample mean, the parameter is zero, and the standard error is estimated through:

$$S_e = S_X/\sqrt{N}.$$
(A.32)

The probability of the subsequent t statistic is assessed against $N - 1$ degrees of freedom. This process is referred to as the *one sample t-test*.

When comparing a sample mean (e.g., experimental mean) against another sample mean (e.g., control mean), the statistic is the experimental mean and the parameter is the control mean. The best estimate of the standard error for this situation is an estimate *pooled* from the two different sample standard deviations:

$$S_e = \sqrt{\frac{(N_1 - 1)S_1^2 + (N_2 - 1)S_2^2}{N_1 + N_2 - 2} \left(\frac{1}{N_1} + \frac{1}{N_2}\right)}, \quad \text{(A.33)}$$

where N_1 is the sample size in Group 1, S_1^2 is the sample variance of Group 1, N_2 is the sample size of Group 2, and S_2^2 is the sample variance of Group 2. The probability of the resulting t statistic is assessed against $N_1 + N_2 - 2$ degrees of freedom. This process is referred to as the *two-sample independent t-test*.

When two samples are mutually dependent (e.g., pretest–posttest), it is inappropriate to compare the two means directly through the two-sample independent *t*-test. Instead, we can take the difference between the pretest and posttest for each subject and compute the mean difference score, which can then be compared against a hypothetical mean difference of zero. Therefore, for the *t*-test of dependent samples, the statistic is the mean difference between each pair of observations, and the parameter is the hypothetical mean difference. The standard error is the dispersion in the sampling distribution of mean differences:

$$S_e = \sqrt{\frac{1}{N} \Sigma \frac{(d - \bar{d})^2}{N - 1}}, \quad \text{(A.34)}$$

where d is the difference between each pair of observations, $\bar{d}$ is the mean difference for all pairs of observations, and N is the number of pairs of observation. The probability of the resulting t statistic is assessed through $N - 1$ degrees of freedom.

The *t*-distribution can also be used to test for the significance of an observed Pearson's r (or Spearman's rho or point-biserial) against a null hypothesis of $\varrho = 0$. The standard error of the sampling distribution of r is:

$$S_e = \sqrt{\frac{1 - r^2}{N - 2}}. \quad \text{(A.35)}$$

The value of t is obtained through Equation A.31, for which the observed r is the statistic, a ϱ of 0 is the parameter, and the standard error is estimated through Equation A.35. The probability of the t is assessed through $N - 2$ degrees of freedom.

Tests Based on the F-Distribution

For situations in which more than two groups are compared simultaneously, the *F*-ratio, which is a ratio of the estimated variance within the groups divided by the estimated variance across the groups, is appropriate. The variance within each group is the variance of all the scores within the group from the mean of the group. The variance between the groups is the variance of all subjects from the grand mean if all subject scores are represented by their respective group means.

When *k* groups of *n* subjects each are drawn from the same population repeatedly and the *F*-ratio is computed from each of the *k* groups, the resulting *F*-ratios will form a sampling distribution of *F*-ratios called the *F*-distribution. The *F*-distributions for the same within-group degree of freedom *and* the same between-group degrees of freedom are identical. The within-group degree of freedom is determined by the total number of subjects across the groups minus the number of groups. The between-group degree of freedom is determined by the number of groups minus one.

The general process used to compare the means across a number of groups through the assessment of the probability of obtaining the subsequent *F*-ratio is called an *analysis of variance* (ANOVA). When the groups are categorized along only one variable, the ANOVA is a one-way ANOVA. When comparisons are to be made among groups that are categorized along two variables, the process is a two-way ANOVA. One may categorize the subjects along *m* variables and compare all the groups simultaneously. The resulting process is then an *m*-way ANOVA. The complexity of the process increases geometrically as new variables are added to the analysis.

For a one-way ANOVA, the between-group and within-group mean squares (MS_b and MS_w) can be assessed as follows. First, the grand mean ($\bar{X}$) of all subjects from all groups can be determined:

$$\bar{X} = \Sigma \ X/N. \tag{A.36}$$

For each of the groups, a group mean can also be obtained:

$$\bar{X}_j = \sum_{i=1}^{N_j} X_i/N_j, \tag{A.37}$$

where N_j is the number of subjects in the *j*th group. The between-group sum of squares (SS_b) across the *k* groups is:

$$SS_b = \sum_{j=1}^{k} N_j(\bar{X}_j - \bar{X})^2. \tag{A.38}$$

For the between-group mean square (MS_b), the degree of freedom is $k - 1$:

$$MS_b = SS_b/(k - 1). \tag{A.39}$$

The within-group sum of squares (SS_w) can be determined by:

$$SS_w = \sum_{j=1}^{k} \sum_{i=1}^{N_j} (X_i - \bar{X}_j)^2. \tag{A.40}$$

For the within-group mean square (MS_w), there are $N - k$ degrees of freedom:

$$MS_w = SS_w/(N - k). \tag{A.41}$$

From the mean square estimates, the F-ratio can be determined by:

$$F = MS_b/MS_w. \tag{A.42}$$

The significance of this F-ratio can be assessed by finding the proportion of F-ratios equal to or greater than this F-ratio in an F-table for $(k - 1)$ and $(N - k)$ degrees of freedom.

When an ANOVA yields a statistically singificant F-ratio, it indicates that at least one of the groups of subjects is significantly different from the other groups. To determine which group(s) is significantly different from others, a post hoc test is needed. The two most common post hoc methods are the Scheffe method (Scheffe, 1959) and the Tukey method (Winer, 1962).

NONPARAMETRIC STATISTICS

Two central assumptions in parametric tests of significance are interval-level data and homoscedasticity (or homogeneity of variances). When these are clearly violated, an alternative is to use one of the nonparametric statistical tests. Nonparametric techniques are also referred to as *distribution-free* statistics.

Tests for Nominal Data

Chi-Square Tests

The chi-square distribution is a theoretical sampling distribution of the total difference between observed frequencies and expected frequencies expressed in the form of a χ^2 statistic. As such, it is very useful for analyses of nominal data. For example, the χ^2 sampling distribution can be used to estimate the probability of drawing a sample with various numbers of cases in each category of a nominal scale from a theoretical population with specific proportion of cases in each category. This use of the χ^2 distribution is referred to as the χ^2 *goodness-of-fit test* or the *one sample* χ^2 *test*. Another use of the χ^2 distribution is the χ^2 *test of independence*. In this case, χ^2 is used to test for the significance of the relationship between two nominal variables or the same nominal variable between two groups of subjects. For example, it can be used to test for the significance of an observed contingency (C) coefficient.

The computation of the χ^2 statistic has been discussed briefly in the previous discussion of the contingency coefficient. In a χ^2 goodness-of-fit test, the contingency table reduces to a single row. The cell frequencies are compared against a set of hypothetical frequencies, and the χ^2 value is computed based on the differences. The probability of obtaining the observed frequencies from a population with the hypothetical distribution is obtained from the sampling distribution of χ^2 values. The sampling distributions of χ^2 values for situations with the same degrees of freedom (df) are identical. The degree of freedom for a test of goodness-of-fit of a variable with k categories is $k - 1$. The degree of freedom for a test of independence in which one variable has n categories and the other variable has k categories is $(n - 1)(k - 1)$.

The χ^2 test of goodness-of-fit or independence will not produce meaningful probability values if more than 20% of the cells have expected frequencies of less than 5. For a goodness-of-fit test involving a dichotomy, each of the two expected frequencies should be at least 5.

Fisher's Exact Probability Test

The Fisher exact probability test is an alternative for 2×2 tables in which more than 20% of the expected frequencies are less than 5. It computes directly the probability of obtaining a particular 2×2 contingency table by chance from a population in which the two variables are not related. For the observed 2×2 frequency table shown in Table A.2, the probability of obtaining such a contingency table by chance is given by:

$$p = \frac{(A + B)!(C + D)!(A + C)!(B + D)!}{N!A!B!C!D!} \tag{A.43}$$

where ! is the factorial operator.

The McNemar Test

A χ^2-based test that is particularly useful for pre- and postinterven-

TABLE A.2
Babbling Behavior Data for Fisher's Exact Test

| | | Gender of the Infant | | |
		Male	Female	Total
Behavior Rating	Babbling	$A = 3$	$B = 1$	4
	Not Babbling	$C = 2$	$D = 4$	6
	Total	5	5	10

tion assessment is the McNemar test. It is appropriate for situations in which the variable is a dichotomy and the research hypothesis is that the behavior tends to change from one category to another as a result of intervention. In a McNemar test, the null hypothesis states that the proportion of cases changing from Category A to Category B is the same as the proportion of cases changing from Category B to Category A, and the observed difference between the number of cases changing in one direction and the other is due to sampling fluctuation. Using the notations in Table A.3, the probability value for a McNemar test can be estimated through the following χ^2 statistic:

$$\chi^2 = \frac{(A - D)^2}{A + D}.$$ (A.44)

The probability can be approximated by comparing the critical value of χ^2 at the desired level of significance against the computed χ^2. To improve the accuracy of the χ^2 value for the McNemar test, the Yates' correction for continuity may be used:

$$\chi^2 = \frac{(|A - D| - 1)^2}{A + D}.$$ (A.45)

Binomial Test

A useful approach to testing the significance of dichotomous data is the binomial test. In a binomial distribution, the proportion of observations scored 1 is represented by p and the proportion scored 0 is represented by a q, which equals $1 - p$. The question in a binomial test is how likely it is to obtain a sample of n observations from a population with parameters

p and q such that r of the n observations are scored 1. The probability is:

$$Pr(r) = \frac{n!}{r!(n - r)!} (p)^r(q)^{n - r}.$$

(A.46)

For large ns, the binomial probability can be assessed through a z-score approximation process:

$$z = \frac{(r \pm .5) - np}{\sqrt{npq}},$$

(A.47)

where the $\pm .5$ is the correction for continuity. If r is less than np, r is corrected by $+.5$. If r is larger than np, r is corrected by $-.5$. The significance of the z value can be assessed directly from a unit-normal z table.

Poisson Test

Another direct approach to testing the significance of discrete dichotomous data is the Poisson test. The Poisson distribution can be viewed as an extremely skewed case of the binomial distribution and provides a more accurate probability estimate than the binomial test when the p value of the population is extremely small. It is also appropriate for the testing of frequency of behavior for an infrequent behavior.

Mathematically, the probability of randomly drawing an event (e.g., a per session frequency of occurrence) with a value of X from all possible events (e.g., all possible frequencies) with a mean value of λ in a Poisson distribution can be computed through:

$$pr(X) = (\lambda^X e^{-\lambda})/X!,$$

(A.48)

where $Pr(X)$ is the probability of obtaining a value of X, λ is the mean value of all possible events (e.g., mean of all possible per session frequen-

TABLE A.3
Contingency Table for McNemar Test

		After Intervention		Total
		Nonviolent	Violent	
Before Intervention	Violent	$A = 8$	$B = 3$	11
	Nonviolent	$C = 88$	$D = 1$	89
		96	4	100

cies of an infrequent behavior), and e is the natural logarithmic constant and is approximately equal to 2.718.

Sign Test

A useful binomial-based test for behavioral observation studies is the sign test. It is appropriate for situations in which the data are expressed in terms of either a + sign, a − sign, or a neutral sign, and the researcher is interested only in determining whether the number of + signs equal the number of − signs. The probability of drawing by chance a sample of n signs with r + signs from a population in which the numbers of + s and − s are equal can be computed through:

$$p = \frac{n!}{r!(n - r)!} .5^n,$$

(A.49)

where n is the total number of + and − signs, ignoring neutral signs.

Tests for Ordinal Data

Much data in behavioral observation fit the definition of ordinal data. This is particularly true with rating scale (see chapter 2). Such data are often analyzed with parametric statistical procedures. However, many statistical tests are available that require only that scores can be ranked meaningfully from highest to lowest. A disadvantage of these statistical tests for ordinal data is that they are typically less powerful than interval statistics. That is, one is more likely to retain a false null hypothesis (Type II error) with an ordinal test than with an interval test. However, in many cases, the difference in power is relatively small.

For a test for difference in central tendencies between two independent samples, the Mann–Whitney U is a test of significance for ranked data that provides the same information that the two-sample independent t-test provides and is slightly less powerful than the t-test. A nonparametric alternative to the one-sample dependent t-test is the Wilcoxon matched-pairs signed-ranks test. It is also slightly less powerful than the dependent t-test. For comparing the central tendencies of k independent samples, the Kruskal–Wallis one-way analysis of variance has a power efficiency ratio of 95.5% compared with the F-ratio analysis of variance. Siegel (1956) and Marascuilo and McSweeney (1977) are two excellent sources on nonparametric ordinal tests.

DIRECT ESTIMATION OF PARAMETERS

An inherent limitation of the significance-testing approach is that it can provide information only on "what is not" (i.e., not zero) but not information on "what is." A supplement to the significance-testing approach is a direct estimation of the parameters. This can be accomplished through either or both of two approaches: point estimation and interval estimation. With point estimation, we derive the most probable value of the parameter based on sample statistic. The limitation is that although the estimate is the most probable value of the parameter, it can in fact be wrong. With interval estimation, we derive the range of possible values for the parameter. Although the latter approach is more conservative and more credible, the result is less precise.

Point Estimates

When the sampe data are random and mutually independent, the best unbiased estimate of the parameter μ is the sample mean $\bar{X}$, and the best unbiased estimate of the parameter σ^2 is the sample variance S^2. However, the sample standard deviation S, because of the quadratic function involved, tends to be an underestimate of the population σ. A better estimate of σ is an S that has been corrected for the expected underestimation (Hays, 1973):

$$\text{unbiased estimate of } \sigma = [1 + \frac{1}{4(N-1)}]S. \tag{A.50}$$

The estimation of the parameter ϱ from a sample Pearson's r is less direct. We can estimate from r^2 as follows:

$$\text{best estimate of } \varrho^2 = \frac{(N-1)r^2 - 1}{(N-1) - r^2}. \tag{A.51}$$

The values of r^2 or ϱ^2 have concrete meanings. Specifically, r^2 is the proportion of uncertainty that is reduced in predicting one variable as a result of knowing another variable. The ϱ^2 is a special case of a more general purpose indicator of the strength of relationship, omega-squared (ω^2). As a measure of the strength of relationship between two or more variables, ω^2 is applicable to most situations in which more than one variable is involved. The underlying parameter ω^2 for a two–sample independent t-test situation can be estimated directly based on the t statistic for the two samples through:

$$\omega^2 = \frac{t^2 - 1}{t^2 + N_1 + N_2 - 1} \tag{A.52}$$

For a one-way analysis-of-variance situation, the strength of the underlying relationship between group membership and scores can be estimated through:

$$\omega^2 = \frac{SS_{between} - (k - 1)MS_{within}}{SS_{total} + MS_{within}}. \tag{A.53}$$

For a two-way ANOVA in which subjects are categorized according to an A variable and a B variable, there are three underlying measures of relationship. These include the reduction in uncertainty with respect to A and B, and to the interaction between A and B. The three parameters can be estimated, respectively, through:

$$\omega_A^2 = \frac{SS_A - (N_A - 1)MS_e}{SS_{total} + MS_e}, \tag{A.54}$$

$$\omega_B^2 = \frac{SS_B - (N_B - 1)MS_e}{SS_{total} + MS_e}, \tag{A.55}$$

and

$$\omega_{AB}^2 = \frac{SS_{AB} - (N_A - 1)(N_B - 1))MS_e}{SS_{total} + MS_e}. \tag{A.56}$$

Interval Estimates

With the confidence-interval approach, one assesses the range of values within which a certain proportion of the sample statistics are expected to fall. The most common application of the confidence-interval estimate is to determine the 95% confidence interval of the mean. If the population standard deviation σ is known, the sampling distribution of the mean is then known to be a z-distribution with a standard error of the mean of $\sigma/\sqrt{N}$. For a z-distribution, it is known that 95% of the cases will fall within the z-scores of $+1.96$ and -1.96. Hence, the 95% confidence interval ($CI_{95\%}$) for the mean is:

$$\begin{aligned} CI_{95\%} &= \bar{X} \pm z_{95\%}(\sigma/\sqrt{N}) \\ &= \bar{X} \pm 1.96(\sigma_e). \end{aligned} \tag{A.57}$$

This will yield two values that define the upper and lower limits of the 95% confidence interval.

When the population standard deviation σ is unknown, the sampling distribution of the mean is no longer a z-distribution but a t-distribution. The 95% confidence interval based on S is:

$$CI_{95\%} = \bar{X} \pm t_{95\%}(S/\sqrt{N}), \tag{A.58}$$

where $\pm t_{95\%}$ are the t values between which 95% of the t values will fall. Unlike $z_{95\%}$, which is known to be 1.96, the value of $t_{95\%}$ is different for different t-distributions with different degrees of freedom. For a t-distribution with 10 degrees of freedom (i.e., $N = 11$), for instance, $t_{95\%}$ is approximately 2.23. For a t-distribution with 100 degrees of freedom, on the other hand, $t_{95\%}$ is about 1.98.

For Pearson's r, the sampling distribution of the Fisher's zeta transformation of rs approximates a normal distribution with a standard error of $\sqrt{1/(N - 3)}$. Hence, the 95% confidence interval of the value of Z_r can be assessed through:

$$CI_{95\%} = Z_r \pm 1.96 \left(\sqrt{\frac{1}{N - 3}} \right).$$

(A.59)

The results will be two Z_r values. The 95% confidence interval of ϱ can be obtained by converting these two Z_r values back to Pearson's rs.

Probabilities of Systematic Error in Single-Subject Time Sampling for Selected Intervals

Interval = 3

B		10	20	30	40	50	60
					T		
10	P	.2686	.0206	.0105	.0103	.0103	.0103
	M	.0206	.0103	.0103	.0103	.0103	.0103
	W	.2686	.2583	.2583	.2583	.2583	.2583
20	P	.2583	.0103	.0014	.0000	.0000	.0000
	M	.0103	.0000	.0000	.0000	.0000	.0000
	W	.0206	.0103	.0103	.0103	.0103	.0103
30	P	.2583	.0103	.0000	.0000	.0000	.0000
	M	.0103	.0000	.0000	.0000	.0000	.0000
	W	.0105	.0014	.0002	.0002	.0002	.0002
40	P	2583	.0103	.0002	.0000	.0000	.0000
	M	.0103	.0000	.0000	.0000	.0000	.0000
	W	.0103	.0000	.0000	.0000	.0000	.0000
50	P	.2583	.0103	.0002	.0000	.0000	.0000
	M	.0103	.0000	.0000	.0000	.0000	.0000
	W	.0103	.0000	.0000	.0000	.0000	.0000
60	P	.2583	.0103	.0002	.0000	.0000	.0000
	M	.0103	.0000	.0000	.0000	.0000	.0000
	W	.0103	.0000	.0000	.0000	.0000	.0000

Note: Probability values are computed through the use of BOSA (Suen & Yue, forthcoming). P = partial-interval sampling; M = momentary sampling; and W = whole-interval sampling.

TABLE
continued
Interval = 5

B		T					
		10	20	30	40	50	60
10	P	.6763	.1341	.0698	.0671	.0670	.0670
	M	.1341	.0671	.0670	.0670	.0670	0670
	W	.6763	.6093	.6092	.6092	.6092	.6092
20	P	.6093	.0671	.0086	.0044	.0033	.0020
	M	.0671	.0044	.0020	.0020	.0020	.0020
	W	.1341	.0671	.0670	.0670	.0670	.0670
30	P	.6092	.0670	.0079	.0020	.0000	.0000
	M	.0670	.0020	.0000	.0000	.0000	.0000
	W	.0698	.0086	.0079	.0079	.0079	.0079
40	P	.6092	.0670	.0079	.0020	.0000	.0000
	M	.0670	.0020	.0000	.0000	.0000	.0000
	W	.0671	.0044	.0020	.0020	.0020	.0020
50	P	.6092	.0670	.0079	.0020	.0000	.0000
	M	.0670	.0020	.0000	.0000	.0000	.0000
	W	.0670	.0033	.0000	.0000	.0000	.0000
60	P	.6092	.0670	.0079	.0020	.0000	.0000
	M	.0670	.0020	.0000	.0000	.0000	.0000
	W	.0670	.0020	.0000	.0000	.0000	.0000

TABLE
continued
Interval = 10

B		T 10	20	30	40	50	60
	P	1.0000	1.0000	.7014	.5938	.5938	.5938
10	M	1.0000	.5938	.5830	.5830	.5830	.5830
	W	1.0000	1.0000	.9796	.9796	.9796	.9796
	P	1.0000	.5938	.1293	.0216	.0114	.0108
20	M	.5938	.0216	.0108	.0108	.0108	.0108
	W	1.0000	.5938	.5830	.5830	.5830	.5830
	P	.9796	.5830	.1185	.0108	.0090	.0046
30	M	.5830	.0108	.0046	.0024	.0024	.0024
	W	.7014	.1293	.1185	.1185	.1185	.1185
	P	.9796	.5830	.1185	.0108	.0087	.0024
40	M	.5830	.0108	.0024	.0000	.0000	.0000
	W	.5938	.0216	.0108	.0108	.0108	.0108
	P	.9796	.5830	.1185	.0108	.0087	.0024
50	M	.5830	.0108	.0024	.0000	.0000	.0000
	W	.5938	.0114	.0090	.0087	.0087	.0087
	P	.9796	.5830	.1185	.0108	.0087	.0024
60	M	.5830	.0108	.0024	.0000	.0000	.0000
	W	.5938	.0108	.0046	.0024	.0024	.0024

TABLE
(continued)
Interval = 20

B		T					
		10	20	30	40	50	60
10	P	1.0000	1.0000	1.0000	1.0000	1.0000	1.0000
	M	1.0000	1.0000	1.0000	1.0000	1.0000	1.0000
	W	1.0000	1.0000	1.0000	1.0000	1.0000	1.0000
20	P	1.0000	1.0000	1.0000	1.0000	1.0000	1.0000
	M	1.0000	1.0000	.5944	.5595	.5591	.5591
	W	1.0000	1.0000	1.0000	1.0000	1.0000	1.0000
30	P	1.0000	1.0000	.9523	.5944	.2208	.0706
	M	1.0000	.5944	.0706	.0357	.0353	.0353
	W	1.0000	1.0000	.9523	.9174	.9170	.9170
40	P	1.0000	1.0000	.9174	.5595	.1859	.0357
	M	1.0000	.5595	.0357	.0037	.0007	.0007
	W	1.0000	1.0000	.5944	.5595	.5591	.5591
50	P	1.0000	1.0000	.9170	.5591	.1855	.0353
	M	1.0000	.5591	.0353	.0007	.0000	.0000
	W	1.0000	1.0000	.2208	.1859	.1855	.1855
60	P	1.0000	1.0000	.9170	.5591	.1855	.0353
	M	1.0000	.5591	.0353	.0007	.0000	.0000
	W	1.0000	1.0000	.0706	.0357	.0353	.0353

TABLE
(continued)
Interval = 30

		T					
B		10	20	30	40	50	60
	P	1.0000	1.0000	1.0000	1.0000	1.0000	1.0000
10	M	1.0000	1.0000	1.0000	1.0000	1.0000	1.0000
	W	1.0000	1.0000	1.0000	1.0000	1.0000	1.0000
	P	1.0000	1.0000	1.0000	1.0000	1.0000	1.0000
20	M	1.0000	1.0000	1.0000	.9833	.9795	.9795
	W	1.0000	1.0000	1.0000	1.0000	1.0000	1.0000
	P	1.0000	1.0000	1.0000	1.0000	.9576	.4987
30	M	1.0000	1.0000	.4987	.2531	.2494	.2494
	W	1.0000	1.0000	1.0000	1.0000	1.0000	1.0000
	P	1.0000	1.0000	1.0000	.9833	.7120	.2531
40	M	1.0000	.9833	.2531	.0540	.0078	.0077
	W	1.0000	1.0000	1.0000	.9833	.9795	.9795
	P	1.0000	1.0000	1.0000	.9795	.7082	.2494
50	M	1.0000	.9795	.2494	.0078	.0064	.0000
	W	1.0000	1.0000	.9576	.7120	.7082	.7082
	P	1.0000	1.0000	1.0000	.9795	.7082	.2494
60	M	1.0000	.9795	.2494	.0077	.0000	.0000
	W	1.0000	1.0000	.4987	.2531	.2494	.2494

Maximum and Minimum Kappa for Given Proportion Agreement Value

MAX KAPPA

p_0 Range*						p_1 Values						
U	L	1.0	0.95	0.90	0.85	0.80	0.75	0.7	0.65	0.60	0.55	0.50
1		0	0.7872	0.7727	1	1	1	1	1	1	1	1
0.95	Any Legitimate Lower Bounds	0	0.6429	0.7727	0.6923	0.8571	0.8750	0.8864	0.8936	0.8980	0.9	0.9
0.9		0	0.4595	0.6154	0.6923	0.7368	0.7647	0.7826	0.7938	0.8	0.8020	0.8
0.85		0	0.3478	0.5000	0.5833	0.6341	0.6667	0.6875	0.7	0.7059	0.7059	0.7
0.8		0	0.2727	0.4118	0.4937	0.5455	0.5789	0.6	0.6117	0.6153	0.6117	0.6
0.75		0	0.2187	0.3421	0.4186	0.4681	0.5	0.5192	0.5283	0.5283	0.5192	0.5
0.7		0	0.1781	0.2857	0.3548	0.4	0.4286	0.4444	0.4495	0.4444	0.4286	0.4
0.65		0	0.1463	0.2391	0.3	0.3396	0.3636	0.375	0.375	0.3637	0.3396	0.3
0.6		0	0.1209	0.2	0.2523	0.2857	0.3043	0.3103	0.3043	0.2857	0.2523	0.2
0.55		0	0.1	0.1667	0.2105	0.2372	0.2500	0.25	0.2373	0.2105	0.1667	0.1
0.50		0	0.0826	0.1379	0.1736	0.1935	0.2000	0.1935	0.1736	0.1397	0.0826	0
0.45		0	0.0678	0.1129	0.1406	0.1538	0.1538	0.1406	0.1129	0.0678	0	− 0.1
0.4		0	0.0551	0.0909	0.1111	0.1176	0.1111	0.0909	0.0551	0	− 0.1009	− 0.2

(Continued)

325

Maximum and Minimum Kappa for Given Proportion Agreement Value
(Continued)

MAX KAPPA

p_0 Range*		p_1 Values										
U	L	1.0	0.95	0.90	0.85	0.80	0.75	0.7	0.65	0.60	0.55	0.50
0.35		0	0.0441	0.0714	0.0845	0.0845	0.0714	0.0441	0	-0.1017	-0.2037	-0.3
0.3		0	0.0345	0.0541	0.0604	0.0541	0.0345	0	-0.1024	-0.2069	-0.3084	-0.4
0.25		0	0.0260	0.0385	0.0385	0.0260	0	-0.1029	-0.2097	-0.3158	-0.4151	-0.5
0.2		0	0.0184	0.0244	0.0184	0	-0.1034	-0.2121	-0.3223	-0.4286	-0.5238	-0.6
0.15		0	0.0116	0.0116	0	-0.1039	-0.2143	-0.3281	-0.4407	-0.5455	-0.6346	-0.7
0.1		0	0.0055	0	-0.1043	-0.2162	-0.3333	-0.4516	-0.5652	-0.6667	-0.7476	-0.8
0.05		0	0	-0.1047	-0.2179	-0.3380	-0.4615	-0.5833	-0.6964	-0.7925	-0.8627	-0.9
0		—	—	—	—	—	—	—	—	—	—	—

Note: This table was constructed by Dr. Patrick S. C. Lee of the Pennsylvania State University and is printed with his permission. Kappa values for $p_1 < .50$ are symmetrical to those of $p_1 > .50$. To find kappa values for $p_1 < .50$, use $(1 - p_1)$ in place of p_1.

*U = upper values of p_0 and L = lower values of p_0.

Any Legitimate Lower Bounds

MIN KAPPA

p_0 Range		p_1 Values										
U	L	1.0	0.95	0.90	0.85	0.80	0.75	6.70	0.65	0.6	0.55	0.5
Any Legitimate Upper Bounds	0.95	0	0.4737	0.7727	0.7727	0.8276	0.8571	0.8750	0.8864	0.8936	0.8980	0.9
	0.9	0	-0.0526	0.4444	0.4595	0.6154	0.6923	0.7368	0.7647	0.7826	0.7938	0.8
	0.85	0	-0.0714	-0.0714	0	0.3478	0.5000	0.5833	0.6341	0.6667	0.6875	0.7
	0.8	0	-0.0811	-0.1111	-0.0811	0	0.2727	0.4118	0.4937	0.5455	0.5789	0.6
	0.75	0	-0.0870	-0.1364	-0.1364	-0.0870	0	0.2187	0.3421	0.4186	0.4681	0.5
	0.7	0	-0.0909	-0.1538	-0.1765	-0.1538	-0.0909	0	0.1781	0.2857	0.3548	0.4
	0.65	0	-0.0938	-0.1667	-0.2069	-0.2069	-0.1667	-0.0938	0	0.1463	0.2391	0.3
	0.6	0	-0.0959	-0.1765	-0.2308	-0.2500	-0.2308	-0.1765	-0.0959	0	0.1209	0.2
	0.55	0	-0.0976	-0.1842	-0.2500	-0.2857	-0.2857	-0.25	-0.1842	-0.0976	0	0.1
	0.5	0	-0.0989	-0.1905	-0.2658	-0.3158	-0.3333	-0.3158	-0.2658	-0.1905	-0.0989	0
	0.45	0	-0.1000	-0.1957	-0.2791	-0.3415	-0.3750	-0.375	-0.3415	-0.2791	-0.1957	-0.1
	0.4	0	-0.1009	-0.2000	-0.2903	-0.3636	-0.4118	-0.4286	-0.4118	-0.3636	-0.2903	-0.2
	0.35	0	-0.1017	-0.2037	-0.3000	-0.3830	-0.4444	-0.4773	-0.4773	-0.4444	-0.3830	-0.3
	0.3	0	-0.1024	-0.2069	-0.3084	-0.4000	-0.4737	-0.5217	-0.5385	-0.5217	-0.4737	-0.4
	0.25	0	-0.1029	-0.2097	-0.3158	-0.4151	-0.5	-0.5625	-0.5957	-0.5957	-0.5625	-0.5
	0.2	0	-0.1034	-0.2121	-0.3223	-0.4286	-0.5238	-0.6	-0.6495	-0.6667	-0.6495	-0.6
	0.15	0	-0.1039	-0.2143	-0.3281	-0.4407	-0.5455	-0.6346	-0.7	-0.7347	-0.7347	-0.7
	0.1	0	-0.1043	-0.2162	-0.3333	-0.4516	-0.5652	-0.6667	-0.7476	-0.8	-0.8182	-0.8
	0.05	0	-0.1047	-0.2179	-0.3380	-0.4615	-0.5833	-0.6964	-0.7925	-0.8627	-0.9	-0.9
	0	0	-0.1050	-0.2195	-0.3423	-0.4706	-0.6000	-0.7241	-0.8349	-0.9231	-0.9802	-1.0

References

Abikoff, H., Gittleman-Klein, R., & Klein, D. F. (1977). Validation of a classroom observation code for hyperactive children. *Journal of Consulting and Clinical Psychology, 45,* 772–783.

Aldrich-Blake, F. P. G. (1970). Problems of social structure in forest monkeys. In J. H. Crook (Ed.), *Social behavior in birds and mammals: Essays on the social ethology of animals and man.* New York: Academic Press.

Allison, P. D., & Liker, J. K. (1982). Analyzing sequential data on dyads: A comment on Gottman. *Psychological Bulletin,* 393–403.

Altmann, J. (1974). Observational study of behavior: Sampling methods. *Behaviour, 49,* 227–267.

Altmann, S. A. (1965). Sociobiology of Rhesus monkeys, II: Stochastic of social communication. *Journal of Theoretical Biology, 8,* 490–522.

American College Testing Program (1973). *Highlights of the ACT technical report.* Iowa City, IA: ACT.

Anastasi, A. (1976). *Psychological testing* (4th ed.). New York: Macmillan.

Araujo, J., & Born, D. G. (1985). Calculating percentage agreement correctly but writing its formula incorrectly. *The Behavior Analyst, 8,* 207–208.

Armitage, P., Blendis, L. M., & Smyllie, H. C. (1966). The measurement of observer disagreement in the recording of signs. *Journal of the Royal Statistical Society, 129,* 98–109.

Arrington, R. E. (1939). Time-sampling studies of child behavior. *Psychological Monographs, 51*(2), 3–185.

Arrington, R. E. (1943). Time sampling in studies of social behavior: A critical review of techniques and results with research suggestions. *Psychological Bulletin, 40,* 81–124.

Ary, D. (1984). Mathematical explanation of error in duration recording using partial interval, whole interval, and momentary time sampling. *Behavioral Assessment, 6,* 221–228.

Ary, D., & Jacobs, L. C. (1976). *Introduction to statistics: Purposes and procedures.* New York: Holt, Rinehart, and Winston.

Ary, D., Jacobs, L. C., & Razavieh, A. (1985). *Introduction to research in education* (3rd ed.). New York: Holt, Rinehart, and Winston.

Ary, D., & Suen, H. K. (1983). The use of momentary time sampling to assess both frequency and duration of behavior. *Journal of Behavioral Assessment, 5*(2), 143–150.

Ary, D., & Suen, H. K. (April 1984). *Determining the number of behaviors to include in sequential time sampling.* Paper presented at the annual meeting of the American Educational Research Association, New Orleans.

Ary, D., & Suen, H. K. (1985). Statistical significance of percent interobserver agreement reliability. *Midwestern Educational Researcher, 6,* 31–33.

Ary, D., Van Acker, R. M., & Karsh, K. L. (April 1986). *Comparing behavior duration reliabilities of momentary time sampling and continuous electronic data gathering.* Paper presented at the annual meeting of the American Educational Research Association, San Francisco.

Aschoff, J. (Ed.). (1981). *Handbook of behavioral neurobiology: Vol. 4. Biological rhythms.* New York: Plenum Press.

Babbie, E. R. (1973). *Survey research methods.* Belmont, CA: Wadsworth.

Baer, D. M. (1977a). Reviewer's comment: Just because it's reliable doesn't mean that you can use it. *Journal of Applied Behavior Analysis, 10,* 117–119.

Baer, D. M. (1977b). Perhaps it would be better not to know everything. *Journal of Applied Behavior Analysis, 10,* 167–172.

Baer, D. M., Wolf, M. M., & Risley, T. R. (1968). Some current dimensions of applied behavior analysis. *Journal of Applied Behavior Analysis, 1,* 91–97.

Bakeman, R. (1978). Untangling streams of behavior: Sequential analysis of observational data. In G. P. Sackett (Ed.), *Observing behavior: Vol. 2. Data collection and analysis methods* (pp. 63–78). Baltimore: University Park Press.

Bakeman, R., & Dabbs, J. J. M. (1976). Social interaction observed: Some approaches to the analysis of behavior streams. *Personality and Social Psychology Bulletin, 2,* 335–345.

Bakeman, R., & Gottman, J. M. (1986). *Observing interaction: An introduction to sequential analysis.* London: Cambridge University Press.

Barker, R. G., & Wright, H. F. (1955). *Midwest and its children: The psychological ecology of an American town.* New York: Row Peterson.

Bartke, J. J. (1966). The intraclass correlation coefficient as a measure of reliability. *Psychological Report, 19,* 3–11.

Bartlett, M. S. (1946). On the theoretical specification of sampling properties of autocorrelated time series. *Journal of the Royal Statistical Society, B8,* 27–41.

Bayley, N. (1933). *The California First-Year Mental Scale.* Berkeley: University of California.

Bayley, N. (1936). *The California Infant Scale of Motor Development*. Berkeley: University of California.

Bayley, N. (1969). *Manual for the Bayley Scales of Infant Development*. New York: Psychological Corporation.

Becker, J. V., Turner, S. M., & Sajwaj, T. E. (1978). Multiple behavioral effects of the use of lemon juice with a ruminating toddler-age child. *Behavior Modification*, *2*, 267–278.

Bejar, I. I. (1983). Achievement testing: Recent advances. In J. L. Sullivan & R. G. Niemi (Eds.), *Quantitative applications in the social sciences* (No. 07–036). Beverly Hills, CA: Sage.

Bell, J. F. (1985). Generalizability theory: The software problem. *Journal of Educational Statistics,10*(1), 19–29.

Bell-Dolan, D. (1985). In defense of the 100 in percentage agreement formulas. *The Behavior Therapist*, *8*, 107.

Berk, R. A. (1979). Generalizability of behavioral observations: A clarification of interobserver agreement and interobserver reliability. *American Journal of Mental Deficiency*, *83*, 460–472.

Berk, R. A. (1984). Selecting the index of reliability. In R. A. Berk (Ed.), *A guide to criterion-referenced test construction* (pp. 231–266). Baltimore: The Johns Hopkins University press.

Berliner, D. (1976). Impediments to the study of teacher effectiveness. *Journal of Teacher Education*, *27*(1), 5–13.

Bijou, S. W., Peterson, R. F., Harris, F. R., Allen, K. E., & Johnston, M. S. (1969). Methodology for experimental studies of young children in natural settings. *Psychological Record*, *19*, 177–210.

Bindra, D., & Blond, J. (1958). A time-sample method for measuring general activity and its components. *Canadian Journal of Psychology*, *12*, 74–76.

Bingham, C., Godfrey, M. D., & Tukey, J. W. (1967). Modern techniques of power spectrum estimation. *Institute of Electrical and Electronic Engineers: Transactions on Audio- and Electroacoustics*, *5*, 56–66.

Birkimer, J. C., & Brown, J. H. (1979). Back to basics: Percentage agreement measures are adequate, but there are easier ways. *Journal of Applied Behavior Analysis*, *12*, 535–543.

Blackman, R. B., & Tukey, J. W. (1958). *The measurement of power spectra*. New York: Dover.

Bloom, M., & Fischer, J. (1982). *Evaluating practice: Guidelines for the accountable professional*. Englewood Cliffs, NJ: Prentice-Hall.

Bloomfield, P. (1976). *Fourier analysis of time series: An introduction*. New York: Wiley.

Bohrnstedt, G. W. (1970). Reliability and validity assessment in attitude measurement. In G. F. Summers (Ed.), *Attitude measurement* (pp. 80–99). Chicago: Rand McNally.

Borg, W. R., & Gall, M. D. (1983). *Educational research: An introduction*. (4th ed.). New York: Longman.

Borgerhoff M. M., & Caro, T. M. (1985). The use of quantitative observational techniques in anthropology. *Current Anthropology*, *26*, 323–335.

Bower, C. P., Padia, W. L., & Glass, G. V. (1974). *TMS: Two Fortran IV programs for the analysis of time-series experiments*. Boulder, CO: Laboratory of Educational Research.

Box, G. E. P., & Jenkins, G. M. (1976). *Time series analysis: Forecasting and control* (rev. ed.). San Francisco: Holden-Day.

Box, G. E. P., & Pierce, D. A. (1970). Distributions of residual autocorrelations in autoregressive-integrated moving average models. *Journal of the American Statistical Association, 65,* 1509–1526.

Boyd, R. D., & DeVault, M. V. (1966). The observation and recording of behavior. *Review of Educational Research, 36,* 529–551.

Bradley, J. V. (1968). *Distribution-free statistical tests.* Englewood Cliffs, NJ: Prentice-Hall.

Brazelton, T. B. (1973). *Neonatal Behavioral Assessment Scale.* Philadelphia: Lippincott.

Brennan, R. L. (1983). *Elements of Generalizability Theory.* Iowa City: ACT Publications.

Brennan, R. L. (1984, April). *Some statistical issues in Generalizability Theory.* Paper presented at the annual meeting of the American Educational Research Association, New Orleans.

Brennan, R. L., & Kane, M. T. (1977a). An index of dependability for mastery tests. *Journal of Educational Measurement, 14,* 277–289.

Brennan, R. L., & Kane, M. T. (1977b). Signal/noise ratios for domain-referenced tests. *Psychometrika, 42,* 609–625.

Brown, M., Solomon, H., & Stephens, M. A. (1977). Estimation of parameters of zero-one process by interval sampling. *Operations Research, 25,* 493–505.

Brulle, A. R., & Repp, A. C. (1984). An investigation of the accuracy of momentary time sampling procedures with time series data. *British Journal of Psychology, 75,* 481–485.

Budescu, D. V. (1984). Tests of lagged dominance in sequential dyadic interaction. *Psychological Bulletin, 56,* 402–414.

Burt, C. (1936). The analysis of examination marks. In P. Hartog & E. C. Rhodes (Eds.), *The marks of examiners* (pp. 245–314). London: Macmillan.

Cairns, R. B. (Ed.). (1979). *The analysis of social interactions: Methods, issues, and illustrations.* Hillsdale, NJ: Lawrence Erlbaum.

Campbell, D. T., & Fiske, D. W. (1959). Convergent and discriminant validation by the multitrait–multimethod matrix. *Psychological Bulletin, 56,* 81–105.

Campbell, D. T., & Stanley, J. C. (1966). *Experimental and quasi-experimental designs for research.* Chicago: Rand McNally.

Cartwright, D. S. (1956). A rapid non-parametric estimate of multi-judge reliability. *Psychometrika, 21,* 17–29.

Celhoffer, L., Boukydis, C., Minde, C., & Muir, E. (1977). The DCR-II event recorder: A portable high-speed digital cassette system with direct computer access. *Behavior Research Methods and Instrumentation, 10,* 563–566.

Chalmers, N. R. (1968). The social behaviour of free living mangabeys in Uganda. *Folia Primatology, 8,* 263–281.

Chatfield, C. & Lemon, R. E. (1970). Analyzing sequences of behavioural events. *Journal of Theoretical Biology, 29,* 427–445.

Ciminero, A. R., Calhoun, K. S., & Adams, H. E. (Eds.) (1977). *Handbook of behavioral assessment.* New York: Wiley.

Clement, P. W. (1976). A formula for computing interobserver agreement. *Psychological Reports, 39,* 257–258.

Cohen, J. (1960). A coefficient of agreement for nominal scales. *Educational and Psychological Measurement, 20,* 37–46.

Cohen, J. (1968). Weighted kappa: Nominal scale agreement with provision for scaled disagreement or partial credit. *Psychological Bulletin, 70,* 213–220.

Cohen, J., & Cohen, P. (1983). *Applied multiple regression/correlation for the behavioral sciences,* (2nd ed.). Hillsdale, NJ: Lawrence Erlbaum.

Colquhoun, W. P. (Ed.). (1971). *Biological rhythms and human performance.* London: Academic Press.

Committee to Develop Joint Technical Standards for Educational and Psychological Testing. (1983). *Draft: Joint technical standards for educational and psychological testing.* Washington, DC: American Educational Research Association, American Psychological Association, and National Council on Measurement in Education.

Cone, J. D. (1977). The relevance of reliability and validity for behavior assessment. *Behavior Therapy, 8,* 411–426.

Cone, J. D. (1982). Validity of direct observation assessment procedures. In D. P. Hartmann (Ed.), *Using observers to study behavior* (pp. 67–80). San Francisco: Jossey-Bass.

Cone, J. D., & Foster, S. L. (1982). Direct observation in clinical psychology. In P. C. Kendall & J. N. Butcher (Eds.), *Handbook of research methods in clinical psychology.* New York: Wiley.

Conners, C. K. (1969). A Teacher Rating Scale for use in drug studies with children. *American Journal of Psychiatry, 126,* 884–888.

Cooley, V. A., & Tukey, J. W. (1965). An algorithm for the machine calculation of complex Fourier series. *Mathematics of Computation, 19,* 297–301.

Costello, A. J. (1973). The reliability of direct observations. *Bulletin of the British Psychological Society, 26,* 105–108.

Crick, J. E., & Brennan, R. L. (1982). *GENOVA: A generalized analysis of variance system (FORTRAN IV computer program and manual).* Dorchester, MA: Computer Facilities, University of Massachusetts at Boston.

Cronbach, L. J., Gleser, G. C., Nanda, H., & Rajaratnam, N. (1972). *The dependability of behavioral measurements: Theory of generalizability for scores and profiles.* New York: John Wiley and Sons.

Crossman, E. K., Williams, J. C., & Chambers, J. H. (1978). Using the PET microcomputer for collecting and analyzing observational data in the classroom. *Behavior Research Methods and Instrumentation, 10,* 563–566.

Crow, E. L. (1979). Approximate confidence intervals for a proportion from a Markov dependent trials. *Communications in Statistics, B8,* 1–24.

Cryer, J. D. (1986). *Time series analysis.* Boston: Duxbury Press.

Darwin, C. (1872). *Expressions of the emotions in man and animals.* London: Murray.

Davidson, P. R., Malcolm, P. B., Lanthier, R. D., Barbaree, H. E., & Ho, T. P. (1981). Penile response measurement: Operating characteristics of the Parks plethysmograph. *Behavioral Assessment, 3,* 137–143.

Davies, N. B. (1982). Behaviour and competition for scarce resources. In King's College Sociobiology Group (Eds.), *Current Problems in Sociobiology.* Cambridge: Cambridge University Press.

Dean, D. G. (1961). Alienation: Its meaning and measurement. *American Sociological Review, 26,* 753–758.

Devore, J. L. (1976). A note on the estimation of parameters in a Bernoulli model with dependence. *Annals of Statistics, 4,* 990–992.

Dice, L. T. (1945). Measures of the amount of ecologic association between species. *Ecology, 26,* 297–302.

Drew, C. J. (1969). Covariate matching: A methodological note. *Perceptual and Motor Skills, 28,* 799–800.

Drew, C. J., & Hardman, M. L. (1985). *Designing and conducting behavioral research.* New York: Pergamon.

Dunbar, R. (1976). Some aspects of research design and their implications in the observational study of behavior. *Behaviour, 58,* 79–98.

Durbin, J., & Watson, G. S. (1950). Testing for serial correlation in least square regression I. *Biometrika, 37,* 409.

Durbin, J., & Watson, G. S. (1951). Testing for serial correlation in least square regression II. *Biometrika, 38,* 145.

Ebel, R. L. (1951). Estimation of the reliability of ratings. *Psychometrika, 16,* 407–424.

Eckerman, C. O., Whatley, J. L., & Kutz, S. L. (1975). Growth of social play with peers during the second year of life. *Developmental Psychology, 11,* 42–49.

Edgington, E. S. (1967). Statistical inference from N = 1 experiments. *Journal of Psychology, 65,* 195–199.

Edgington, E. S. (1975). Randomization tests for one-subject operant experiments. *Journal of Psychology, 90,* 57–68.

Edgington, E. S. (1982). Nonparametric tests for single-subject multiple schedule experiments. *Behavioral Assessment, 4,* 83–91.

Edwards, A. L. (1968). *Experimental design in psychological research* (3rd ed.). New York: Holt, Rinehart, and Winston.

Enright, J. T. (1981). Data analysis. In J. Aschoff (Ed.), *Handbook of behavioral neurobiology: Vol. 4. Biological rhythms* (pp. 21–39). New York: Plenum.

Evans, I. M. (1985). Building systems models as a strategy for target behavior selection in clinical assessment. *Behavioral Assessment, 7,* 21–32.

Eysenck, H. J. (1960). *Behaviour therapy and the neuroses.* Oxford: Pergamon.

Eysenck, M. W., & Eysenck, H. J. (1980). Mischel and the concept of personality. *British Journal of Psychology, 71,* 191–204.

Eysenck, H. J., Wakefield, J. A., & Friedman, A. F. (1983). Diagnosis and clinical assessment: The DSM-III. *Annual Review of Psychology, 34,* 167–193.

Farrell, A. D., Rabinowitz, J. A., Wallander, J. L., & Curran, J. P. (1985). An evaluation of two formats for the intermediate-level assessment of social skills. *Behavioral Assessment, 7,* 155–171.

Fassnacht, G. (1982). *Theory and practice of observing behaviour.* London: Academic Press.

Fernald, R. D., & Heinecke, P. (1974). A computer compatible multi-purpose event recorder. *Behaviour, 49,* 268–275.

Fetterman, D. M. (1982). Ethnography in educational research: The dynamics of diffusion. *Educational Researcher, 11*(3), 17–22.

Fiske, D. W. (1978). *Strategies for personality research: The observation versus interpretation of behavior.* San Francisco: Jossey-Bass.

Flanders, N. A. (1967). Estimating reliability. In E. J. Amidon & J. B. Hough (Eds.), *Interaction analysis: Theory, research, and application.* Reading, MA: Addison-Wesley.

Flanders, N. A. (1970). *Analyzing teaching behavior.* Boston: Addison-Wesley.

Fleiss, J. L. (1975). Measuring agreement between two judges on the presence and absence of a trait. *Biometrics, 31,* 651–659.

Foster, S. L., & Cone, J. D. (1980). Current issues in direct observation. *Behavioral Assessment, 2,* 313–338.

Frame, R. B. (1979). Interobserver agreement as a function of the number of behaviors recorded simultaneously. *The Psychological Record, 29,* 287–296.

Francis, S. H. (1966). *An ethological study of mentally retarded individuals and normal infants.* Unpublished doctoral dissertation, University of Cambridge.

Frick, T., & Semmel, M. I. (1978). Observer agreement and reliability of classroom observational measures. *Review of Educational Research, 48,* 157–184.

Froman, T. W., & Llabre, M. M. (April, 1984). *The equivalence of kappa and del.* Paper presented at the annual meeting of the American Educational Research Association, New Orleans.

Gardner, W., Hartman, D. P., & Mitchell, C. (1982). The effects of serial dependency on the use of chi-square for analyzing sequential data. *Behavioral Assessment, 4,* 75–82.

Garrett, C. S. (1972). *Modification of the Scott coefficient as an observer agreement estimate for marginal form observation scale data* (Occasional Paper #6). Bloomington: Indiana University, Center for Innovation in Teaching the Handicapped.

Garrett, F. D. (1972). *Feedback and Flanders interaction analysis related to change in the indirect teaching behavior of student teachers.* Unpublished doctoral dissertation. Northern Illinois University, DeKalb, IL.

Gass, C. L. (1977). A digital encoder for field recording of behavioral, temporal, and spacial information in directly computer-accessible form. *Behavior Research Methods and Instrumentation, 9,* 5–11.

Gaylord-Ross, R. T., Haring, T. G., Breen, C., & Pitts-Conway, V. (1984). The training and generalization of social interaction skills with autistic youth. *Journal of Applied Behavior Analysis, 17,* 229–247.

Geary, R. C. (1970). Relative efficiency of count of sign changes for assessing residual autoregression in least square regression. *Biometrika, 57,* 123.

Geertz, C. (1973). *The interpretation of cultures.* New York: Basic Books.

Gelfand, D. M., & Hartmann, D. P. (1975). *Child behavior analysis and therapy.* New York: Pergamon.

Gilbert, J. P., Light, R. J., & Mosteller, F. (1975). Assessing social innovation: An empirical base for policy. In C. A. Bennet & A. A. Lumsdaine (Eds.), *Evaluation and experiment.* New York: Academic Press.

Glass, G. V., & Hopkins, K. D. (1984). *Statistical methods in education and psychology* (2nd ed.). Englewood Cliffs, NJ: Prentice-Hall.

Glass, G. V., Willson, V. L., & Gottman, J. M. (1975). *Design and analysis of time-series experiments.* Boulder, CO: University of Colorado Press.

Goldfried, M. R., & Linehan, M. M. (1977). Basic issues in behavioral assessment. In A. R. Ciminero, K. S. Calhoun, & H. E. Adams (Eds.), *Handbook of behavioral assessment.* New York: Wiley.

Goodenough, F. L. (1928). Measuring behavior traits by means of repeated short samples. *Journal of Juvenile Research, 12,* 230–235.

Goodenough, F. L. (1949). *Mental testing.* New York: Rinehart.

Goodman, L. A., & Kruskal, W. H. (1954). Measures of association for cross classifications. *Journal of the American Statistical Association, 49*, 732–764.

Gottman, J. M. (1979). Detecting cyclicity in social interaction. *Psychological Bulletin, 86*, 338–348.

Gottman, J. M. (1985). Observational measures of behavior therapy outcome: A reply to Jacobson. *Behavioral Assessment, 7*, 317–322.

Gottman, J. M., & Glass, G. V. (1978). Analysis of interrupted time-series experiments. In T. R. Kratochwill (Ed.), *Single subject research: Strategies for evaluating change* (pp. 197–236.) New York: Academic Press.

Gottman, J. M., Markman, H., & Notarius, C. (1977). The topography of marital conflict: A sequential analysis of verbal and nonverbal behavior. *Journal of Marriage and Family, 39*, 461–477.

Gottman, J. M., & Notarius, C. (1978). Sequential analysis of observational data using Markov Chains. In T. R. Kratochwill (Ed.), *Single subject research: Strategies for evaluating change* (pp. 237–286). New York: Academic Press.

Green, S. B., & Alverson, L. G. (1978). A comparison of indirect measures of long-duration behaviors. *Journal of Applied Behavior Analysis, 11*, 530.

Griffin, B., & Adams, R. (1983). A parametric model for estimating prevalence, incidence, and mean bout duration from point sampling. *American Journal of Primatology, 4*, 261–271.

Gronlund, N. E. (1981). *Measurement and evaluation in teaching* (4th ed.). New York: MacMillan.

Habibagahi, H., & Pratschke, J. L. (1972). A comparison of the power of the Von Neumann ratio, Durbin-Watson and Geary tests. *Review of Economics and Statistics*, 179–185.

Haggard, E. A. (1958). *Intraclass correlation and the analysis of variance.* New York: Dryden Press.

Halberg, F., Carandente, F., Cornelissen, G., & Katinas, G. S. (1977). Glossary of chronobiology. *Chronobiologia*, Supplement 1.

Halberg, F., Tong, Y. L., & Johnson, E. A. (1967). Circadian system phase—An aspect of temporal morphology: procedures and illustrative examples. In H. von Mayersbach (Ed.), *The cellular aspects of biorhythms.* Berlin: Springer.

Hambleton, R. A., & Swaminathan, H. (1985). *Item response theory: Principles and applications.* Boston, MA: Kluwer-Nijhoff.

Hansen, D. J., Tisdelle, D. A., & O'Dell, S. L. (1985). Audio recorded and directly observed parent-child interactions: A comparison of observation methods. *Behavioral Assessment, 7*, 389–399.

Hart, B. (1983). Assessing spontaneous speech. *Behavioral Assessment, 5*, 71–82.

Hartmann, D. P. (1977). Considerations in the choice of interobserver reliability estimates. *Journal of Applied Behavior Analysis, 10*, 103–116.

Hartmann, D. P. (1981). Editorial note. *Behavioral Assessment, 3*, 1–3.

Hartmann, D. P. (1982). Assessing the dependability of observational data. In D. P. Hartmann (Ed.), *Using observers to study behavior* (pp. 51–66). San Francisco: Jossey-Bass.

Hartmann, D. P., & Gardner, W. (1979). On the not so recent invention of interobserver reliability statistics: A commentary on two articles by Birkimer and Brown. *Journal of Applied Behavior Analysis, 12*, 559–560.

Hartmann, D. P., Gottman, J. M., Jones, R. R., Gardner, W., Kazdin, A. E., & Vaught, R. S. (1980). Interrupted time-series analysis and its application to behavioral data. *Journal of Applied Behavior Analysis, 13*, 543–559.

Hartmann, D. P., & Wood, D. D. (1982). Observational methods. In A. S. Bellack, M. Hersen, & A. E. Kazdin (Eds.), *International handbook of behavior modification and therapy* (pp. 109–138). New York: Plenum.

Hawkins, R. P. (1982). Developing a behavior code. In D. P. Hartmann (Ed.), *Using observers to study behavior* (pp. 21–36). San Francisco: Jossey-Bass.

Hawkins, R. P. (1983). A frequent error in calculation or reporting of interobserver agreement. *The Behavior Therapist, 6,* 109.

Hawkins, R. P., Axelrod, S., & Hall, R. V. (1976). Teachers as behavior analysts: Precisely monitoring student performance. In J. A. Brigham, R. Hawkins, J. Scott, & T. R. McLaughlin (Eds.), *Behavior analysis in education: Self-control and reading.* Dubuque, IA: Kendall-Hunt.

Hawkins, R. P., & Dotson, V. A. (1975). Reliability scores that delude: An Alice in Wonderland trip through the misleading characteristics of interobserver agreement scores in interval recording. In E. Ramp & G. Semb (Eds.), *Behavior analysis: Areas of research and application* (pp. 359–376). Englewood Cliffs, NJ: Prentice-Hall.

Haynes, S. N. (1978). *Principles of behavioral assessment.* New York: Gardner.

Haynes, S. N., & Wilson, C. C. (1979). *Behavioral assessment.* San Francisco: Jossey-Bass.

Hays, W. L. (1973). *Statistics for the social sciences.* New York: Holt, Rinehart, and Winston.

Hedges, L. V. (1981). Distribution theory for Glass's estimator of effect size and related estimators. *Journal of Educational Statistics, 6,* 107–128.

Heise, D. R. (1969). Separating reliability and stability in test-retest correlations. *American Sociological Review, 34,* 93–101.

Helmer, O., & Rescher, N. (1959). On the epistemology of the inexact sciences. *Management Science, 6,* 25–52.

Henryssen, S. (1971). Gathering, analyzing, and using data on test items. In R. L. Thorndike (Ed.), *Educational measurement* (2nd ed., pp. 130–159). Washington, DC: American Council on Education.

Herbert, J., & Attridge, C. A. (1975). A guide for developers and users of observation systems and manuals. *American Educational Research Journal, 12,* 1–20.

Hersen, M., & Barlow, D. H. (1976). *Single case experimental designs.* New York: Pergamon Press.

Heuer, E., & Wiersma, W. (1977). A design for the content validation of standardized achievement tests. *AIGE Forum, 2*(3), 18–20.

Hildebrand, D. K., Laing, J. D., & Rosenthal, H. (1974). Prediction logic: A method for empirical evaluation of formal theory. *Journal of Mathematical Sociology, 3,* 163–185.

Hildebrand, D. K., Laing, J. D., & Rosenthal, H. (1977). *Prediction analysis of cross classification.* New York: John Wiley and Sons.

Hinkle, D. E., Wiersma, W., & Jurs, S. G. (1979). *Applied statistics for the behavioral sciences.* Boston, MA: Houghton Mifflin.

Hoge, R. D. (1985). The validity of direct observation measures of pupil classroom behavior. *Review of Educational Research, 55,* 469–483.

Homer, A. L., & Peterson, L. (1980). Differential reinforcement of other behavior: A preferred response elimination procedure. *Behavior Therapy, 11,* 449–471.

Homer, A. L., Peterson, L., & Wonderlich, S. A. (1983). Subject selection in applied behavior analysis. *The Behavior Analyst, 6,* 39–45.

Hopkins, B. L., & Hermann, J. A. (1977). Evaluating interobserver reliability of interval data. *Journal of Applied Behavior Analysis, 10,* 121–126.

House, A. E., Farber, J., & Nier, L. L. (1980). *Accuracy and speed of reliability calculation using different measures of interobserver agreement.* Paper presented at the Association for the Advancement of Behavior Therapy Convention, New York.

House, A. E., House, B. J., & Campbell, M. B. (1981). Measures of interobserver agreement: Calculation formulas and distribution effects. *Journal of Behavioral Assessment, 3,* 37–57.

Hoyt, C. J. (1941). Test reliability estimated by analysis of variance. *Psychometrika, 6,* 153–160.

Huitema, B. E. (1985). Autocorrelation in applied behavior analysis: A myth. *Behavioral Assessment, 7,* 107–118.

Hutt, S. J., & Hutt, C. (1970). *Direct observation and measurement of behavior.* Springfield, IL: Thomas.

Issacson, D. L., & Madsen, R. W. (1976). *Markov chains theory and application.* New York: John Wiley and Sons.

Jackson, R. W. B., & Ferguson, G. (1941). *Studies on the reliability of tests.* Toronto: University of Toronto.

Jacobson, N. S. (1985a). The role of observational measures in behavior therapy outcome research. *Behavioral Assessment, 7,* 297–308.

Jacobson, N. S. (1985b). Uses versus abuses of observational measures. *Behavioral Assessment, 7,* 323–330.

Jacobson, N. S., Elwood, R. W., & Dallas, M. (1981). Assessment of marital dysfunction. In D. H. Barlow (Ed.), *Behavioral assessment of adult disorders* (pp. 439–479). New York: Guilford Press.

Jaffe, J., & Feldstein, S. (1970). *Rhythms of dialogue.* New York: Academic Press.

Jason, L. A., and Liotta, R. F. (1982). Reduction of cigarette smoking in a university cafeteria. *Journal of Applied Behavior Analysis, 15,* 573–577.

Jenkins, G. M., & Watts, D. G. (1969). *Spectral analysis and its applications.* San Francisco: Holden-Day.

Jensen, A. R. (1959). The reliability of projective techniques: Methodology. *Acta Psychologica, 16,* 108–136.

Johnson, L. C. (1975). Sleep. In P. H. Venables & M. J. Christies (Eds.), *Research in psychophysiology* (pp. 125–152). New York: John Wiley and Sons.

Johnson, S. M., and Bolstad, O. D. (1973). Methodological issues in naturalistic observation: Some problems and solutions for field research. In L. A. Hamerlynck, L. C. Hardy, and E. J. Mash (Eds.), *Behavior change: Methodology, concepts, and practice* (pp. 7–67). Champaign, IL: Research Press.

Johnston, J. (1966). *Econometric methods.* New York: McGraw-Hill.

Johnston, J. M., & Pennypacker, H. S. (1980). *Strategies and tactics of human behavioral research.* Hillsdale, NJ: Lawrence Erlbaum.

Jones, M. C. (1924). The elimination of children's fears. *Journal of Experimental Psychology, 7,* 383–390.

Jones, R. R., Vaught, R. S., & Weinrott, M. (1977). Time-series analysis in operant research. *Journal of Applied Behavior Analysis, 10,* 151–166.

Jones, R. R., Weinrott, M., & Vaught, R. S. (1978). Effects of serial dependency on the agreement between visual and statistical inference. *Journal of Applied Behavior Analysis, 11,* 277–283.

Kaestner, N. F., & Ross, H. L. (1974). Highway safety programs: How do we know they work? *North Carolina Symposium on Highway Safety, 10,* 1–67.

Kanfer, F. H. (1985). Target selection for clinical change programs. *Behavioral Assessment, 7,* 7–20.

Kanfer, F. H., & Saslow, G. (1965). Behavioral analysis: An alternative to diagnostic classification. *Archives of General Psychiatry, 12,* 529–538.

Kazdin, A. E. (1974). Self-monitoring and behavior change. In M. J. Mahoney & C. E. Thoresen (Eds.), *Self-control: Power to the person* (pp. 218–246.) Monterey, CA: Brooks/Cole.

Kazdin, A. E. (1977). Artifacts, bias, and complexity of assessment: The ABC's of reliability. *Journal of Applied Behavior Analysis, 10,* 141–150.

Kazdin, A. E. (1985). Selection of target behaviors: The relationship of the treatment focus to clinical dysfunction. *Behavioral Assessment, 7,* 33–47.

Kelly, M. B. (1977). A review of the observational data-collection and reliability procedures in *The Journal of Applied Behavior Analysis. Journal of Applied Behavior Analysis, 10,* 97–101.

Kelly, M. L., & Stokes, T. F. (1982). Contingency contracting with disadvantaged youth: Improving classroom performance. *Journal of Applied Behavior Analysis, 15,* 447–454.

Kemeny, J. G., & Snell, J. L. (1960). *Finite Markov chains.* Princeton: Van Nostrand.

Kendall, M. G. (1948). The advanced theory of statistics (Vol. 1, 4th ed.). London: Griffin.

Kendall, M. G. (1973). *Time series.* London: Griffin.

Kendall, M. G., & Stuart, A. (1973). *The advanced theory of statistics, Vol. II.* New York: Hafner.

Keppel, G., & Saufley, W. H., Jr. (1980). *Introduction to design and analysis: A student's handbook.* San Francisco: Freeman.

Kerlinger, F. N. (1973). *Foundations of behavioral research,* (2nd ed.). New York: Holt, Rinehart, and Winston.

Kerlinger, F. N. (1986). *Foundations of behavioral research* (3rd ed.). New York: Holt, Rinehart, and Winston.

Kim, S., & Bai, D. S. (1980). On parameter estimation in Bernoulli trials with dependence. *Communications in Statistics, A9,* 1401–1410.

Klotz, J. (1973). Statistical inference in Bernoulli trials with dependence. *Annals of Statistics, 1,* 373–379.

Kmenta, J. (1971). *Elements of econometrics.* New York: Macmillan.

Koopmans, L. H. (1974). *The spectral analysis of time series.* New York: Academic Press.

Kraemer, H. C. (1979). One-zero sampling in the study of primate behavior. *Primates, 20,* 237–244.

Kratochwill, T. R., & Wetzel, R. J. (1977). Observer agreement, credibility, and judgment: Some considerations in presenting observer agreement data. *Journal of Applied Behavior Analysis, 10,* 133–139.

Krebs, J. R., & Davies, N. B. (1981). *An introduction to behavioural ecology*. Oxford: Blackwell Scientific Publications.

Kubany, E., & Slogett, B. (1973). Coding procedures for teachers. *Journal of Applied Behavior Analysis, 6*, 339–344.

Lamb, M. E. (1978). Infant social cognition and "second-order" effects. *Infant Behavior and Development, 1*, 1–10.

Landis, J. R., & Koch, G. G. (1977). The measurement of observer agreement for categorical data. *Biometrics, 33*, 159–174.

Lazarus, A. A. (1966). Broad spectrum behavior therapy and the treatment of agoraphobia. *Behaviour Research and Therapy, 4*, 95–97.

Lee, P. S. C., & Suen, H. K. (1984). The estimation of kappa from percentage agreement interobserver reliability. *Behavioral Assessment, 6*, 375–378.

Legar, D. (1977). An empirical evaluation of instantaneous and one-zero sampling of chimpanzee behavior. *Primates, 18*, 387–393.

Lehner, P. N. (1979). *Handbook of ethological methods*. New York: Garland STPM Press.

Lemon, R. E., & Chatfield, C. (1971). Organization of song in cardinals. *Animal Behavior, 19*, 1–17.

Levin, J. R., Marascuilo, L. A., & Hubert, L. J. (1978). N = 1 nonparametric randomization tests. In T. R. Kratochwill (Ed.), *Single subject research: Strategies for evaluating change* (pp. 167–196) New York: Academic Press.

Lewin, L. M., & Wakefield, J. A. (1979). Percentage agreement to phi: A conversion table. *Journal of Applied Behavior Analysis, 12*, 299–301.

Licht, M. H., Paul, G. L., Power, C. T., & Engel, K. L. (1980). The comparative effectiveness of two modes of observer training on the Staff-Resident Interaction Chronograph. *Journal of Behavioral Assessment, 2*, 175–205.

Lienert, G. A. (1972). Note on tests concerning the G index of agreement. *Educational and Psychological Measurement, 32*, 281–288.

Lindquist, E. F. (1953). *Design and analysis of experiments in psychology and education*. Boston: Houghton-Mifflin.

Linqvist, B. (1978). A note on Bernoulli trials with dependence. *Scandinavian Journal of Statistics, 5*, 205–208.

Ljung, G. M., & Box, G. E. P. (1978). On a measure of lack of fit in time series models. *Biometrika, 65*, 67–72.

Longabaugh, R. (1980). The systematic observation of behavior in naturalistic settings. In H. C. Triandis & J. W. Berry (Eds.), *Handbook of cross-cultural psychology: Methodology* (Vol. 2., pp. 57–126) Boston: Allyn and Bacon.

Lord, F. M. (1980). *Applications of item response theory to practical testing problems*. Hillsdale, NJ: Lawrence Erlbaum.

Lytton, H. (1971). Observation studies of parent-child interaction: A methodological review. *Child Development, 42*, 651–684.

Marascuilo, L. A., & McSweeney, M. (1977). *Nonparametric and distribution-free methods for the social sciences*. Monterey, CA: Brooks/Cole.

Martin, P., & Bateson, P. (1986). *Measuring behaviour: An introductory guide*. London: Cambridge University Press.

Mash, E. J., & Tedral, L. G. (1981). Behavioral assessment of childhood distur-
bance. In E. J. Mash & L. G. Terdal (Eds.), *Behavioral assessment of childhood dis-
turbance.* New York: Guilford.

Mash, E. J., Tedral, L. G., & Anderson, K. (1973). The response-class matrix: A
procedure for recording parent-child interactions. *Journal of Consulting and Clinical
Psychology, 40,* 163–164.

Maxwell, A. E. (1968). The effect of correlated errors on estimates of reliability
coefficients. *Educational and Psychological Measurement, 28,* 803–811.

Maxwell, A. E., & Pilliner, A. E. G. (1968). Deriving coefficients of reliability
and agreement for ratings. *British Journal of Mathematical and Statistical Psychology, 21,* 105–116.

McCain, L. J., & McCleary, R. (1979). The statistical analysis of the simple interrupted time-series quasi-experiment. In T. D. Cook & D. T. Campbell (Eds.),
Quasi-experimentation: Design and analysis issues for field settings (pp. 233–293). Chicago: Rand McNally.

McDowall, D., McCleary, R., Meidinger, E. E., & Hay, R. A., Jr. (1980). Interrupted time series analysis. In J. L. Sullivan (Ed.), *Quantitative applications in the
social sciences.* Beverly Hills, CA: Sage.

McDowell, E. (1973). Comparison of time-sampling and continuous recording
techniques for observing developmental change in caretaker and infant behaviors.
Journal of Genetic Psychology, 123, 99–105.

McFall, R. M. (1977). Analogue methods in behavioral assessment. In J. D. Cone
& R. P. Hawkins (Eds.), *Behavioral assessment: New directions in clinical psychology.* New York: Brunner/Mazel.

McSweeney, A. J. (1977). Time series analysis and research in behavior modification: Some answers. *AABT Newsletter, 4,* 22–23.

Meier-Koll, A., Fels, Th., Kofler, B., Schulz-Weber, U., & Thiessen, M. (1977).
Basic rest activity cycle and stereotyped behavior of a mentally defective child.
Neuropadiatrie, 8, 172–180.

Meier-Koll, A., & Pohl, P. (1981). Chronobiological aspects of stereotyped motor behavior in mentally retarded children. *International Journal of Chronobiology,
6,* 191–209.

Messick, S. (1975). The standard problem: Meaning and values in measurement
and evaluation. *American Psychologist, 30,* 955–966.

Meyer, V., & Crisp, A. H. (1966). Some problems in behaviour therapy. *British
Journal of Psychiatry, 112,* 367–381.

Michael, J. (1974). Statistical inference for individual organism research: Mixed
blessing or curse? *Journal of Applied Behavior Analysis, 7,* 647–653.

Michener, G. R. (1980). The measurement and interpretation of interaction rates:
An example with adult Richardson's ground squirrels. *Biology of Behavior, 5,*
371–384.

Milar, C., & Hawkins, R. (1976). Distorted results from the use of interval recording
techniques. In T. Brigham, R. Hawkins, J. Scott, & T. Laughlin (Eds.), *Behaviour
analysis in education: Self-control and reading* (pp. 261–273). Dubuque, IA: Ken-
dall/Hunt.

Miller, D. C. (1977). *Handbook of research design and social measurement* (3rd ed.). New York: David McKay.

Mitchell, S. K. (1979). Interobserver agreement, reliability, and generalizability of data collected in observational studies. *Psychological Bulletin, 86*, 376–390.

Murphy, G., & Goodall, E. (1980). Measurement error in direct observations: A comparison of common recording methods. *Behavior Research and Therapy, 18*, 147–150.

Murphy, H. A., Hutchinson, J. M., & Bailey, J. S. (1983). Behavioral school psychology goes outdoors: The effect of organized games and playground aggression. *Journal of Applied Behavior Analysis, 16*, 29–35.

Nelson, R. O., & Hayes, S. C. (1979). Some current dimensions of behavioral assessment. *Behavioral Assessment, 1*, 1–16.

Nunnally, J. C. (1978). *Psychometric theory*. New York: McGraw-Hill.

O'Leary, K. D. (1979). Behavioral assessment. *Behavioral Assessment, 1*, 31–36.

O'Leary, K. D., Kent, R. N., & Kanowitz, J. (1975). Shaping data collection congruent with experimental hypothesis. *Journal of Applied Behavior Analysis, 8*, 43–51.

Olson, W. C. (1929). *The measurement of nervous habits in normal children*. Minneapolis: University of Minnesota Press.

Orr, W. C., & Naitoh, P. (1975). The coherence spectrum: An extension of correlation analysis with applications to chronobiology. *International Journal of Chronobiology, 3*, 171–192.

Ostrom, C. W., Jr. (1978). Time series analysis: Regression techniques. In E. M. Uslaner (Ed.), *Quantitative applications in the social sciences*. Beverly Hills, CA: Sage. Hills, CA: Sage.

Pack, D. J. (1977). *A computer program for the analysis of time series models using the Box–Jenkins philosophy*. Columbus, OH: Ohio State University, Data Center.

Parsonson, B. S., & Baer, D. M. (1978). The analysis and presentation of graphic data. In T. R. Kratochwill (Ed.), *Single subject research: Strategies for evaluating change*. (pp. 101–166). New York: Academic Press.

Patterson, G. R., & Maerov, S. L. (1978). Observation as a mode of investigation. In J. B. Reid (Ed.), *A social learning approach to family intervention: Vol. 2. Observation in home settings*. Eugene, OR: Castalia.

Paul, G. L., & Lentz, R. J. (1977). *Psychological treatment of chronic mental patients: Milieu versus social learning programs*. Cambridge, MA: Harvard University Press.

Pearson, E. S., & Hartley, H. O. (1966). *Biometrika tables for statisticians: Vol. I* (3rd ed.). London: Cambridge University Press.

Pedhazur, E. J. (1982). *Multiple regression in behavioral research: Explanation and prediction* (2nd ed.). New York: Holt, Rinehart, and Winston.

Pohl, P. (1977). Voluntary control of stereotyped behaviour in mentally retarded children: Preliminary experimental findings. *Developmental Medicine and Child Neurology, 19*, 811–817.

Powell, J. (1984). Some empirical justification for a modest proposal regarding data acquisition via intermittent direct observation. *Journal of Behavioral Assessment, 6*, 71–80.

Powell, J., Martindale, A., & Kulp, S. (1975). An evaluation of time-sample measures of behavior. *Journal of Applied Behavior Analysis, 8*, 463–469.

Powell, J., Martindale, B., Kulp, S., Martindale, A., & Bauman, R. (1977). Taking a closer look: Time sampling and measurement error. *Journal of Applied Behavior Analysis, 10,* 325–332.

Powell, J., & Rockinson, R. (1978). On the inability of interval time sampling to reflect frequency of occurrence data. *Journal of Applied Behavior Analysis, 11,* 531–532.

Prehm, H. J. (1966). Verbal learning research in mental retardation. *American Journal of Mental Deficiency, 71,* 42–47.

Quenouille, M. H. (1949). Approximate tests of correlation in time series. *Journal of the Royal Statistical Society, B11,* 68–83.

Raiffe, H., & Schlaiffer, R. (1961). *Applied statistical decision theory.* Boston: Division of Research, Graduate School of Business Administration, Harvard University.

Rasch, G. (1980). *Probabilistic models for some intelligence and attainment tests.* Chicago: University of Chicago Press.

Raush, H. L. (1972). Process and change: A Markov model for interaction. *Family Process, 11,* 275–298.

Reid, J. B. (1982). Observer training in naturalistic research. In D. P. Hartmann (Ed.), *Using observers to study behavior* (pp. 37–50). San Francisco: Jossey-Bass.

Repp, A. C., Deitz, D. E. D., Boles, S. M., Deitz, S. M., & Repp, C.F. (1976). Differences among common methods for calculating interobserver agreement. *Journal of Applied Behavior Analysis, 9,* 109–113.

Repp, A. C., Harman, M. L., Felce, D., Van Acker, R., & Karsh, K. L. (1985, September). *A real-time, parallel entry, portable computer system for observational research.* Paper presented at the annual meeting of the Midwestern Educational Research Association. Chicago.

Rhine, R. J., & Flanigon, M. (1978). An empirical comparison of one–zero, focal-animal, and instantaneous methods of sampling spontaneous primate social behavior. *Primates, 19,* 353–361.

Rhine, R. J., & Linville, A. K. (1980). Properties of one–zero scores in observational studies of primate social behavior: The effect of assumptions on empirical analysis. *Primates, 21,* 111–122.

Roberts, R. R., & Renzaglia, G. A. (1965). The influence of tape recording on counseling. *Journal of Counseling Psychology, 12,* 10–16.

Rogot, E., & Goldberg, I. D. (1966). A proposed index for measuring agreement in test-retest studies. *Journal of Chronic Diseases, 19,* 991–1006.

Rosenblum, L. A. (1978). The creation of a behavioral taxonomy. In G. P. Sackett (Ed.), *Observing behavior: Vol. 2. Data collection and analysis methods* (pp. 15–24). Baltimore: University Park Press.

Rosenshine, B., & Furst, N. F. (1973). The use of direct observation to study teaching. In N. L. Gage (Ed.), *Handbook of research on teaching* (2nd. ed., pp. 122–183). Chicago: Rand McNally.

Rosenthal, R., & Rubin, D. B. (1978). Interpersonal expectancy effects: The first 345 studies. *The behavioural and brain sciences, 1,* 377–415.

Sackett, G. P. (1974). *A nonparametric lag sequential analysis for studying dependency among responses in observational scoring systems.* Unpublished manuscript, University of Washington, Seattle.

Sackett, G. P. (1978). Measurement in observational research. In G. P. Sackett (Ed.), *Observing behavior: (Vol. 2). Data collection and analysis methods* (pp. 25–44). Baltimore: University Park Press.

Sackett, G. P., Stephenson, E., & Rupenthal, G. C. (1973). Digital data acquisition systems for observing behavior in laboratory and field settings. *Behavior Research Methodology and Instrumentation, 5,* 344–348.

Sade, D. S. (1966). *Ontogeny of social relations in a group of free-ranging rhesus monkeys (Macaca mulatta Zimmerman).* Doctoral dissertation, University of California, Berkeley.

Sanson-Fisher, R. W., Poole, A. D., & Dunn, J. (1980). An empirical method for determining an appropriate interval length for recording behavior. *Journal of Applied Behavior Analysis, 13,* 493–500.

Sanson-Fisher, R. W., Poole, A. D., Small, G. A., & Fleming, I. R. (1979). Data acquisition in real time—an improved system for naturalistic observations. *Behavior Therapy, 10,* 543–554.

Scheffe, H. (1959). *The analysis of variance.* New York: John Wiley.

Scott, W. A. (1955). Reliability of content analysis: The case of nominal scale coding. *Public Opinion Quarterly, 19,* 321–325.

Sharpley, C. F., & Alavosius, M. P. (In press). Autocorrelation in behavioral data: Some facts. *Behavioral Assessment.*

Shavelson, R., & Webb, N. (1981). Generalizability theory: 1973–1980. *British Journal of Mathematical and Statistical Psychology, 34,* 133–166.

Sidman, M. (1960). *Tactics of scientific research.* New York: Basic Books.

Siegel, S. (1956). *Nonparametric statistics.* New York: McGraw-Hill.

Simpson, M. J. A., & Simpson, A. E. (1977). One-zero and scan-methods for sampling behavior. *Animal behavior, 25,* 726–731.

Smith, P. K. (1985). The reliability and validity of one-zero sampling: Misconceived criticisms and unacknowledged assumptions. *British Educational Research Journal, 11,* 215–220.

Sorosky, A. D., Ornitz, E. M., Brown, M. B., & Ritvo, E. R. (1968). Systematic observations of autistic behavior. *Archive of Genetic Psychology, 18,* 439.

Stephenson, G. R., & Roberts, T. W. (1977). The SSR system 7: A general encoding system with computerized transcription. *Behavior Research Methods and Instrumentation, 9,* 434–441.

Stoline, M. R., Huitema, B. E., & Mitchell, B. T. (1980). Intervention time-series model with different pre- and postintervention first-order autoregressive parameters. *Psychological Bulletin, 88,* 46–53.

Stuart, R. B. (1971). Behavioral contracting within the families of delinquents. *Journal of Behavior Therapy and Experimental Psychiatry.*

Suen, H. K. (1984). A procedure for the derivation of the best estimate when empirical data are unattainable. *Evaluation Review, 8*(5), 734–743.

Suen, H. K. (1986a). On the utility of a post hoc correction procedure for one-zero sampling duration estimates. *Primates, 27*(2), 237–244.

Suen, H. K. (1986b, May). *Single-facet generalizability study of binary observational data with k observers.* Paper presented at the annual meeting of the Association for Behavior Analysis, Milwaukee.

Suen, H. K. (1987). On the epistemology of autocorrelation in applied behavior analysis. *Behavioral Assessment, 9,* 113–124.

Suen, H. K., & Ary, D. (1984a). Simplified conversion of percentage agreement to phi. *Behavioral Assessment, 6,* 283–284.

Suen, H. K., & Ary, D. (1984b). Variables influencing one-zero and instantaneous time sampling outcomes. *Primates, 25,* 89–94.

Suen, H. K., & Ary, D. (1986a). Poisson cumulative probabilities of systematic errors in single-subject and multiple-subject time sampling. *Behavioral Assessment, 8,* 155–169.

Suen, H. K., & Ary, D. (1986b). A post hoc correction procedure for systematic errors in time sampling duration estimates. *Journal of Psychopathology and Behavioral Assessment, 8*(1), 31–38.

Suen, H. K., & Ary, D. (1987). Autocorrelation in applied behavior analysis: Myth or reality? *Behavioral Assessment, 9,* 125–130.

Suen, H. K., Ary, D., & Ary, R. (1986). A note on the relationship among eight indices of interobserver agreement. *Behavioral Assessment, 8,* 301–303.

Suen, H. K., Ary, D., & Greenspan, S. (In press). Generalizability assessment of behavioral observation data. In R. Barrett & J. Matson (Eds.), *Advances in developmental disorders: A research annual.* Greenwich, CT: JAI press.

Suen, H. K., & Karabinus, R. A. (1986). Assessment of judgmental prior distributions in the Bayesian inferential process. *Mid-Western Educational Researcher, 1*(3), 9–16.

Suen, H. K., & Lee, P. S. C. (1985). Effects of the use of percentage agreement on behavioral observation reliabilities: A reassessment. *Journal of Psychopathology and Behavioral Assessment, 7,* 221–234.

Suen, H. K., & Lee, P. S. C. (1987a, April). *An aggregate-segregate approach to the generalizability study of data with correlated errors.* Paper presented at the annual meeting of the American Educational Research Association, Washington, DC.

Suen, H. K., & Lee, P. S. C. (1987b, October). *Generalizability assessment of autocorrelated data via Box-Jenkins backforecasting.* Paper presented at the annual meeting of the Midwestern Educational Research Association, Chicago, IL.

Suen, H. K., Lee, P. S. C., & Prochnow-LaGrow, J. E. (1985). A critical review of the S/L reliability index. *Journal of Psychopathology and Behavioral Assessment, 7,* 277–287.

Suen, H. K., & Yue, K. T. (forthcoming). *User's manual for BOSA (Behavioral Observation Statistical Analysis).* Hillsdale, NJ: Lawrence Erlbaum.

Swan, G. E., & MacDonald, M. L. (1978). Behavior therapy in practice: A national survey of behavior therapists. *Behavior Therapy, 9,* 799–807.

Symonds, R. J., & Unwin, D. M. (1982). The use of a microcomputer to collect activity data. *Physiological Entomology, 7,* 91–98.

Thomson, C., Holmberg, M., & Baer, D. M. (1974). A brief report on a comparison of time-sampling procedures. *Journal of Applied Behavior Analysis, 7,* 623–626.

Thrall, T., & Engelman, L. (1981). PIT: Univariate and bivariate spectral analysis. In W. J. Dixon et al. (Eds.), *BMDP statistical software, 1981.* (pp. 604–638). Berkeley, CA: University of California Press.

Timm, N. H. (1975). *Multivariate analysis with applications in education and psychology.* Belmont, CA: Wadsworth.

Tinsley, H. E. A., & Weiss, D. J. (1975). Interrater reliability and agreement of subjective judgments. *Journal of Counseling Psychology, 22,* 358–276.

Torgerson, L. (1977). Datamyte 900. *Behavior Research Methods and Instrumentation,*

9, 405–406.

Tronick, E., & Brazelton, T. B. (1975). Clinical uses of the Brazelton Neonatal Behavioral Assessment. In B. Z. Friedlander, G. M. Sterritt, & G. E. Kirk (Eds.), *Exceptional infant, Vol. 3*. New York: Brunner/Mazel.

Tryon, W. W. (1982). A simplified time-series analysis for evaluating treatment interventions. *Journal of Applied Behavior Analysis, 15*, 423–429.

Tukey, J. W. (1967). An introduction to the calculation of numerical spectrum analysis. In B. Harris (Ed.), *Spectral analysis of time series* (pp. 25–46). New York: Wiley.

Ullmann, L. P., & Krasner, L. (Eds.) (1965). *Case studies in behavior modification*. New York: Holt, Rinehart and Winston.

Underwood, B. J. (1966). *Experimental psychology* (2nd ed.). New York: Appleton-Century-Crofts.

Van Cauter, E., & Huyberechts, S. (1973). Problems in the statistical analysis of biological time series: The cosinor test and the periodogram. *Journal of Interdisciplinary Cycle Research, 4*, 41–57.

Vandaele, W. (1983). *Applied time series and Box-Jenkins models*. New York: Academic Press.

Voeltz, L. M., & Evans, I. M. (1983). Educational validity: Procedures to evaluate outcomes of programs for severely handicapped learners. *Journal of the Association for the Severely Handicapped, 8*, 3–15.

Wade, T. C., Baker, T. B., & Hartmann, D. P. (1979). Behavior therapists' self-reported views and practices. *The Behavior Therapist, 2*, 3–6.

Wakefield, J. A. (1980). Relationship between two expressions of reliability: Percentage agreement and phi. *Educational and Psychological Measurement, 40*, 593–597.

Wallander, J. L., Conger, A. J., & Conger, J. C. (1985). Development and evaluation of a behaviorally referenced rating system for heterosocial skills. *Behavioral Assessment, 7*, 137–153.

Warm, T. A. (1978). *A primer of item response theory*. Springfield, VA: National Technical Information Service.

Watson, J. B., & Rayner, R. (1920). Conditioned emotional reactions. *Journal of Experimental Psychology, 3*, 1–12.

Weick, K. E. (1968). Systematic observational methods. In G. Lindzey & E. Aronson (Eds.), *The handbook of social psychology* (2nd ed., pp. 357–451). Reading, MA: Addison-Wesley.

Weiss, R. L., & Frohman, P. E. (1985). Behavioral observation as outcome measures: Not through a glass darkly. *Behavioral Assessment, 7*, 309–316.

Whiting, B. B., & Whiting, J. W. M. (1973). Methods for observing and recording behavior. In R. Naroll & R. Cohen (Eds.), *Handbook of methods in cultural anthropology*. New York: Columbia University Press.

Wiersma, W., & Jurs, S. G. (1985). *Educational measurement and testing*. Boston: Allyn and Bacon.

Wiggins, J. S. (1973). *Personality and prediction: Principles of personality assessment*. Reading, MA: Addison-Wesley.

Winer, B. J. (1962). *Statistical principles in experimental design*. New York: McGraw-Hill.

Winkler, R. L. (1968). The consensus of subject probability distributions. *Management Science, 15,* 61–75.

Wright, B. D., & Stone, M. H. (1979). *Best test design: Rasch measurement.* Chicago, IL: Mesa.

Wright, H. F. (1960). Observational child study. In P. Mussen (Ed.), *Handbook of research methods in child development* (pp. 71–139). New York: Wiley.

Yalow, E. S., & Popham, W. J. (1983). Content validity at the crossroads. *Educational Researcher, 12,* 10–14, 21.

Yelton, A. R., Wildman, B. G., & Erickson, M. T. (1977). A probability-based formula for calculating interobserver agreement. *Journal of Applied Behavior Analysis, 10,* 127–131.

Young, L. C. (1941). On randomness in ordered sequences. *Annals of Mathematical Statistics, 12,* 293–300.

Yule, G. U. (1927). On a method of investigating periodicities in disturbed series, with special inference to Wolfer's sunspot numbers. *Philosophical Transactions, A226,* 267–298.

Author Index

Subject Index